# SÍ, SE PUEDE

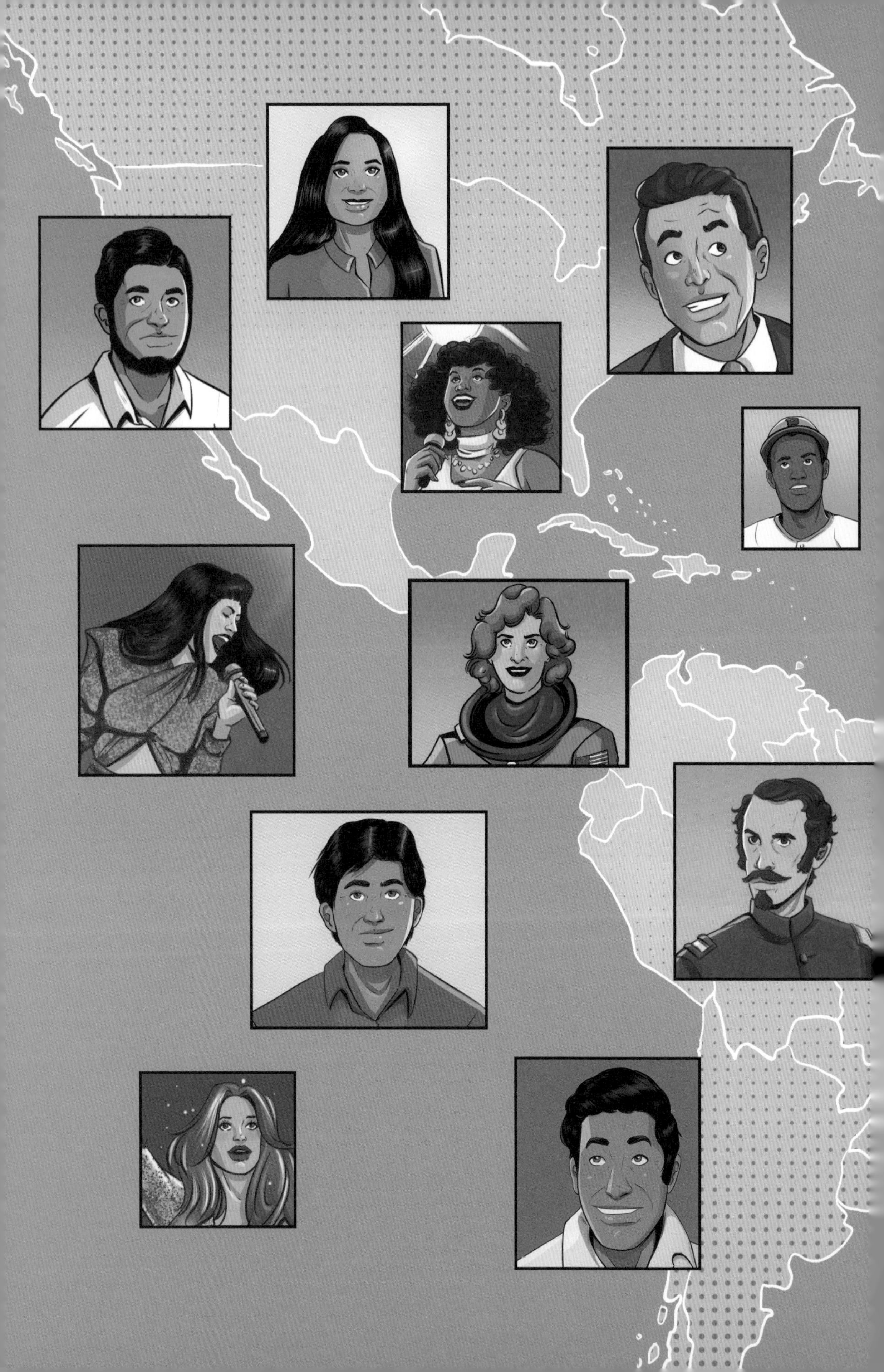

# SÍ, SE PUEDE

## THE LATINO HEROES WHO CHANGED THE UNITED STATES

JULIO ANTA

ILLUSTRATED BY
YASMÍN FLORES MONTAÑEZ

COLORS BY FABI MARQUES

LETTERS BY HASSAN OTSMANE-ELHAOU

TEN SPEED GRAPHIC
An imprint of TEN SPEED PRESS
California | New York

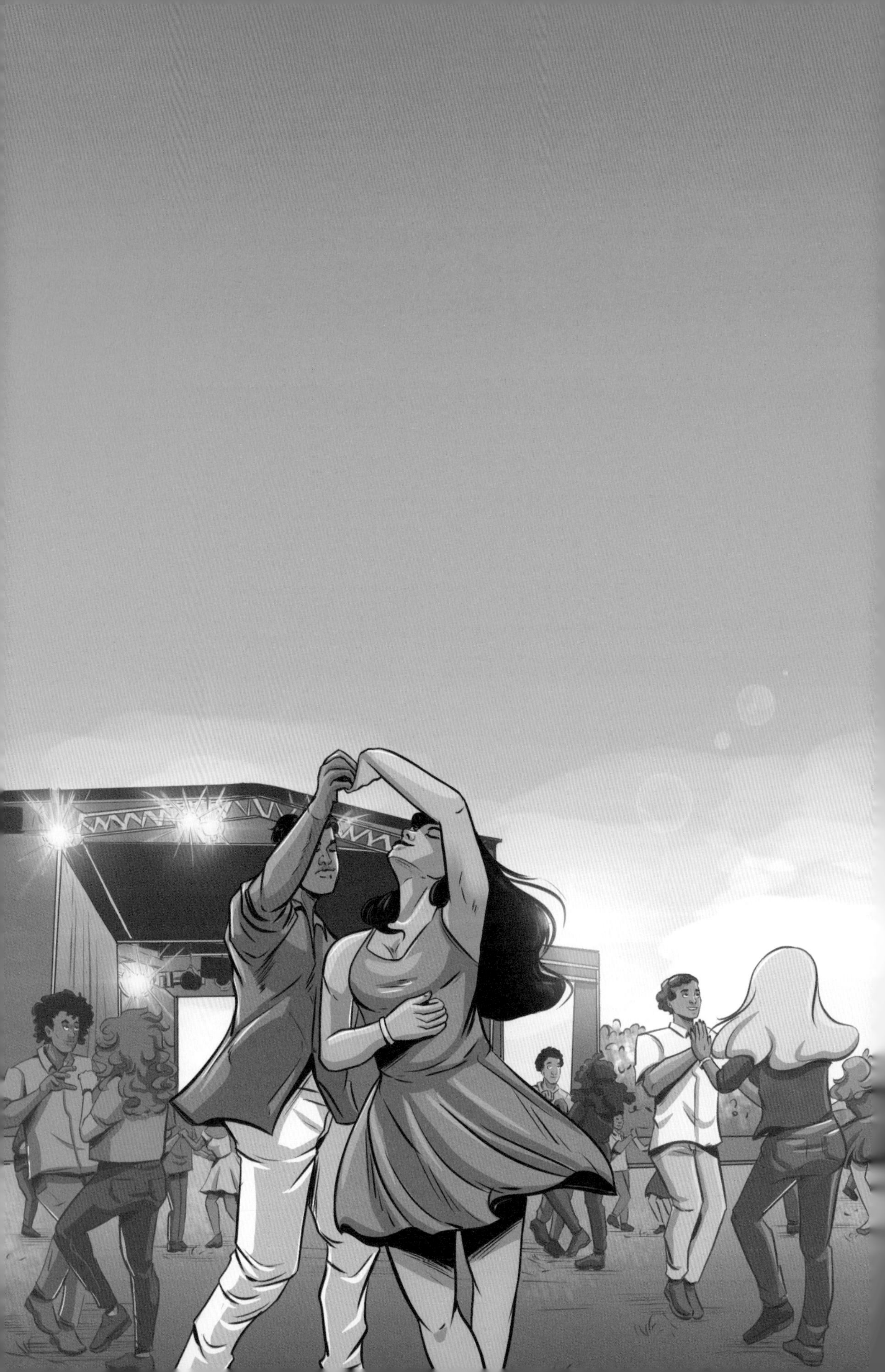

# TABLE OF CONTENTS

# FOREWORD

A few years ago, when I was chair of the Congressional Hispanic Caucus, I convened a meeting with a group of top U.S. publishers to talk about Latino representation. The folks in the room were titans of industry, responsible for producing the textbooks that millions of schoolchildren read, as well as the best-selling novels and comics that become source material for generations of movies and television shows.

To start the conversation, I turned to the CEO of one of the top five publishing companies in the country, and I asked him a simple question.

Could he name three Latinos or Latinas who made a significant impact on American history?

He thought for a moment, and then admitted that he couldn't.

It was an earnest conversation, and he wasn't trying to be dismissive. Our country is nearly 20 percent Latino, but I expect that most Americans—including many of our own children—would give you the same answer.

Latinos have shaped the history of the United States since the beginning and played an undeniable role in our nation's prosperity. But it's rare to see a grade school textbook that highlights Latino stories, or to get genuine Latino representation in books or movies. By and large, Latino history has been written out of the American narrative, making it far too easy to perpetuate the idea that we do not belong.

Thankfully, a new generation of writers, illustrators, and creative minds are breaking down barriers to highlight how Latinos have changed the world. In *Sí, Se Puede*, Julio Anta takes readers on a spectacular journey through thousands of years of history, navigating complex issues through the eyes of a multigenerational group of museum visitors and their talented tour guide.

*Sí, Se Puede* lionizes a litany of heroes—from César Chávez and Roberto Clemente to twenty-first-century leaders like Mario Molina and Ellen Ochoa. Anta does not shy away from difficult topics like colonialism and colorism, but the overriding theme of the graphic novel is joy and pride in the past, present, and future of America's diverse and powerful Latino community. The graphic novel's masterful storytelling is brought to life through vibrant illustrations by Yasmín Flores Montañez, who takes care to illustrate the broad, multiracial coalitions that stood side by side with some of our community's greatest heroes.

At a time when candid portrayals of American history are under attack, *Sí, Se Puede* is a must-read for all ages. This graphic novel belongs on the bookshelves of every home and library as a reminder of who Latinos are—and what we can achieve.

Congressman Joaquin Castro
San Antonio, Texas
February 2023

# CHAPTER 1: A DIVERSE AND UNIQUE HISTORY

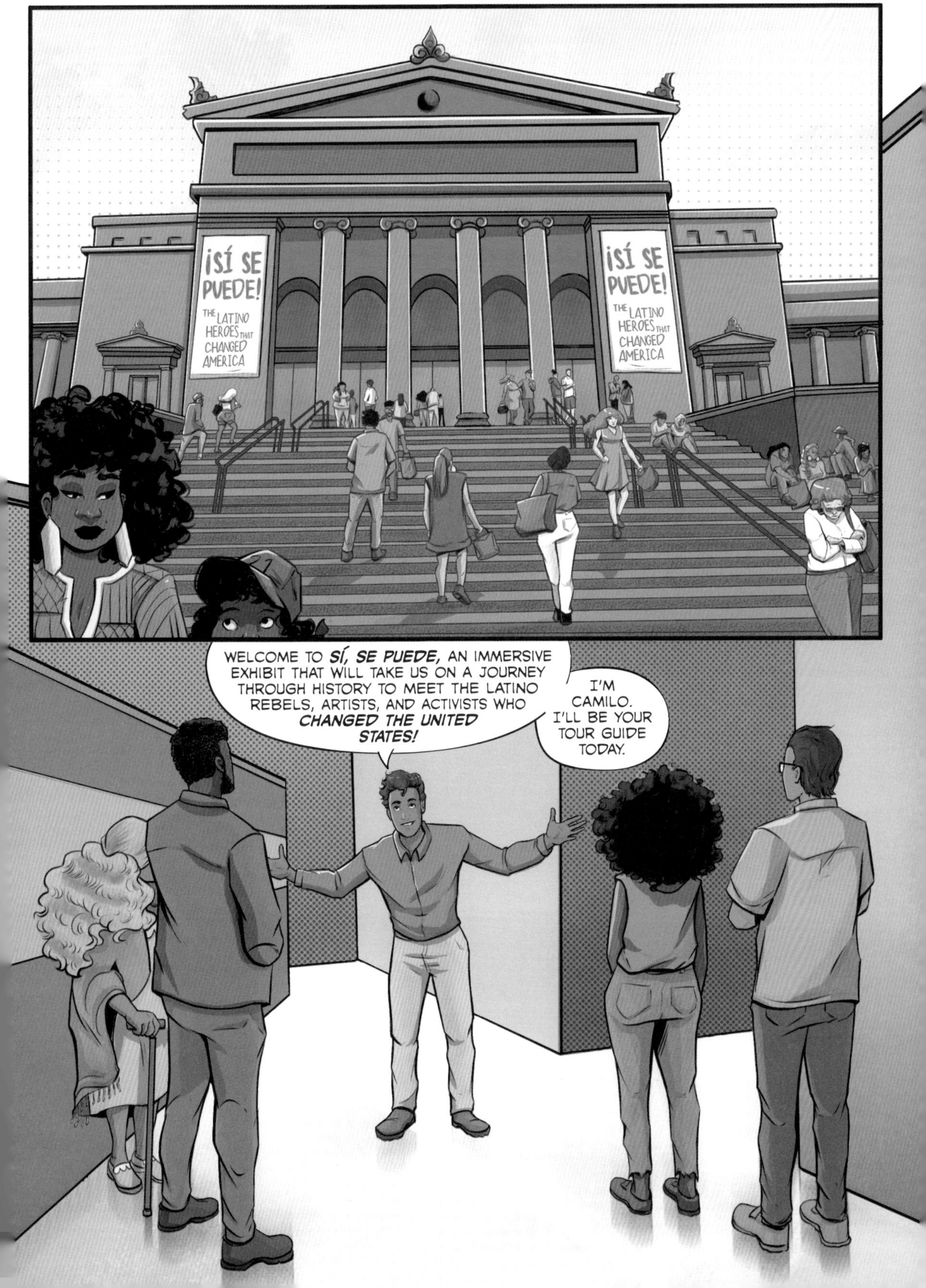
¡SÍ SE PUEDE! THE LATINO HEROES THAT CHANGED AMERICA
¡SÍ SE PUEDE! THE LATINO HEROES THAT CHANGED AMERICA
WELCOME TO SÍ, SE PUEDE, AN IMMERSIVE EXHIBIT THAT WILL TAKE US ON A JOURNEY THROUGH HISTORY TO MEET THE LATINO REBELS, ARTISTS, AND ACTIVISTS WHO CHANGED THE UNITED STATES!
I'M CAMILO. I'LL BE YOUR TOUR GUIDE TODAY.

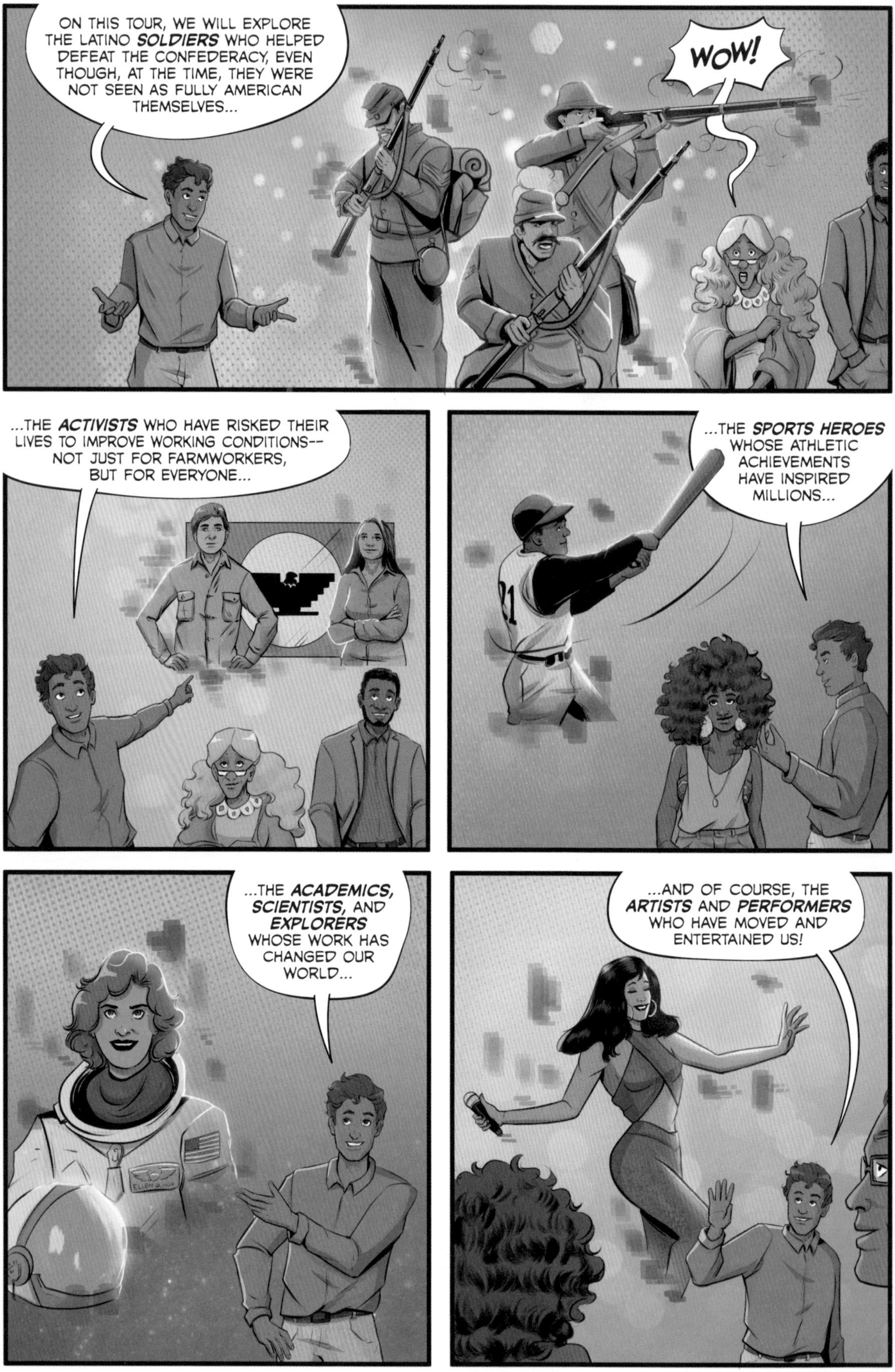
ON THIS TOUR, WE WILL EXPLORE THE LATINO SOLDIERS WHO HELPED DEFEAT THE CONFEDERACY, EVEN THOUGH, AT THE TIME, THEY WERE NOT SEEN AS FULLY AMERICAN THEMSELVES...
WOW!
...THE ACTIVISTS WHO HAVE RISKED THEIR LIVES TO IMPROVE WORKING CONDITIONS-- NOT JUST FOR FARMWORKERS, BUT FOR EVERYONE...
...THE SPORTS HEROES WHOSE ATHLETIC ACHIEVEMENTS HAVE INSPIRED MILLIONS...
21
...THE ACADEMICS, SCIENTISTS, AND EXPLORERS WHOSE WORK HAS CHANGED OUR WORLD...
...AND OF COURSE, THE ARTISTS AND PERFORMERS WHO HAVE MOVED AND ENTERTAINED US!

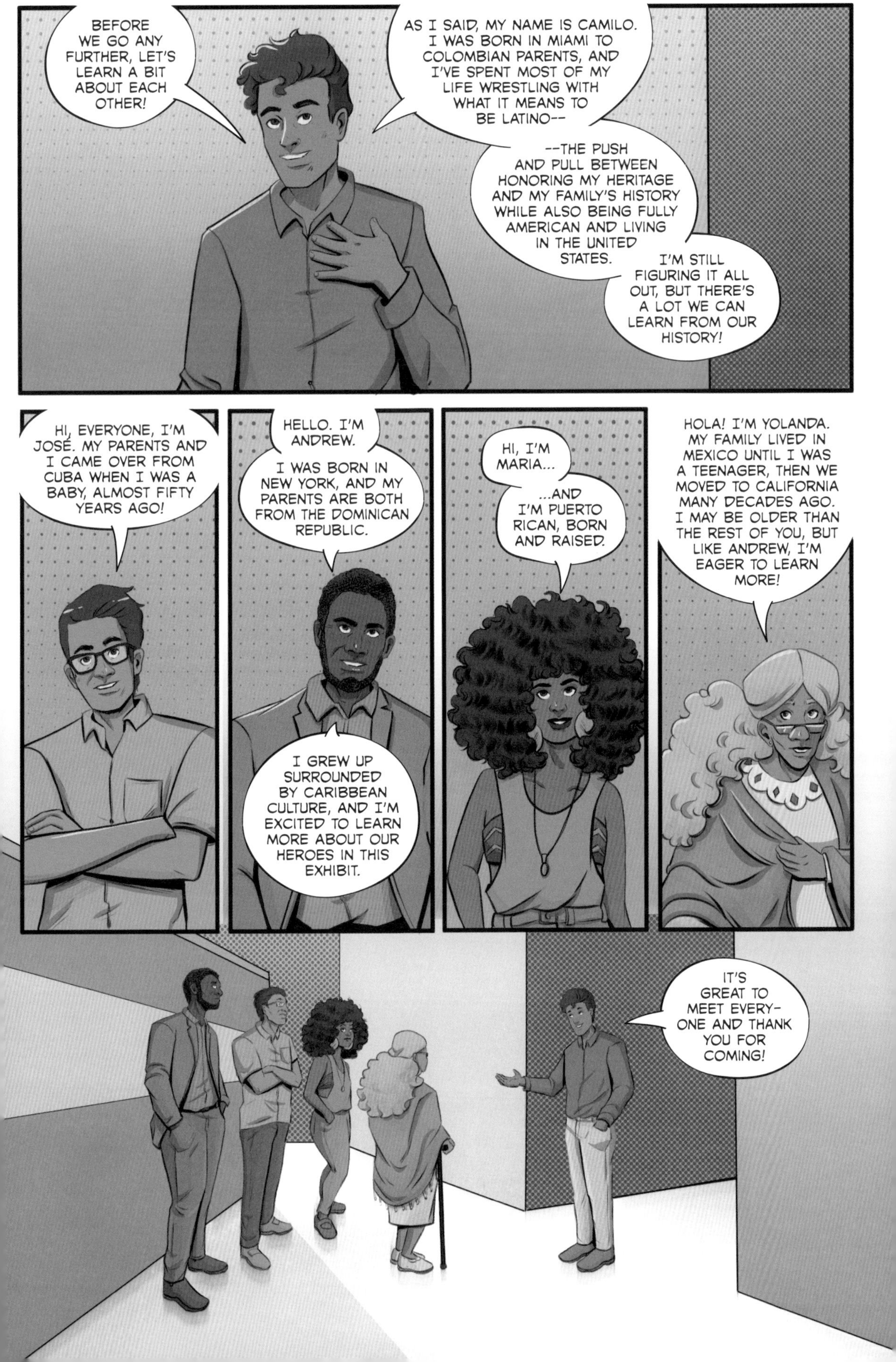

BEFORE WE GO ANY FURTHER, LET'S LEARN A BIT ABOUT EACH OTHER!
AS I SAID, MY NAME IS CAMILO. I WAS BORN IN MIAMI TO COLOMBIAN PARENTS, AND I'VE SPENT MOST OF MY LIFE WRESTLING WITH WHAT IT MEANS TO BE LATINO--
--THE PUSH AND PULL BETWEEN HONORING MY HERITAGE AND MY FAMILY'S HISTORY WHILE ALSO BEING FULLY AMERICAN AND LIVING IN THE UNITED STATES.
I'M STILL FIGURING IT ALL OUT, BUT THERE'S A LOT WE CAN LEARN FROM OUR HISTORY!
HI, EVERYONE, I'M JOSÉ. MY PARENTS AND I CAME OVER FROM CUBA WHEN I WAS A BABY, ALMOST FIFTY YEARS AGO!
HELLO. I'M ANDREW.
I WAS BORN IN NEW YORK, AND MY PARENTS ARE BOTH FROM THE DOMINICAN REPUBLIC.
I GREW UP SURROUNDED BY CARIBBEAN CULTURE, AND I'M EXCITED TO LEARN MORE ABOUT OUR HEROES IN THIS EXHIBIT.
HI, I'M MARIA...
...AND I'M PUERTO RICAN, BORN AND RAISED.
HOLA! I'M YOLANDA. MY FAMILY LIVED IN MEXICO UNTIL I WAS A TEENAGER, THEN WE MOVED TO CALIFORNIA MANY DECADES AGO. I MAY BE OLDER THAN THE REST OF YOU, BUT LIKE ANDREW, I'M EAGER TO LEARN MORE!
IT'S GREAT TO MEET EVERY-ONE AND THANK YOU FOR COMING!

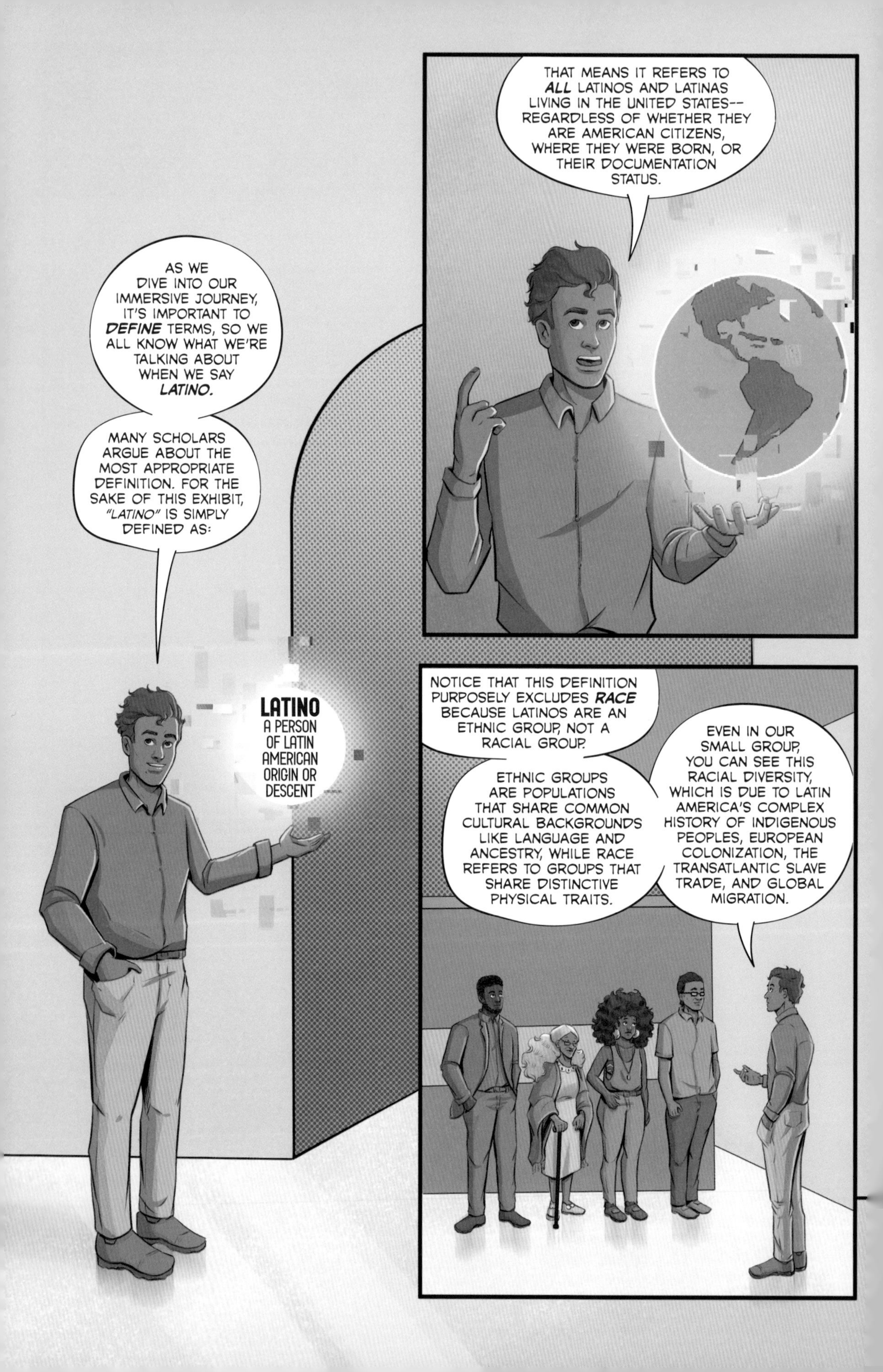
AS WE DIVE INTO OUR IMMERSIVE JOURNEY, IT'S IMPORTANT TO *DEFINE* TERMS, SO WE ALL KNOW WHAT WE'RE TALKING ABOUT WHEN WE SAY *LATINO.*
MANY SCHOLARS ARGUE ABOUT THE MOST APPROPRIATE DEFINITION. FOR THE SAKE OF THIS EXHIBIT, *"LATINO"* IS SIMPLY DEFINED AS:
**LATINO** A PERSON OF LATIN AMERICAN ORIGIN OR DESCENT
THAT MEANS IT REFERS TO *ALL* LATINOS AND LATINAS LIVING IN THE UNITED STATES-- REGARDLESS OF WHETHER THEY ARE AMERICAN CITIZENS, WHERE THEY WERE BORN, OR THEIR DOCUMENTATION STATUS.
NOTICE THAT THIS DEFINITION PURPOSELY EXCLUDES *RACE* BECAUSE LATINOS ARE AN ETHNIC GROUP, NOT A RACIAL GROUP.
ETHNIC GROUPS ARE POPULATIONS THAT SHARE COMMON CULTURAL BACKGROUNDS LIKE LANGUAGE AND ANCESTRY, WHILE RACE REFERS TO GROUPS THAT SHARE DISTINCTIVE PHYSICAL TRAITS.
EVEN IN OUR SMALL GROUP, YOU CAN SEE THIS RACIAL DIVERSITY, WHICH IS DUE TO LATIN AMERICA'S COMPLEX HISTORY OF INDIGENOUS PEOPLES, EUROPEAN COLONIZATION, THE TRANSATLANTIC SLAVE TRADE, AND GLOBAL MIGRATION.

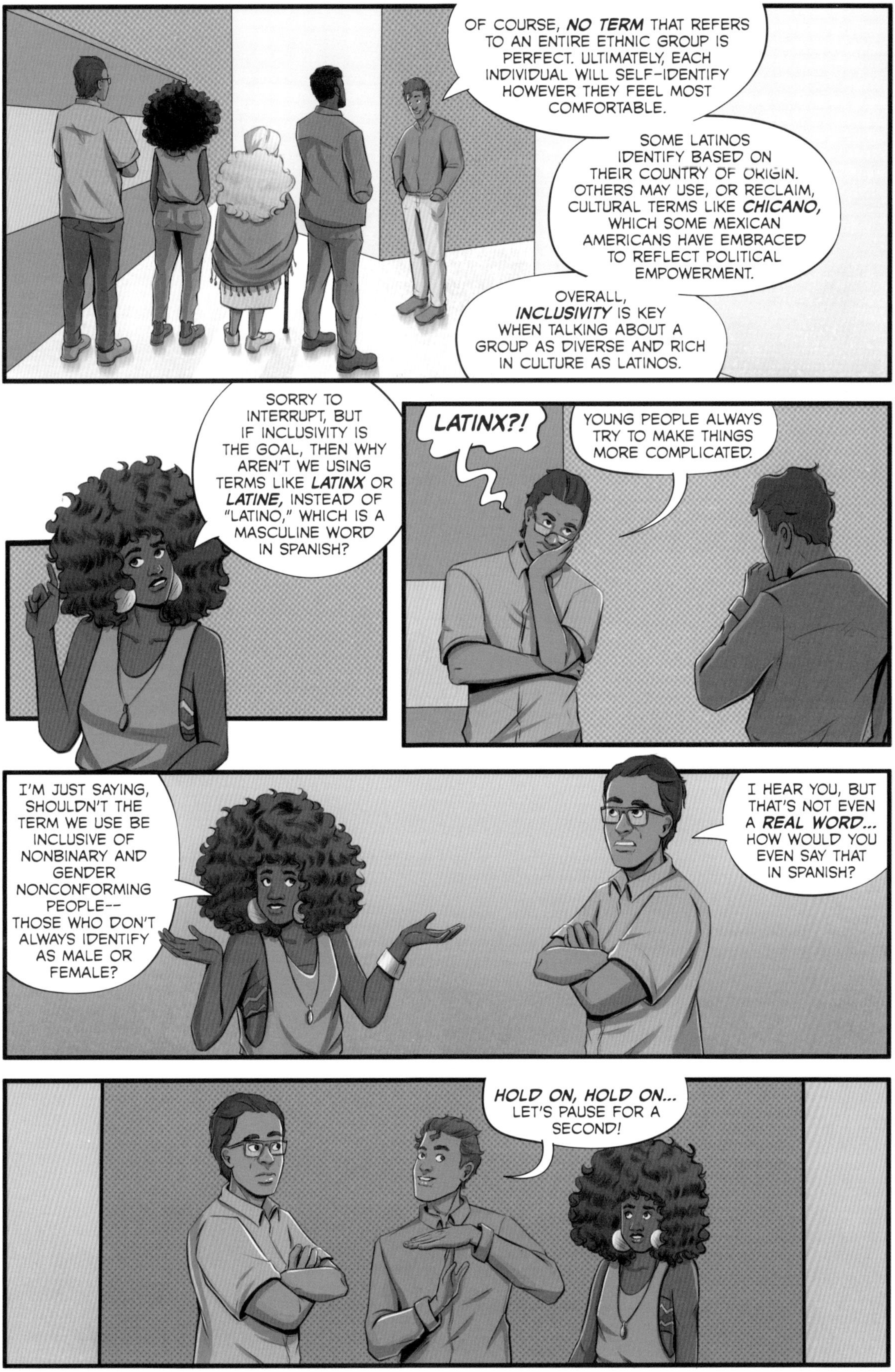
OF COURSE, **NO TERM** THAT REFERS TO AN ENTIRE ETHNIC GROUP IS PERFECT. ULTIMATELY, EACH INDIVIDUAL WILL SELF-IDENTIFY HOWEVER THEY FEEL MOST COMFORTABLE.
SOME LATINOS IDENTIFY BASED ON THEIR COUNTRY OF ORIGIN. OTHERS MAY USE, OR RECLAIM, CULTURAL TERMS LIKE **CHICANO,** WHICH SOME MEXICAN AMERICANS HAVE EMBRACED TO REFLECT POLITICAL EMPOWERMENT.
OVERALL, **INCLUSIVITY** IS KEY WHEN TALKING ABOUT A GROUP AS DIVERSE AND RICH IN CULTURE AS LATINOS.
SORRY TO INTERRUPT, BUT IF INCLUSIVITY IS THE GOAL, THEN WHY AREN'T WE USING TERMS LIKE **LATINX** OR **LATINE,** INSTEAD OF "LATINO," WHICH IS A MASCULINE WORD IN SPANISH?
**LATINX?!**
YOUNG PEOPLE ALWAYS TRY TO MAKE THINGS MORE COMPLICATED.
I'M JUST SAYING, SHOULDN'T THE TERM WE USE BE INCLUSIVE OF NONBINARY AND GENDER NONCONFORMING PEOPLE-- THOSE WHO DON'T ALWAYS IDENTIFY AS MALE OR FEMALE?
I HEAR YOU, BUT THAT'S NOT EVEN A **REAL WORD...** HOW WOULD YOU EVEN SAY THAT IN SPANISH?
**HOLD ON, HOLD ON...** LET'S PAUSE FOR A SECOND!

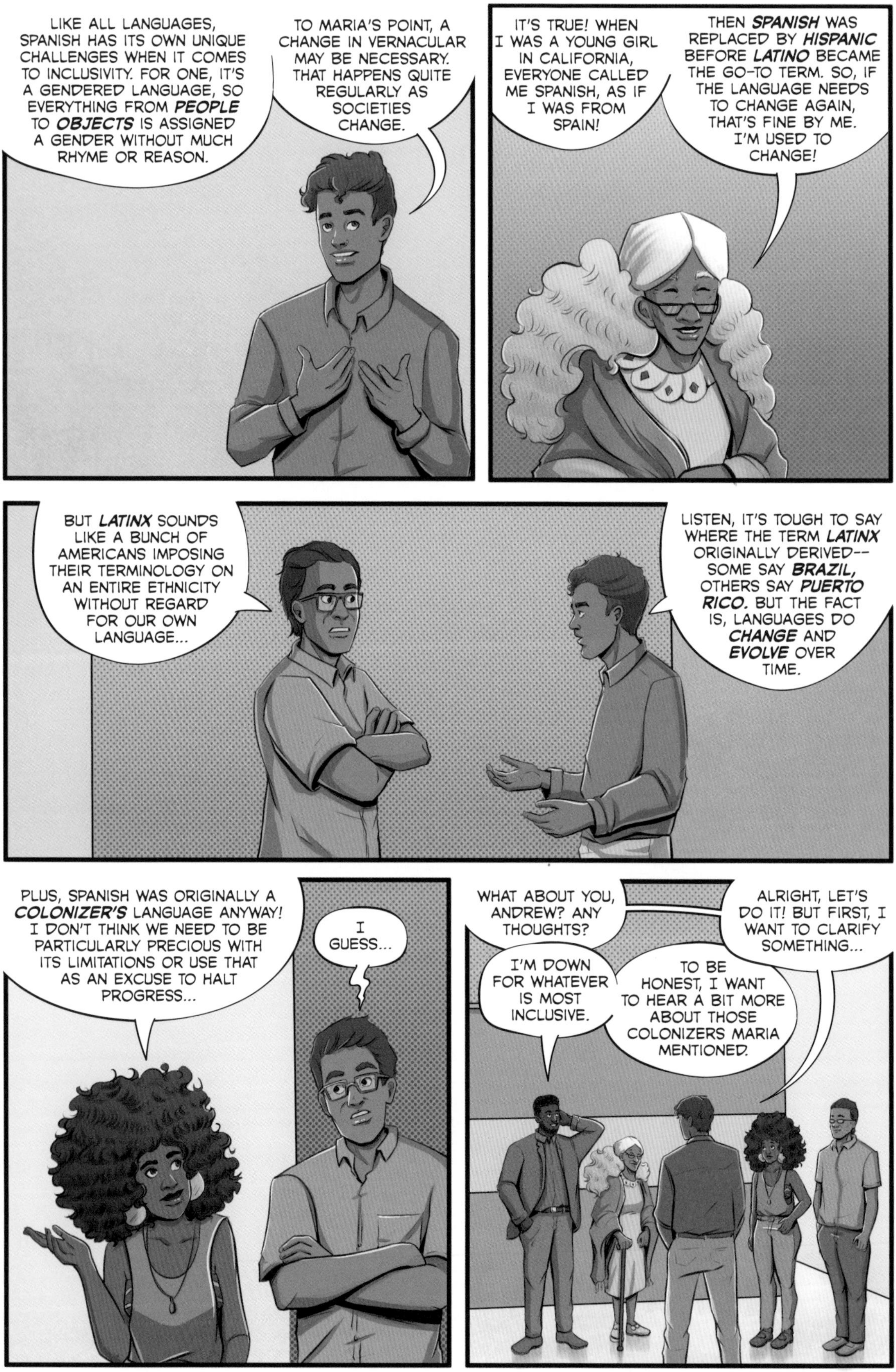
LIKE ALL LANGUAGES, SPANISH HAS ITS OWN UNIQUE CHALLENGES WHEN IT COMES TO INCLUSIVITY. FOR ONE, IT'S A GENDERED LANGUAGE, SO EVERYTHING FROM PEOPLE TO OBJECTS IS ASSIGNED A GENDER WITHOUT MUCH RHYME OR REASON.
TO MARIA'S POINT, A CHANGE IN VERNACULAR MAY BE NECESSARY. THAT HAPPENS QUITE REGULARLY AS SOCIETIES CHANGE.
IT'S TRUE! WHEN I WAS A YOUNG GIRL IN CALIFORNIA, EVERYONE CALLED ME SPANISH, AS IF I WAS FROM SPAIN!
THEN SPANISH WAS REPLACED BY HISPANIC BEFORE LATINO BECAME THE GO-TO TERM. SO, IF THE LANGUAGE NEEDS TO CHANGE AGAIN, THAT'S FINE BY ME. I'M USED TO CHANGE!
BUT LATINX SOUNDS LIKE A BUNCH OF AMERICANS IMPOSING THEIR TERMINOLOGY ON AN ENTIRE ETHNICITY WITHOUT REGARD FOR OUR OWN LANGUAGE...
LISTEN, IT'S TOUGH TO SAY WHERE THE TERM LATINX ORIGINALLY DERIVED-- SOME SAY BRAZIL, OTHERS SAY PUERTO RICO. BUT THE FACT IS, LANGUAGES DO CHANGE AND EVOLVE OVER TIME.
PLUS, SPANISH WAS ORIGINALLY A COLONIZER'S LANGUAGE ANYWAY! I DON'T THINK WE NEED TO BE PARTICULARLY PRECIOUS WITH ITS LIMITATIONS OR USE THAT AS AN EXCUSE TO HALT PROGRESS...
I GUESS...
WHAT ABOUT YOU, ANDREW? ANY THOUGHTS?
I'M DOWN FOR WHATEVER IS MOST INCLUSIVE.
ALRIGHT, LET'S DO IT! BUT FIRST, I WANT TO CLARIFY SOMETHING...
TO BE HONEST, I WANT TO HEAR A BIT MORE ABOUT THOSE COLONIZERS MARIA MENTIONED.

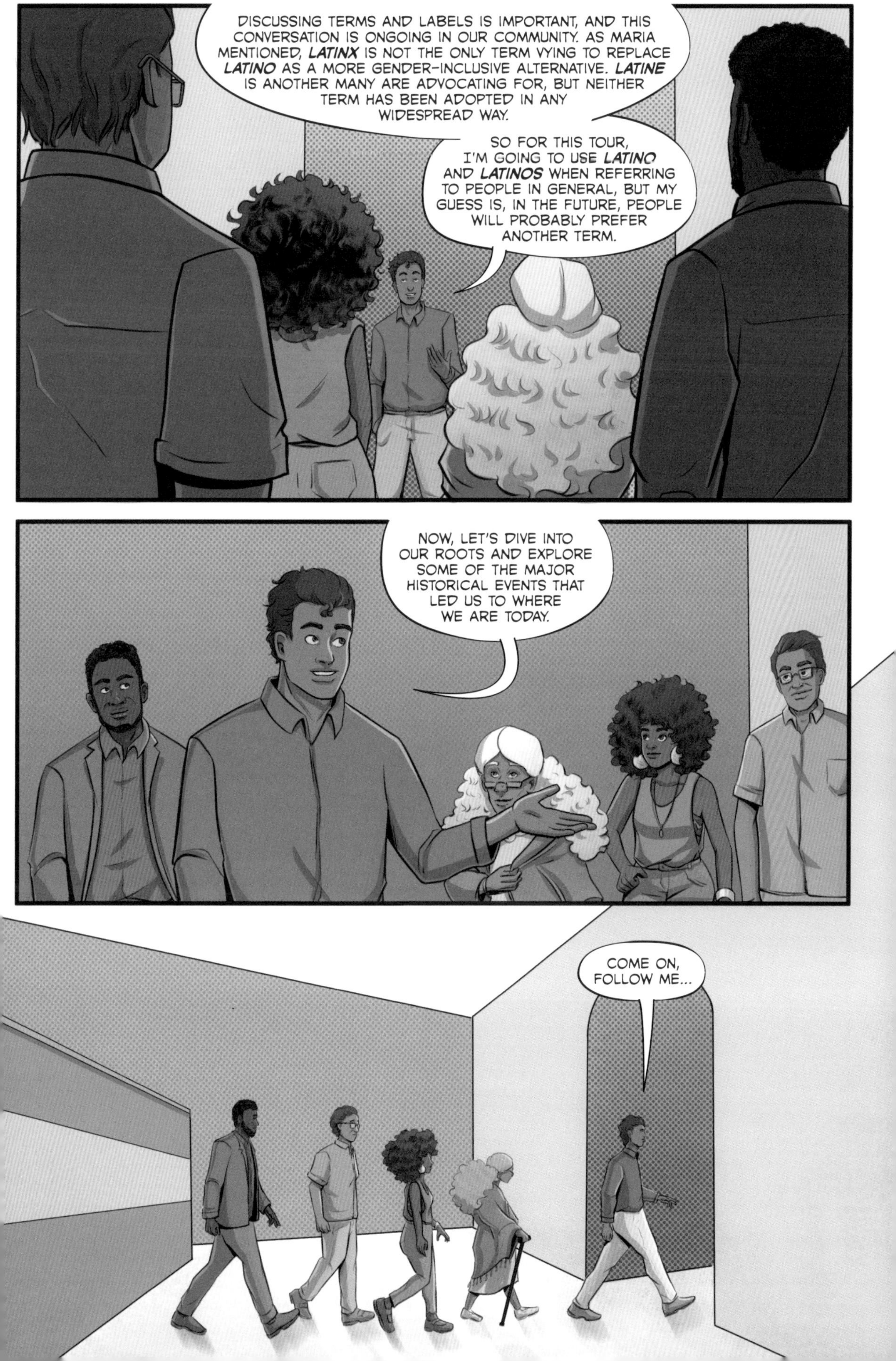
DISCUSSING TERMS AND LABELS IS IMPORTANT, AND THIS CONVERSATION IS ONGOING IN OUR COMMUNITY. AS MARIA MENTIONED, *LATINX* IS NOT THE ONLY TERM VYING TO REPLACE *LATINO* AS A MORE GENDER-INCLUSIVE ALTERNATIVE. *LATINE* IS ANOTHER MANY ARE ADVOCATING FOR, BUT NEITHER TERM HAS BEEN ADOPTED IN ANY WIDESPREAD WAY.
SO FOR THIS TOUR, I'M GOING TO USE *LATINO* AND *LATINOS* WHEN REFERRING TO PEOPLE IN GENERAL, BUT MY GUESS IS, IN THE FUTURE, PEOPLE WILL PROBABLY PREFER ANOTHER TERM.
NOW, LET'S DIVE INTO OUR ROOTS AND EXPLORE SOME OF THE MAJOR HISTORICAL EVENTS THAT LED US TO WHERE WE ARE TODAY.
COME ON, FOLLOW ME...

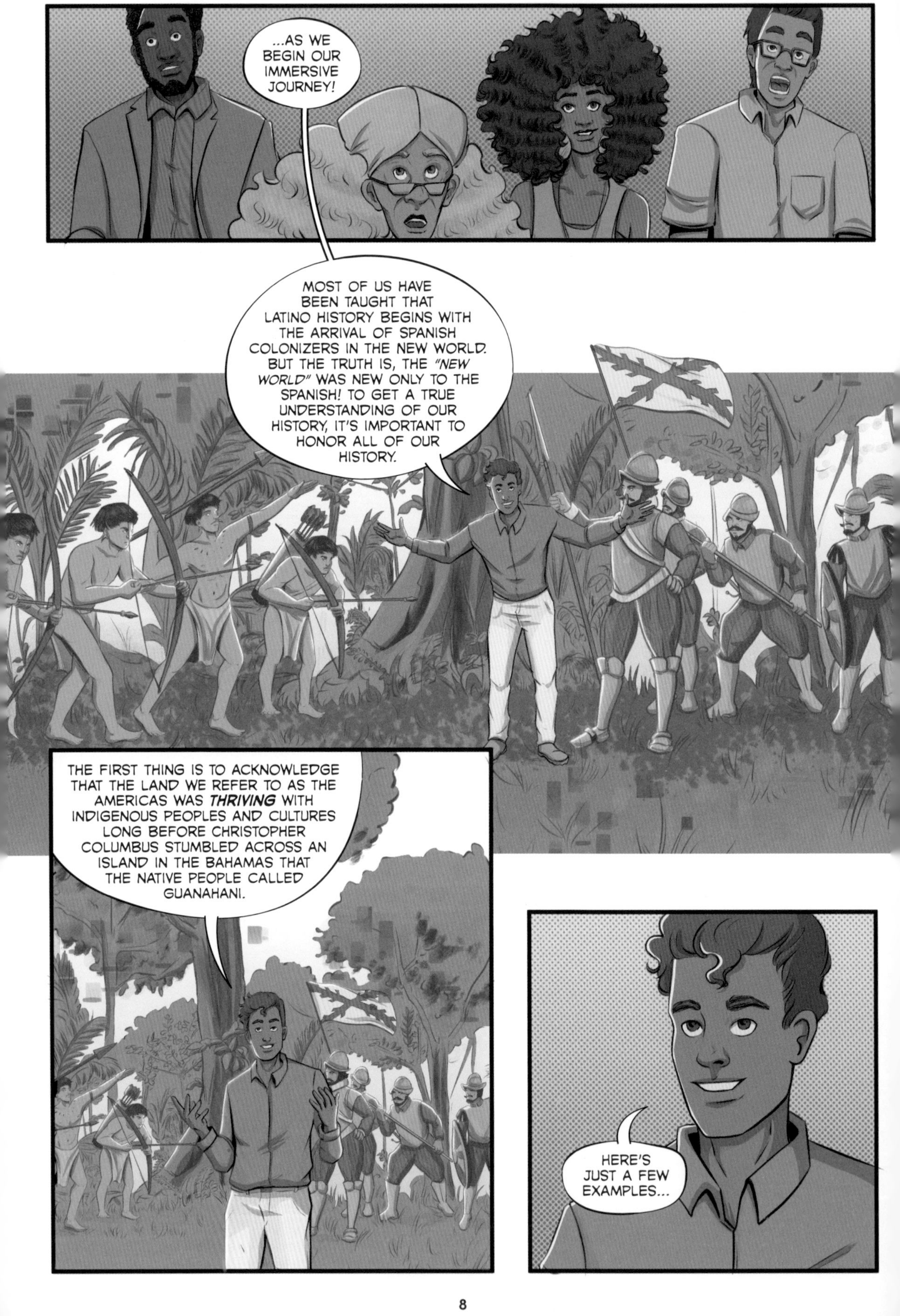
...AS WE BEGIN OUR IMMERSIVE JOURNEY!
MOST OF US HAVE BEEN TAUGHT THAT LATINO HISTORY BEGINS WITH THE ARRIVAL OF SPANISH COLONIZERS IN THE NEW WORLD. BUT THE TRUTH IS, THE *"NEW WORLD"* WAS NEW ONLY TO THE SPANISH! TO GET A TRUE UNDERSTANDING OF OUR HISTORY, IT'S IMPORTANT TO HONOR ALL OF OUR HISTORY.
THE FIRST THING IS TO ACKNOWLEDGE THAT THE LAND WE REFER TO AS THE AMERICAS WAS ***THRIVING*** WITH INDIGENOUS PEOPLES AND CULTURES LONG BEFORE CHRISTOPHER COLUMBUS STUMBLED ACROSS AN ISLAND IN THE BAHAMAS THAT THE NATIVE PEOPLE CALLED GUANAHANI.
HERE'S JUST A FEW EXAMPLES...

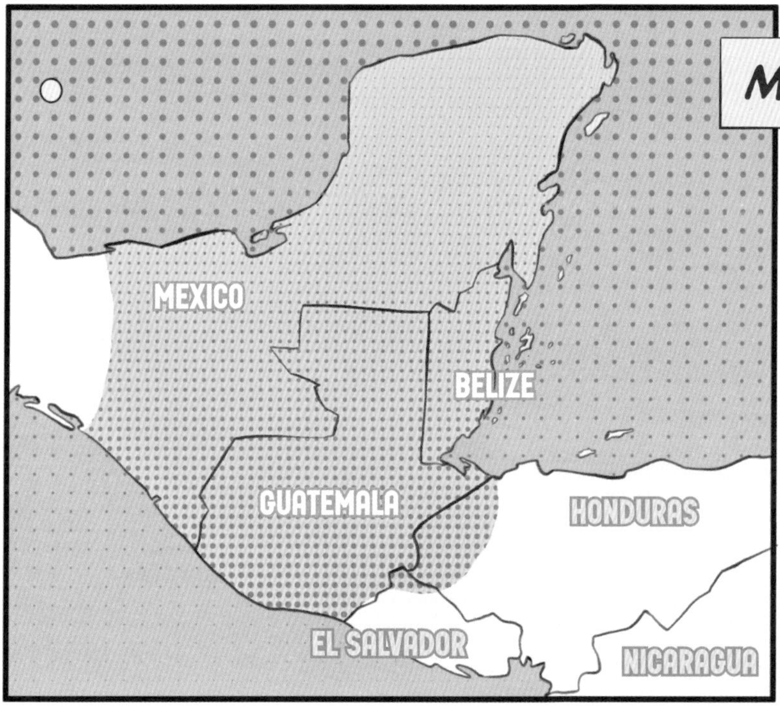
MEXICO
BELIZE
GUATEMALA
HONDURAS
EL SALVADOR
NICARAGUA

## MAYA EMPIRE

"THE MAYA CIVILIZATION STRETCHED FROM THE SOUTH OF MODERN-DAY MEXICO TO GUATEMALA, BELIZE, AND PARTS OF EL SALVADOR AND HONDURAS.

"ESTABLISHED AROUND 2000 BC, THE MAYA STEADILY BUILT A MASSIVE EMPIRE OF LARGE CITIES THAT WERE EACH HOME TO TENS OF THOUSANDS OF PEOPLE. BY THE END OF THE "CLASSIC PERIOD" (AD 250–900), THE TOTAL MAYA POPULATION IS ESTIMATED TO HAVE BEEN IN THE MILLIONS.

"THE MAYA WERE KNOWN FOR THEIR WRITING, SYMBOLIC ART, ARCHITECTURE, AND ADVANCED UNDERSTANDING OF MATHEMATICS AND ASTRONOMY. THEIR COMPLEX CALENDAR SYSTEM, FOR EXAMPLE, IS STILL THE SUBJECT OF SCHOLARLY DEBATE AND END-OF-THE-WORLD CONSPIRACY THEORIES TO THIS DAY."

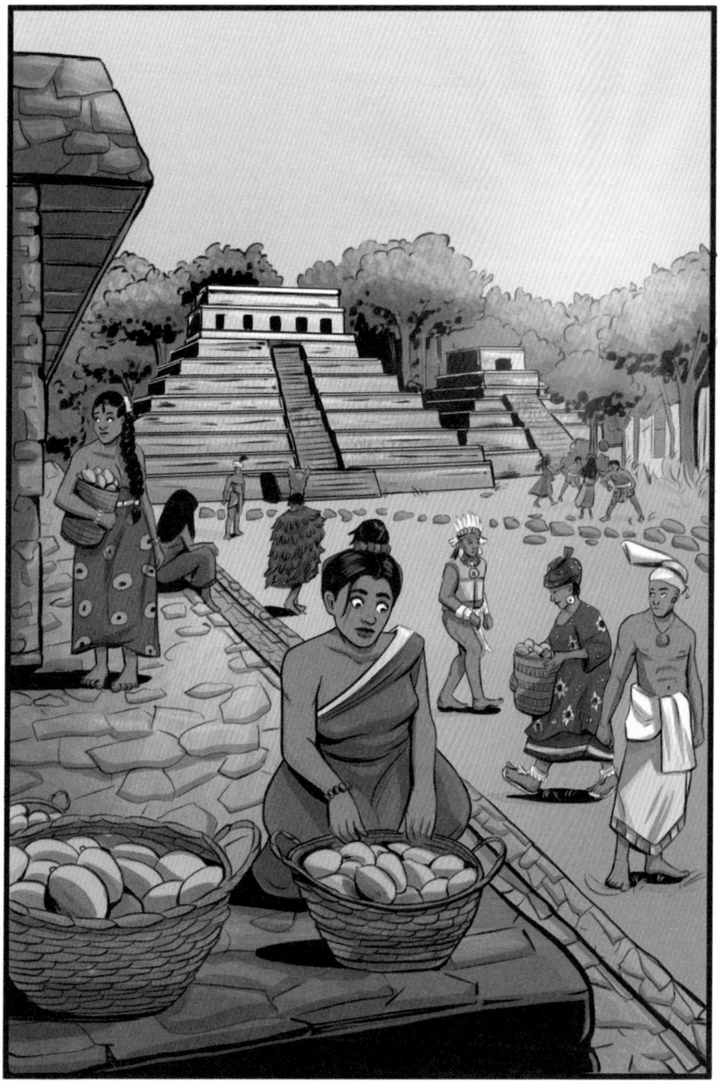

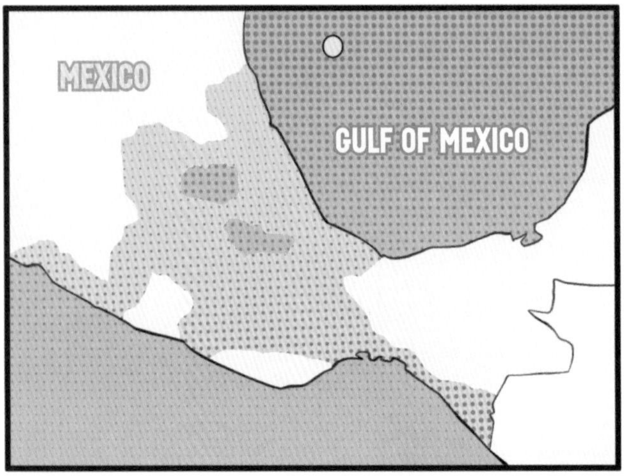
MEXICO
GULF OF MEXICO

# AZTEC EMPIRE

"NORTH OF THE MAYA IN MODERN-DAY CENTRAL MEXICO WAS THE AZTEC EMPIRE, AN ALLIANCE BETWEEN THE THREE CITY-STATES OF TENOCHTITLAN, TETZCOCO, AND TLACOPAN.

"THE AZTECS WERE A MESOAMERICAN CIVILIZATION THAT SHARED MANY OF THE SAME BASIC CULTURAL TRAITS AS THE MAYA. THEY BUILT PYRAMIDS TO HONOR THEIR GODS, DEVELOPED FARMING AND IRRIGATION SYSTEMS, AND MAINTAINED COMPLEX SOCIAL CLASS SYSTEMS.

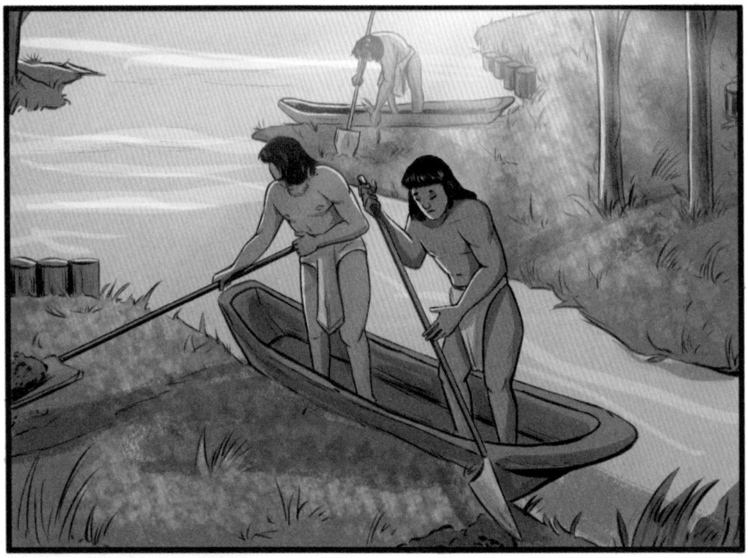

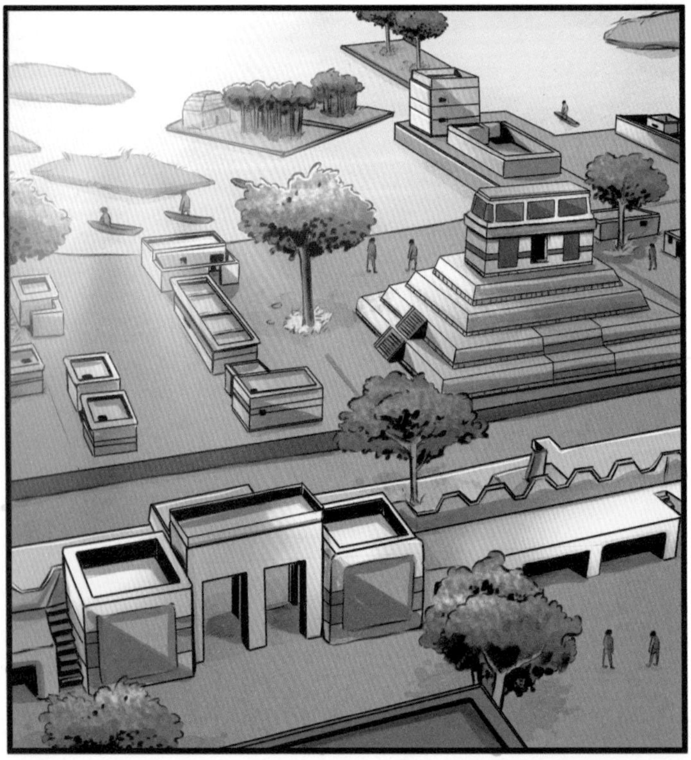

"THE AZTEC CAPITAL OF TENOCHTITLAN WAS A SPRAWLING METROPOLIS CONSTRUCTED ON AN ISLAND ON LAKE TEXCOCO. THE CITY'S POPULATION BOASTED OVER 200,000 PEOPLE-- FOUR TIMES AS MANY AS LIVED IN LONDON AT THE TIME, AND AT LEAST 50,000 MORE THAN LIVED IN PARIS. THIS LIKELY MADE TENOCHTITLAN THE LARGEST CITY IN THE WORLD. TENOCHTITLAN CONTAINED PALACES, SINGLE-FAMILY HOMES, BOTANICAL GARDENS, AND EVEN A ZOO."

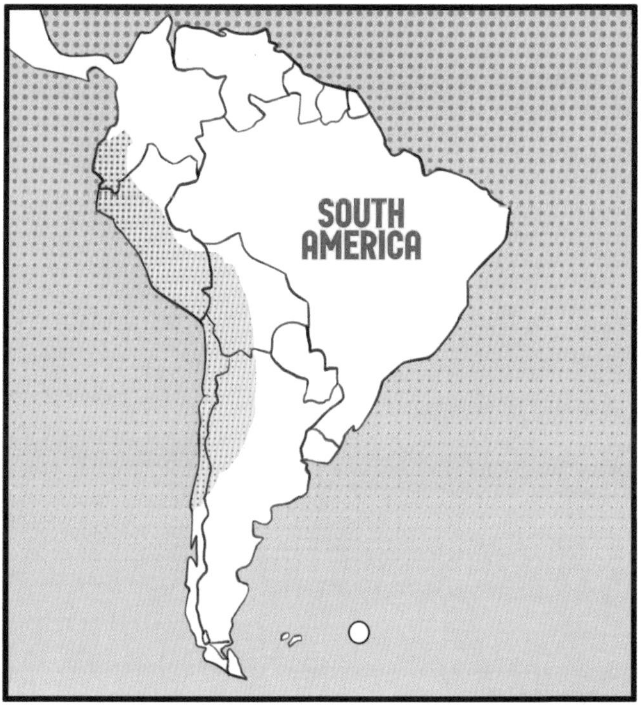
SOUTH AMERICA

## INCA EMPIRE

"MEANWHILE, CONTROLLING OVER 3,000 MILES OF LAND ALONG THE PACIFIC COAST OF MODERN-DAY PERU, BOLIVIA, ECUADOR, ARGENTINA, AND CHILE, THE INCA EMPIRE WAS THE LARGEST KINGDOM IN THE WESTERN HEMISPHERE.

"THE INCA CIVILIZATION BEGAN IN THE PERUVIAN HIGHLANDS SOMETIME IN THE EARLY THIRTEENTH CENTURY BEFORE GROWING INTO A HIGHLY CULTURED EMPIRE THAT VALUED MUSIC, ART, AND POETRY. THE INCAS DEVELOPED MEDICAL PRACTICES THAT EVEN INCLUDED PERFORMING BRAIN SURGERIES USING EARLY FORMS OF ANESTHESIA."

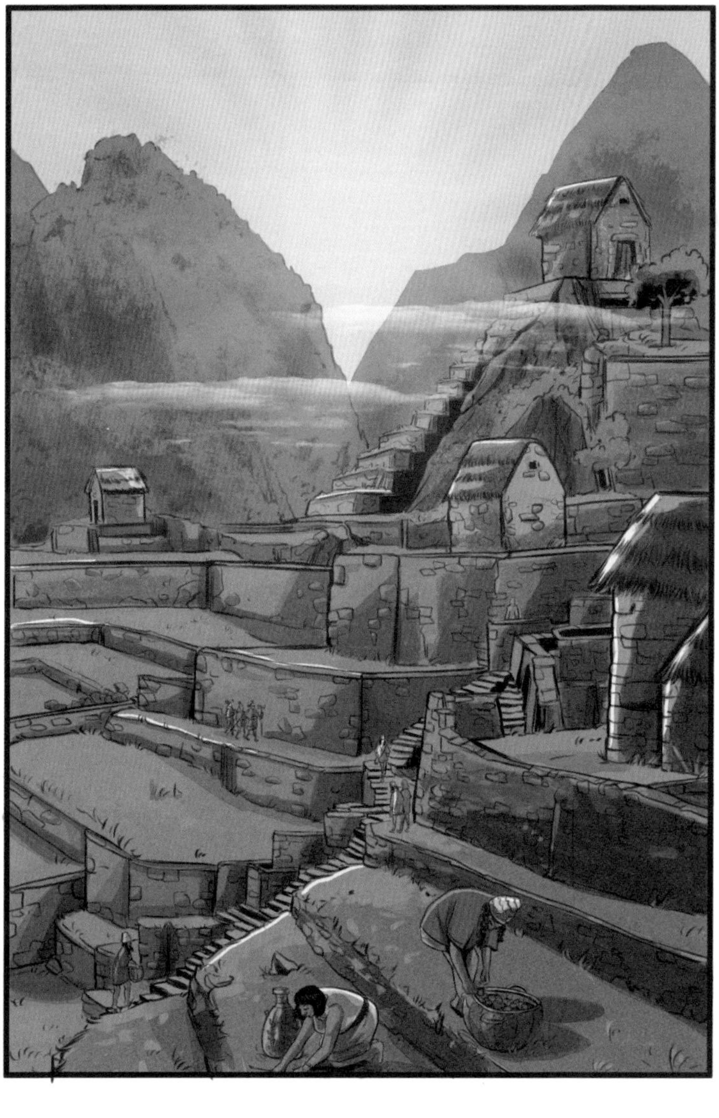

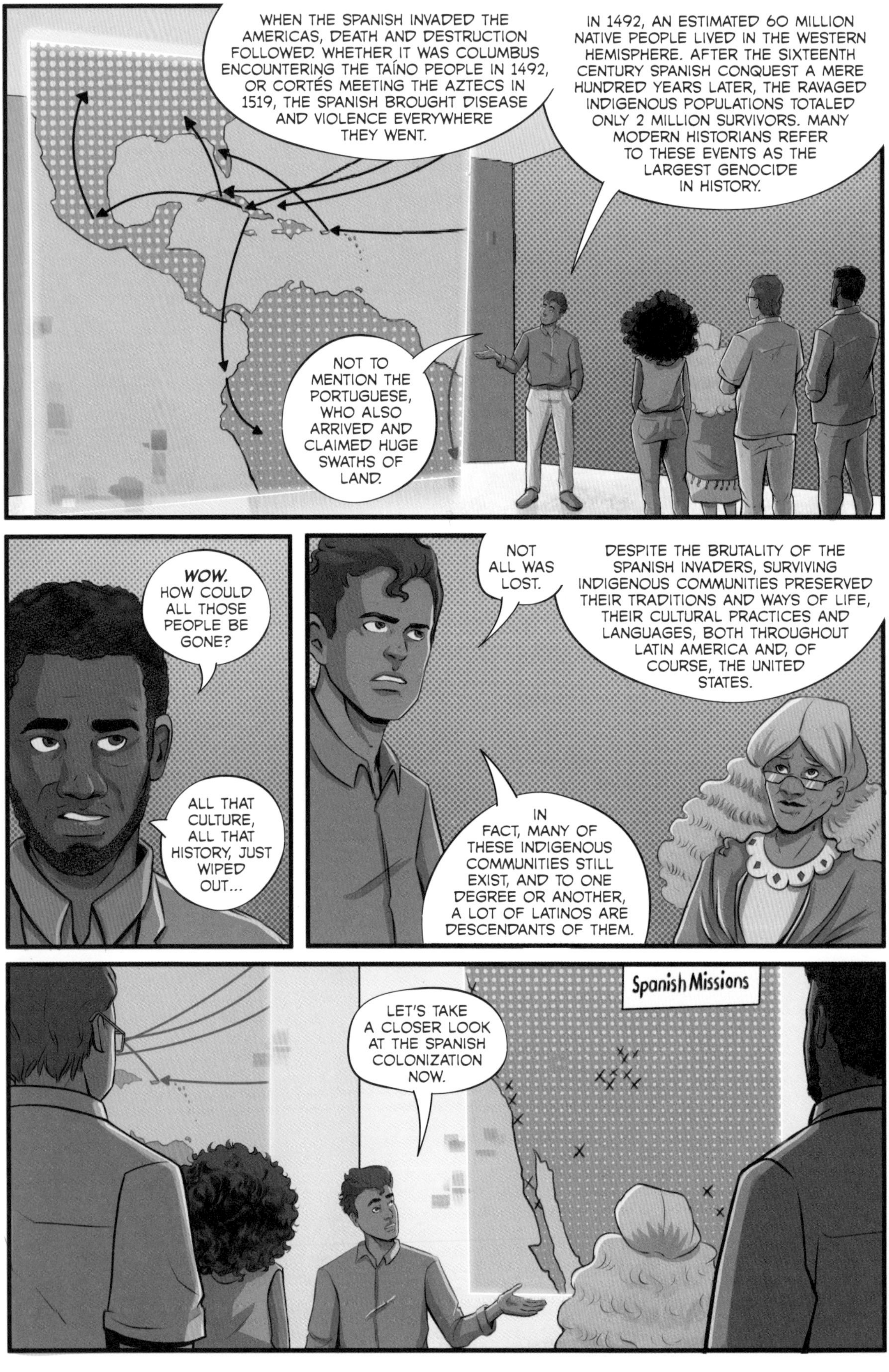
WHEN THE SPANISH INVADED THE AMERICAS, DEATH AND DESTRUCTION FOLLOWED. WHETHER IT WAS COLUMBUS ENCOUNTERING THE TAÍNO PEOPLE IN 1492, OR CORTÉS MEETING THE AZTECS IN 1519, THE SPANISH BROUGHT DISEASE AND VIOLENCE EVERYWHERE THEY WENT.
IN 1492, AN ESTIMATED 60 MILLION NATIVE PEOPLE LIVED IN THE WESTERN HEMISPHERE. AFTER THE SIXTEENTH CENTURY SPANISH CONQUEST A MERE HUNDRED YEARS LATER, THE RAVAGED INDIGENOUS POPULATIONS TOTALED ONLY 2 MILLION SURVIVORS. MANY MODERN HISTORIANS REFER TO THESE EVENTS AS THE LARGEST GENOCIDE IN HISTORY.
NOT TO MENTION THE PORTUGUESE, WHO ALSO ARRIVED AND CLAIMED HUGE SWATHS OF LAND.
*WOW.* HOW COULD ALL THOSE PEOPLE BE GONE?
ALL THAT CULTURE, ALL THAT HISTORY, JUST WIPED OUT...
NOT ALL WAS LOST.
DESPITE THE BRUTALITY OF THE SPANISH INVADERS, SURVIVING INDIGENOUS COMMUNITIES PRESERVED THEIR TRADITIONS AND WAYS OF LIFE, THEIR CULTURAL PRACTICES AND LANGUAGES, BOTH THROUGHOUT LATIN AMERICA AND, OF COURSE, THE UNITED STATES.
IN FACT, MANY OF THESE INDIGENOUS COMMUNITIES STILL EXIST, AND TO ONE DEGREE OR ANOTHER, A LOT OF LATINOS ARE DESCENDANTS OF THEM.
Spanish Missions
LET'S TAKE A CLOSER LOOK AT THE SPANISH COLONIZATION NOW.

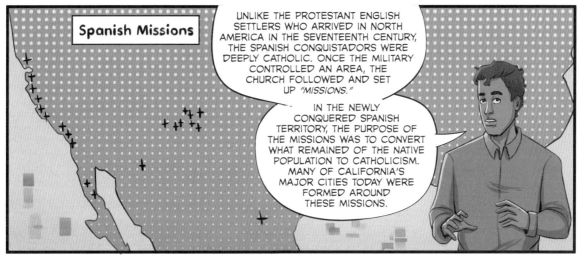

Spanish Missions

UNLIKE THE PROTESTANT ENGLISH SETTLERS WHO ARRIVED IN NORTH AMERICA IN THE SEVENTEENTH CENTURY, THE SPANISH CONQUISTADORS WERE DEEPLY CATHOLIC. ONCE THE MILITARY CONTROLLED AN AREA, THE CHURCH FOLLOWED AND SET UP *"MISSIONS."*

IN THE NEWLY CONQUERED SPANISH TERRITORY, THE PURPOSE OF THE MISSIONS WAS TO CONVERT WHAT REMAINED OF THE NATIVE POPULATION TO CATHOLICISM. MANY OF CALIFORNIA'S MAJOR CITIES TODAY WERE FORMED AROUND THESE MISSIONS.

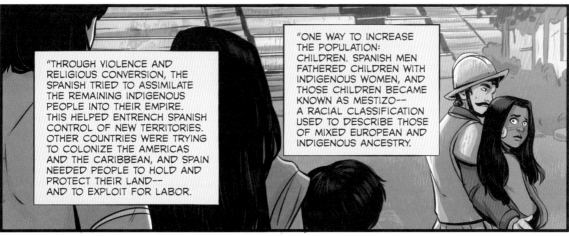

"THROUGH VIOLENCE AND RELIGIOUS CONVERSION, THE SPANISH TRIED TO ASSIMILATE THE REMAINING INDIGENOUS PEOPLE INTO THEIR EMPIRE. THIS HELPED ENTRENCH SPANISH CONTROL OF NEW TERRITORIES. OTHER COUNTRIES WERE TRYING TO COLONIZE THE AMERICAS AND THE CARIBBEAN, AND SPAIN NEEDED PEOPLE TO HOLD AND PROTECT THEIR LAND-- AND TO EXPLOIT FOR LABOR.

"ONE WAY TO INCREASE THE POPULATION: CHILDREN. SPANISH MEN FATHERED CHILDREN WITH INDIGENOUS WOMEN, AND THOSE CHILDREN BECAME KNOWN AS MESTIZO-- A RACIAL CLASSIFICATION USED TO DESCRIBE THOSE OF MIXED EUROPEAN AND INDIGENOUS ANCESTRY.

"ANOTHER WAY TO GAIN POPULATION: RELIGIOUS CONVERSION. AS THE SPANISH BAPTIZED NATIVE AMERICANS AND ACCEPTED THE IDEA THAT INDIGENOUS PEOPLE POSSESSED SOULS, *SOME* OF THE MOST BRUTAL FORMS OF ABUSE AND FORCED LABOR SUBSIDED.

"HOWEVER, THEN THE SPANISH EMPIRE NEEDED ANOTHER GROUP OF PEOPLE TO EXPLOIT FOR LABOR. SO THEY ABDUCTED AND ENSLAVED PEOPLE FROM AFRICA, WHICH CEMENTED MOST OF THE RACIAL MAKE-UP WE NOW SEE IN LATIN AMERICA AS WELL AS IN LATINOS IN THE UNITED STATES."

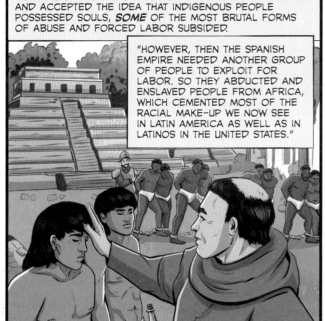

WOW, THAT'S PRETTY BLEAK, CAMILO...

...THAT'S SOME SERIOUS GENERATIONAL TRAUMA.

IT IS. OUR HISTORY IS ADMITTEDLY OFF TO A PRETTY DEPRESSING START...

...BUT FORTUNATELY, THE STORY DOESN'T END THERE.

13

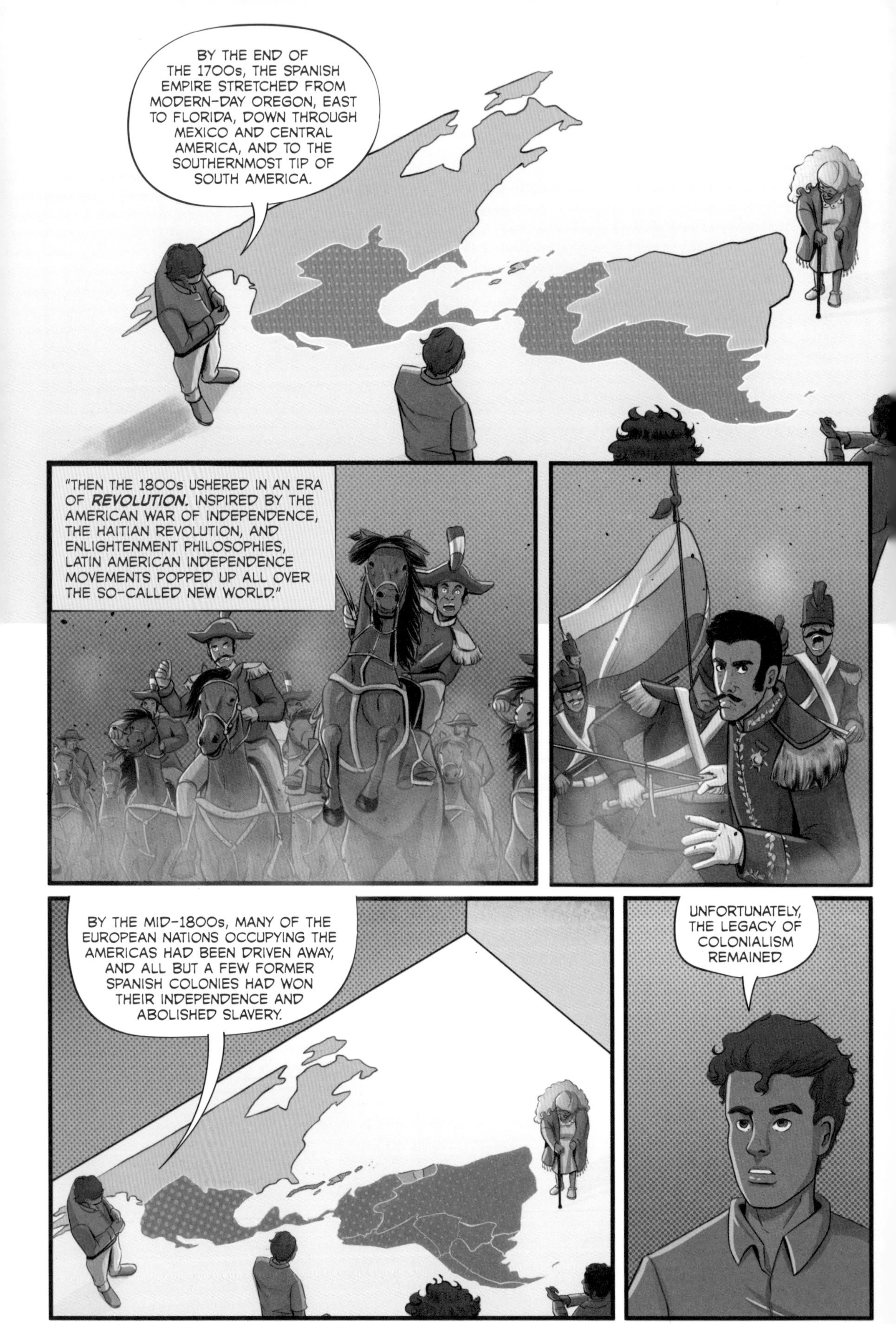
BY THE END OF THE 1700s, THE SPANISH EMPIRE STRETCHED FROM MODERN-DAY OREGON, EAST TO FLORIDA, DOWN THROUGH MEXICO AND CENTRAL AMERICA, AND TO THE SOUTHERNMOST TIP OF SOUTH AMERICA.
"THEN THE 1800s USHERED IN AN ERA OF REVOLUTION. INSPIRED BY THE AMERICAN WAR OF INDEPENDENCE, THE HAITIAN REVOLUTION, AND ENLIGHTENMENT PHILOSOPHIES, LATIN AMERICAN INDEPENDENCE MOVEMENTS POPPED UP ALL OVER THE SO-CALLED NEW WORLD."
BY THE MID-1800s, MANY OF THE EUROPEAN NATIONS OCCUPYING THE AMERICAS HAD BEEN DRIVEN AWAY, AND ALL BUT A FEW FORMER SPANISH COLONIES HAD WON THEIR INDEPENDENCE AND ABOLISHED SLAVERY.
UNFORTUNATELY, THE LEGACY OF COLONIALISM REMAINED.

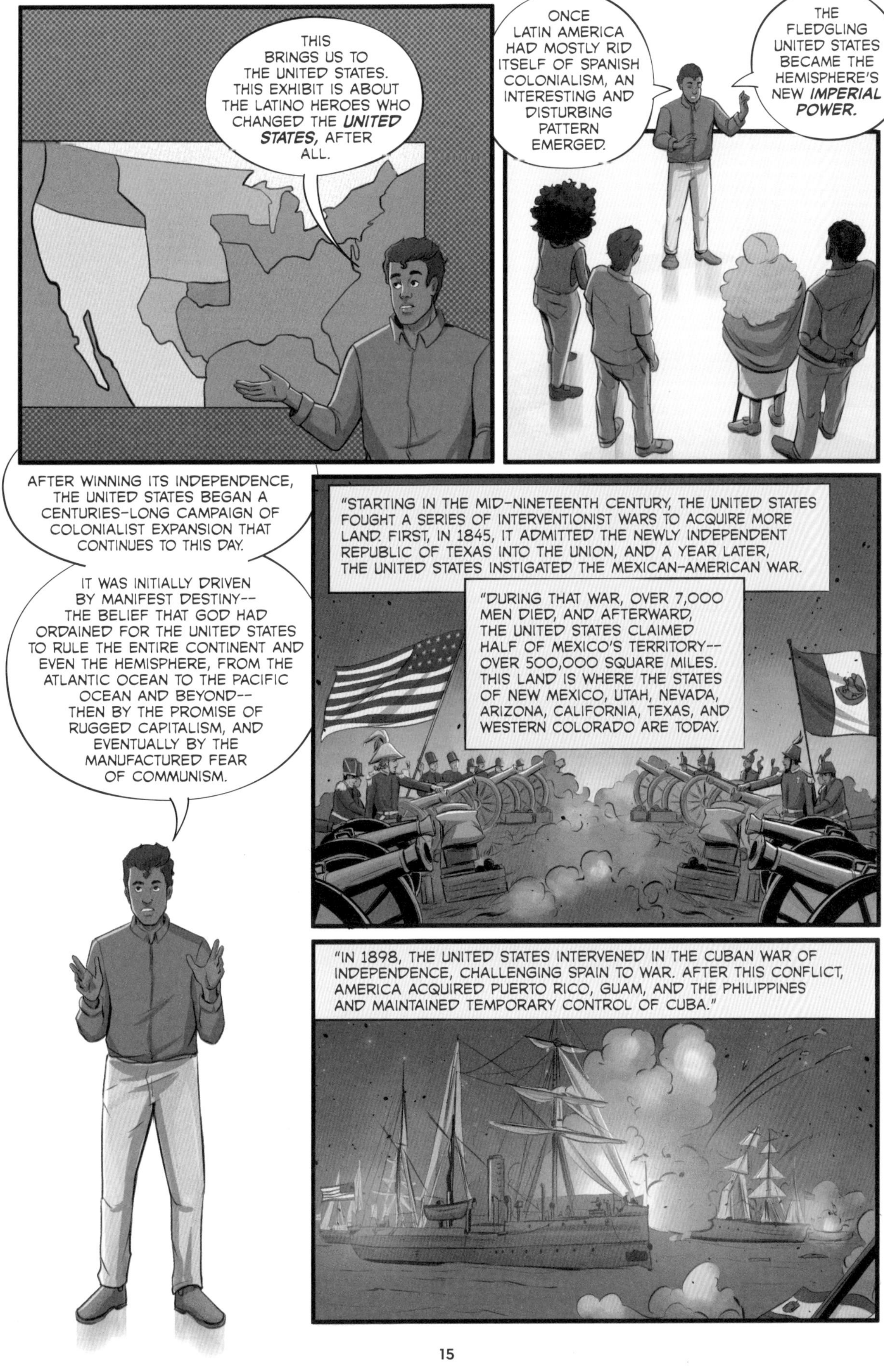
THIS BRINGS US TO THE UNITED STATES. THIS EXHIBIT IS ABOUT THE LATINO HEROES WHO CHANGED THE *UNITED STATES,* AFTER ALL.
ONCE LATIN AMERICA HAD MOSTLY RID ITSELF OF SPANISH COLONIALISM, AN INTERESTING AND DISTURBING PATTERN EMERGED.
THE FLEDGLING UNITED STATES BECAME THE HEMISPHERE'S NEW ***IMPERIAL POWER.***
AFTER WINNING ITS INDEPENDENCE, THE UNITED STATES BEGAN A CENTURIES-LONG CAMPAIGN OF COLONIALIST EXPANSION THAT CONTINUES TO THIS DAY.
IT WAS INITIALLY DRIVEN BY MANIFEST DESTINY-- THE BELIEF THAT GOD HAD ORDAINED FOR THE UNITED STATES TO RULE THE ENTIRE CONTINENT AND EVEN THE HEMISPHERE, FROM THE ATLANTIC OCEAN TO THE PACIFIC OCEAN AND BEYOND-- THEN BY THE PROMISE OF RUGGED CAPITALISM, AND EVENTUALLY BY THE MANUFACTURED FEAR OF COMMUNISM.
"STARTING IN THE MID-NINETEENTH CENTURY, THE UNITED STATES FOUGHT A SERIES OF INTERVENTIONIST WARS TO ACQUIRE MORE LAND. FIRST, IN 1845, IT ADMITTED THE NEWLY INDEPENDENT REPUBLIC OF TEXAS INTO THE UNION, AND A YEAR LATER, THE UNITED STATES INSTIGATED THE MEXICAN-AMERICAN WAR.
"DURING THAT WAR, OVER 7,000 MEN DIED, AND AFTERWARD, THE UNITED STATES CLAIMED HALF OF MEXICO'S TERRITORY-- OVER 500,000 SQUARE MILES. THIS LAND IS WHERE THE STATES OF NEW MEXICO, UTAH, NEVADA, ARIZONA, CALIFORNIA, TEXAS, AND WESTERN COLORADO ARE TODAY.
"IN 1898, THE UNITED STATES INTERVENED IN THE CUBAN WAR OF INDEPENDENCE, CHALLENGING SPAIN TO WAR. AFTER THIS CONFLICT, AMERICA ACQUIRED PUERTO RICO, GUAM, AND THE PHILIPPINES AND MAINTAINED TEMPORARY CONTROL OF CUBA."

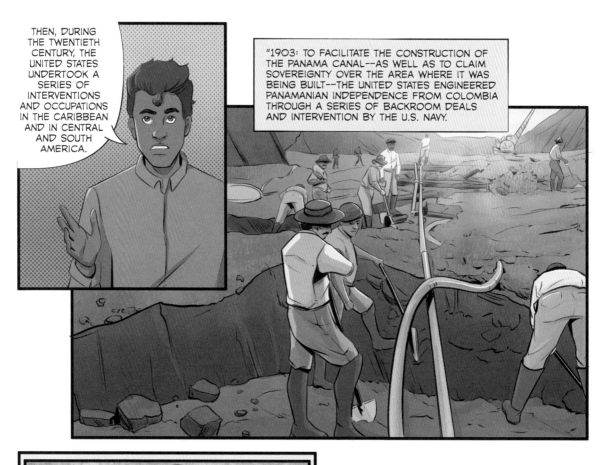

THEN, DURING THE TWENTIETH CENTURY, THE UNITED STATES UNDERTOOK A SERIES OF INTERVENTIONS AND OCCUPATIONS IN THE CARIBBEAN AND IN CENTRAL AND SOUTH AMERICA.

"1903: TO FACILITATE THE CONSTRUCTION OF THE PANAMA CANAL--AS WELL AS TO CLAIM SOVEREIGNTY OVER THE AREA WHERE IT WAS BEING BUILT--THE UNITED STATES ENGINEERED PANAMANIAN INDEPENDENCE FROM COLOMBIA THROUGH A SERIES OF BACKROOM DEALS AND INTERVENTION BY THE U.S. NAVY.

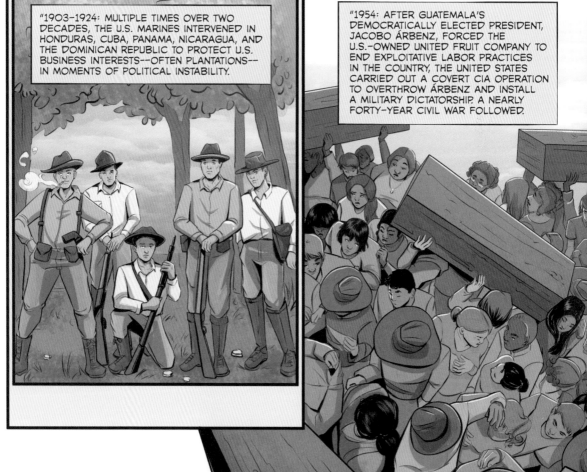

"1903-1924: MULTIPLE TIMES OVER TWO DECADES, THE U.S. MARINES INTERVENED IN HONDURAS, CUBA, PANAMA, NICARAGUA, AND THE DOMINICAN REPUBLIC TO PROTECT U.S. BUSINESS INTERESTS--OFTEN PLANTATIONS-- IN MOMENTS OF POLITICAL INSTABILITY.

"1954: AFTER GUATEMALA'S DEMOCRATICALLY ELECTED PRESIDENT, JACOBO ÁRBENZ, FORCED THE U.S.-OWNED UNITED FRUIT COMPANY TO END EXPLOITATIVE LABOR PRACTICES IN THE COUNTRY, THE UNITED STATES CARRIED OUT A COVERT CIA OPERATION TO OVERTHROW ÁRBENZ AND INSTALL A MILITARY DICTATORSHIP. A NEARLY FORTY-YEAR CIVIL WAR FOLLOWED.

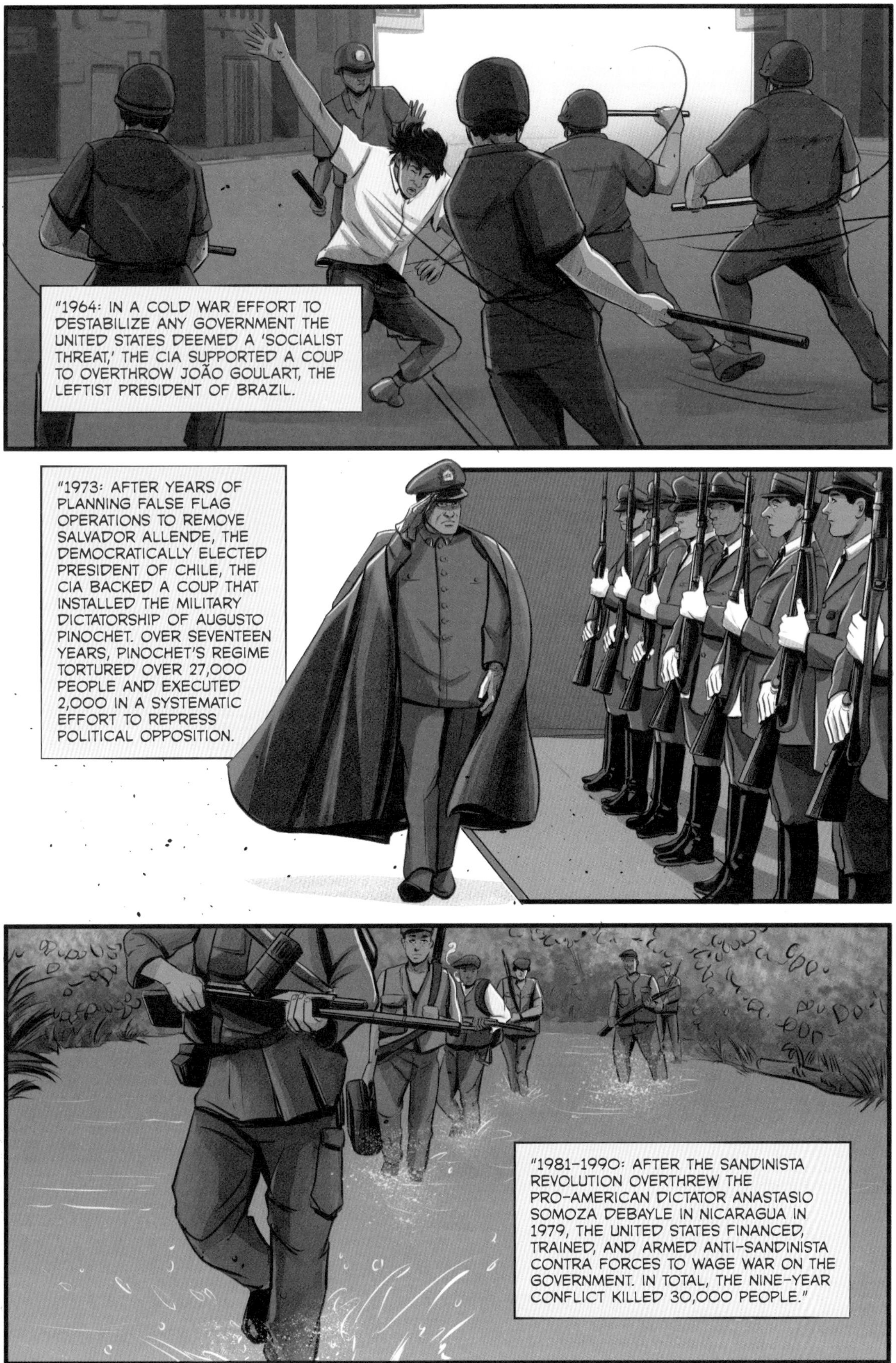
"1964: IN A COLD WAR EFFORT TO DESTABILIZE ANY GOVERNMENT THE UNITED STATES DEEMED A 'SOCIALIST THREAT,' THE CIA SUPPORTED A COUP TO OVERTHROW JOÃO GOULART, THE LEFTIST PRESIDENT OF BRAZIL.
"1973: AFTER YEARS OF PLANNING FALSE FLAG OPERATIONS TO REMOVE SALVADOR ALLENDE, THE DEMOCRATICALLY ELECTED PRESIDENT OF CHILE, THE CIA BACKED A COUP THAT INSTALLED THE MILITARY DICTATORSHIP OF AUGUSTO PINOCHET. OVER SEVENTEEN YEARS, PINOCHET'S REGIME TORTURED OVER 27,000 PEOPLE AND EXECUTED 2,000 IN A SYSTEMATIC EFFORT TO REPRESS POLITICAL OPPOSITION.
"1981–1990: AFTER THE SANDINISTA REVOLUTION OVERTHREW THE PRO-AMERICAN DICTATOR ANASTASIO SOMOZA DEBAYLE IN NICARAGUA IN 1979, THE UNITED STATES FINANCED, TRAINED, AND ARMED ANTI-SANDINISTA CONTRA FORCES TO WAGE WAR ON THE GOVERNMENT. IN TOTAL, THE NINE-YEAR CONFLICT KILLED 30,000 PEOPLE."

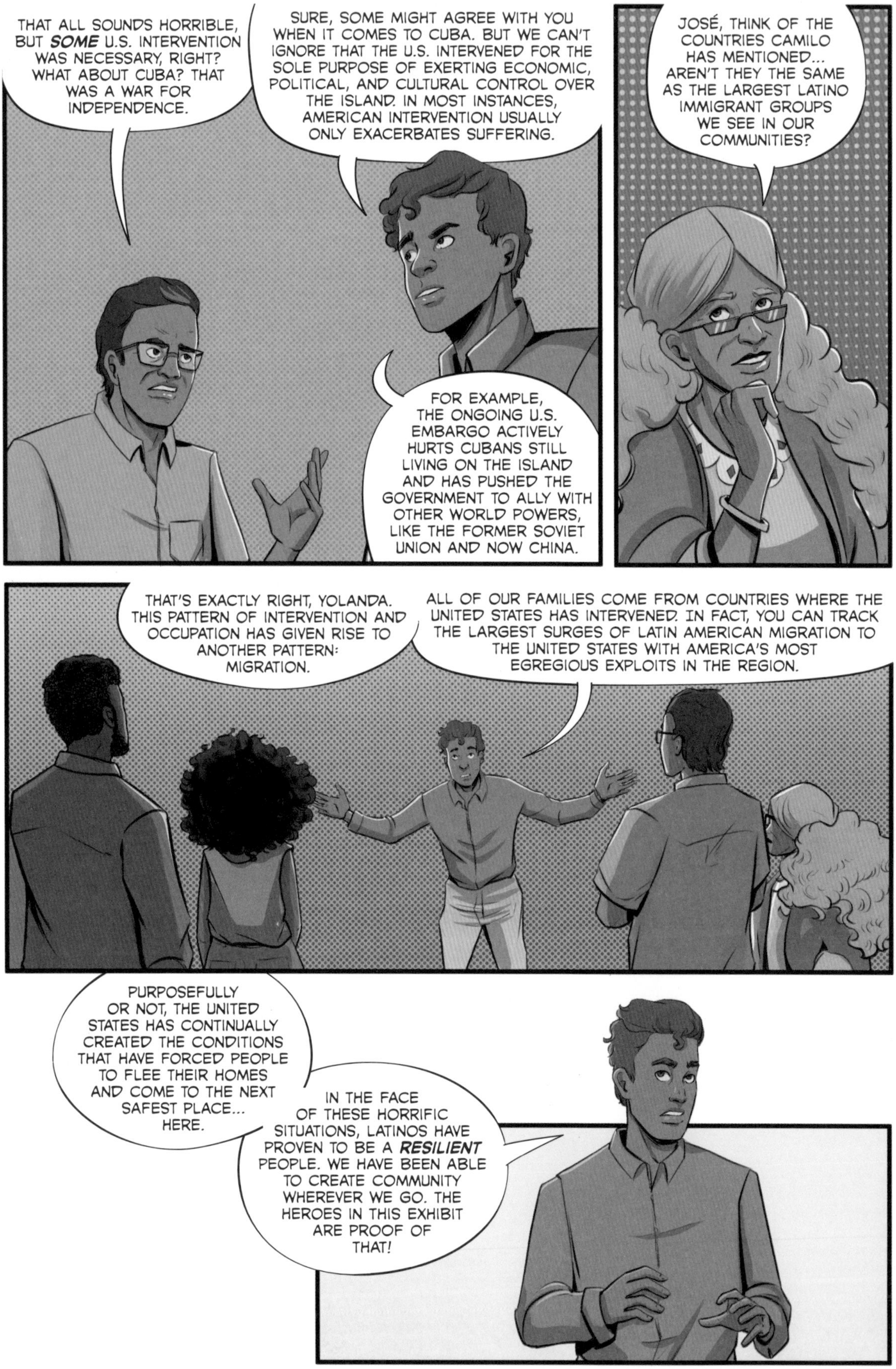
THAT ALL SOUNDS HORRIBLE, BUT *SOME* U.S. INTERVENTION WAS NECESSARY, RIGHT? WHAT ABOUT CUBA? THAT WAS A WAR FOR INDEPENDENCE.
SURE, SOME MIGHT AGREE WITH YOU WHEN IT COMES TO CUBA. BUT WE CAN'T IGNORE THAT THE U.S. INTERVENED FOR THE SOLE PURPOSE OF EXERTING ECONOMIC, POLITICAL, AND CULTURAL CONTROL OVER THE ISLAND. IN MOST INSTANCES, AMERICAN INTERVENTION USUALLY ONLY EXACERBATES SUFFERING.
FOR EXAMPLE, THE ONGOING U.S. EMBARGO ACTIVELY HURTS CUBANS STILL LIVING ON THE ISLAND AND HAS PUSHED THE GOVERNMENT TO ALLY WITH OTHER WORLD POWERS, LIKE THE FORMER SOVIET UNION AND NOW CHINA.
JOSÉ, THINK OF THE COUNTRIES CAMILO HAS MENTIONED... AREN'T THEY THE SAME AS THE LARGEST LATINO IMMIGRANT GROUPS WE SEE IN OUR COMMUNITIES?
THAT'S EXACTLY RIGHT, YOLANDA. THIS PATTERN OF INTERVENTION AND OCCUPATION HAS GIVEN RISE TO ANOTHER PATTERN: MIGRATION.
ALL OF OUR FAMILIES COME FROM COUNTRIES WHERE THE UNITED STATES HAS INTERVENED. IN FACT, YOU CAN TRACK THE LARGEST SURGES OF LATIN AMERICAN MIGRATION TO THE UNITED STATES WITH AMERICA'S MOST EGREGIOUS EXPLOITS IN THE REGION.
PURPOSEFULLY OR NOT, THE UNITED STATES HAS CONTINUALLY CREATED THE CONDITIONS THAT HAVE FORCED PEOPLE TO FLEE THEIR HOMES AND COME TO THE NEXT SAFEST PLACE... HERE.
IN THE FACE OF THESE HORRIFIC SITUATIONS, LATINOS HAVE PROVEN TO BE A *RESILIENT* PEOPLE. WE HAVE BEEN ABLE TO CREATE COMMUNITY WHEREVER WE GO. THE HEROES IN THIS EXHIBIT ARE PROOF OF THAT!

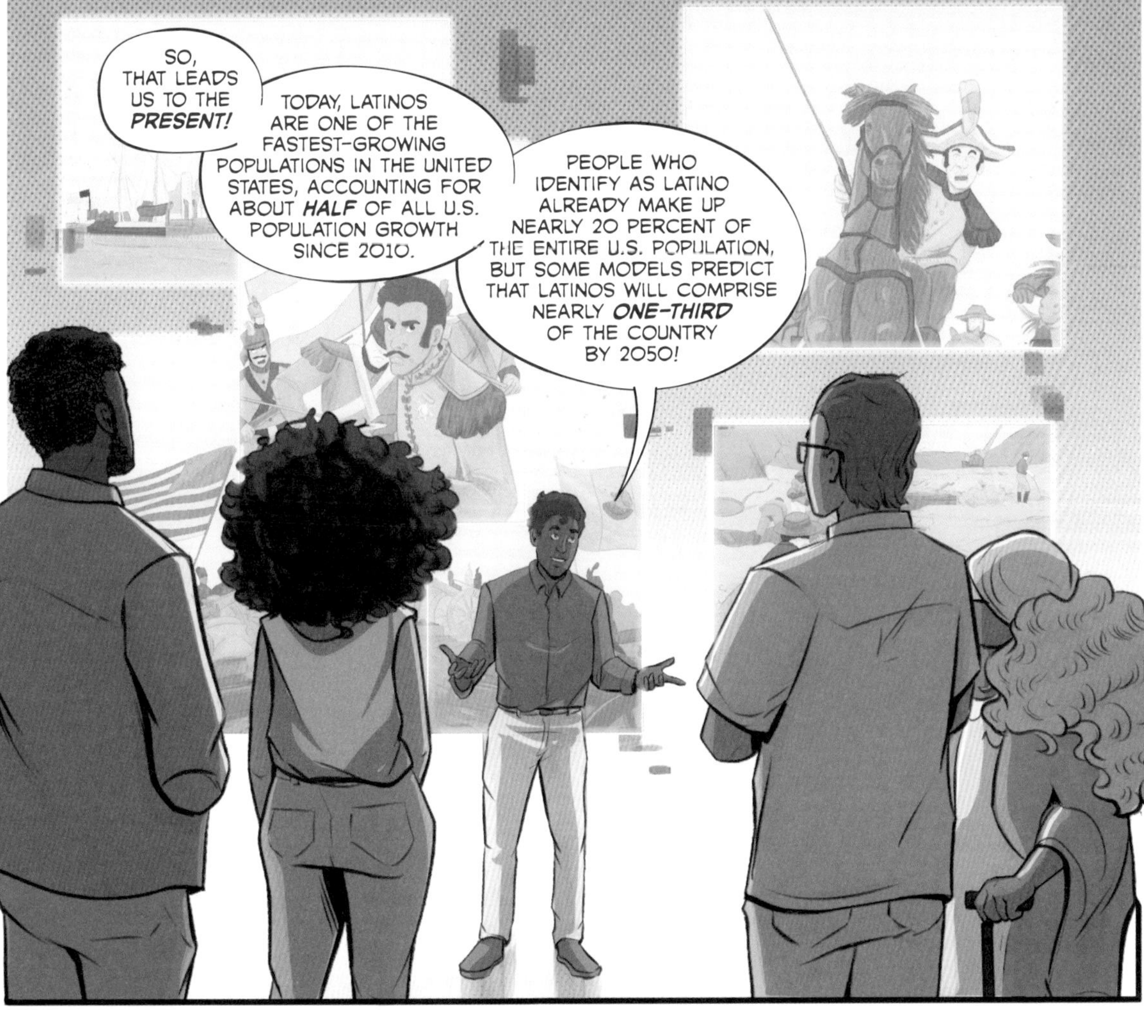
SO, THAT LEADS US TO THE *PRESENT!*
TODAY, LATINOS ARE ONE OF THE FASTEST-GROWING POPULATIONS IN THE UNITED STATES, ACCOUNTING FOR ABOUT *HALF* OF ALL U.S. POPULATION GROWTH SINCE 2010.
PEOPLE WHO IDENTIFY AS LATINO ALREADY MAKE UP NEARLY 20 PERCENT OF THE ENTIRE U.S. POPULATION, BUT SOME MODELS PREDICT THAT LATINOS WILL COMPRISE NEARLY *ONE-THIRD* OF THE COUNTRY BY 2050!

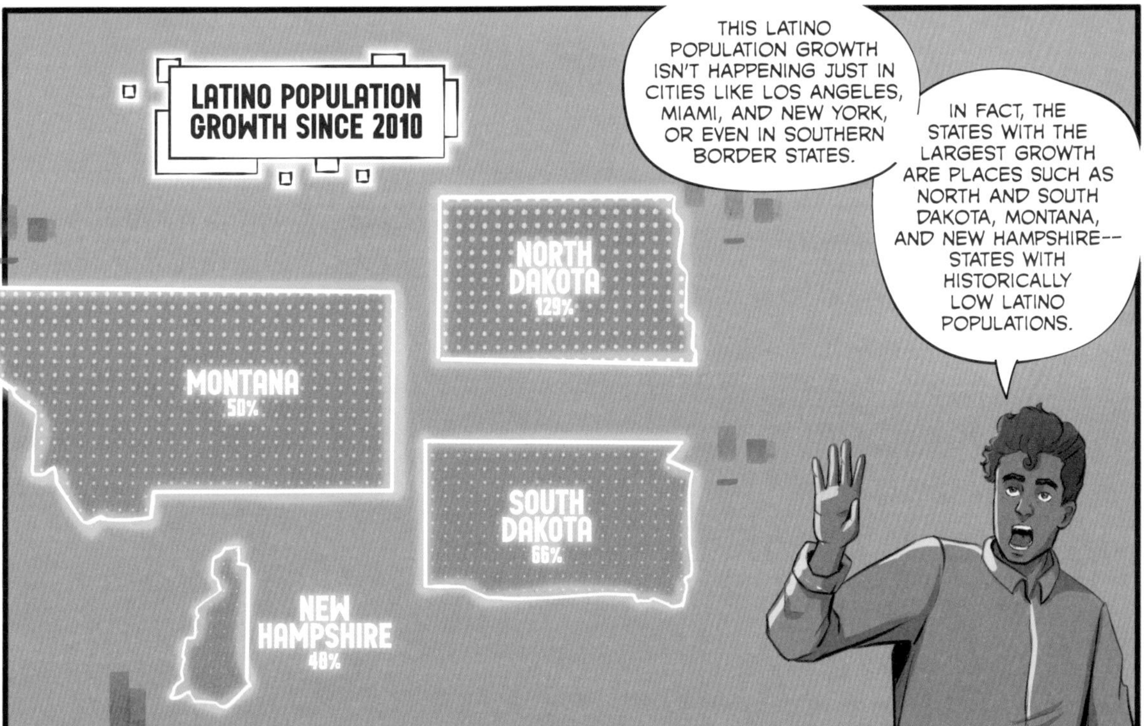
LATINO POPULATION GROWTH SINCE 2010
THIS LATINO POPULATION GROWTH ISN'T HAPPENING JUST IN CITIES LIKE LOS ANGELES, MIAMI, AND NEW YORK, OR EVEN IN SOUTHERN BORDER STATES.
IN FACT, THE STATES WITH THE LARGEST GROWTH ARE PLACES SUCH AS NORTH AND SOUTH DAKOTA, MONTANA, AND NEW HAMPSHIRE-- STATES WITH HISTORICALLY LOW LATINO POPULATIONS.
NORTH DAKOTA 129%
MONTANA 50%
SOUTH DAKOTA 66%
NEW HAMPSHIRE 40%

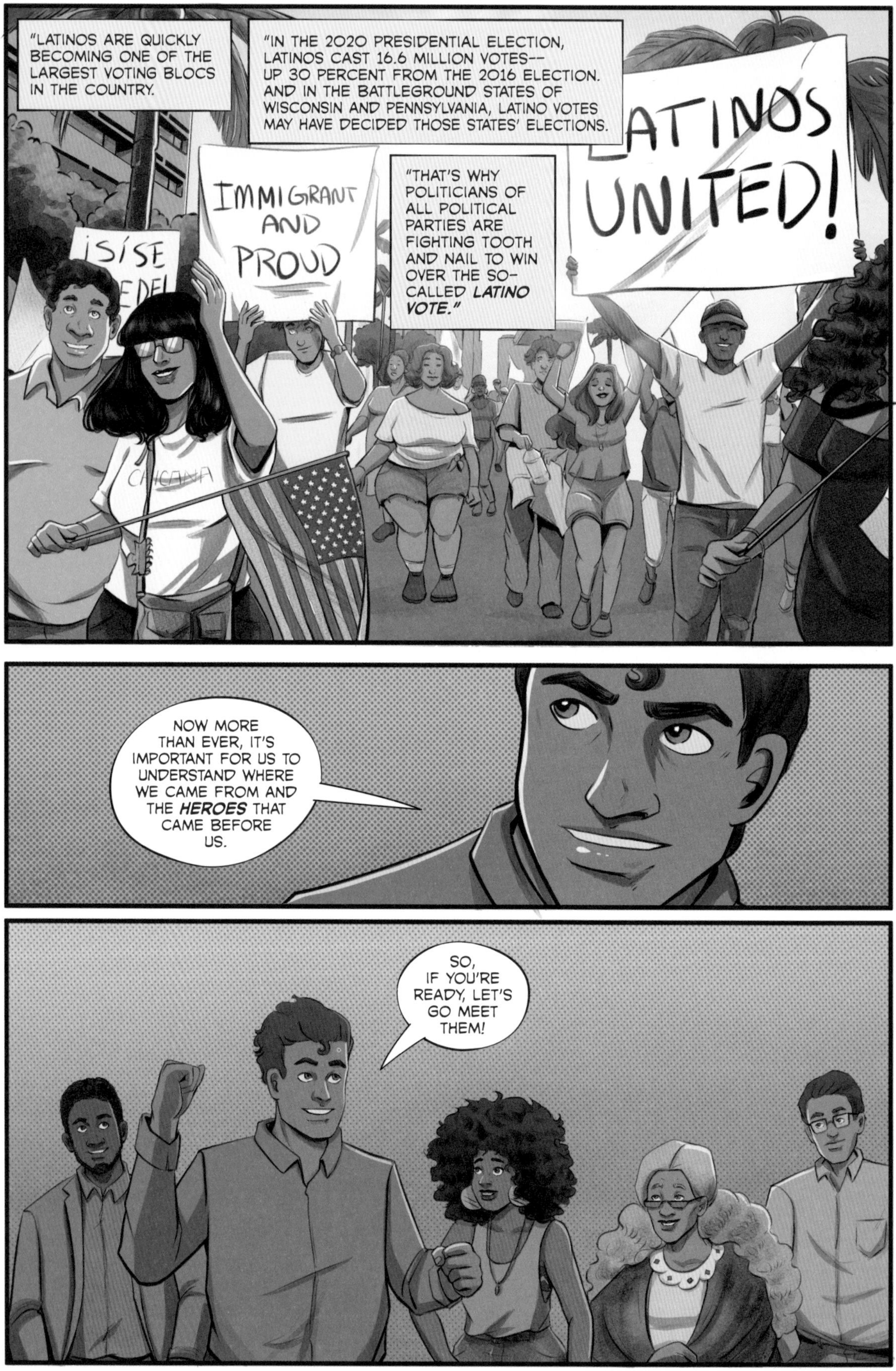
"LATINOS ARE QUICKLY BECOMING ONE OF THE LARGEST VOTING BLOCS IN THE COUNTRY.
"IN THE 2020 PRESIDENTIAL ELECTION, LATINOS CAST 16.6 MILLION VOTES-- UP 30 PERCENT FROM THE 2016 ELECTION. AND IN THE BATTLEGROUND STATES OF WISCONSIN AND PENNSYLVANIA, LATINO VOTES MAY HAVE DECIDED THOSE STATES' ELECTIONS.
LATINOS UNITED!
IMMIGRANT AND PROUD
"THAT'S WHY POLITICIANS OF ALL POLITICAL PARTIES ARE FIGHTING TOOTH AND NAIL TO WIN OVER THE SO-CALLED *LATINO VOTE.*"
NOW MORE THAN EVER, IT'S IMPORTANT FOR US TO UNDERSTAND WHERE WE CAME FROM AND THE ***HEROES*** THAT CAME BEFORE US.
SO, IF YOU'RE READY, LET'S GO MEET THEM!

# CHAPTER 2: THE LATINO UNION SOLDIERS OF THE CIVIL WAR

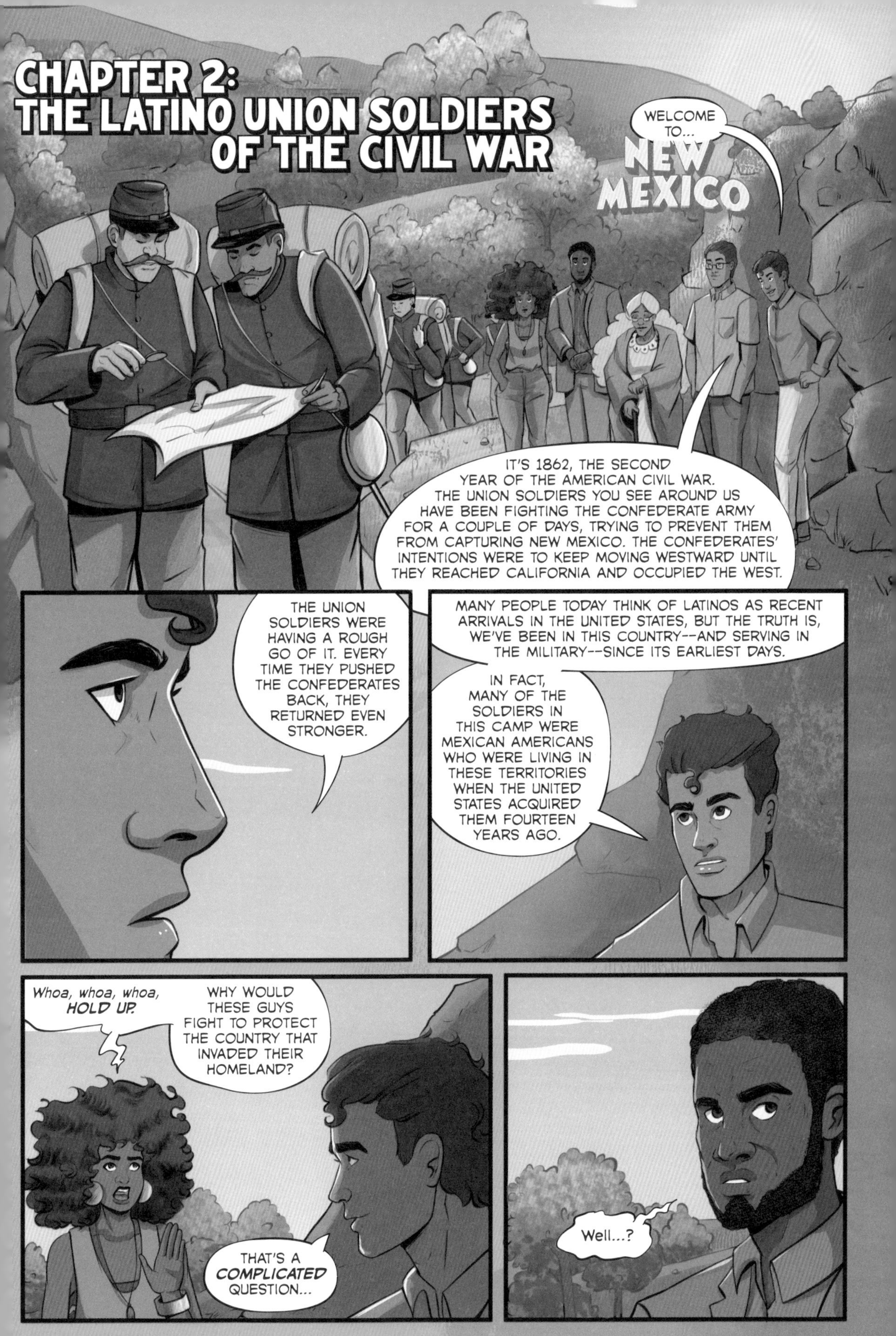

WELCOME TO...
NEW MEXICO
IT'S 1862, THE SECOND YEAR OF THE AMERICAN CIVIL WAR. THE UNION SOLDIERS YOU SEE AROUND US HAVE BEEN FIGHTING THE CONFEDERATE ARMY FOR A COUPLE OF DAYS, TRYING TO PREVENT THEM FROM CAPTURING NEW MEXICO. THE CONFEDERATES' INTENTIONS WERE TO KEEP MOVING WESTWARD UNTIL THEY REACHED CALIFORNIA AND OCCUPIED THE WEST.
THE UNION SOLDIERS WERE HAVING A ROUGH GO OF IT. EVERY TIME THEY PUSHED THE CONFEDERATES BACK, THEY RETURNED EVEN STRONGER.
MANY PEOPLE TODAY THINK OF LATINOS AS RECENT ARRIVALS IN THE UNITED STATES, BUT THE TRUTH IS, WE'VE BEEN IN THIS COUNTRY--AND SERVING IN THE MILITARY--SINCE ITS EARLIEST DAYS.
IN FACT, MANY OF THE SOLDIERS IN THIS CAMP WERE MEXICAN AMERICANS WHO WERE LIVING IN THESE TERRITORIES WHEN THE UNITED STATES ACQUIRED THEM FOURTEEN YEARS AGO.
*Whoa, whoa, whoa,* ***HOLD UP.***
WHY WOULD THESE GUYS FIGHT TO PROTECT THE COUNTRY THAT INVADED THEIR HOMELAND?
THAT'S A ***COMPLICATED*** QUESTION...
Well...?

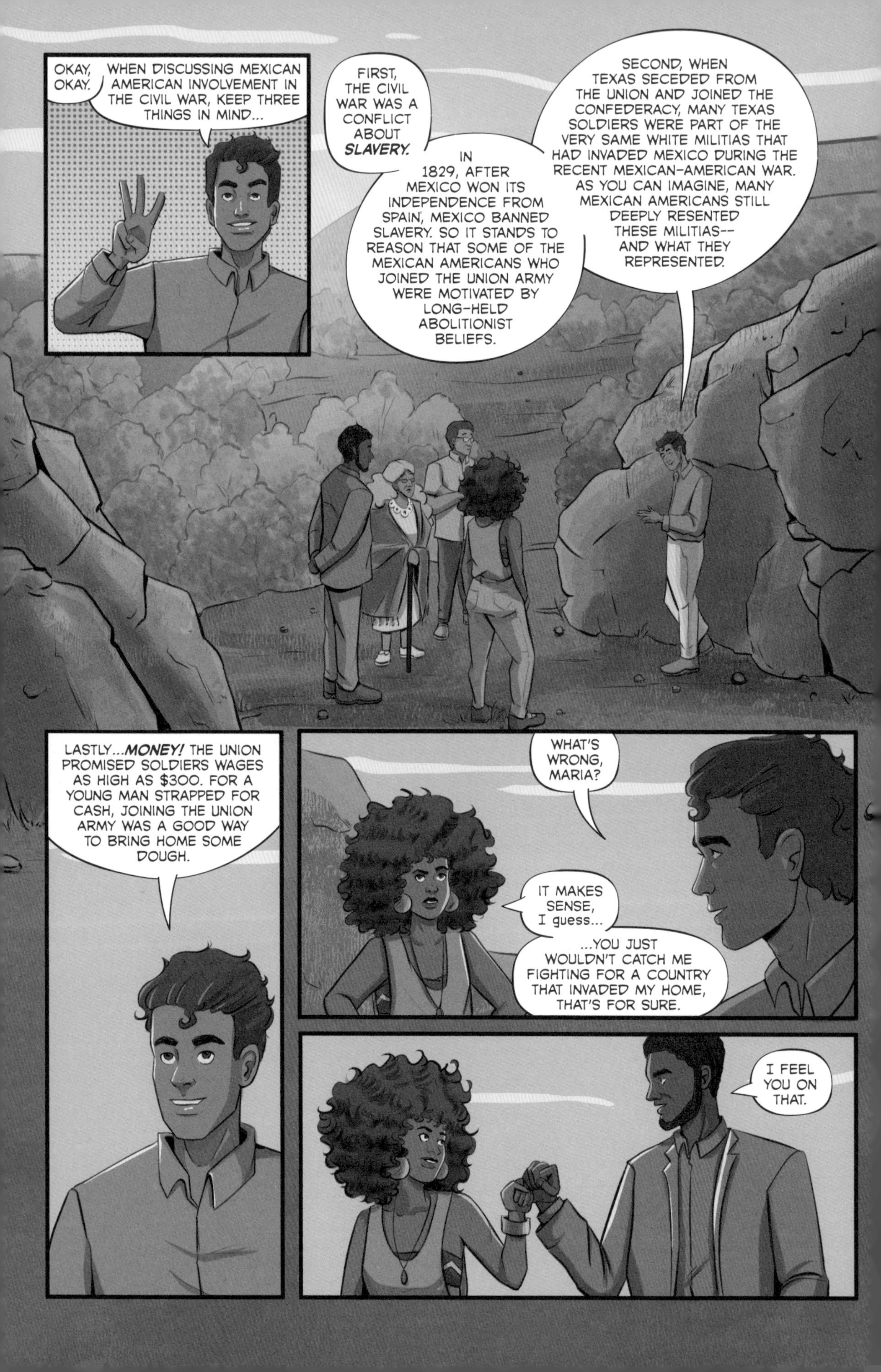
OKAY, OKAY.
WHEN DISCUSSING MEXICAN AMERICAN INVOLVEMENT IN THE CIVIL WAR, KEEP THREE THINGS IN MIND...
FIRST, THE CIVIL WAR WAS A CONFLICT ABOUT ***SLAVERY.***
IN 1829, AFTER MEXICO WON ITS INDEPENDENCE FROM SPAIN, MEXICO BANNED SLAVERY. SO IT STANDS TO REASON THAT SOME OF THE MEXICAN AMERICANS WHO JOINED THE UNION ARMY WERE MOTIVATED BY LONG-HELD ABOLITIONIST BELIEFS.
SECOND, WHEN TEXAS SECEDED FROM THE UNION AND JOINED THE CONFEDERACY, MANY TEXAS SOLDIERS WERE PART OF THE VERY SAME WHITE MILITIAS THAT HAD INVADED MEXICO DURING THE RECENT MEXICAN-AMERICAN WAR. AS YOU CAN IMAGINE, MANY MEXICAN AMERICANS STILL DEEPLY RESENTED THESE MILITIAS-- AND WHAT THEY REPRESENTED.
LASTLY...***MONEY!*** THE UNION PROMISED SOLDIERS WAGES AS HIGH AS $300. FOR A YOUNG MAN STRAPPED FOR CASH, JOINING THE UNION ARMY WAS A GOOD WAY TO BRING HOME SOME DOUGH.
WHAT'S WRONG, MARIA?
IT MAKES SENSE, I guess...
...YOU JUST WOULDN'T CATCH ME FIGHTING FOR A COUNTRY THAT INVADED MY HOME, THAT'S FOR SURE.
I FEEL YOU ON THAT.

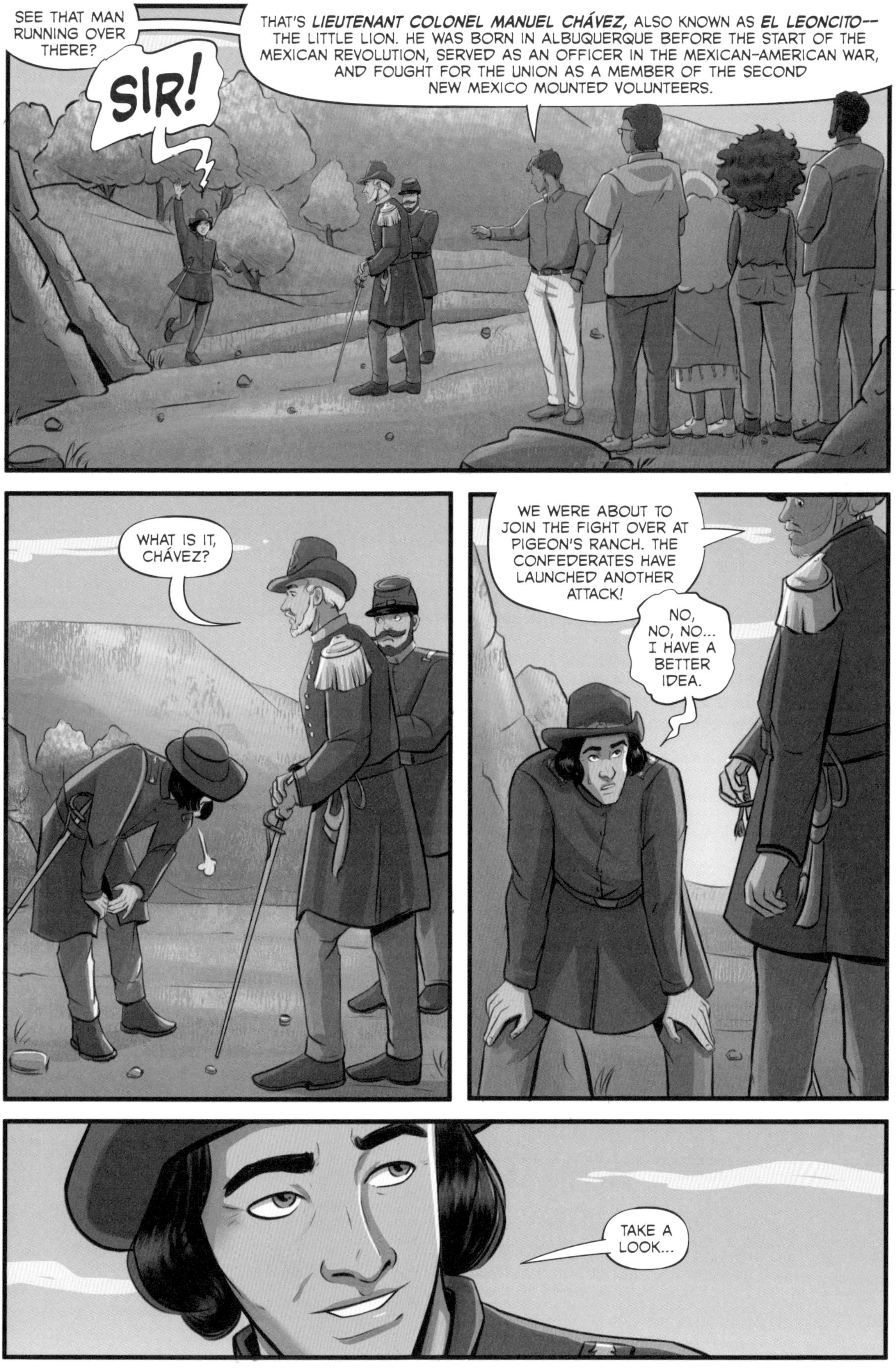
SEE THAT MAN RUNNING OVER THERE?
THAT'S *LIEUTENANT COLONEL MANUEL CHÁVEZ,* ALSO KNOWN AS *EL LEONCITO*-- THE LITTLE LION. HE WAS BORN IN ALBUQUERQUE BEFORE THE START OF THE MEXICAN REVOLUTION, SERVED AS AN OFFICER IN THE MEXICAN-AMERICAN WAR, AND FOUGHT FOR THE UNION AS A MEMBER OF THE SECOND NEW MEXICO MOUNTED VOLUNTEERS.
SIR!
WHAT IS IT, CHÁVEZ?
WE WERE ABOUT TO JOIN THE FIGHT OVER AT PIGEON'S RANCH. THE CONFEDERATES HAVE LAUNCHED ANOTHER ATTACK!
NO, NO, NO... I HAVE A BETTER IDEA.
TAKE A LOOK...

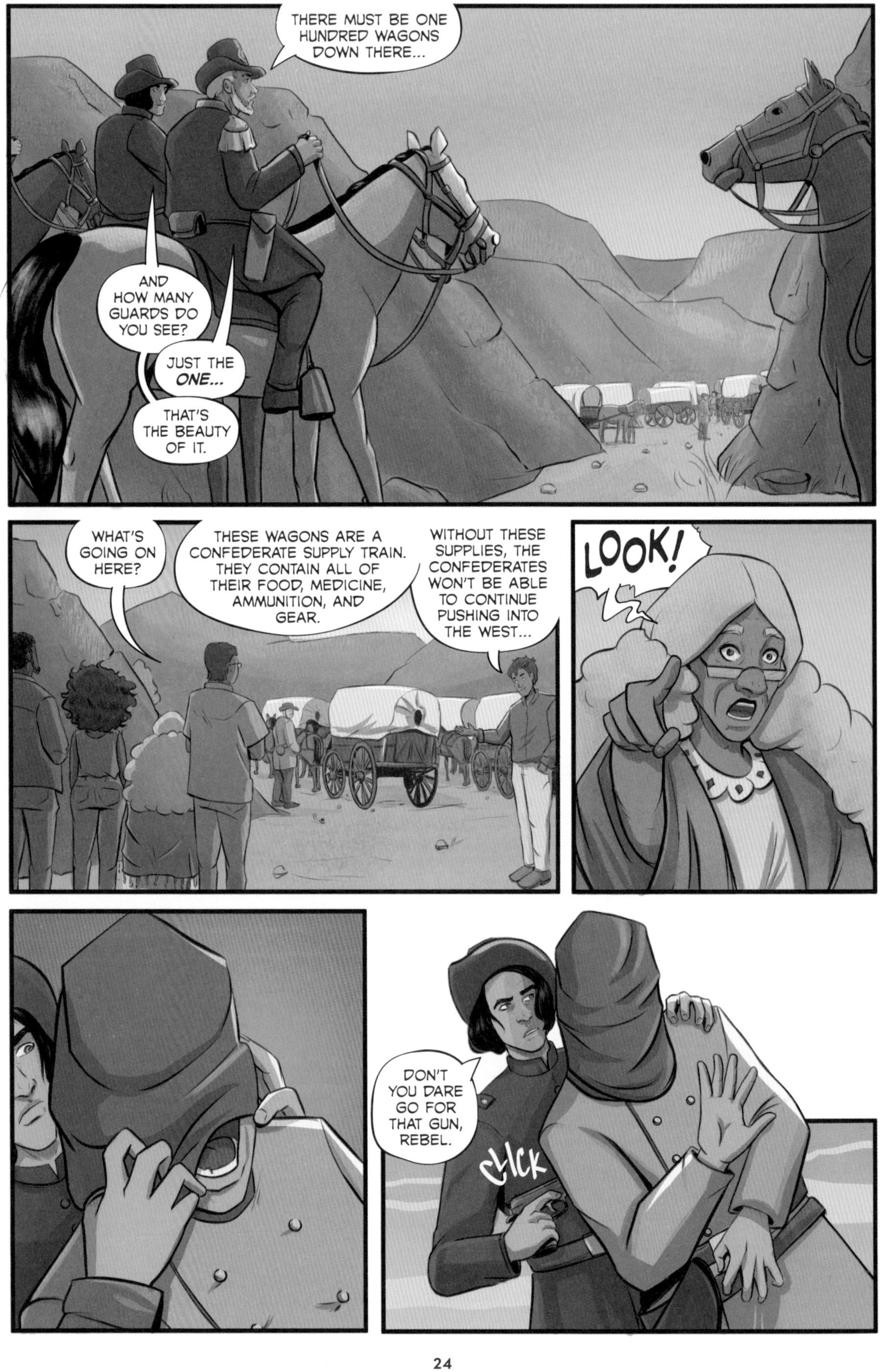
THERE MUST BE ONE HUNDRED WAGONS DOWN THERE...
AND HOW MANY GUARDS DO YOU SEE?
JUST THE *ONE...*
THAT'S THE BEAUTY OF IT.
WHAT'S GOING ON HERE?
THESE WAGONS ARE A CONFEDERATE SUPPLY TRAIN. THEY CONTAIN ALL OF THEIR FOOD, MEDICINE, AMMUNITION, AND GEAR.
WITHOUT THESE SUPPLIES, THE CONFEDERATES WON'T BE ABLE TO CONTINUE PUSHING INTO THE WEST...
LOOK!
DON'T YOU DARE GO FOR THAT GUN, REBEL.
CLICK

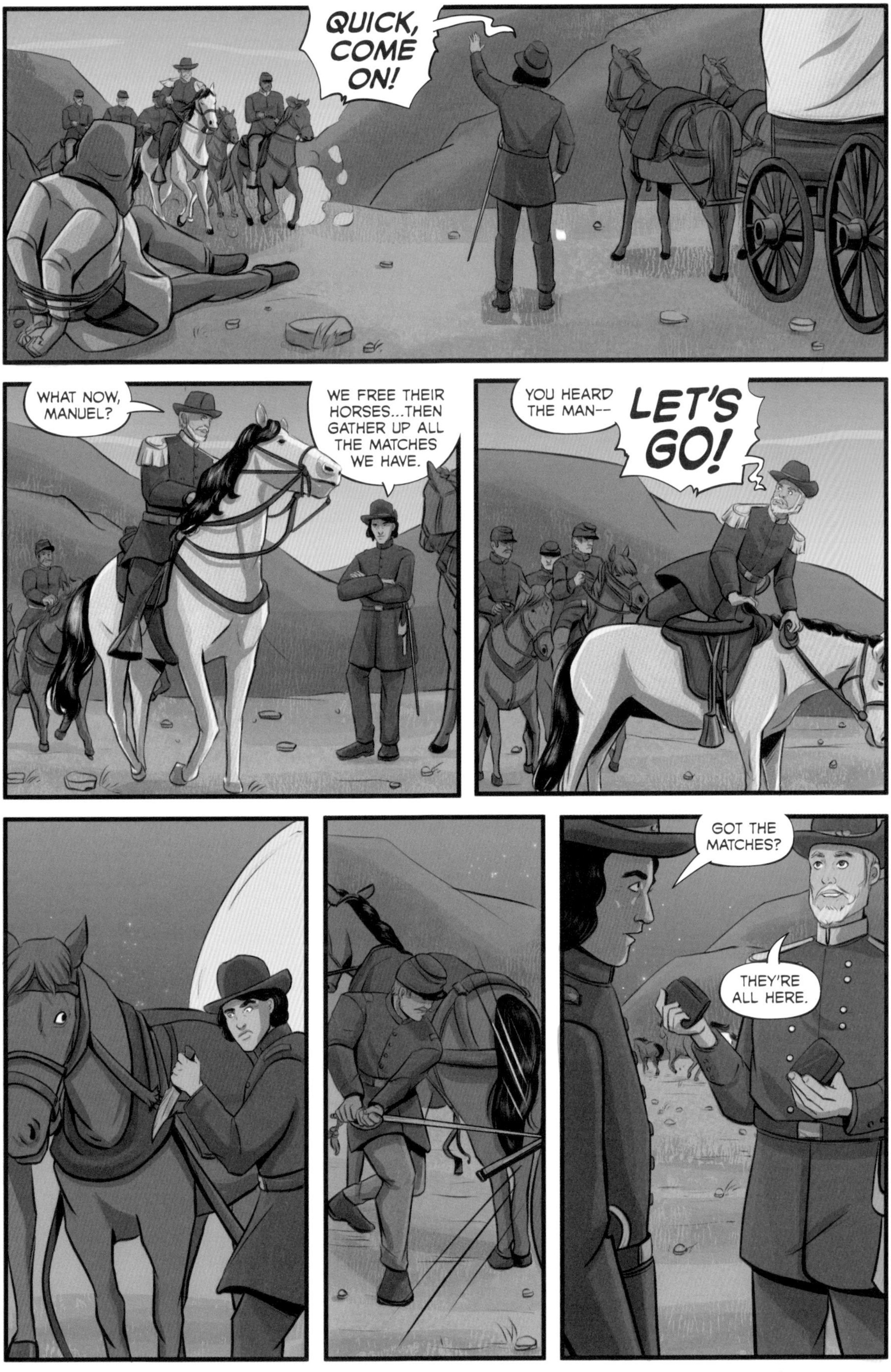
QUICK, COME ON!
WHAT NOW, MANUEL?
WE FREE THEIR HORSES...THEN GATHER UP ALL THE MATCHES WE HAVE.
YOU HEARD THE MAN--
LET'S GO!
GOT THE MATCHES?
THEY'RE ALL HERE.

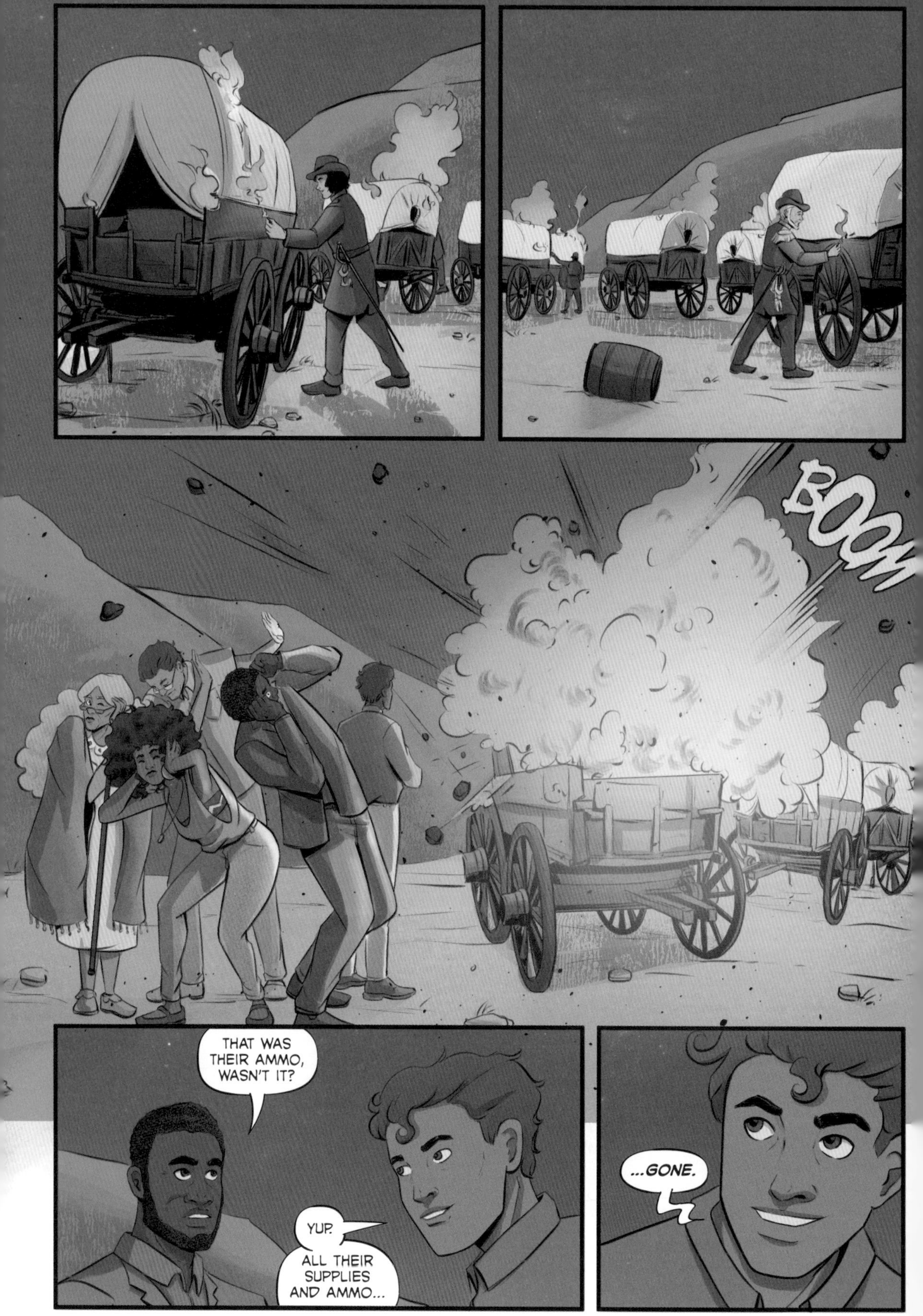
BOOM
THAT WAS THEIR AMMO, WASN'T IT?
YUP.
ALL THEIR SUPPLIES AND AMMO...
...GONE.

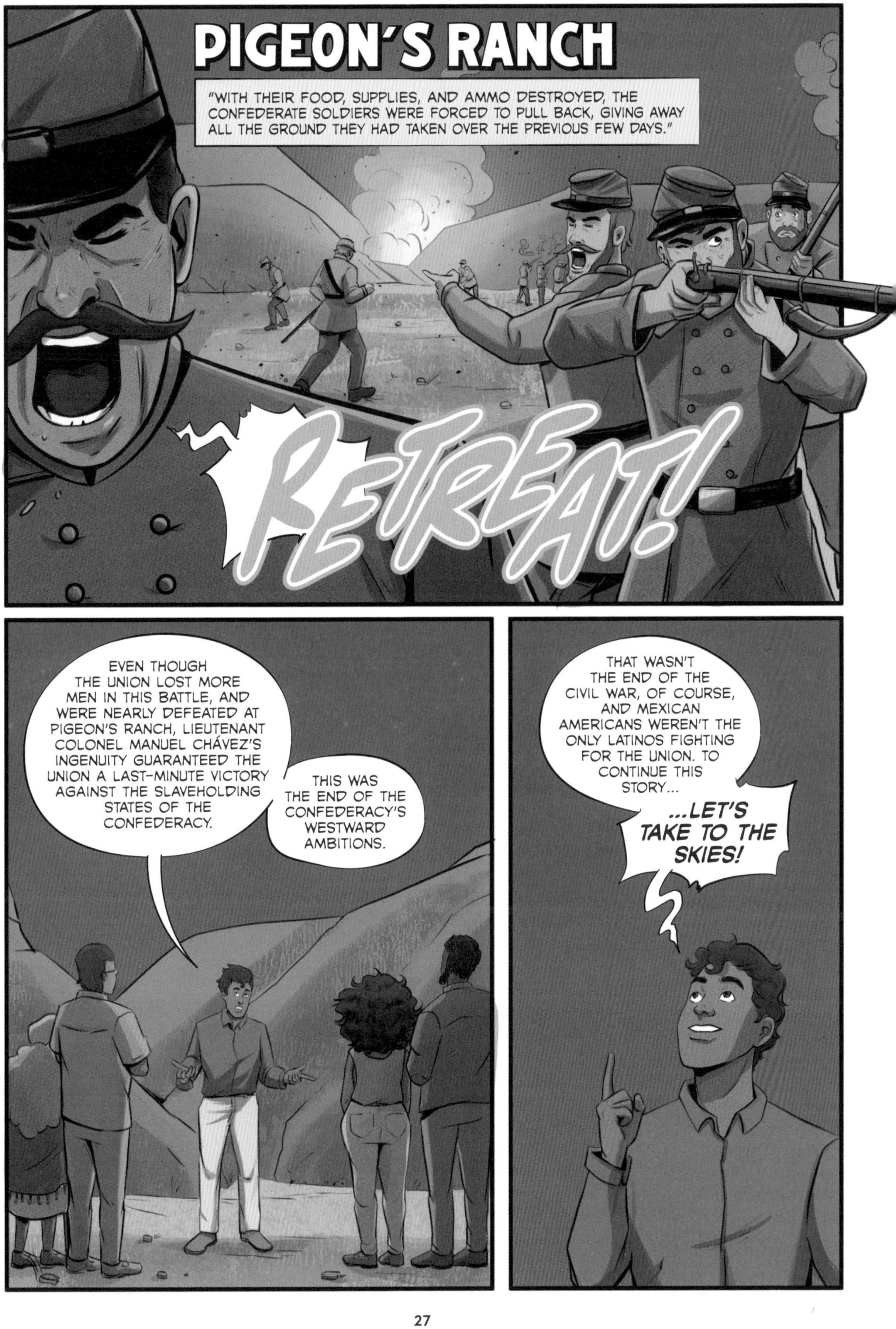
PIGEON'S RANCH
"WITH THEIR FOOD, SUPPLIES, AND AMMO DESTROYED, THE CONFEDERATE SOLDIERS WERE FORCED TO PULL BACK, GIVING AWAY ALL THE GROUND THEY HAD TAKEN OVER THE PREVIOUS FEW DAYS."
RETREAT!
EVEN THOUGH THE UNION LOST MORE MEN IN THIS BATTLE, AND WERE NEARLY DEFEATED AT PIGEON'S RANCH, LIEUTENANT COLONEL MANUEL CHÁVEZ'S INGENUITY GUARANTEED THE UNION A LAST-MINUTE VICTORY AGAINST THE SLAVEHOLDING STATES OF THE CONFEDERACY.
THIS WAS THE END OF THE CONFEDERACY'S WESTWARD AMBITIONS.
THAT WASN'T THE END OF THE CIVIL WAR, OF COURSE, AND MEXICAN AMERICANS WEREN'T THE ONLY LATINOS FIGHTING FOR THE UNION. TO CONTINUE THIS STORY...
...LET'S TAKE TO THE SKIES!

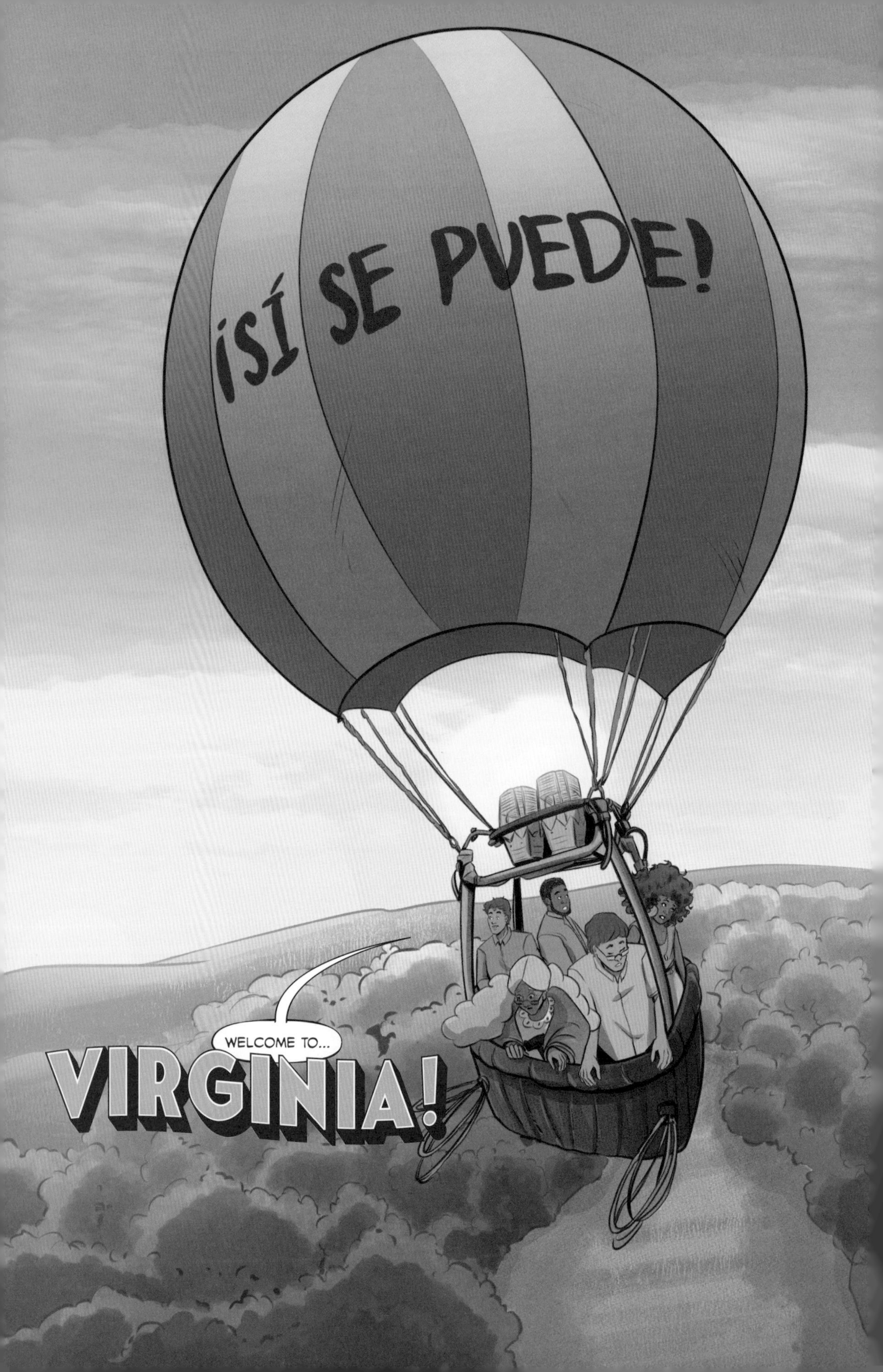
¡SÍ SE PUEDE!
WELCOME TO...
VIRGINIA!

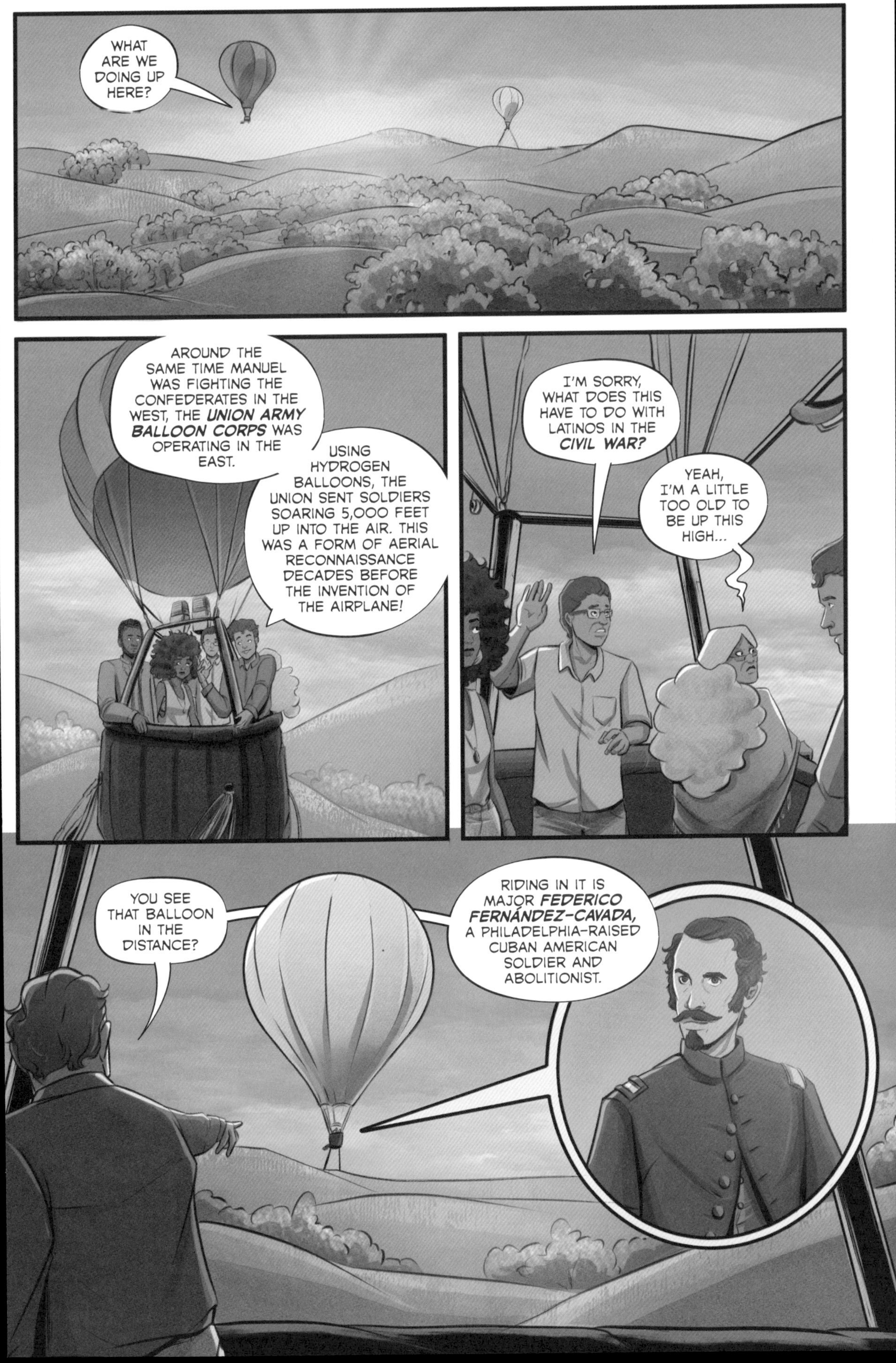
WHAT ARE WE DOING UP HERE?
AROUND THE SAME TIME MANUEL WAS FIGHTING THE CONFEDERATES IN THE WEST, THE UNION ARMY BALLOON CORPS WAS OPERATING IN THE EAST.
USING HYDROGEN BALLOONS, THE UNION SENT SOLDIERS SOARING 5,000 FEET UP INTO THE AIR. THIS WAS A FORM OF AERIAL RECONNAISSANCE DECADES BEFORE THE INVENTION OF THE AIRPLANE!
I'M SORRY, WHAT DOES THIS HAVE TO DO WITH LATINOS IN THE CIVIL WAR?
YEAH, I'M A LITTLE TOO OLD TO BE UP THIS HIGH...
YOU SEE THAT BALLOON IN THE DISTANCE?
RIDING IN IT IS MAJOR FEDERICO FERNÁNDEZ-CAVADA, A PHILADELPHIA-RAISED CUBAN AMERICAN SOLDIER AND ABOLITIONIST.

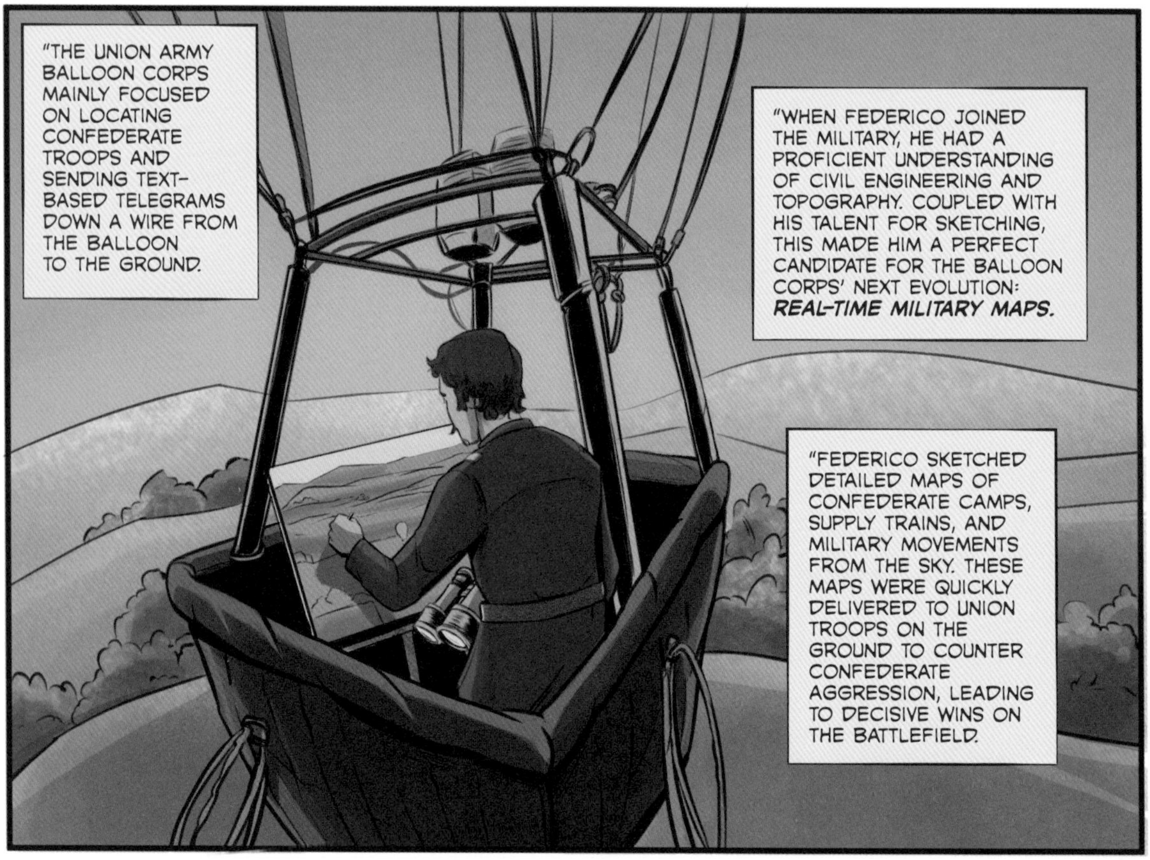
"THE UNION ARMY BALLOON CORPS MAINLY FOCUSED ON LOCATING CONFEDERATE TROOPS AND SENDING TEXT-BASED TELEGRAMS DOWN A WIRE FROM THE BALLOON TO THE GROUND.
"WHEN FEDERICO JOINED THE MILITARY, HE HAD A PROFICIENT UNDERSTANDING OF CIVIL ENGINEERING AND TOPOGRAPHY. COUPLED WITH HIS TALENT FOR SKETCHING, THIS MADE HIM A PERFECT CANDIDATE FOR THE BALLOON CORPS' NEXT EVOLUTION: ***REAL-TIME MILITARY MAPS.***
"FEDERICO SKETCHED DETAILED MAPS OF CONFEDERATE CAMPS, SUPPLY TRAINS, AND MILITARY MOVEMENTS FROM THE SKY. THESE MAPS WERE QUICKLY DELIVERED TO UNION TROOPS ON THE GROUND TO COUNTER CONFEDERATE AGGRESSION, LEADING TO DECISIVE WINS ON THE BATTLEFIELD.

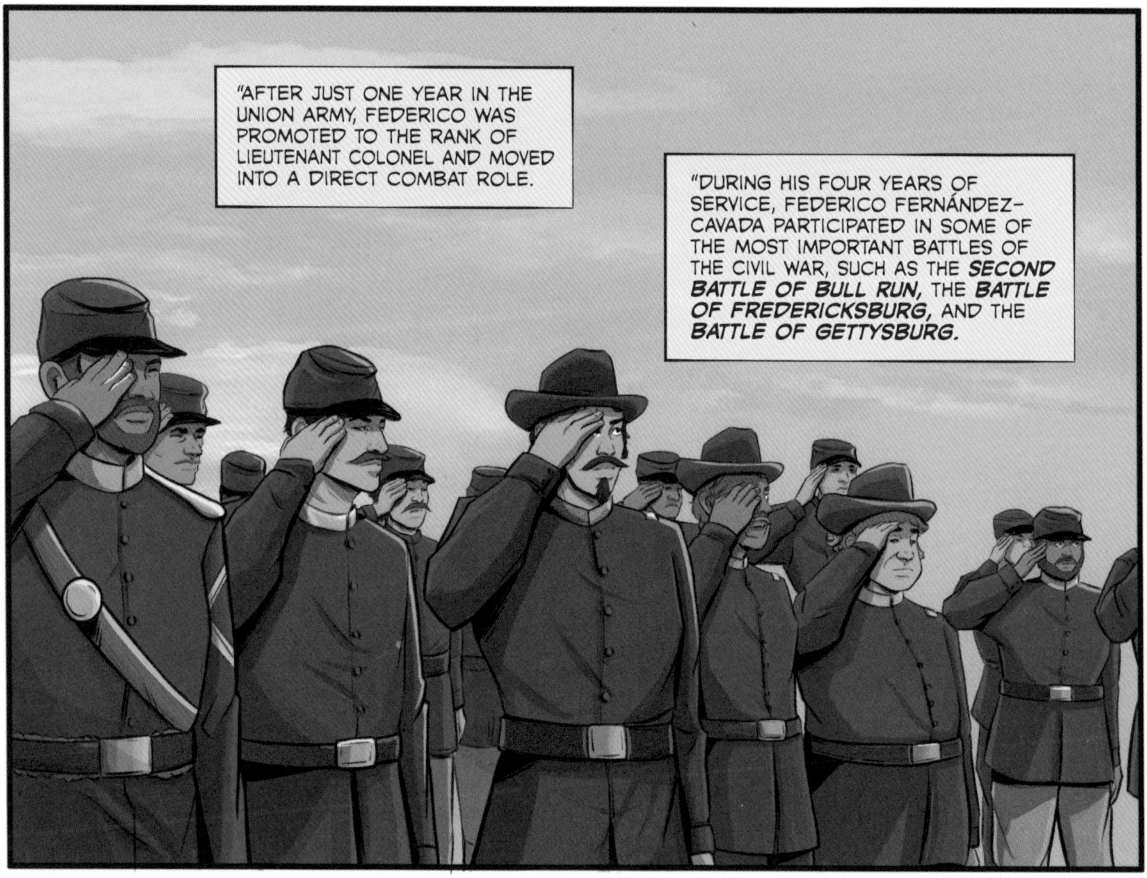
"AFTER JUST ONE YEAR IN THE UNION ARMY, FEDERICO WAS PROMOTED TO THE RANK OF LIEUTENANT COLONEL AND MOVED INTO A DIRECT COMBAT ROLE.
"DURING HIS FOUR YEARS OF SERVICE, FEDERICO FERNÁNDEZ-CAVADA PARTICIPATED IN SOME OF THE MOST IMPORTANT BATTLES OF THE CIVIL WAR, SUCH AS THE ***SECOND BATTLE OF BULL RUN,*** THE ***BATTLE OF FREDERICKSBURG,*** AND THE ***BATTLE OF GETTYSBURG.***

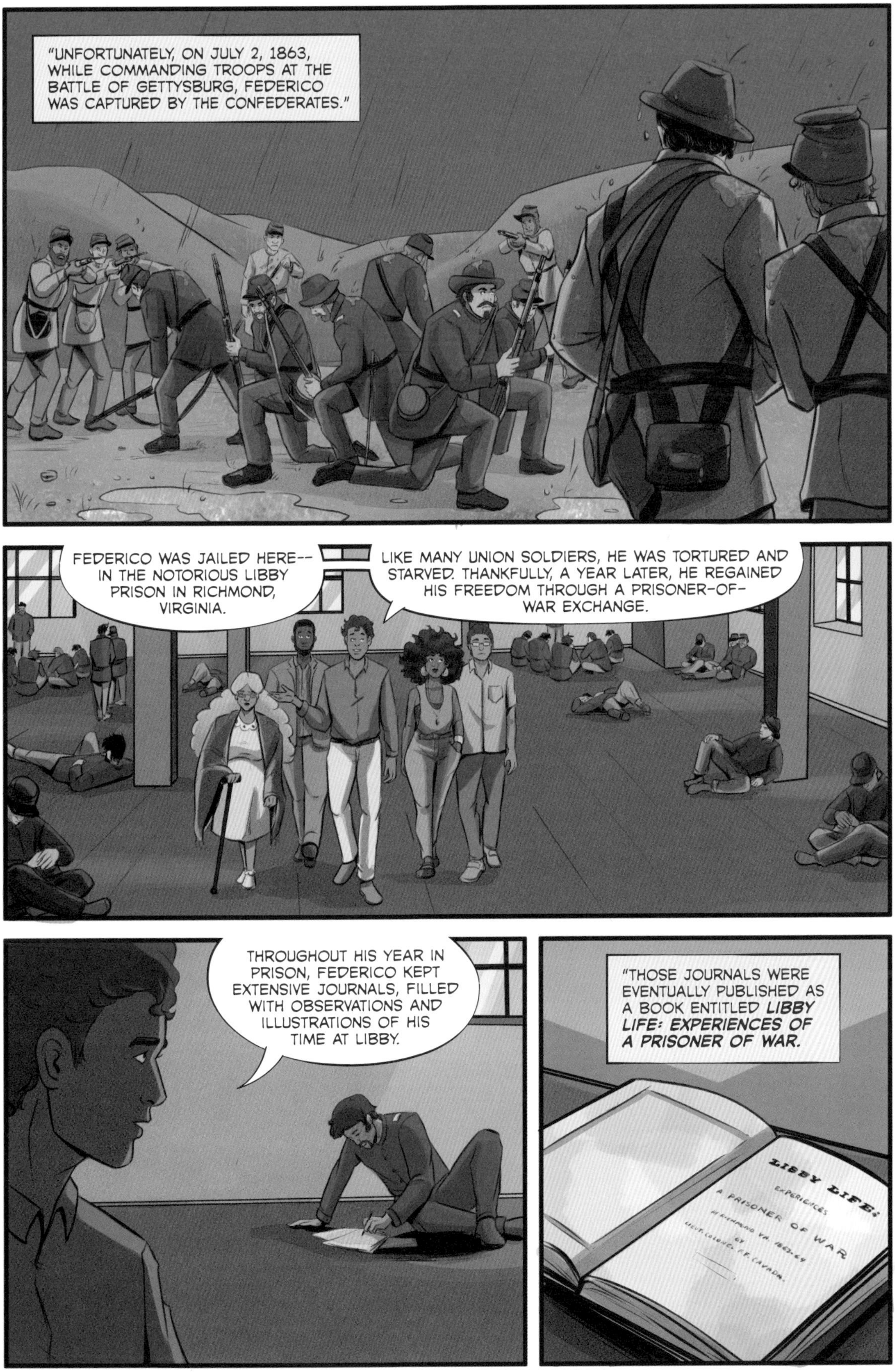
"UNFORTUNATELY, ON JULY 2, 1863, WHILE COMMANDING TROOPS AT THE BATTLE OF GETTYSBURG, FEDERICO WAS CAPTURED BY THE CONFEDERATES."
FEDERICO WAS JAILED HERE-- IN THE NOTORIOUS LIBBY PRISON IN RICHMOND, VIRGINIA.
LIKE MANY UNION SOLDIERS, HE WAS TORTURED AND STARVED. THANKFULLY, A YEAR LATER, HE REGAINED HIS FREEDOM THROUGH A PRISONER-OF-WAR EXCHANGE.
THROUGHOUT HIS YEAR IN PRISON, FEDERICO KEPT EXTENSIVE JOURNALS, FILLED WITH OBSERVATIONS AND ILLUSTRATIONS OF HIS TIME AT LIBBY.
"THOSE JOURNALS WERE EVENTUALLY PUBLISHED AS A BOOK ENTITLED ***LIBBY LIFE: EXPERIENCES OF A PRISONER OF WAR.***
LIBBY LIFE:
A PRISONER OF WAR

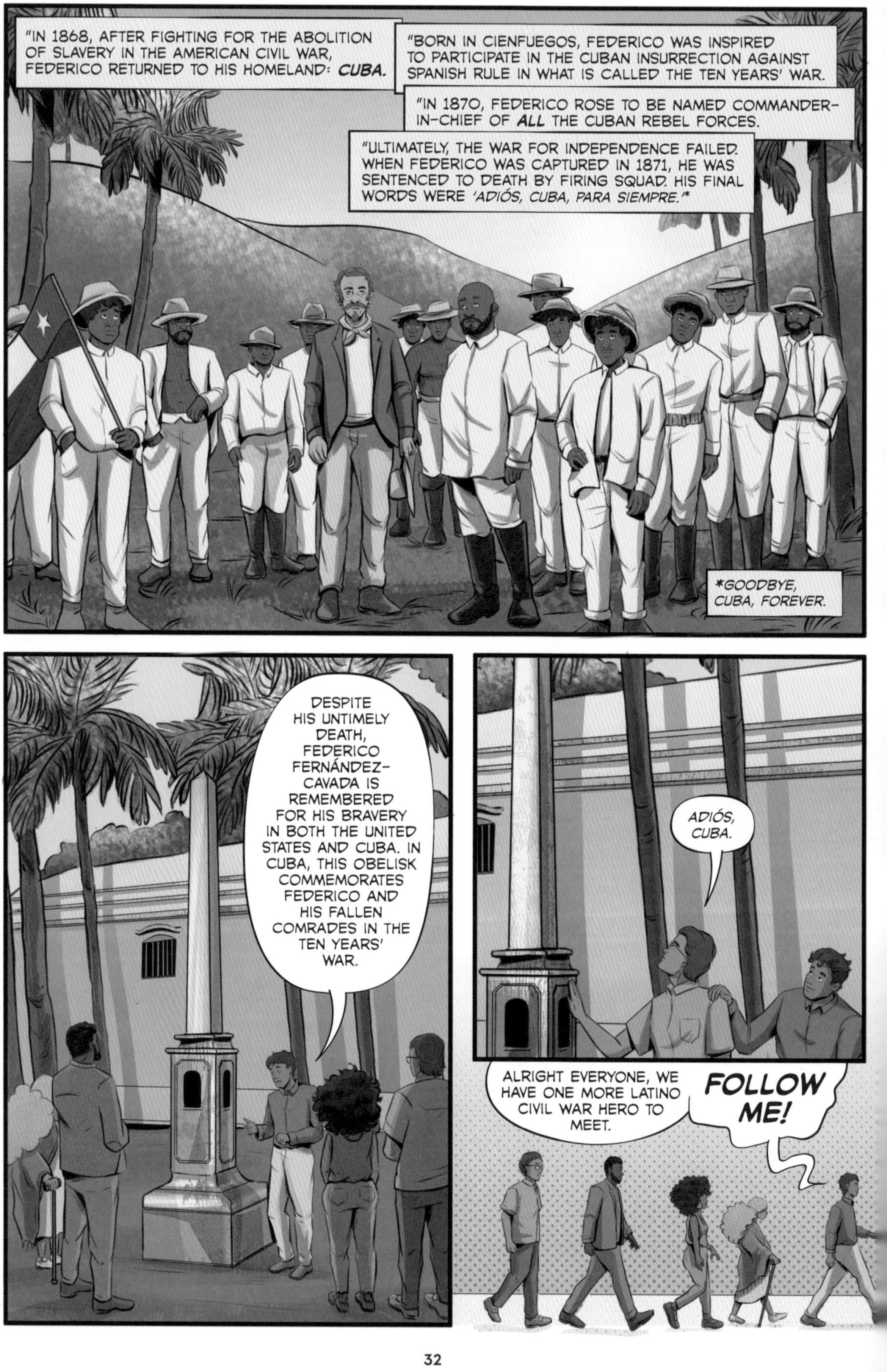
"IN 1868, AFTER FIGHTING FOR THE ABOLITION OF SLAVERY IN THE AMERICAN CIVIL WAR, FEDERICO RETURNED TO HIS HOMELAND: *CUBA.*
"BORN IN CIENFUEGOS, FEDERICO WAS INSPIRED TO PARTICIPATE IN THE CUBAN INSURRECTION AGAINST SPANISH RULE IN WHAT IS CALLED THE TEN YEARS' WAR.
"IN 1870, FEDERICO ROSE TO BE NAMED COMMANDER-IN-CHIEF OF **ALL** THE CUBAN REBEL FORCES.
"ULTIMATELY, THE WAR FOR INDEPENDENCE FAILED. WHEN FEDERICO WAS CAPTURED IN 1871, HE WAS SENTENCED TO DEATH BY FIRING SQUAD. HIS FINAL WORDS WERE *'ADIÓS, CUBA, PARA SIEMPRE.'**
**GOODBYE, CUBA, FOREVER.*
DESPITE HIS UNTIMELY DEATH, FEDERICO FERNÁNDEZ-CAVADA IS REMEMBERED FOR HIS BRAVERY IN BOTH THE UNITED STATES AND CUBA. IN CUBA, THIS OBELISK COMMEMORATES FEDERICO AND HIS FALLEN COMRADES IN THE TEN YEARS' WAR.
*ADIÓS, CUBA.*
ALRIGHT EVERYONE, WE HAVE ONE MORE LATINO CIVIL WAR HERO TO MEET.
**FOLLOW ME!**

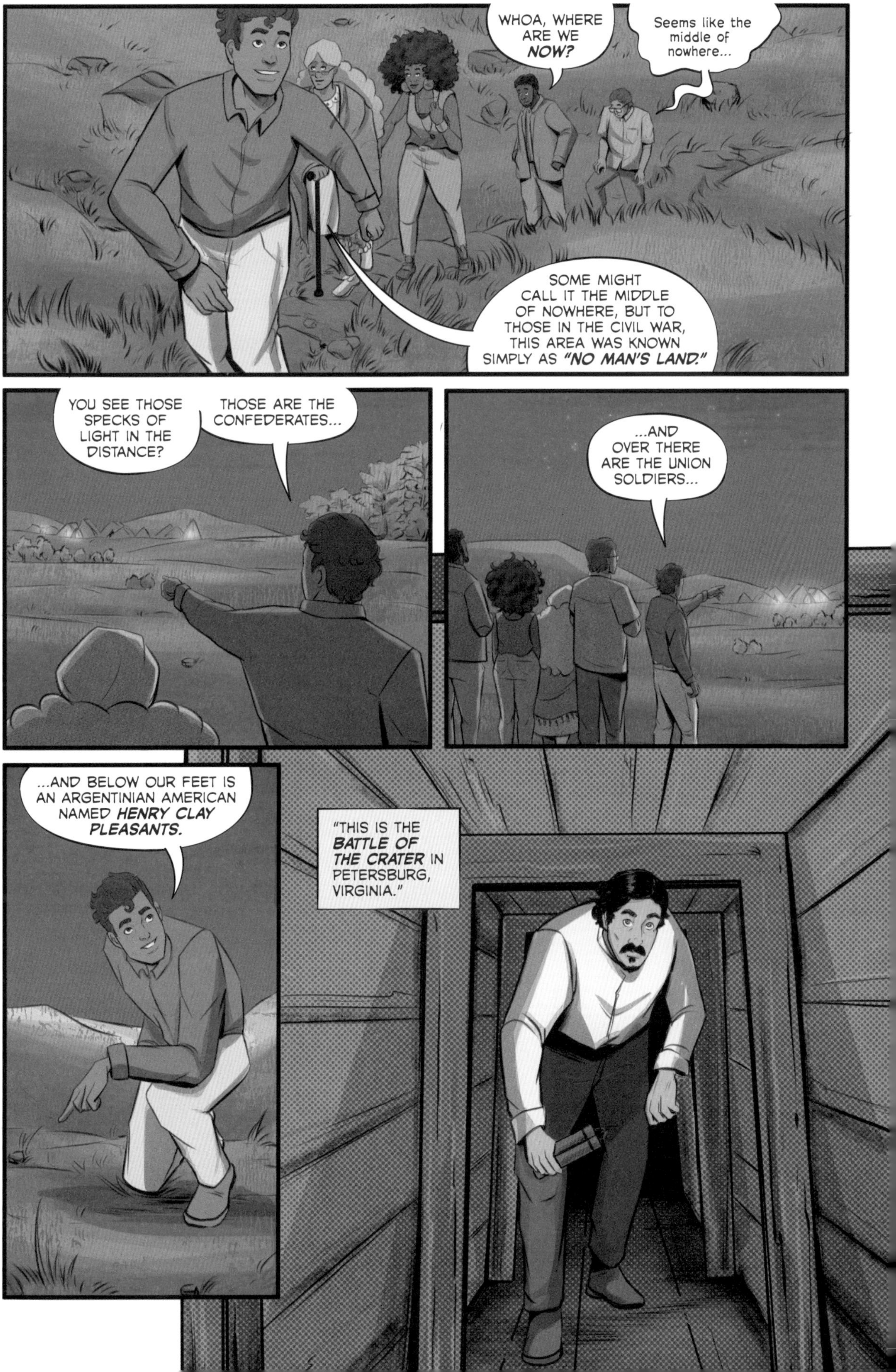
WHOA, WHERE ARE WE *NOW?*
Seems like the middle of nowhere...
SOME MIGHT CALL IT THE MIDDLE OF NOWHERE, BUT TO THOSE IN THE CIVIL WAR, THIS AREA WAS KNOWN SIMPLY AS ***"NO MAN'S LAND."***
YOU SEE THOSE SPECKS OF LIGHT IN THE DISTANCE?
THOSE ARE THE CONFEDERATES...
...AND OVER THERE ARE THE UNION SOLDIERS...
...AND BELOW OUR FEET IS AN ARGENTINIAN AMERICAN NAMED ***HENRY CLAY PLEASANTS.***
"THIS IS THE ***BATTLE OF THE CRATER*** IN PETERSBURG, VIRGINIA."

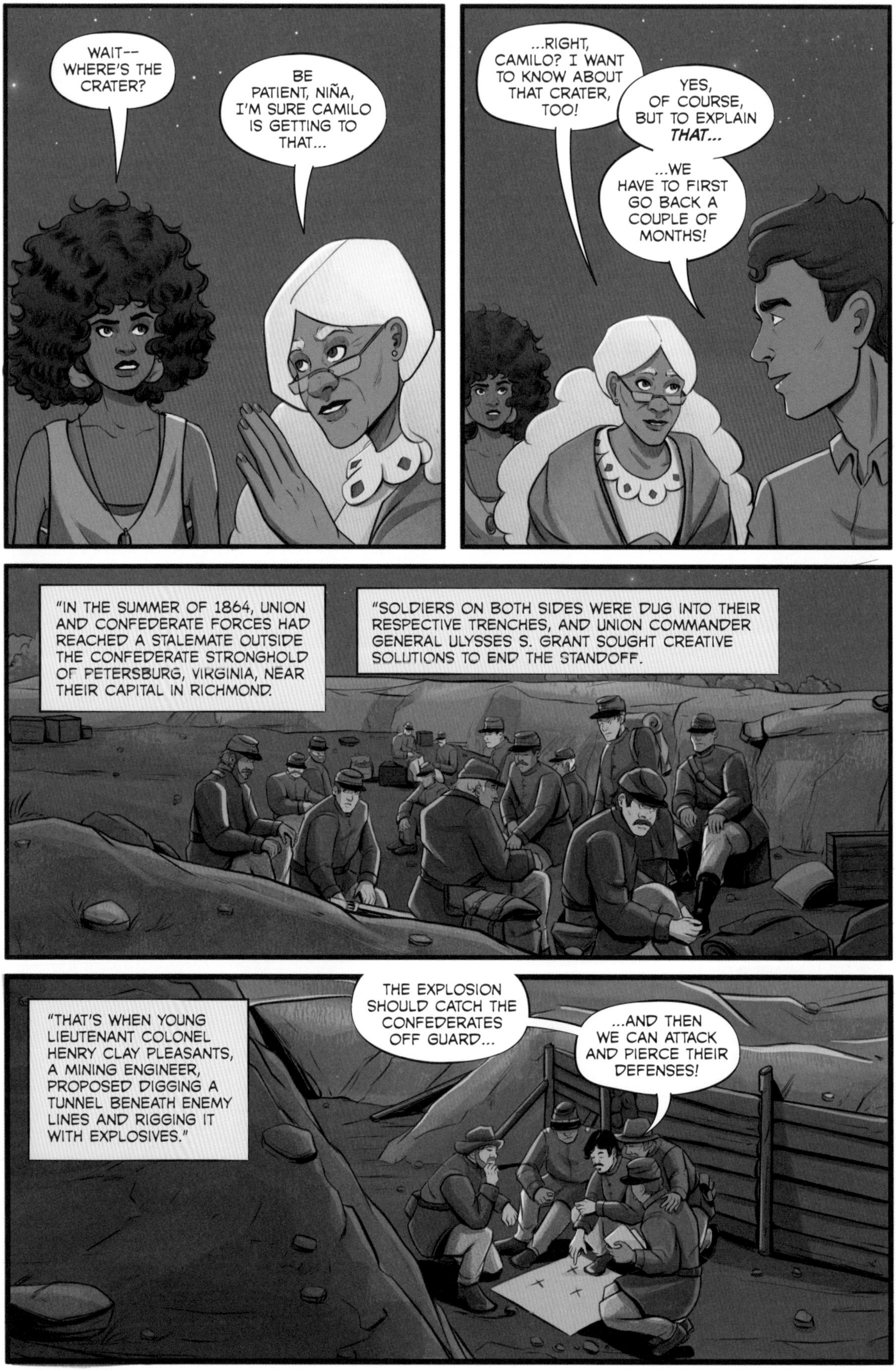
WAIT-- WHERE'S THE CRATER?
BE PATIENT, NIÑA, I'M SURE CAMILO IS GETTING TO THAT...
...RIGHT, CAMILO? I WANT TO KNOW ABOUT THAT CRATER, TOO!
YES, OF COURSE, BUT TO EXPLAIN *THAT...*
...WE HAVE TO FIRST GO BACK A COUPLE OF MONTHS!
"IN THE SUMMER OF 1864, UNION AND CONFEDERATE FORCES HAD REACHED A STALEMATE OUTSIDE THE CONFEDERATE STRONGHOLD OF PETERSBURG, VIRGINIA, NEAR THEIR CAPITAL IN RICHMOND.
"SOLDIERS ON BOTH SIDES WERE DUG INTO THEIR RESPECTIVE TRENCHES, AND UNION COMMANDER GENERAL ULYSSES S. GRANT SOUGHT CREATIVE SOLUTIONS TO END THE STANDOFF.
"THAT'S WHEN YOUNG LIEUTENANT COLONEL HENRY CLAY PLEASANTS, A MINING ENGINEER, PROPOSED DIGGING A TUNNEL BENEATH ENEMY LINES AND RIGGING IT WITH EXPLOSIVES."
THE EXPLOSION SHOULD CATCH THE CONFEDERATES OFF GUARD...
...AND THEN WE CAN ATTACK AND PIERCE THEIR DEFENSES!

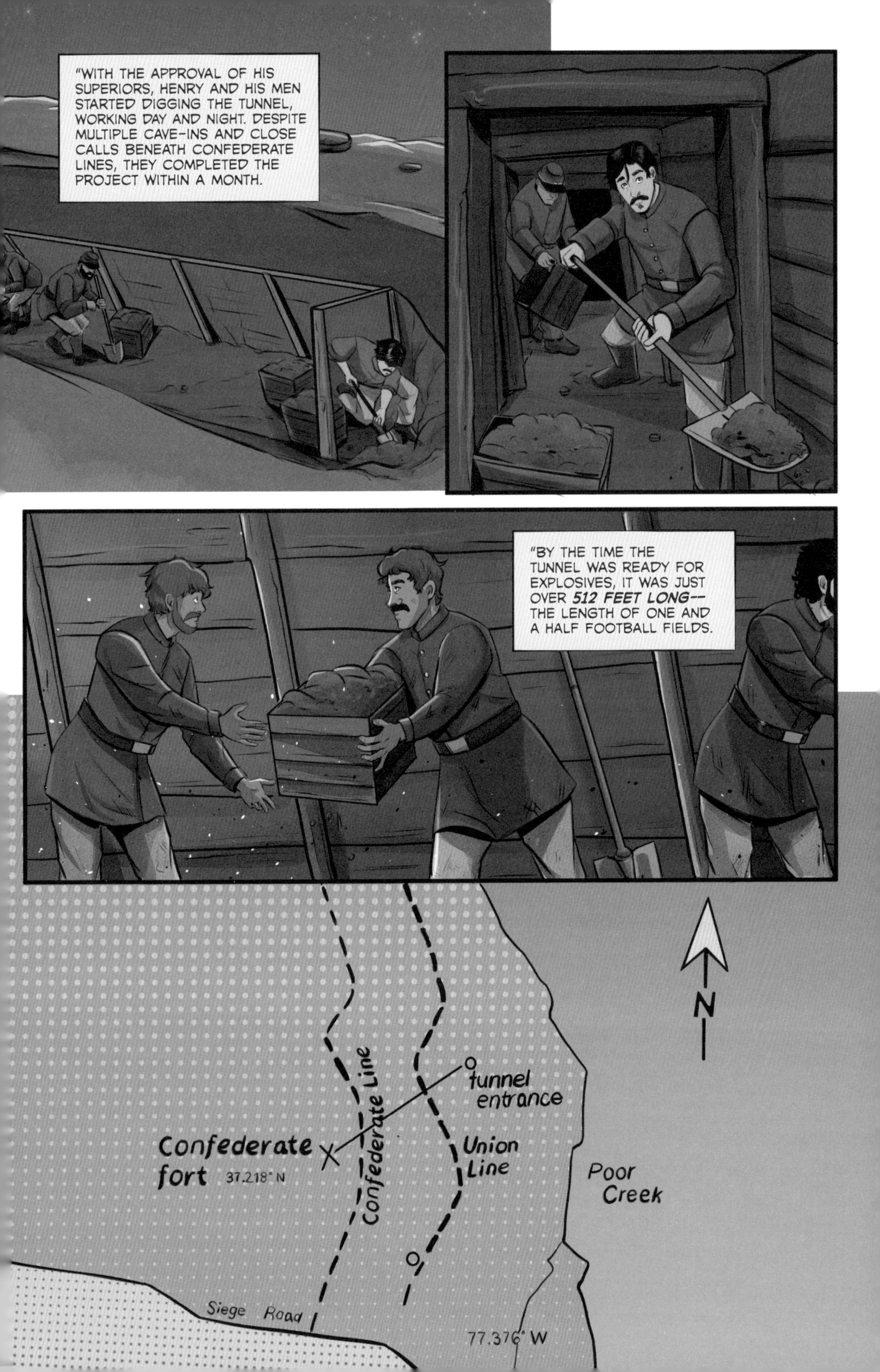
"WITH THE APPROVAL OF HIS SUPERIORS, HENRY AND HIS MEN STARTED DIGGING THE TUNNEL, WORKING DAY AND NIGHT. DESPITE MULTIPLE CAVE-INS AND CLOSE CALLS BENEATH CONFEDERATE LINES, THEY COMPLETED THE PROJECT WITHIN A MONTH.
"BY THE TIME THE TUNNEL WAS READY FOR EXPLOSIVES, IT WAS JUST OVER **512 FEET LONG**-- THE LENGTH OF ONE AND A HALF FOOTBALL FIELDS.
N
tunnel entrance
Confederate Line
Confederate fort
37.218° N
Union Line
Poor Creek
Siege Road
77.376° W

"IT TOOK UNION SOLDIERS THREE DAYS TO FILL HENRY'S TUNNEL WITH 320 KEGS OF GUNPOWDER, TOTALING OVER 8,000 POUNDS.

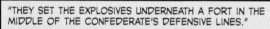

"THEY SET THE EXPLOSIVES UNDERNEATH A FORT IN THE MIDDLE OF THE CONFEDERATE'S DEFENSIVE LINES."

GUN POWDER

GUN POWDER

THEN, ON THE MORNING OF JULY 30, 1864...

...WITH THEIR PLAN IN PLACE, IT WAS TIME TO *EXECUTE* IT.

WATCH...

THE FUSE IS SET!

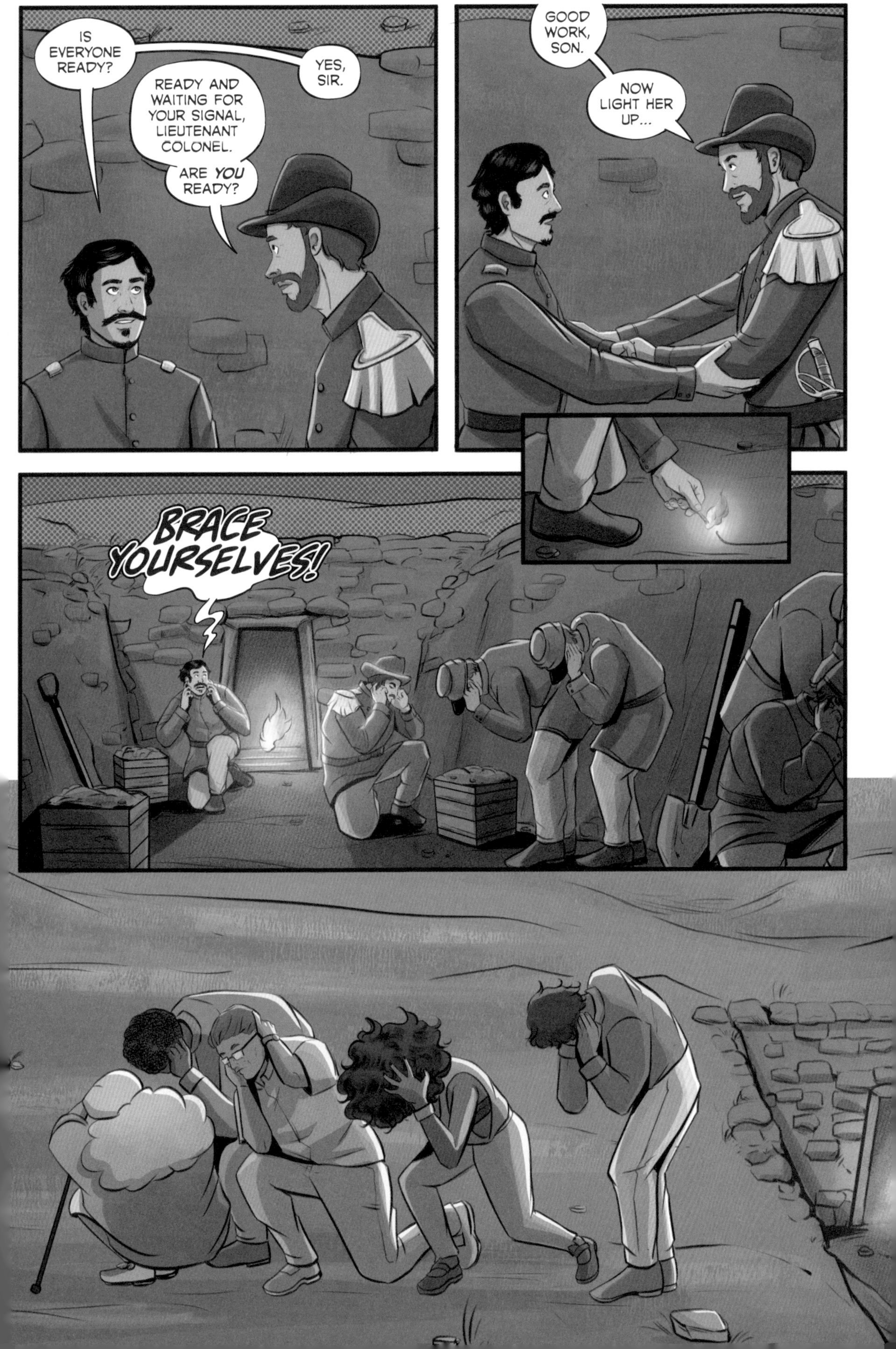
IS EVERYONE READY?
YES, SIR.
READY AND WAITING FOR YOUR SIGNAL, LIEUTENANT COLONEL.
ARE YOU READY?
GOOD WORK, SON.
NOW LIGHT HER UP...
BRACE YOURSELVES!

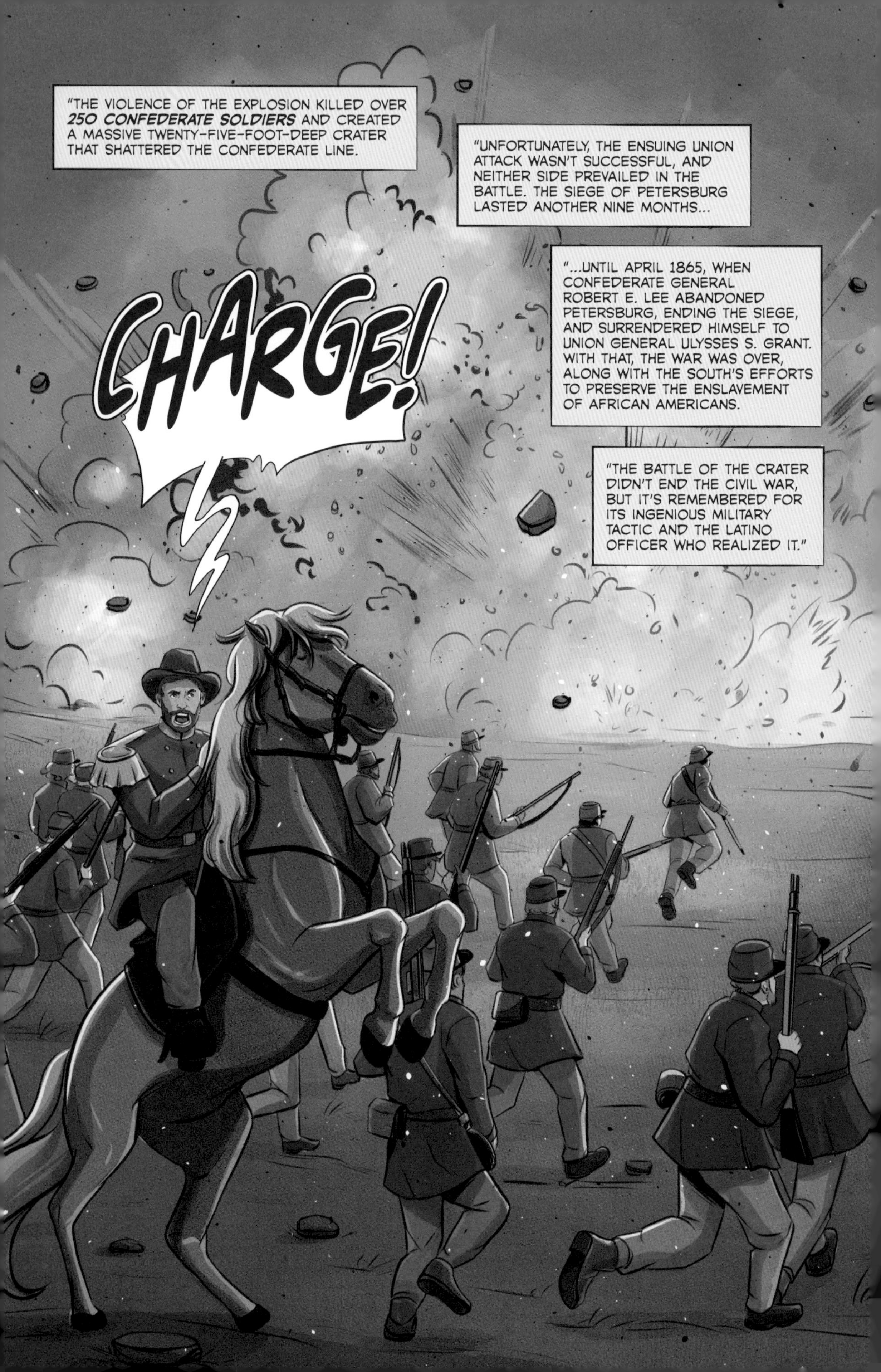
"THE VIOLENCE OF THE EXPLOSION KILLED OVER ***250 CONFEDERATE SOLDIERS*** AND CREATED A MASSIVE TWENTY-FIVE-FOOT-DEEP CRATER THAT SHATTERED THE CONFEDERATE LINE.
"UNFORTUNATELY, THE ENSUING UNION ATTACK WASN'T SUCCESSFUL, AND NEITHER SIDE PREVAILED IN THE BATTLE. THE SIEGE OF PETERSBURG LASTED ANOTHER NINE MONTHS...
CHARGE!
"...UNTIL APRIL 1865, WHEN CONFEDERATE GENERAL ROBERT E. LEE ABANDONED PETERSBURG, ENDING THE SIEGE, AND SURRENDERED HIMSELF TO UNION GENERAL ULYSSES S. GRANT. WITH THAT, THE WAR WAS OVER, ALONG WITH THE SOUTH'S EFFORTS TO PRESERVE THE ENSLAVEMENT OF AFRICAN AMERICANS.
"THE BATTLE OF THE CRATER DIDN'T END THE CIVIL WAR, BUT IT'S REMEMBERED FOR ITS INGENIOUS MILITARY TACTIC AND THE LATINO OFFICER WHO REALIZED IT."

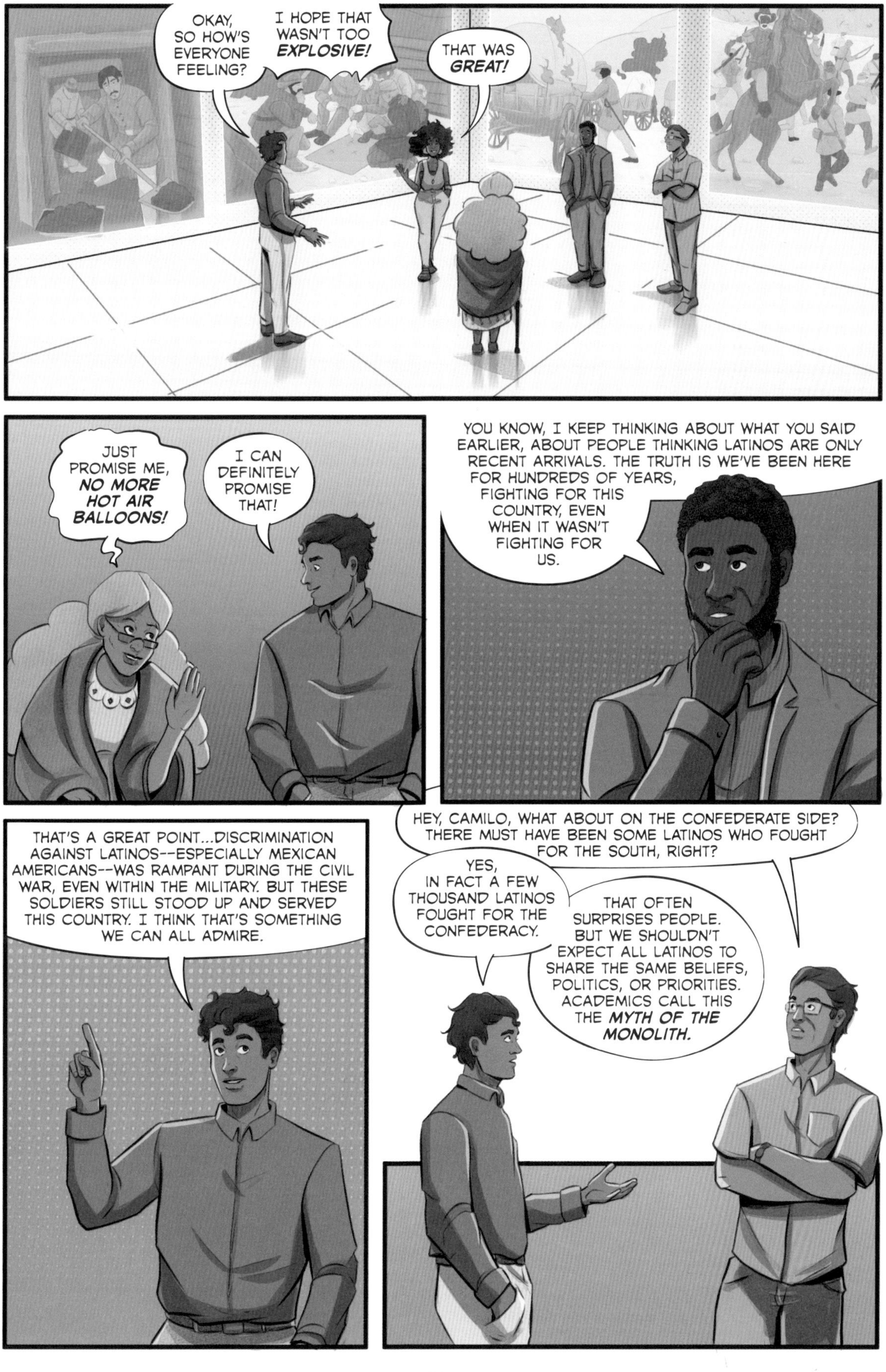
OKAY, SO HOW'S EVERYONE FEELING?
I HOPE THAT WASN'T TOO *EXPLOSIVE!*
THAT WAS *GREAT!*
JUST PROMISE ME, ***NO MORE HOT AIR BALLOONS!***
I CAN DEFINITELY PROMISE THAT!
YOU KNOW, I KEEP THINKING ABOUT WHAT YOU SAID EARLIER, ABOUT PEOPLE THINKING LATINOS ARE ONLY RECENT ARRIVALS. THE TRUTH IS WE'VE BEEN HERE FOR HUNDREDS OF YEARS, FIGHTING FOR THIS COUNTRY, EVEN WHEN IT WASN'T FIGHTING FOR US.
THAT'S A GREAT POINT...DISCRIMINATION AGAINST LATINOS--ESPECIALLY MEXICAN AMERICANS--WAS RAMPANT DURING THE CIVIL WAR, EVEN WITHIN THE MILITARY. BUT THESE SOLDIERS STILL STOOD UP AND SERVED THIS COUNTRY. I THINK THAT'S SOMETHING WE CAN ALL ADMIRE.
HEY, CAMILO, WHAT ABOUT ON THE CONFEDERATE SIDE? THERE MUST HAVE BEEN SOME LATINOS WHO FOUGHT FOR THE SOUTH, RIGHT?
YES, IN FACT A FEW THOUSAND LATINOS FOUGHT FOR THE CONFEDERACY.
THAT OFTEN SURPRISES PEOPLE. BUT WE SHOULDN'T EXPECT ALL LATINOS TO SHARE THE SAME BELIEFS, POLITICS, OR PRIORITIES. ACADEMICS CALL THIS THE ***MYTH OF THE MONOLITH.***

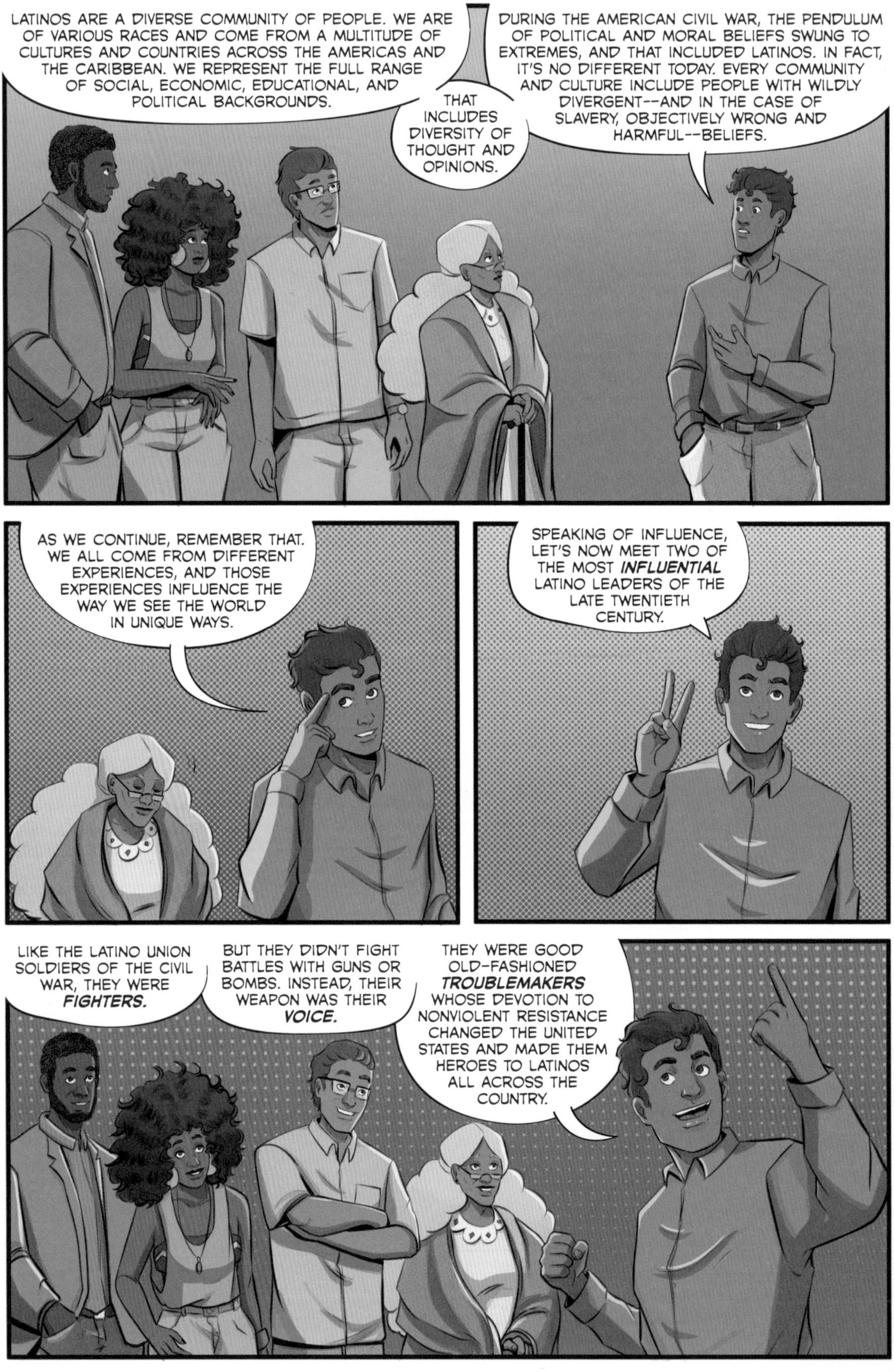
LATINOS ARE A DIVERSE COMMUNITY OF PEOPLE. WE ARE OF VARIOUS RACES AND COME FROM A MULTITUDE OF CULTURES AND COUNTRIES ACROSS THE AMERICAS AND THE CARIBBEAN. WE REPRESENT THE FULL RANGE OF SOCIAL, ECONOMIC, EDUCATIONAL, AND POLITICAL BACKGROUNDS.
THAT INCLUDES DIVERSITY OF THOUGHT AND OPINIONS.
DURING THE AMERICAN CIVIL WAR, THE PENDULUM OF POLITICAL AND MORAL BELIEFS SWUNG TO EXTREMES, AND THAT INCLUDED LATINOS. IN FACT, IT'S NO DIFFERENT TODAY. EVERY COMMUNITY AND CULTURE INCLUDE PEOPLE WITH WILDLY DIVERGENT--AND IN THE CASE OF SLAVERY, OBJECTIVELY WRONG AND HARMFUL--BELIEFS.
AS WE CONTINUE, REMEMBER THAT. WE ALL COME FROM DIFFERENT EXPERIENCES, AND THOSE EXPERIENCES INFLUENCE THE WAY WE SEE THE WORLD IN UNIQUE WAYS.
SPEAKING OF INFLUENCE, LET'S NOW MEET TWO OF THE MOST ***INFLUENTIAL*** LATINO LEADERS OF THE LATE TWENTIETH CENTURY.
LIKE THE LATINO UNION SOLDIERS OF THE CIVIL WAR, THEY WERE ***FIGHTERS.***
BUT THEY DIDN'T FIGHT BATTLES WITH GUNS OR BOMBS. INSTEAD, THEIR WEAPON WAS THEIR ***VOICE.***
THEY WERE GOOD OLD-FASHIONED ***TROUBLEMAKERS*** WHOSE DEVOTION TO NONVIOLENT RESISTANCE CHANGED THE UNITED STATES AND MADE THEM HEROES TO LATINOS ALL ACROSS THE COUNTRY.

# CHAPTER 3: CÉSAR CHÁVEZ AND DOLORES HUERTA

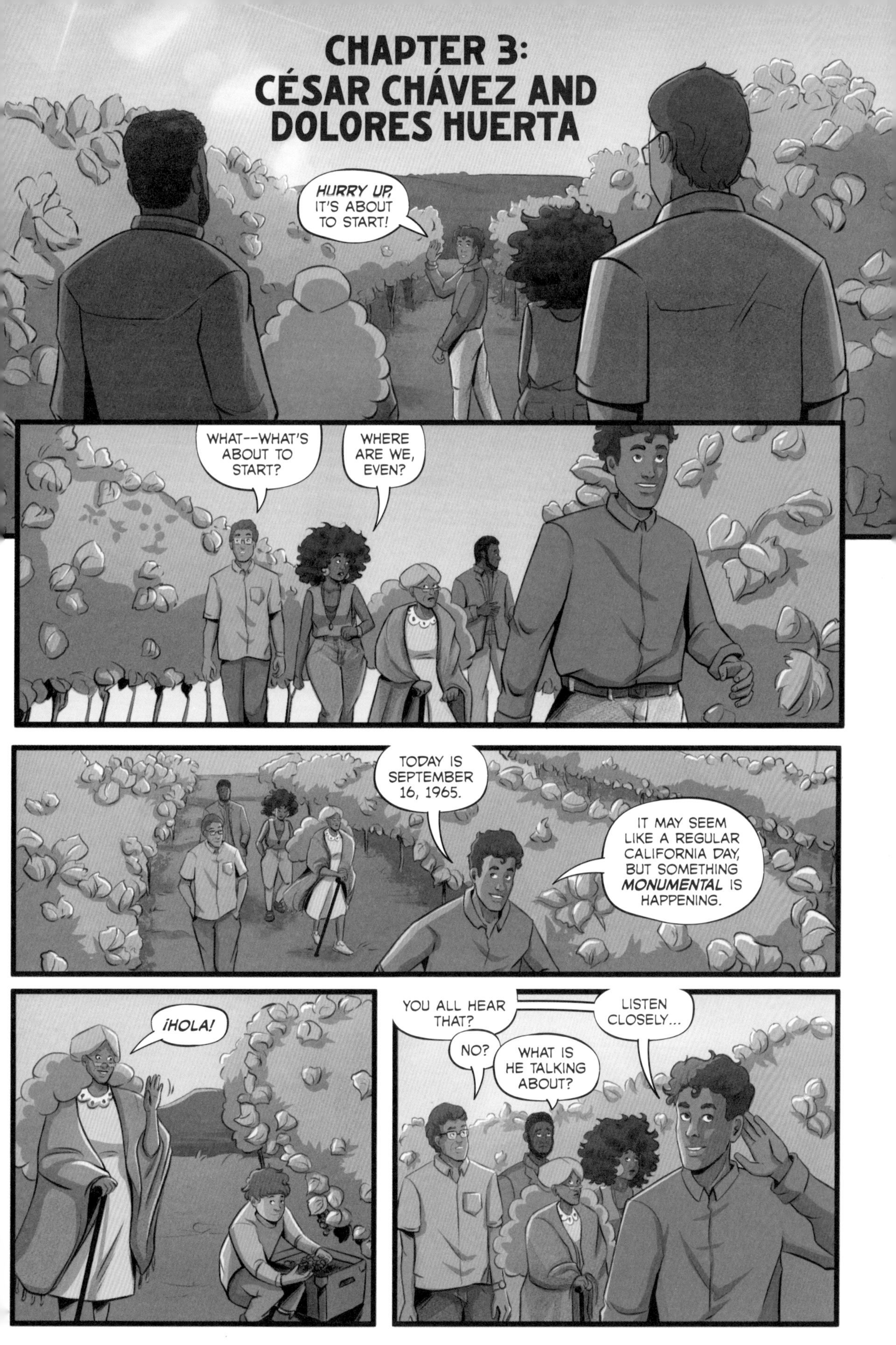

HURRY UP, IT'S ABOUT TO START!
WHAT--WHAT'S ABOUT TO START?
WHERE ARE WE, EVEN?
TODAY IS SEPTEMBER 16, 1965.
IT MAY SEEM LIKE A REGULAR CALIFORNIA DAY, BUT SOMETHING MONUMENTAL IS HAPPENING.
¡HOLA!
YOU ALL HEAR THAT?
LISTEN CLOSELY...
NO?
WHAT IS HE TALKING ABOUT?

¡HUELGA!
FARM WORKERS UNITED
FARM WORKERS
FARM WORKERS
¡HUELGA!
FARM WORKERS
¡SÍ SE PUEDE!
HIGHER WAGES NOW
HIGHER WAGES NOW!

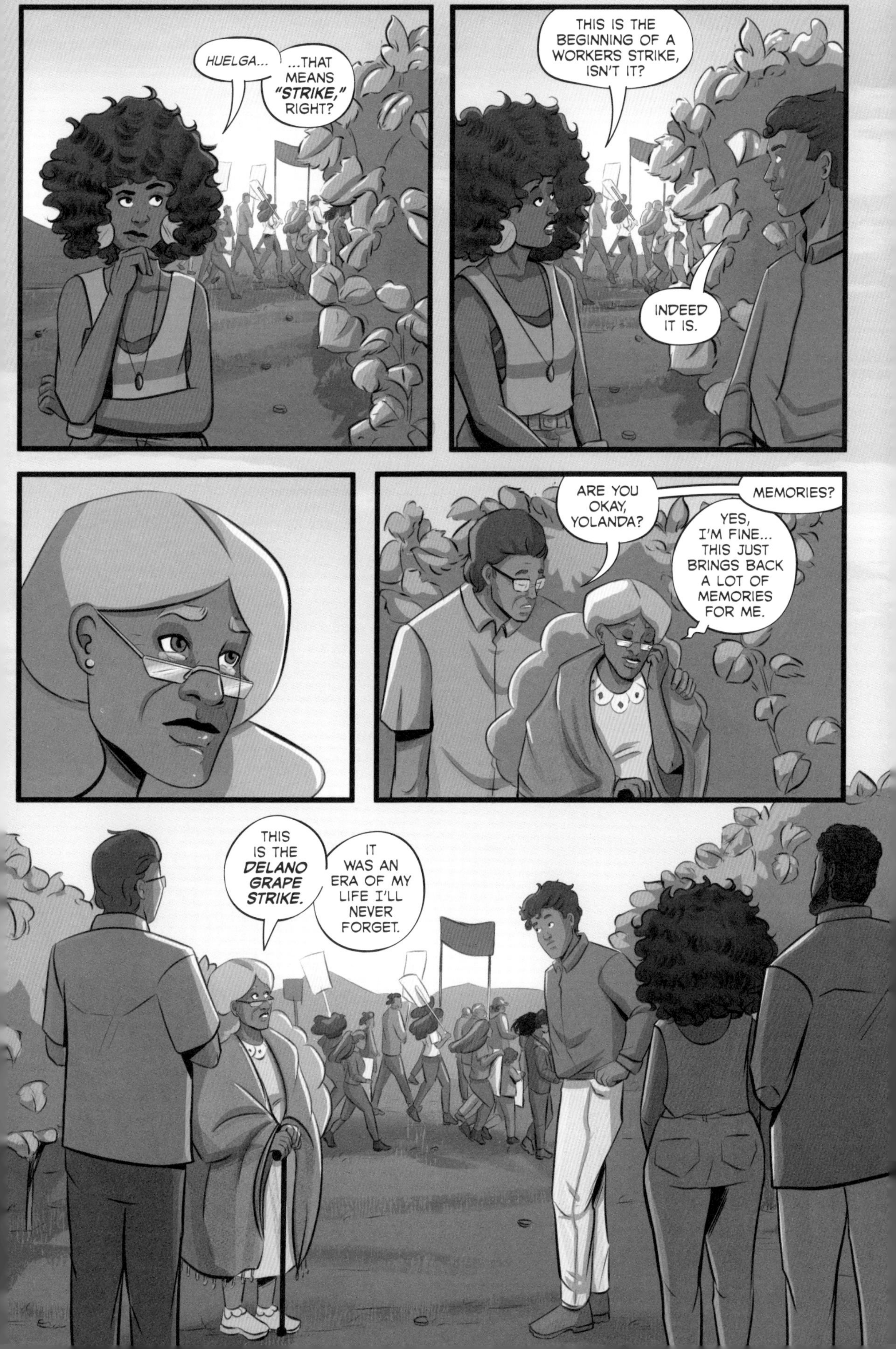
HUELGA...
...THAT MEANS "STRIKE," RIGHT?
THIS IS THE BEGINNING OF A WORKERS STRIKE, ISN'T IT?
INDEED IT IS.
ARE YOU OKAY, YOLANDA?
YES, I'M FINE... THIS JUST BRINGS BACK A LOT OF MEMORIES FOR ME.
MEMORIES?
THIS IS THE DELANO GRAPE STRIKE.
IT WAS AN ERA OF MY LIFE I'LL NEVER FORGET.

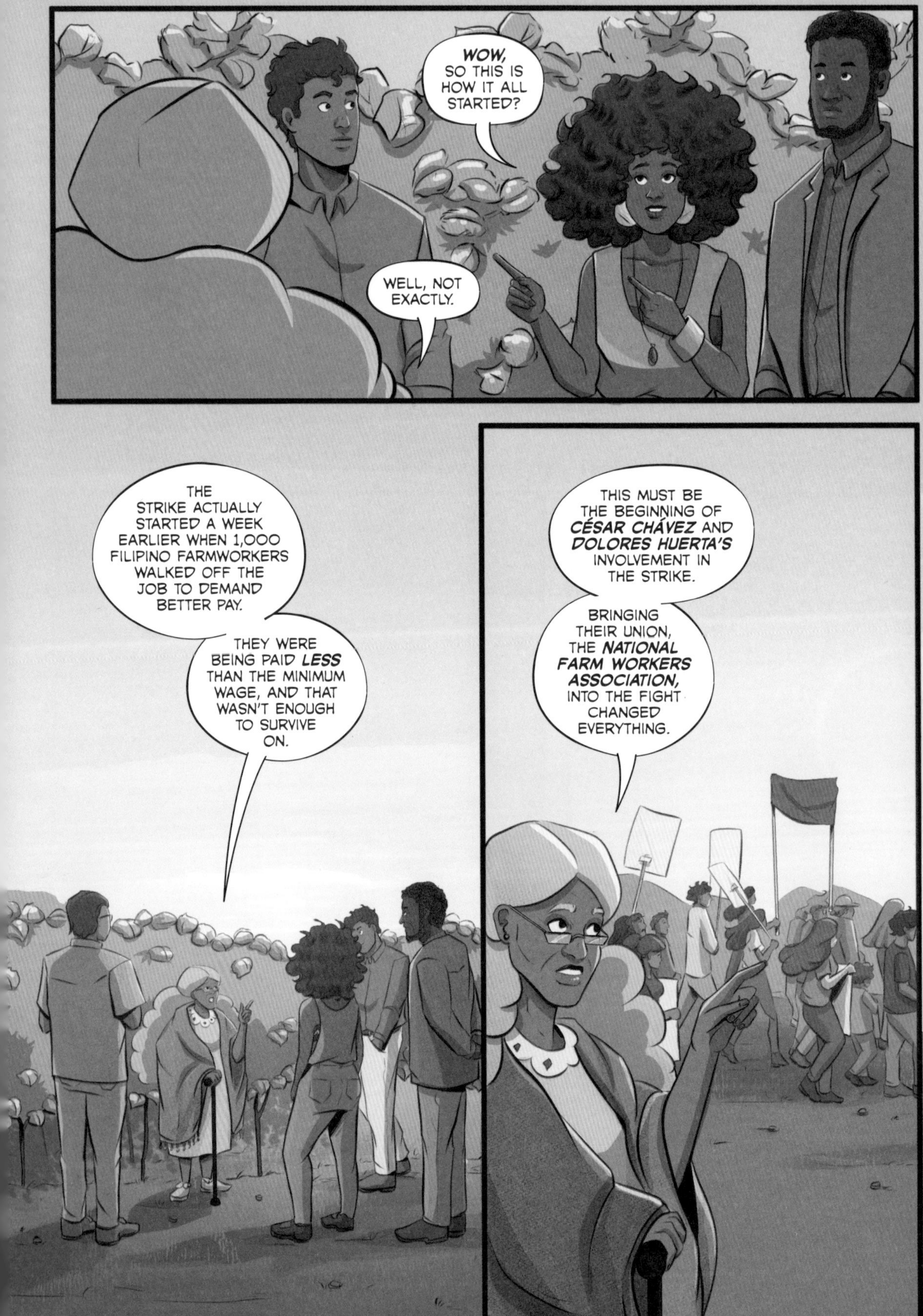
WOW, SO THIS IS HOW IT ALL STARTED?
WELL, NOT EXACTLY.
THE STRIKE ACTUALLY STARTED A WEEK EARLIER WHEN 1,000 FILIPINO FARMWORKERS WALKED OFF THE JOB TO DEMAND BETTER PAY.
THEY WERE BEING PAID LESS THAN THE MINIMUM WAGE, AND THAT WASN'T ENOUGH TO SURVIVE ON.
THIS MUST BE THE BEGINNING OF CÉSAR CHÁVEZ AND DOLORES HUERTA'S INVOLVEMENT IN THE STRIKE.
BRINGING THEIR UNION, THE NATIONAL FARM WORKERS ASSOCIATION, INTO THE FIGHT CHANGED EVERYTHING.

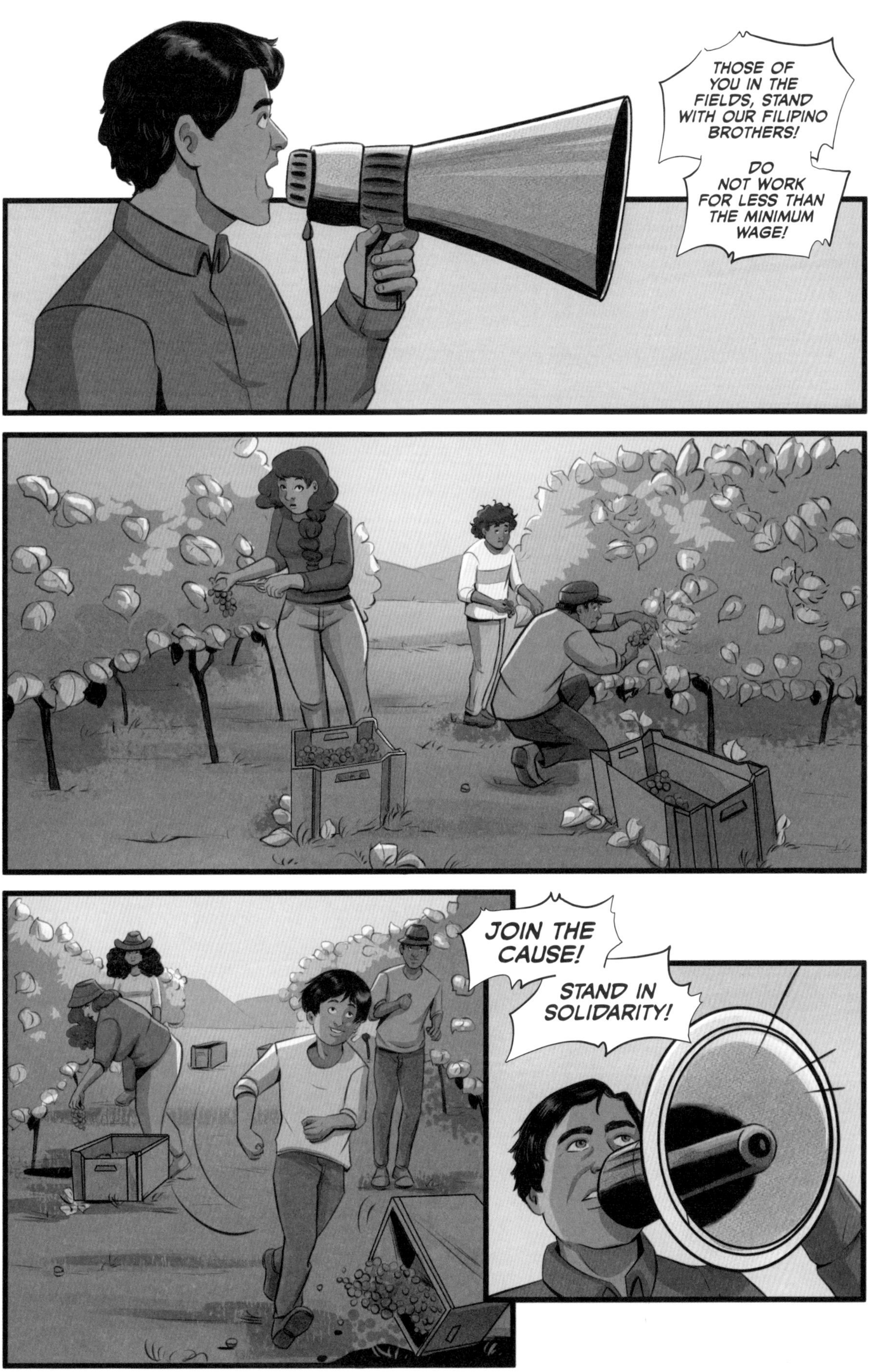
THOSE OF YOU IN THE FIELDS, STAND WITH OUR FILIPINO BROTHERS!
DO NOT WORK FOR LESS THAN THE MINIMUM WAGE!
JOIN THE CAUSE!
STAND IN SOLIDARITY!

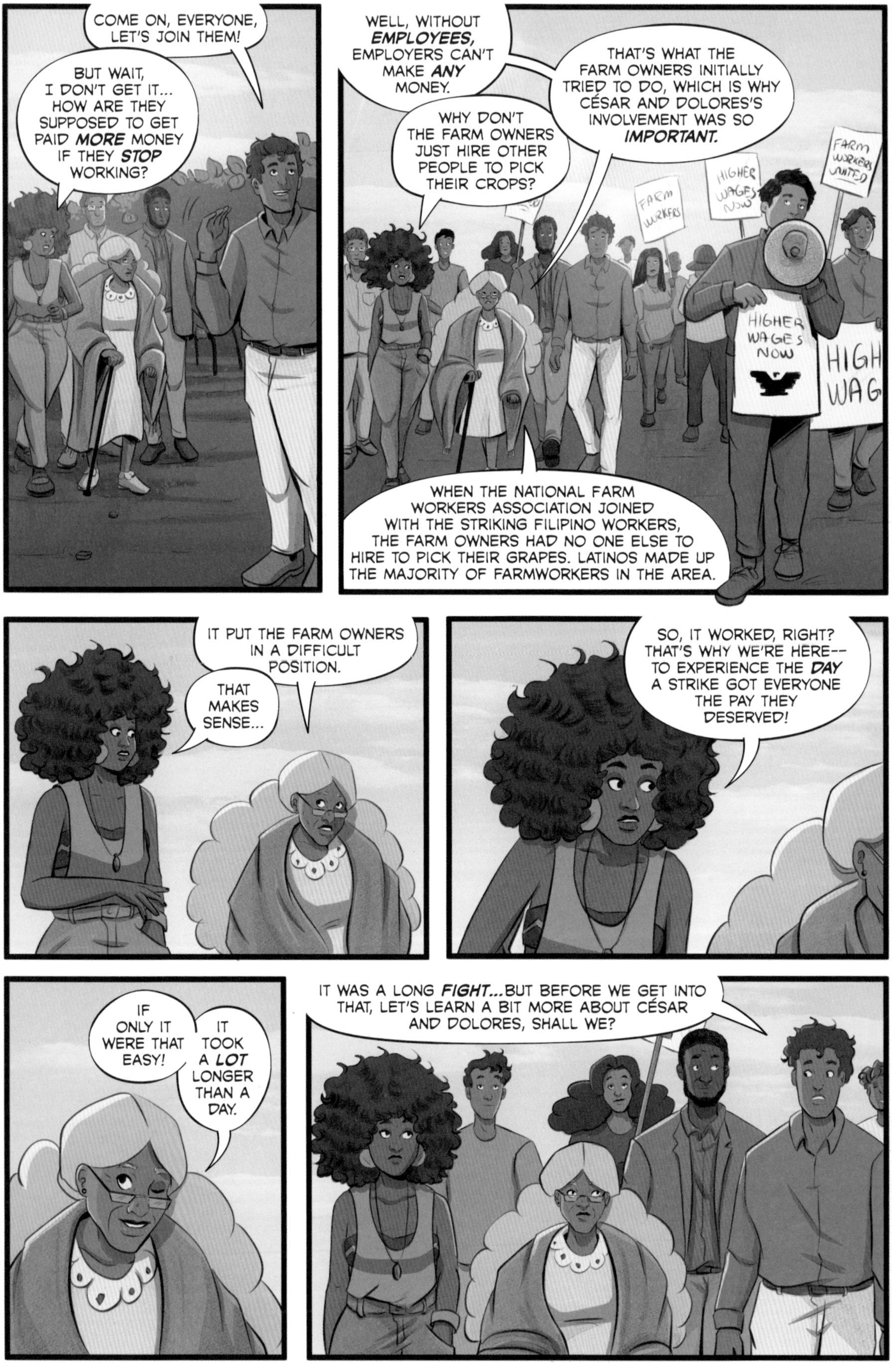
COME ON, EVERYONE, LET'S JOIN THEM!
BUT WAIT, I DON'T GET IT... HOW ARE THEY SUPPOSED TO GET PAID *MORE* MONEY IF THEY *STOP* WORKING?
WELL, WITHOUT *EMPLOYEES,* EMPLOYERS CAN'T MAKE *ANY* MONEY.
WHY DON'T THE FARM OWNERS JUST HIRE OTHER PEOPLE TO PICK THEIR CROPS?
THAT'S WHAT THE FARM OWNERS INITIALLY TRIED TO DO, WHICH IS WHY CÉSAR AND DOLORES'S INVOLVEMENT WAS SO *IMPORTANT.*
FARM WORKERS
HIGHER WAGES NOW
FARM WORKERS UNITED
HIGHER WAGES NOW
WHEN THE NATIONAL FARM WORKERS ASSOCIATION JOINED WITH THE STRIKING FILIPINO WORKERS, THE FARM OWNERS HAD NO ONE ELSE TO HIRE TO PICK THEIR GRAPES. LATINOS MADE UP THE MAJORITY OF FARMWORKERS IN THE AREA.
IT PUT THE FARM OWNERS IN A DIFFICULT POSITION.
THAT MAKES SENSE...
SO, IT WORKED, RIGHT? THAT'S WHY WE'RE HERE-- TO EXPERIENCE THE *DAY* A STRIKE GOT EVERYONE THE PAY THEY DESERVED!
IF ONLY IT WERE THAT EASY!
IT TOOK A *LOT* LONGER THAN A DAY.
IT WAS A LONG *FIGHT...* BUT BEFORE WE GET INTO THAT, LET'S LEARN A BIT MORE ABOUT CÉSAR AND DOLORES, SHALL WE?

CÉSAR CHÁVEZ

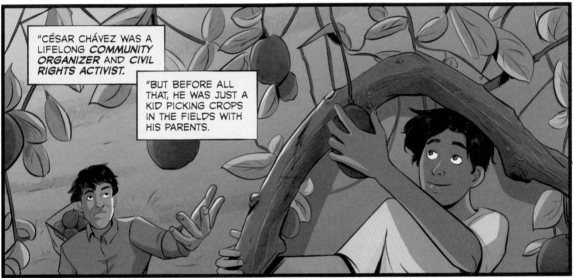

"CÉSAR CHÁVEZ WAS A LIFELONG *COMMUNITY ORGANIZER* AND *CIVIL RIGHTS ACTIVIST.*

"BUT BEFORE ALL THAT, HE WAS JUST A KID PICKING CROPS IN THE FIELDS WITH HIS PARENTS.

"GROWING UP, HE CAME TO KNOW FIRSTHAND THE BRUTAL WORKING CONDITIONS MANY LATINO FARMWORKERS EXPERIENCED-- THE INCREDIBLY LONG HOURS, POOR WAGES, AND INADEQUATE LIVING CONDITIONS.

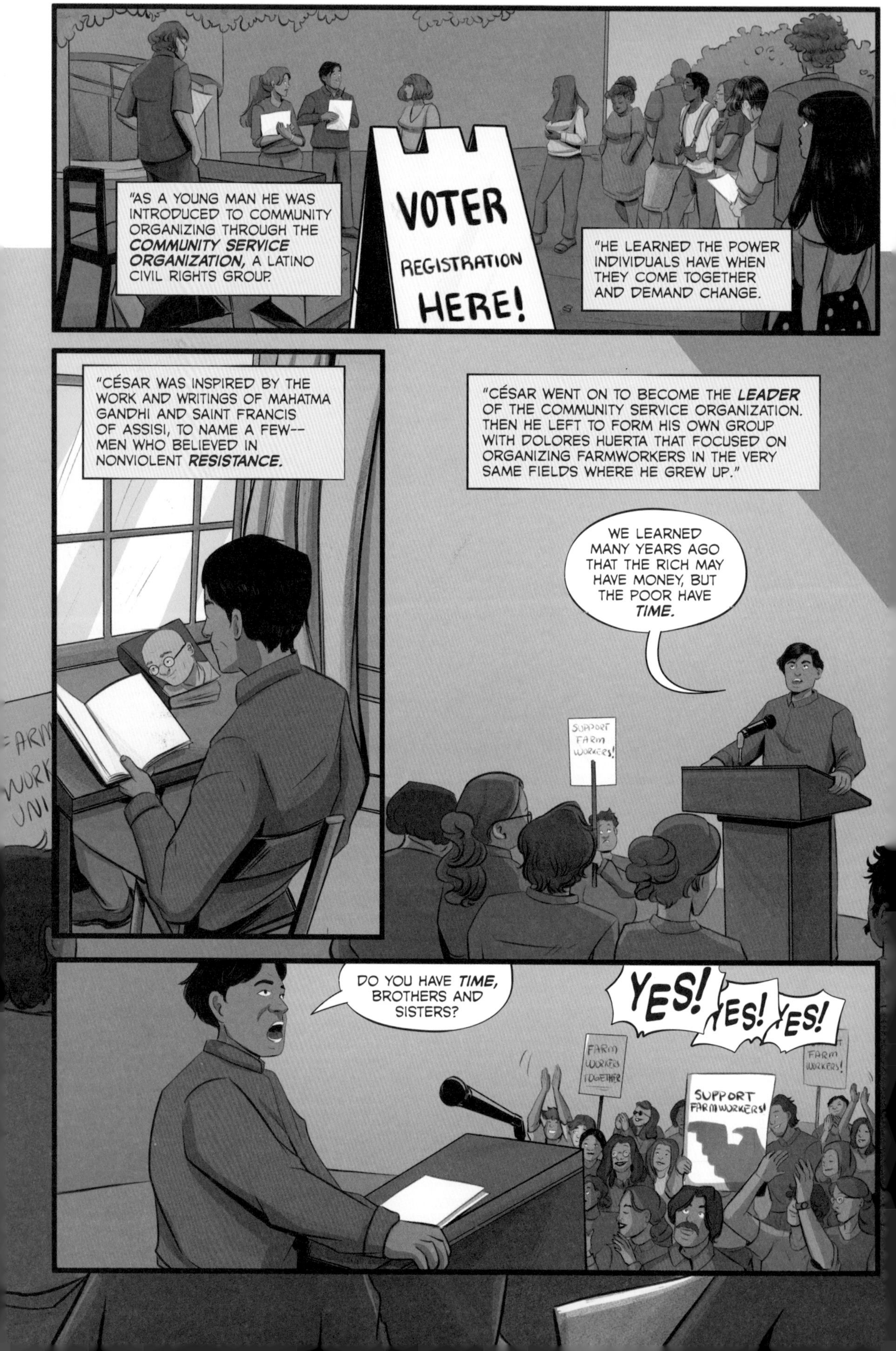
"AS A YOUNG MAN HE WAS INTRODUCED TO COMMUNITY ORGANIZING THROUGH THE COMMUNITY SERVICE ORGANIZATION, A LATINO CIVIL RIGHTS GROUP.
VOTER REGISTRATION HERE!
"HE LEARNED THE POWER INDIVIDUALS HAVE WHEN THEY COME TOGETHER AND DEMAND CHANGE.
"CÉSAR WAS INSPIRED BY THE WORK AND WRITINGS OF MAHATMA GANDHI AND SAINT FRANCIS OF ASSISI, TO NAME A FEW-- MEN WHO BELIEVED IN NONVIOLENT RESISTANCE.
"CÉSAR WENT ON TO BECOME THE LEADER OF THE COMMUNITY SERVICE ORGANIZATION. THEN HE LEFT TO FORM HIS OWN GROUP WITH DOLORES HUERTA THAT FOCUSED ON ORGANIZING FARMWORKERS IN THE VERY SAME FIELDS WHERE HE GREW UP."
WE LEARNED MANY YEARS AGO THAT THE RICH MAY HAVE MONEY, BUT THE POOR HAVE TIME.
SUPPORT FARM WORKERS!
DO YOU HAVE TIME, BROTHERS AND SISTERS?
YES!
YES!
YES!
FARM WORKERS TOGETHER
SUPPORT FARMWORKERS!
FARM WORKERS!

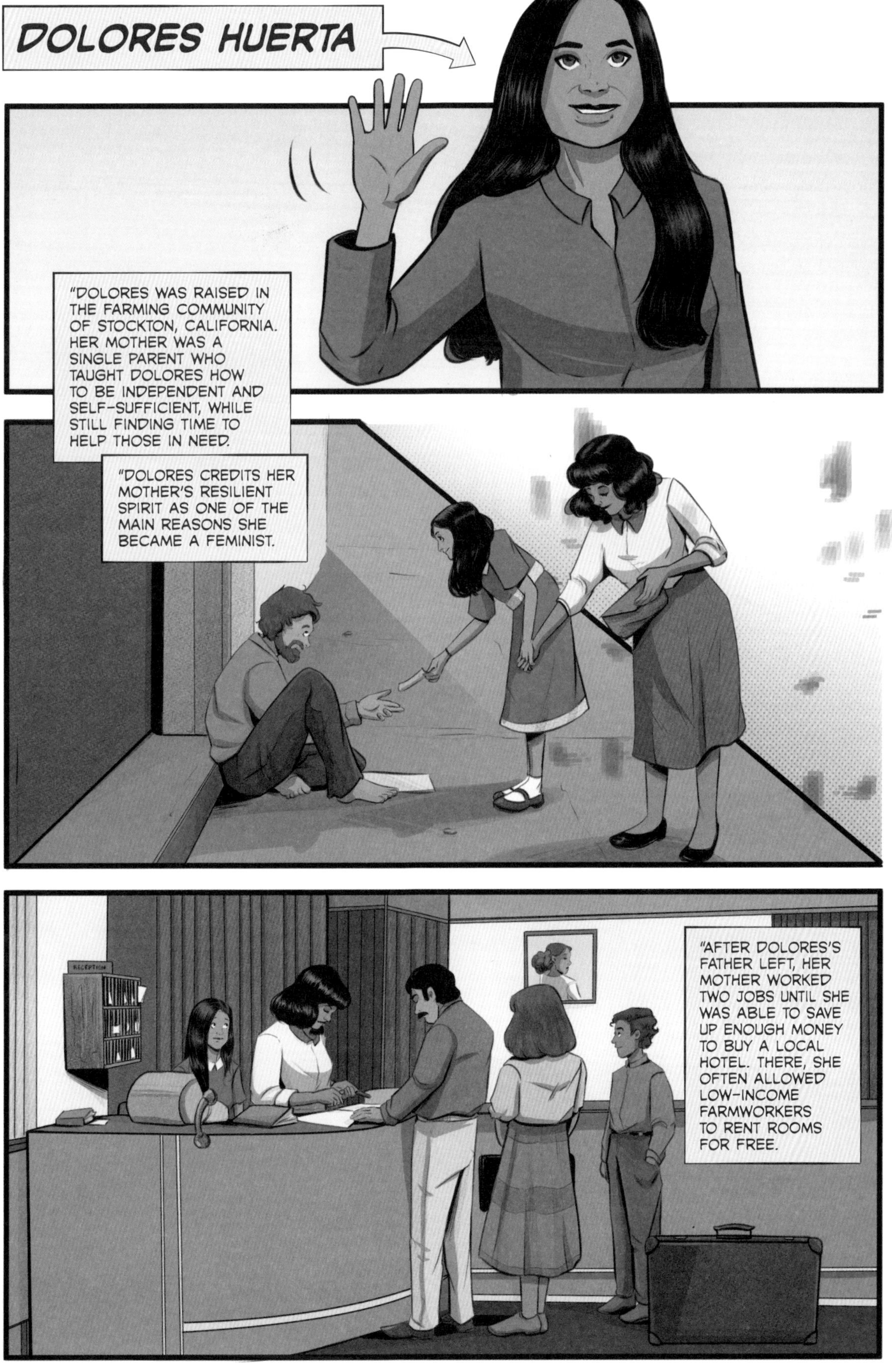
DOLORES HUERTA
"DOLORES WAS RAISED IN THE FARMING COMMUNITY OF STOCKTON, CALIFORNIA. HER MOTHER WAS A SINGLE PARENT WHO TAUGHT DOLORES HOW TO BE INDEPENDENT AND SELF-SUFFICIENT, WHILE STILL FINDING TIME TO HELP THOSE IN NEED.
"DOLORES CREDITS HER MOTHER'S RESILIENT SPIRIT AS ONE OF THE MAIN REASONS SHE BECAME A FEMINIST.
"AFTER DOLORES'S FATHER LEFT, HER MOTHER WORKED TWO JOBS UNTIL SHE WAS ABLE TO SAVE UP ENOUGH MONEY TO BUY A LOCAL HOTEL. THERE, SHE OFTEN ALLOWED LOW-INCOME FARMWORKERS TO RENT ROOMS FOR FREE.

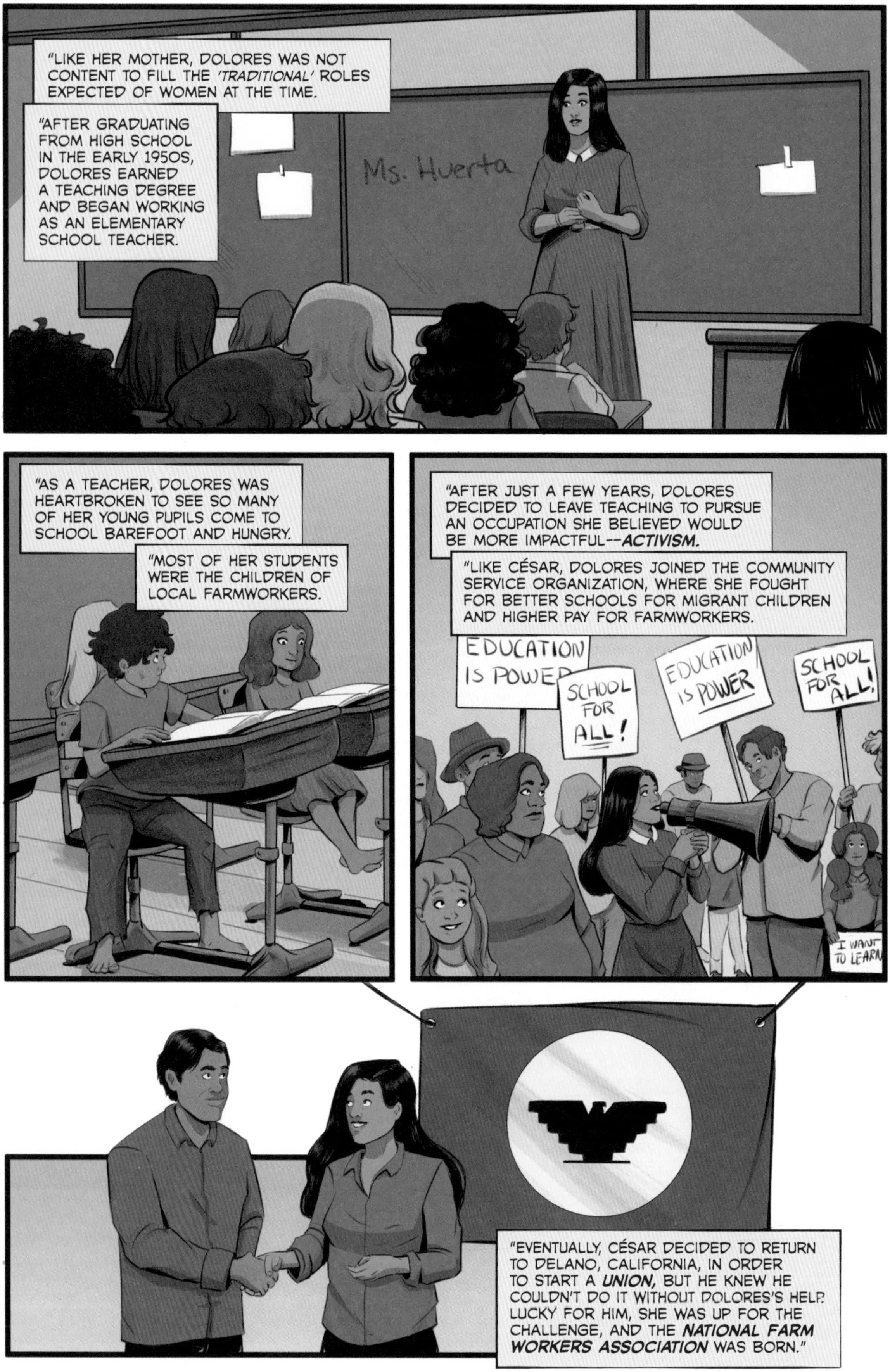

"LIKE HER MOTHER, DOLORES WAS NOT CONTENT TO FILL THE *'TRADITIONAL'* ROLES EXPECTED OF WOMEN AT THE TIME.
"AFTER GRADUATING FROM HIGH SCHOOL IN THE EARLY 1950S, DOLORES EARNED A TEACHING DEGREE AND BEGAN WORKING AS AN ELEMENTARY SCHOOL TEACHER.
Ms. Huerta
"AS A TEACHER, DOLORES WAS HEARTBROKEN TO SEE SO MANY OF HER YOUNG PUPILS COME TO SCHOOL BAREFOOT AND HUNGRY.
"MOST OF HER STUDENTS WERE THE CHILDREN OF LOCAL FARMWORKERS.
"AFTER JUST A FEW YEARS, DOLORES DECIDED TO LEAVE TEACHING TO PURSUE AN OCCUPATION SHE BELIEVED WOULD BE MORE IMPACTFUL--***ACTIVISM.***
"LIKE CÉSAR, DOLORES JOINED THE COMMUNITY SERVICE ORGANIZATION, WHERE SHE FOUGHT FOR BETTER SCHOOLS FOR MIGRANT CHILDREN AND HIGHER PAY FOR FARMWORKERS.
EDUCATION IS POWER
SCHOOL FOR ALL!
EDUCATION IS POWER
SCHOOL FOR ALL!
I WANT TO LEARN
"EVENTUALLY, CÉSAR DECIDED TO RETURN TO DELANO, CALIFORNIA, IN ORDER TO START A ***UNION,*** BUT HE KNEW HE COULDN'T DO IT WITHOUT DOLORES'S HELP. LUCKY FOR HIM, SHE WAS UP FOR THE CHALLENGE, AND THE ***NATIONAL FARM WORKERS ASSOCIATION*** WAS BORN."

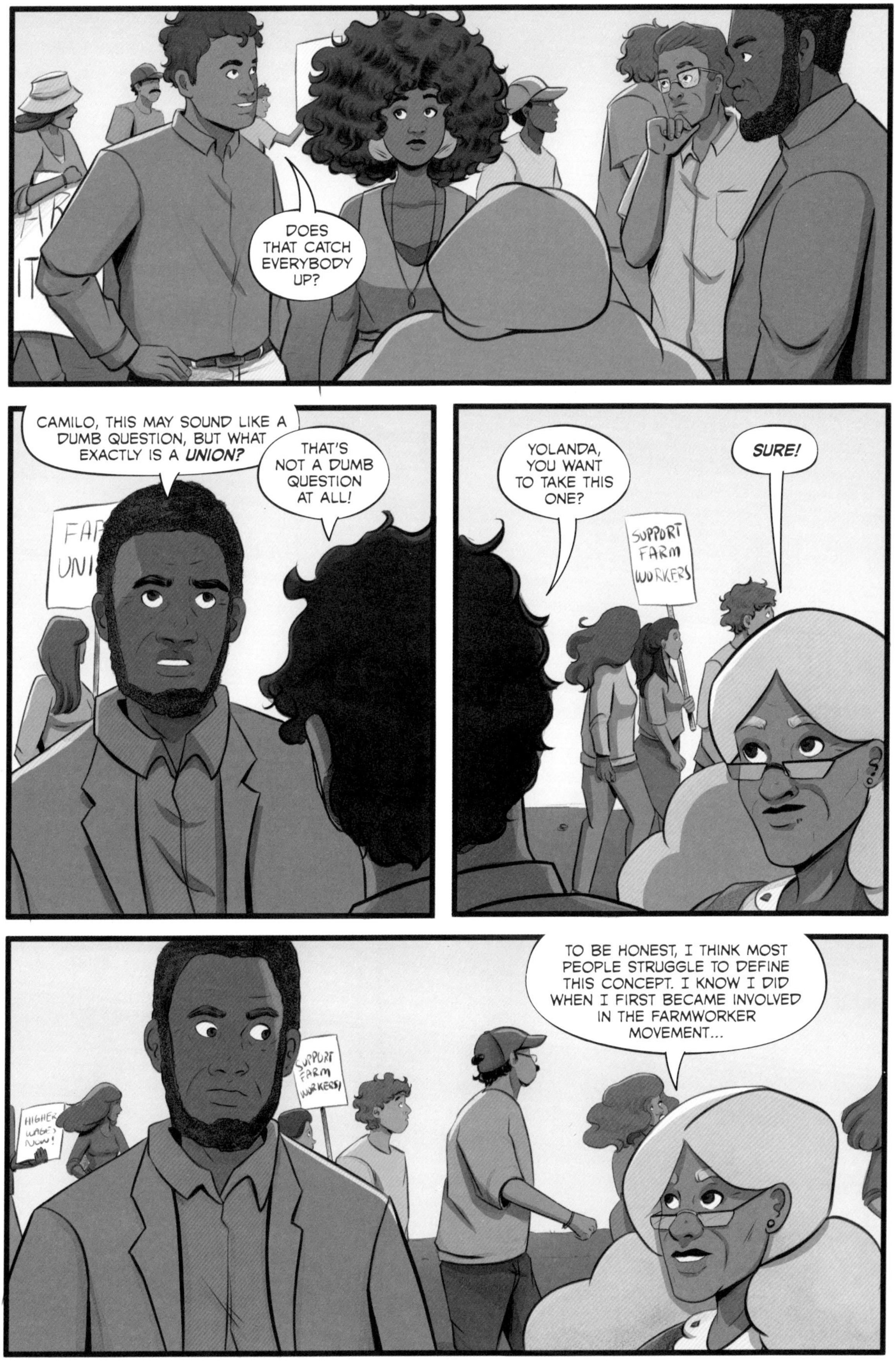
DOES THAT CATCH EVERYBODY UP?
CAMILO, THIS MAY SOUND LIKE A DUMB QUESTION, BUT WHAT EXACTLY IS A *UNION?*
THAT'S NOT A DUMB QUESTION AT ALL!
YOLANDA, YOU WANT TO TAKE THIS ONE?
*SURE!*
SUPPORT FARM WORKERS
TO BE HONEST, I THINK MOST PEOPLE STRUGGLE TO DEFINE THIS CONCEPT. I KNOW I DID WHEN I FIRST BECAME INVOLVED IN THE FARMWORKER MOVEMENT...
HIGHER WAGES NOW!
SUPPORT FARM WORKERS!

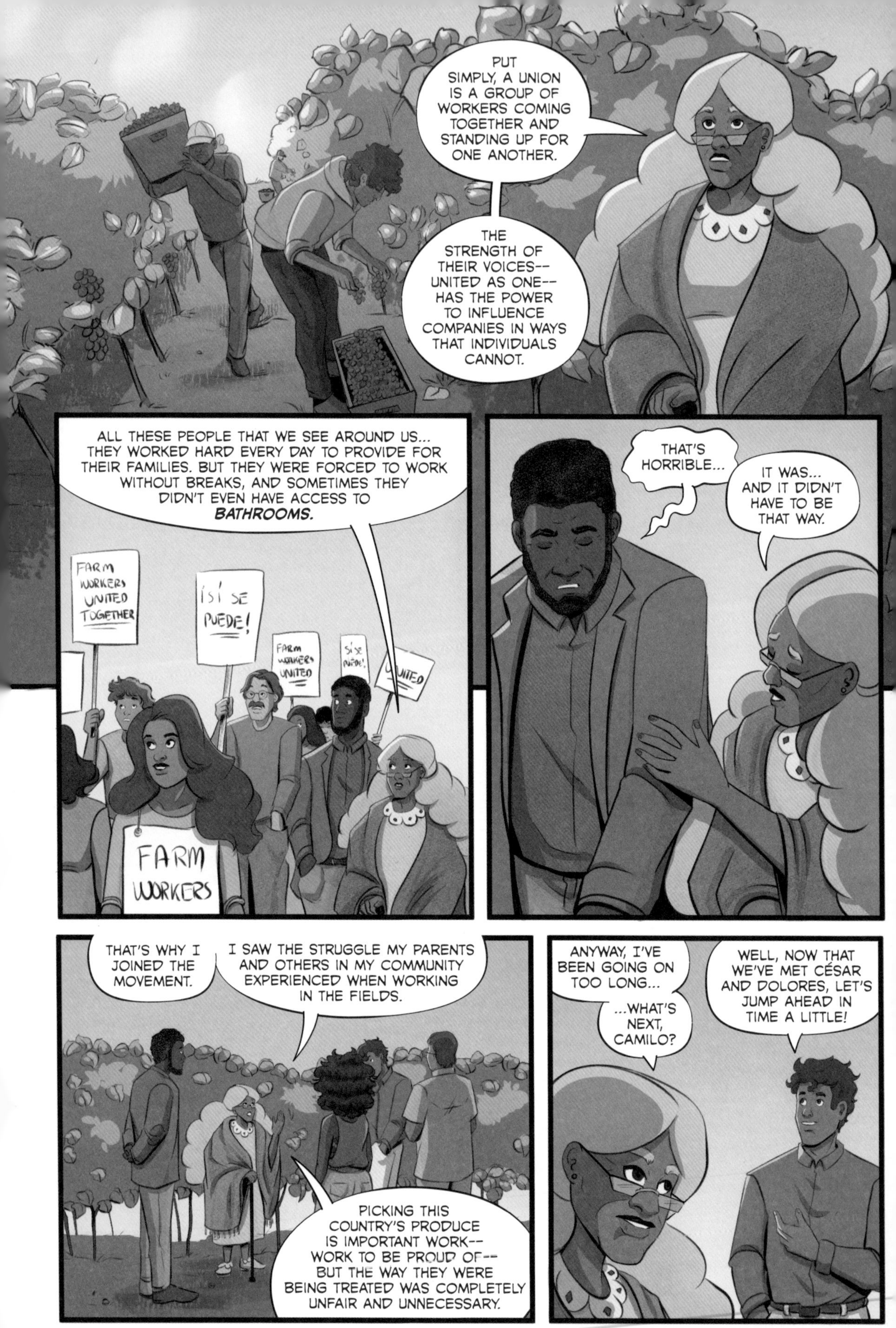
PUT SIMPLY, A UNION IS A GROUP OF WORKERS COMING TOGETHER AND STANDING UP FOR ONE ANOTHER.
THE STRENGTH OF THEIR VOICES--UNITED AS ONE--HAS THE POWER TO INFLUENCE COMPANIES IN WAYS THAT INDIVIDUALS CANNOT.
ALL THESE PEOPLE THAT WE SEE AROUND US... THEY WORKED HARD EVERY DAY TO PROVIDE FOR THEIR FAMILIES. BUT THEY WERE FORCED TO WORK WITHOUT BREAKS, AND SOMETIMES THEY DIDN'T EVEN HAVE ACCESS TO ***BATHROOMS.***
FARM WORKERS UNITED TOGETHER
¡SÍ SE PUEDE!
FARM WORKERS UNITED
SÍ SE PUEDE!
UNITED
FARM WORKERS
THAT'S HORRIBLE...
IT WAS... AND IT DIDN'T HAVE TO BE THAT WAY.
THAT'S WHY I JOINED THE MOVEMENT.
I SAW THE STRUGGLE MY PARENTS AND OTHERS IN MY COMMUNITY EXPERIENCED WHEN WORKING IN THE FIELDS.
PICKING THIS COUNTRY'S PRODUCE IS IMPORTANT WORK--WORK TO BE PROUD OF--BUT THE WAY THEY WERE BEING TREATED WAS COMPLETELY UNFAIR AND UNNECESSARY.
ANYWAY, I'VE BEEN GOING ON TOO LONG...
...WHAT'S NEXT, CAMILO?
WELL, NOW THAT WE'VE MET CÉSAR AND DOLORES, LET'S JUMP AHEAD IN TIME A LITTLE!

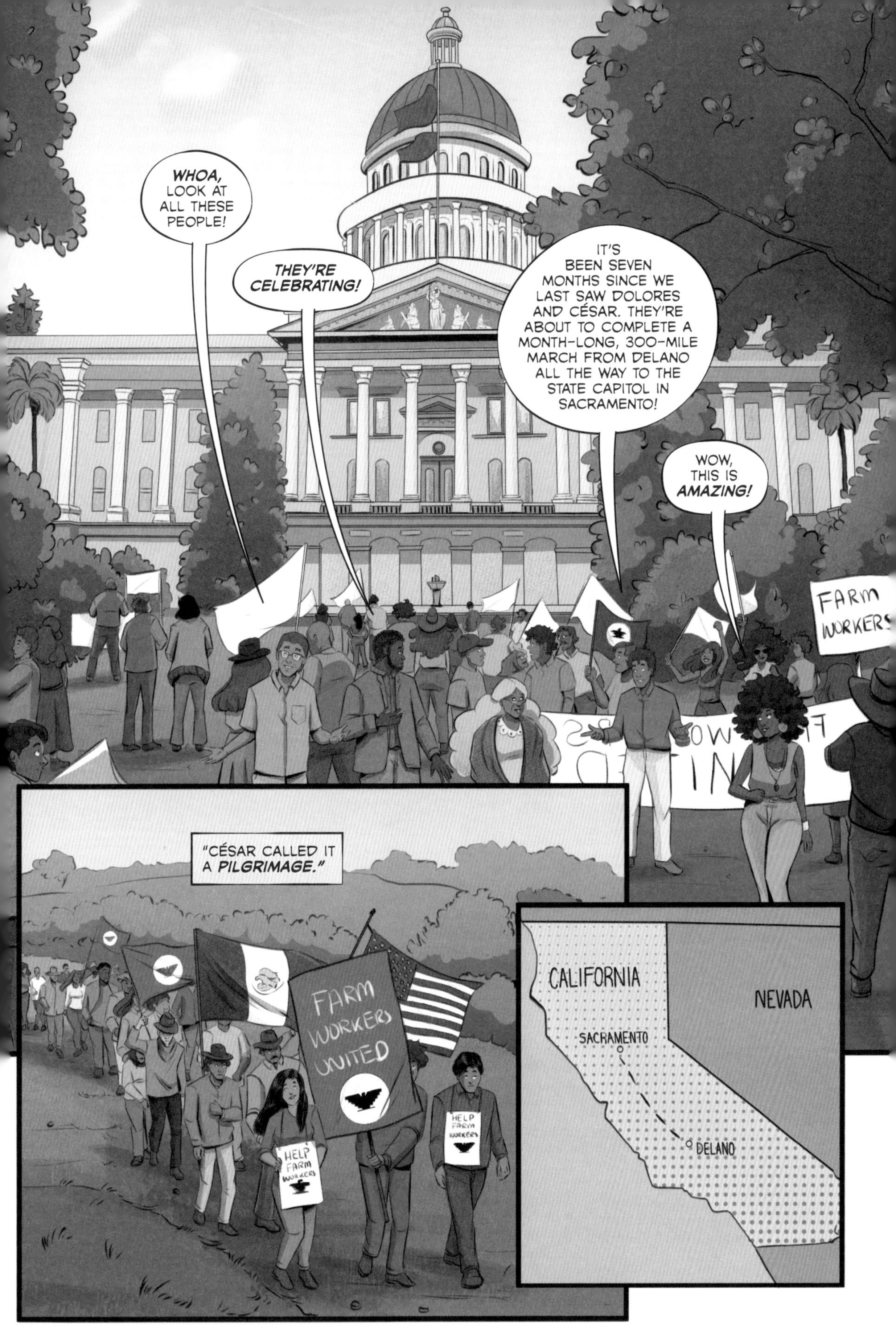
WHOA, LOOK AT ALL THESE PEOPLE!
THEY'RE CELEBRATING!
IT'S BEEN SEVEN MONTHS SINCE WE LAST SAW DOLORES AND CÉSAR. THEY'RE ABOUT TO COMPLETE A MONTH-LONG, 300-MILE MARCH FROM DELANO ALL THE WAY TO THE STATE CAPITOL IN SACRAMENTO!
WOW, THIS IS AMAZING!
FARM WORKERS
"CÉSAR CALLED IT A PILGRIMAGE."
FARM WORKERS UNITED
HELP FARM WORKERS
HELP FARM WORKERS
CALIFORNIA
NEVADA
SACRAMENTO
DELANO

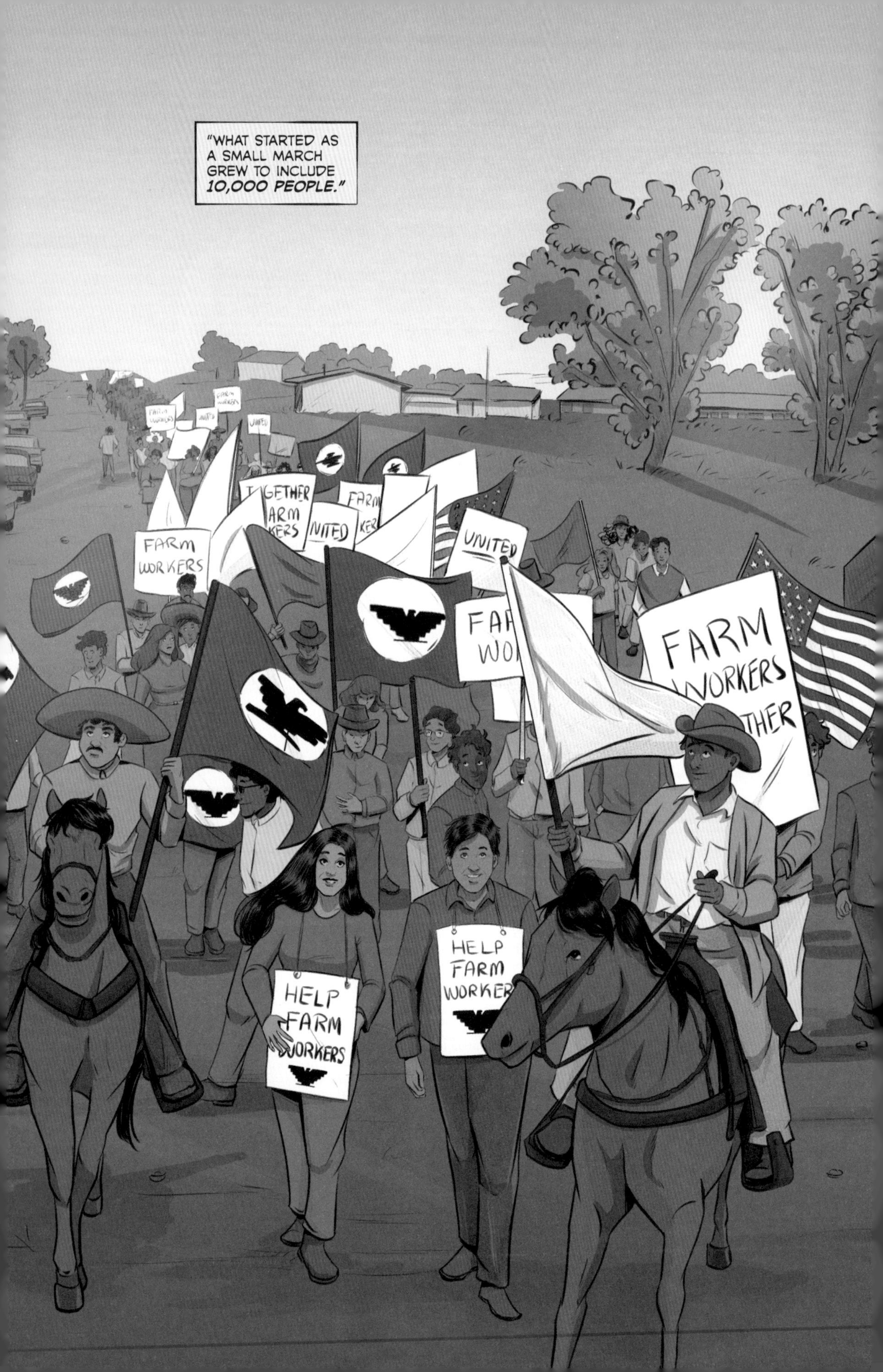
"WHAT STARTED AS A SMALL MARCH GREW TO INCLUDE *10,000 PEOPLE.*"
FARM WORKERS
UNITED
UNITED
UNITED
HELP FARM WORKERS
HELP FARM WORKERS

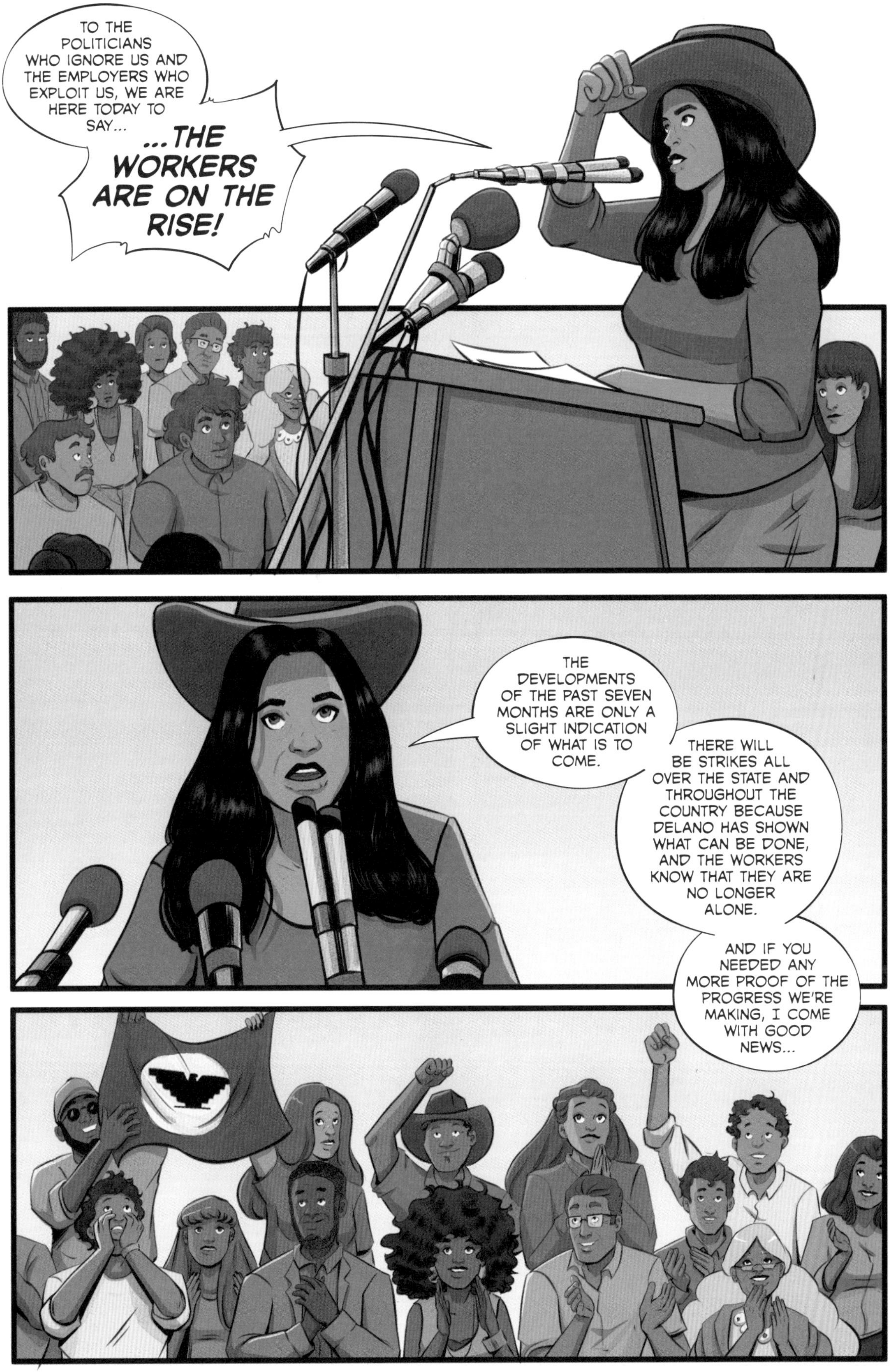
TO THE POLITICIANS WHO IGNORE US AND THE EMPLOYERS WHO EXPLOIT US, WE ARE HERE TODAY TO SAY...
...THE WORKERS ARE ON THE RISE!
THE DEVELOPMENTS OF THE PAST SEVEN MONTHS ARE ONLY A SLIGHT INDICATION OF WHAT IS TO COME.
THERE WILL BE STRIKES ALL OVER THE STATE AND THROUGHOUT THE COUNTRY BECAUSE DELANO HAS SHOWN WHAT CAN BE DONE, AND THE WORKERS KNOW THAT THEY ARE NO LONGER ALONE.
AND IF YOU NEEDED ANY MORE PROOF OF THE PROGRESS WE'RE MAKING, I COME WITH GOOD NEWS...

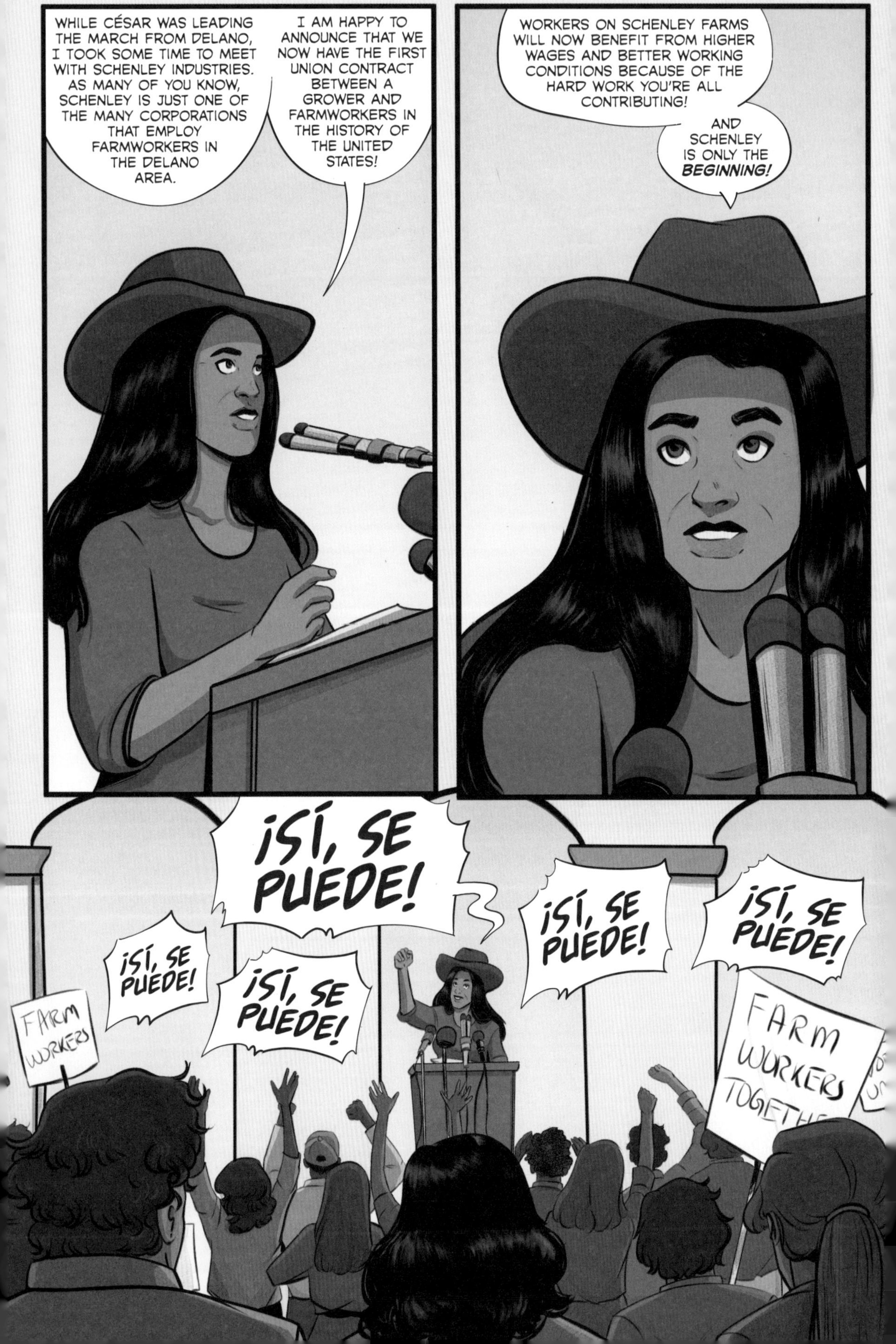

WHILE CÉSAR WAS LEADING THE MARCH FROM DELANO, I TOOK SOME TIME TO MEET WITH SCHENLEY INDUSTRIES. AS MANY OF YOU KNOW, SCHENLEY IS JUST ONE OF THE MANY CORPORATIONS THAT EMPLOY FARMWORKERS IN THE DELANO AREA.
I AM HAPPY TO ANNOUNCE THAT WE NOW HAVE THE FIRST UNION CONTRACT BETWEEN A GROWER AND FARMWORKERS IN THE HISTORY OF THE UNITED STATES!
WORKERS ON SCHENLEY FARMS WILL NOW BENEFIT FROM HIGHER WAGES AND BETTER WORKING CONDITIONS BECAUSE OF THE HARD WORK YOU'RE ALL CONTRIBUTING!
AND SCHENLEY IS ONLY THE ***BEGINNING!***
¡SÍ, SE PUEDE!
¡SÍ, SE PUEDE!
¡SÍ, SE PUEDE!
¡SÍ, SE PUEDE!
¡SÍ, SE PUEDE!
FARM WORKERS
FARM WORKERS TOGETHE

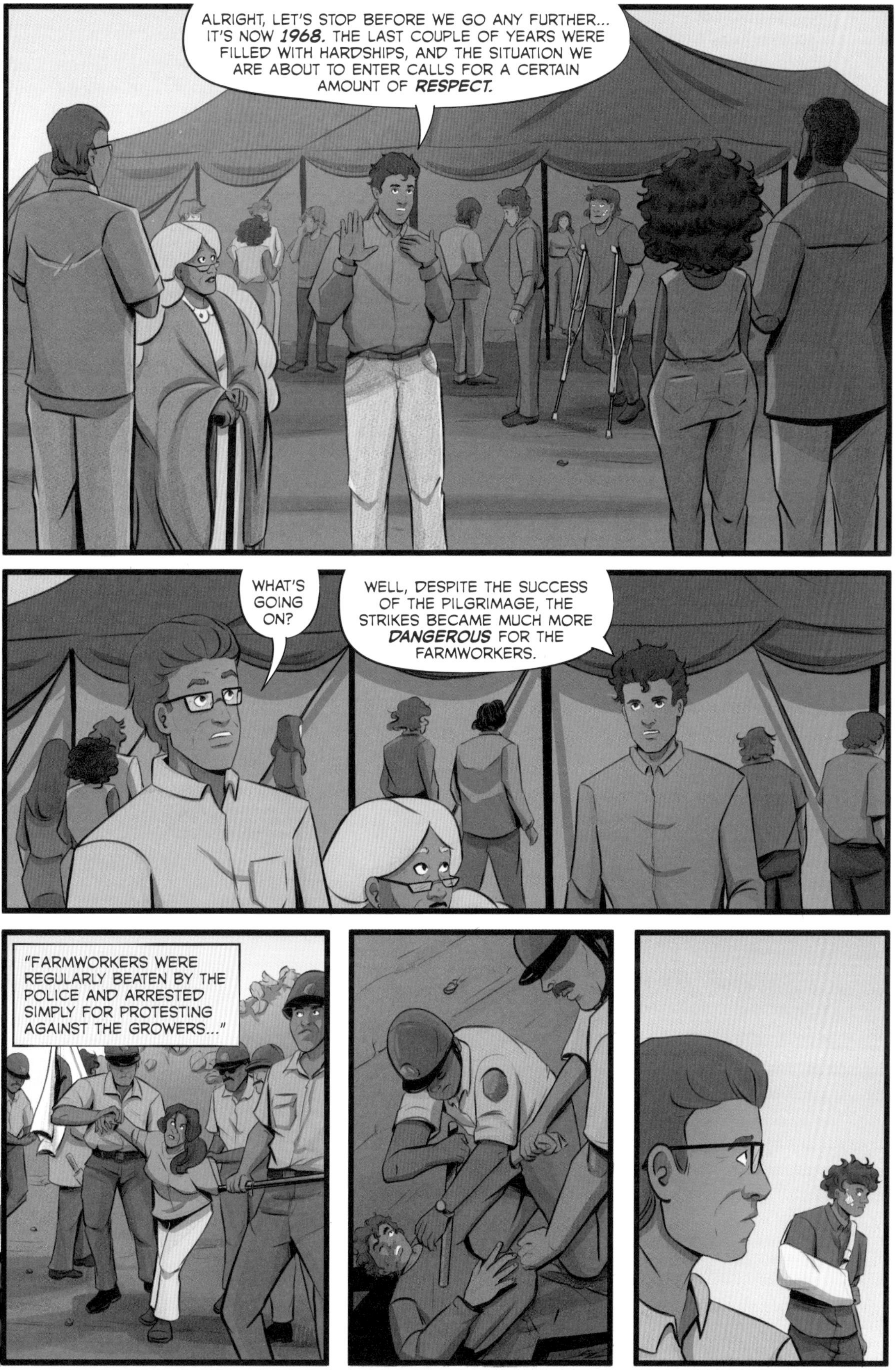
ALRIGHT, LET'S STOP BEFORE WE GO ANY FURTHER... IT'S NOW 1968. THE LAST COUPLE OF YEARS WERE FILLED WITH HARDSHIPS, AND THE SITUATION WE ARE ABOUT TO ENTER CALLS FOR A CERTAIN AMOUNT OF RESPECT.
WHAT'S GOING ON?
WELL, DESPITE THE SUCCESS OF THE PILGRIMAGE, THE STRIKES BECAME MUCH MORE DANGEROUS FOR THE FARMWORKERS.
"FARMWORKERS WERE REGULARLY BEATEN BY THE POLICE AND ARRESTED SIMPLY FOR PROTESTING AGAINST THE GROWERS..."

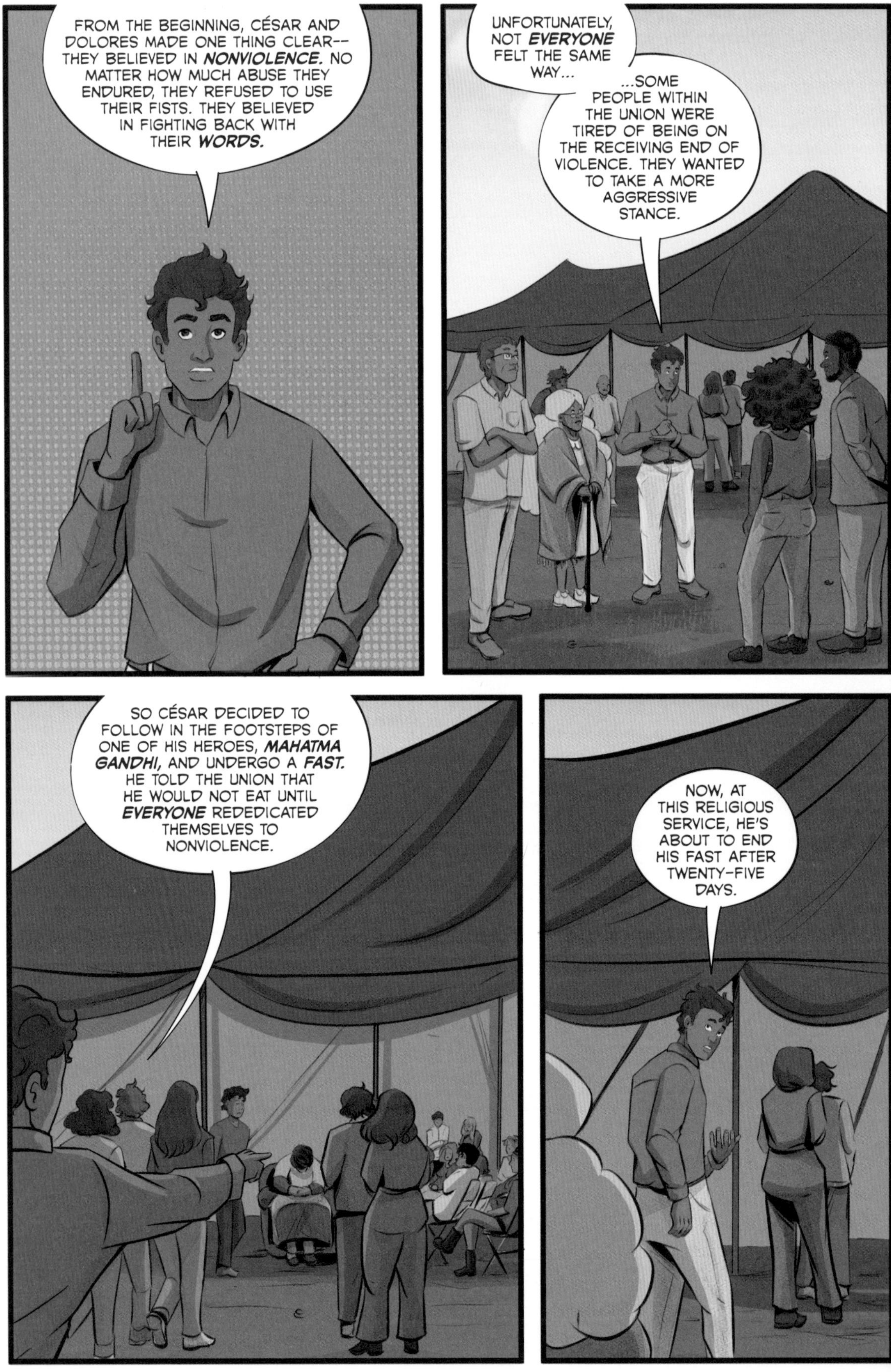
FROM THE BEGINNING, CÉSAR AND DOLORES MADE ONE THING CLEAR-- THEY BELIEVED IN NONVIOLENCE. NO MATTER HOW MUCH ABUSE THEY ENDURED, THEY REFUSED TO USE THEIR FISTS. THEY BELIEVED IN FIGHTING BACK WITH THEIR WORDS.
UNFORTUNATELY, NOT EVERYONE FELT THE SAME WAY...
...SOME PEOPLE WITHIN THE UNION WERE TIRED OF BEING ON THE RECEIVING END OF VIOLENCE. THEY WANTED TO TAKE A MORE AGGRESSIVE STANCE.
SO CÉSAR DECIDED TO FOLLOW IN THE FOOTSTEPS OF ONE OF HIS HEROES, MAHATMA GANDHI, AND UNDERGO A FAST. HE TOLD THE UNION THAT HE WOULD NOT EAT UNTIL EVERYONE REDEDICATED THEMSELVES TO NONVIOLENCE.
NOW, AT THIS RELIGIOUS SERVICE, HE'S ABOUT TO END HIS FAST AFTER TWENTY-FIVE DAYS.

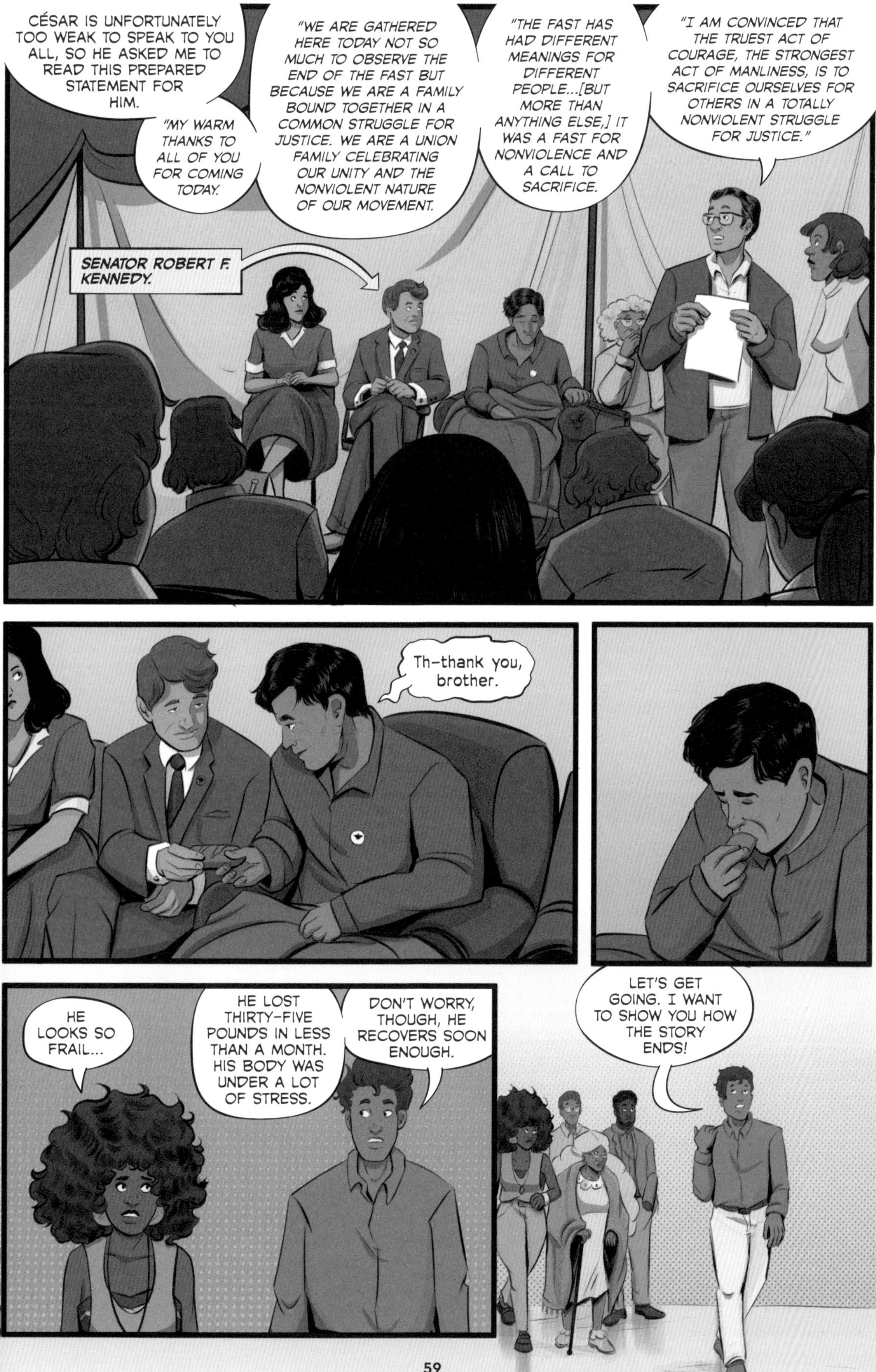
CÉSAR IS UNFORTUNATELY TOO WEAK TO SPEAK TO YOU ALL, SO HE ASKED ME TO READ THIS PREPARED STATEMENT FOR HIM.
"MY WARM THANKS TO ALL OF YOU FOR COMING TODAY.
"WE ARE GATHERED HERE TODAY NOT SO MUCH TO OBSERVE THE END OF THE FAST BUT BECAUSE WE ARE A FAMILY BOUND TOGETHER IN A COMMON STRUGGLE FOR JUSTICE. WE ARE A UNION FAMILY CELEBRATING OUR UNITY AND THE NONVIOLENT NATURE OF OUR MOVEMENT.
"THE FAST HAS HAD DIFFERENT MEANINGS FOR DIFFERENT PEOPLE...[BUT MORE THAN ANYTHING ELSE,] IT WAS A FAST FOR NONVIOLENCE AND A CALL TO SACRIFICE.
"I AM CONVINCED THAT THE TRUEST ACT OF COURAGE, THE STRONGEST ACT OF MANLINESS, IS TO SACRIFICE OURSELVES FOR OTHERS IN A TOTALLY NONVIOLENT STRUGGLE FOR JUSTICE."
SENATOR ROBERT F. KENNEDY.
Th-thank you, brother.
HE LOOKS SO FRAIL...
HE LOST THIRTY-FIVE POUNDS IN LESS THAN A MONTH. HIS BODY WAS UNDER A LOT OF STRESS.
DON'T WORRY, THOUGH, HE RECOVERS SOON ENOUGH.
LET'S GET GOING. I WANT TO SHOW YOU HOW THE STORY ENDS!

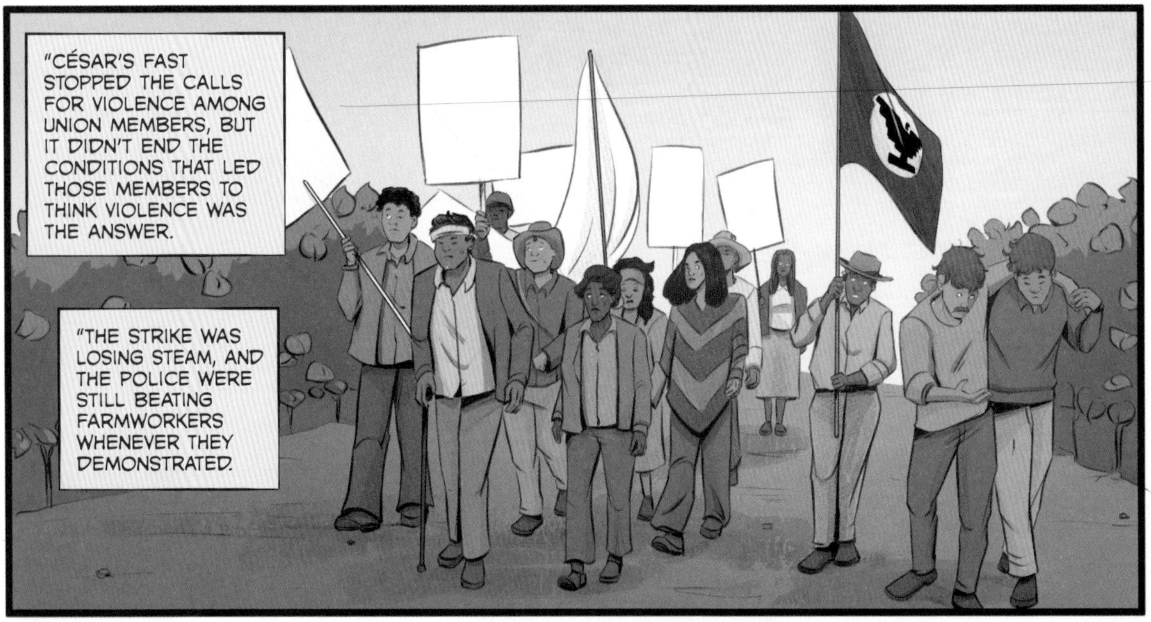
"CÉSAR'S FAST STOPPED THE CALLS FOR VIOLENCE AMONG UNION MEMBERS, BUT IT DIDN'T END THE CONDITIONS THAT LED THOSE MEMBERS TO THINK VIOLENCE WAS THE ANSWER.
"THE STRIKE WAS LOSING STEAM, AND THE POLICE WERE STILL BEATING FARMWORKERS WHENEVER THEY DEMONSTRATED.

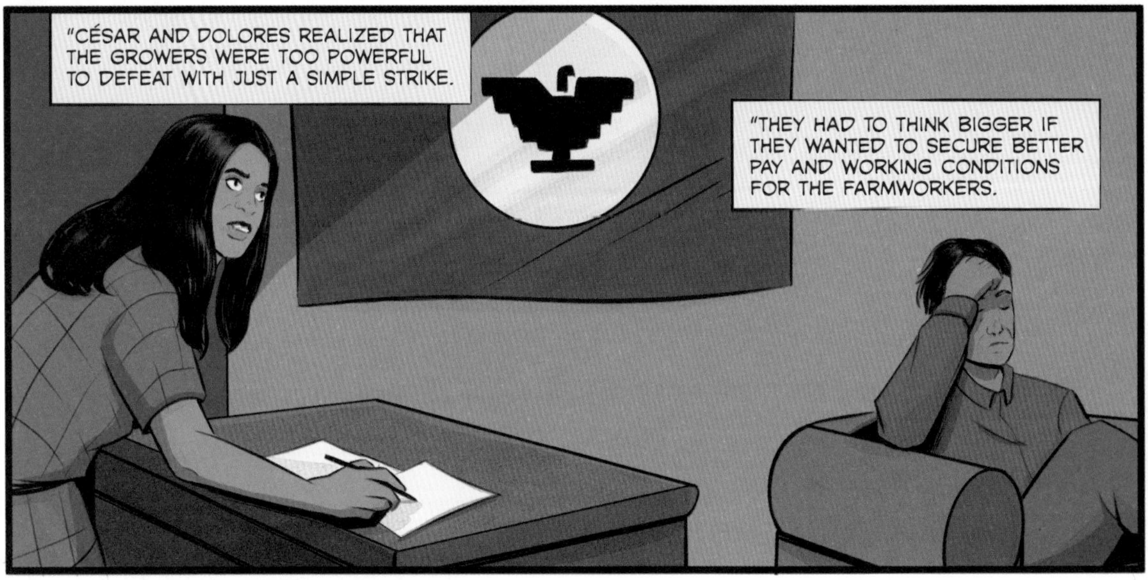
"CÉSAR AND DOLORES REALIZED THAT THE GROWERS WERE TOO POWERFUL TO DEFEAT WITH JUST A SIMPLE STRIKE.
"THEY HAD TO THINK BIGGER IF THEY WANTED TO SECURE BETTER PAY AND WORKING CONDITIONS FOR THE FARMWORKERS.

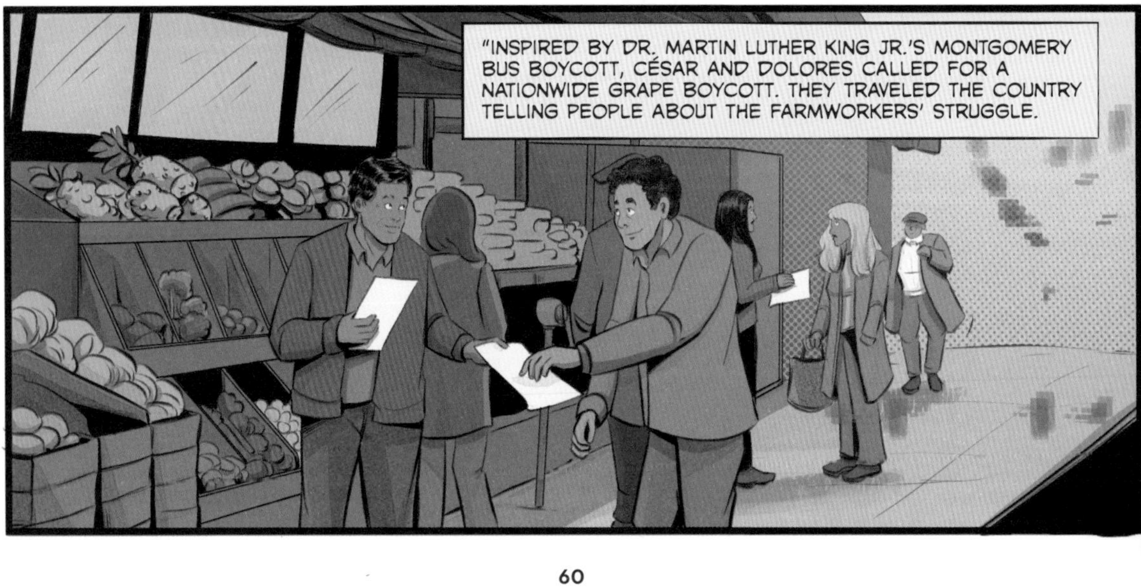
"INSPIRED BY DR. MARTIN LUTHER KING JR.'S MONTGOMERY BUS BOYCOTT, CÉSAR AND DOLORES CALLED FOR A NATIONWIDE GRAPE BOYCOTT. THEY TRAVELED THE COUNTRY TELLING PEOPLE ABOUT THE FARMWORKERS' STRUGGLE.

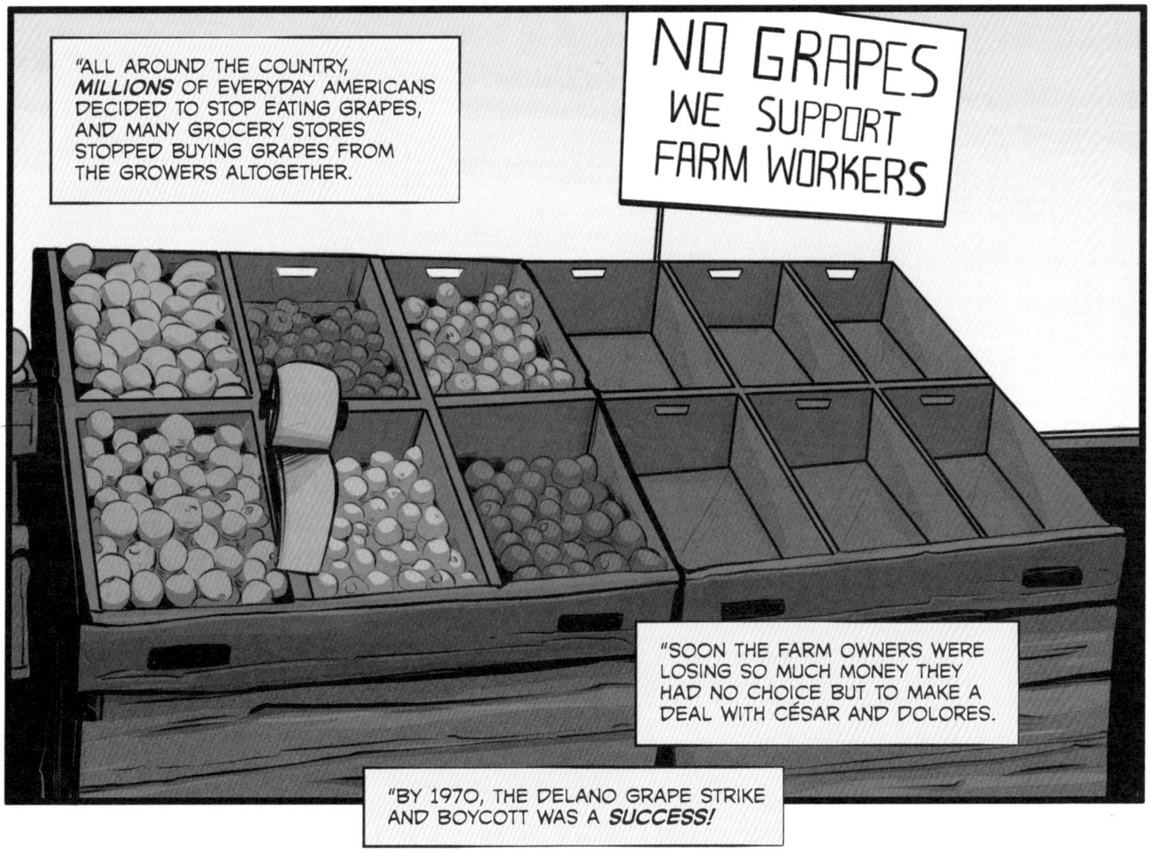
"ALL AROUND THE COUNTRY, **MILLIONS** OF EVERYDAY AMERICANS DECIDED TO STOP EATING GRAPES, AND MANY GROCERY STORES STOPPED BUYING GRAPES FROM THE GROWERS ALTOGETHER.
NO GRAPES WE SUPPORT FARM WORKERS
"SOON THE FARM OWNERS WERE LOSING SO MUCH MONEY THEY HAD NO CHOICE BUT TO MAKE A DEAL WITH CÉSAR AND DOLORES.
"BY 1970, THE DELANO GRAPE STRIKE AND BOYCOTT WAS A **SUCCESS!**

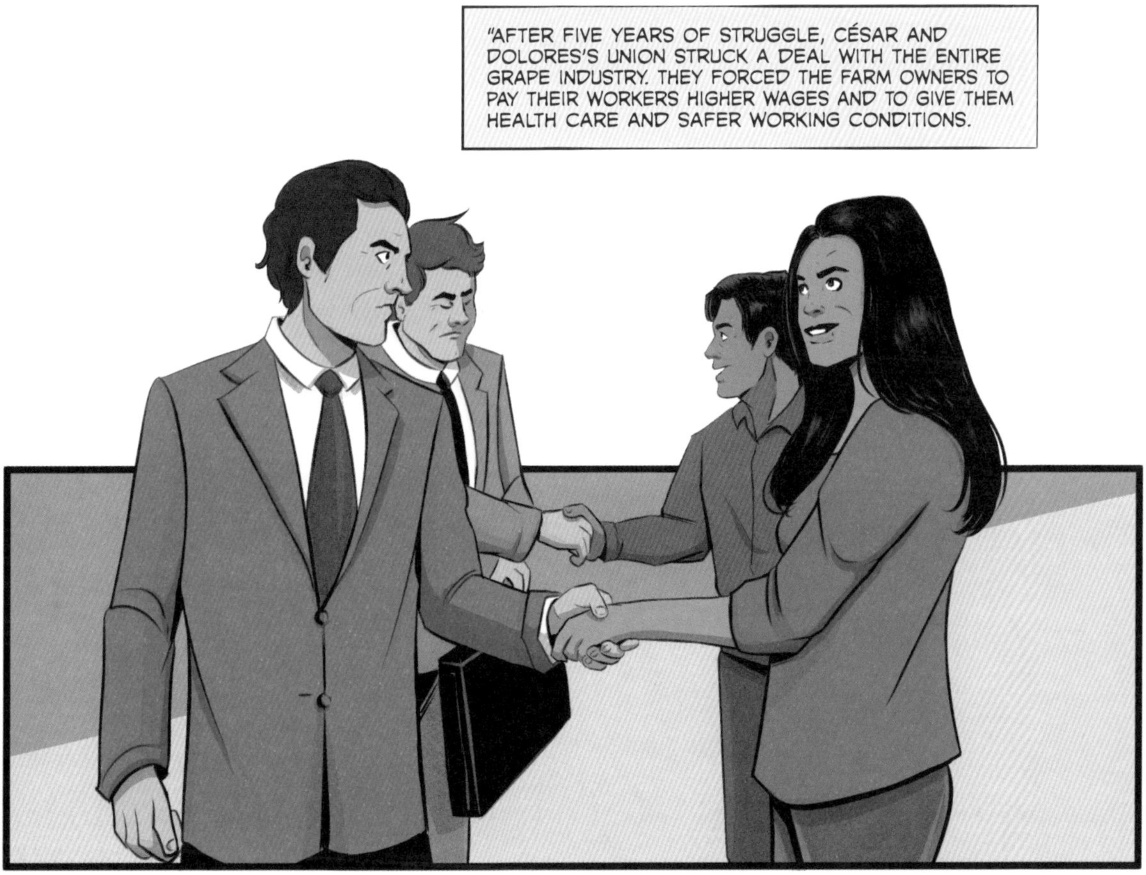
"AFTER FIVE YEARS OF STRUGGLE, CÉSAR AND DOLORES'S UNION STRUCK A DEAL WITH THE ENTIRE GRAPE INDUSTRY. THEY FORCED THE FARM OWNERS TO PAY THEIR WORKERS HIGHER WAGES AND TO GIVE THEM HEALTH CARE AND SAFER WORKING CONDITIONS.

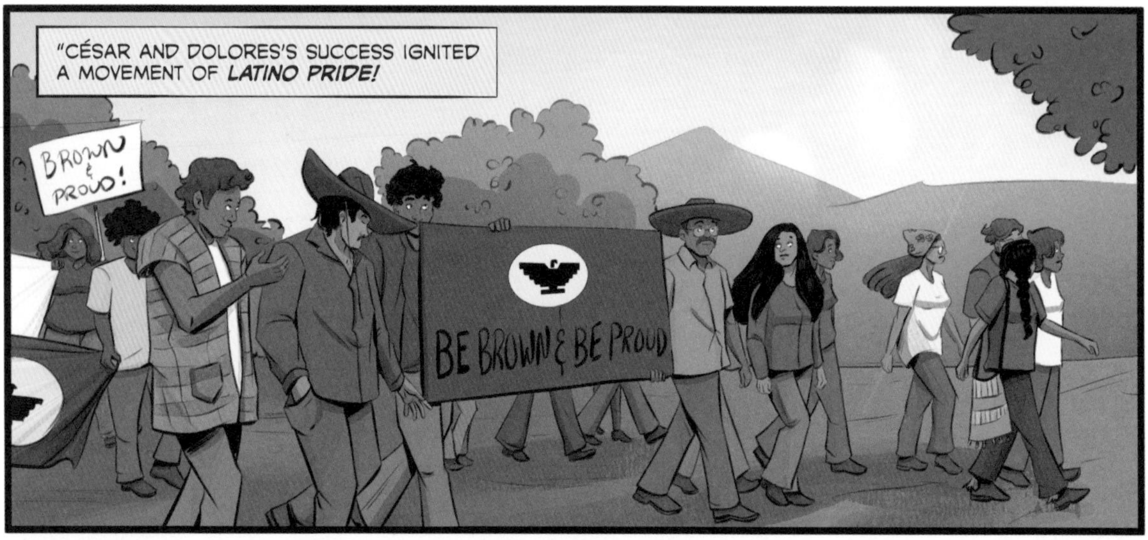
"CÉSAR AND DOLORES'S SUCCESS IGNITED A MOVEMENT OF LATINO PRIDE!
BROWN & PROUD!
BE BROWN & BE PROUD

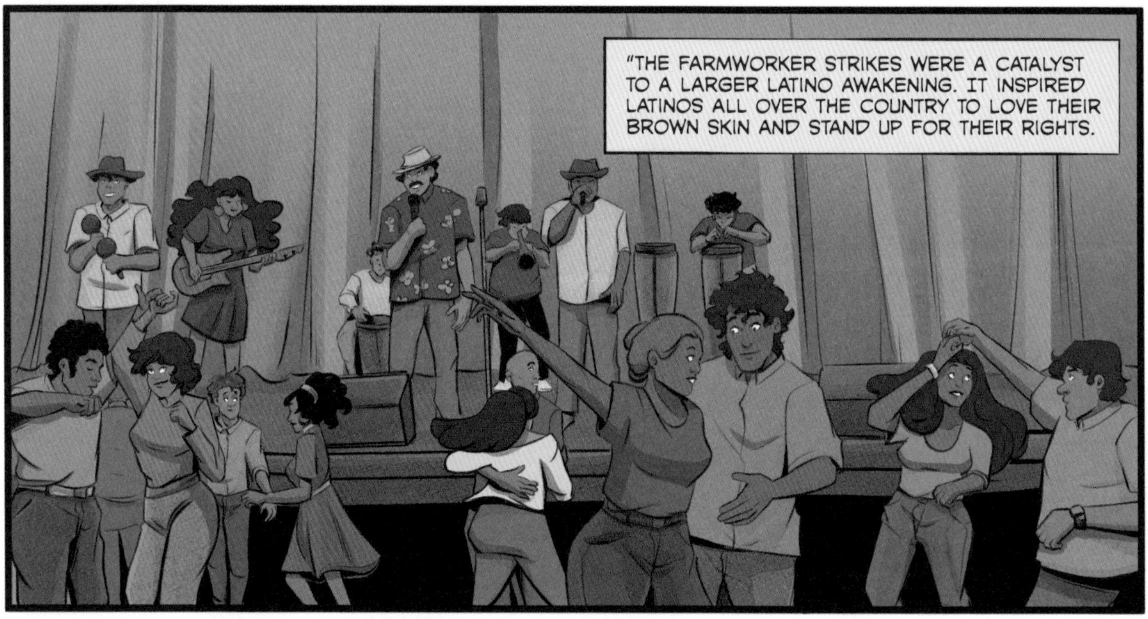
"THE FARMWORKER STRIKES WERE A CATALYST TO A LARGER LATINO AWAKENING. IT INSPIRED LATINOS ALL OVER THE COUNTRY TO LOVE THEIR BROWN SKIN AND STAND UP FOR THEIR RIGHTS.

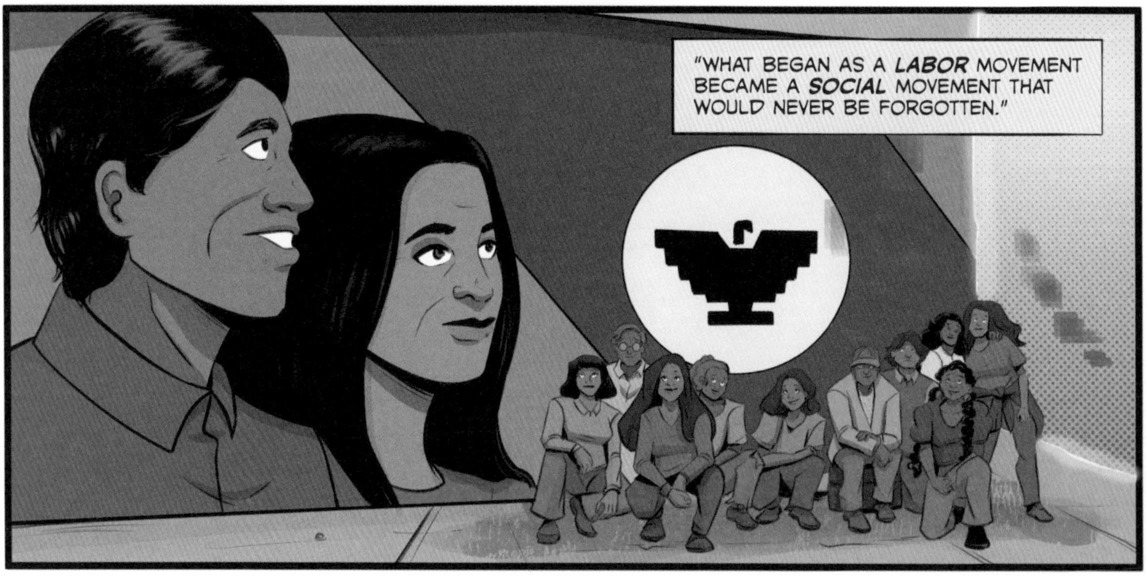
"WHAT BEGAN AS A LABOR MOVEMENT BECAME A SOCIAL MOVEMENT THAT WOULD NEVER BE FORGOTTEN."

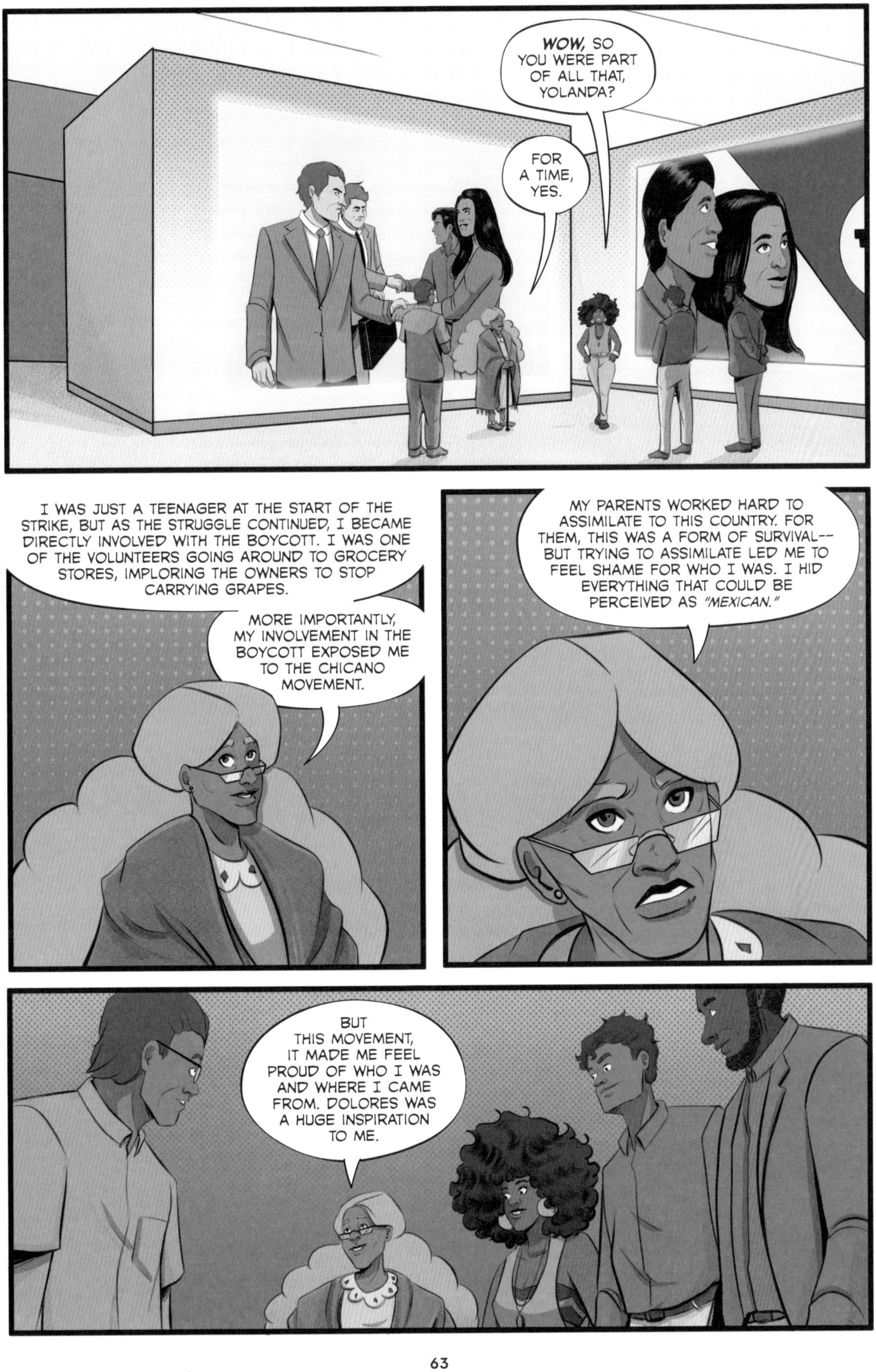
*WOW,* SO YOU WERE PART OF ALL THAT, YOLANDA?
FOR A TIME, YES.
I WAS JUST A TEENAGER AT THE START OF THE STRIKE, BUT AS THE STRUGGLE CONTINUED, I BECAME DIRECTLY INVOLVED WITH THE BOYCOTT. I WAS ONE OF THE VOLUNTEERS GOING AROUND TO GROCERY STORES, IMPLORING THE OWNERS TO STOP CARRYING GRAPES.
MORE IMPORTANTLY, MY INVOLVEMENT IN THE BOYCOTT EXPOSED ME TO THE CHICANO MOVEMENT.
MY PARENTS WORKED HARD TO ASSIMILATE TO THIS COUNTRY. FOR THEM, THIS WAS A FORM OF SURVIVAL--BUT TRYING TO ASSIMILATE LED ME TO FEEL SHAME FOR WHO I WAS. I HID EVERYTHING THAT COULD BE PERCEIVED AS *"MEXICAN."*
BUT THIS MOVEMENT, IT MADE ME FEEL PROUD OF WHO I WAS AND WHERE I CAME FROM. DOLORES WAS A HUGE INSPIRATION TO ME.

WHAT HAPPENED TO CÉSAR AND DOLORES AFTER THE BOYCOTT?

THEY CONTINUED WORKING WITH FARMWORKERS FOR MANY YEARS AND HELPED PASS LEGISLATION THAT ENSURED SOME OF THE RIGHTS THEY FOUGHT FOR IN THE STRIKE BECAME LAW.

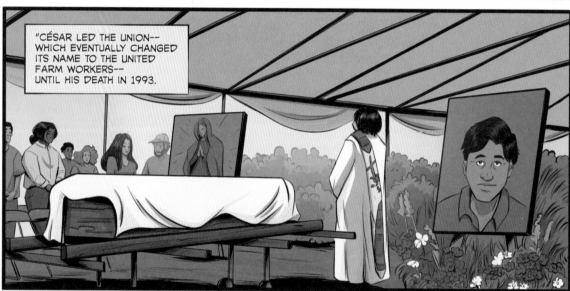

"CÉSAR LED THE UNION-- WHICH EVENTUALLY CHANGED ITS NAME TO THE UNITED FARM WORKERS-- UNTIL HIS DEATH IN 1993.

"CÉSAR'S DEATH LED TO A VERY SAD TIME, AND IT CREATED UNCERTAINTY WITHIN THE MOVEMENT. LUCKILY, THERE WAS NO SHORTAGE OF GREAT PEOPLE WITHIN THE ORGANIZATION TO MAKE SURE THE WORK CONTINUED."

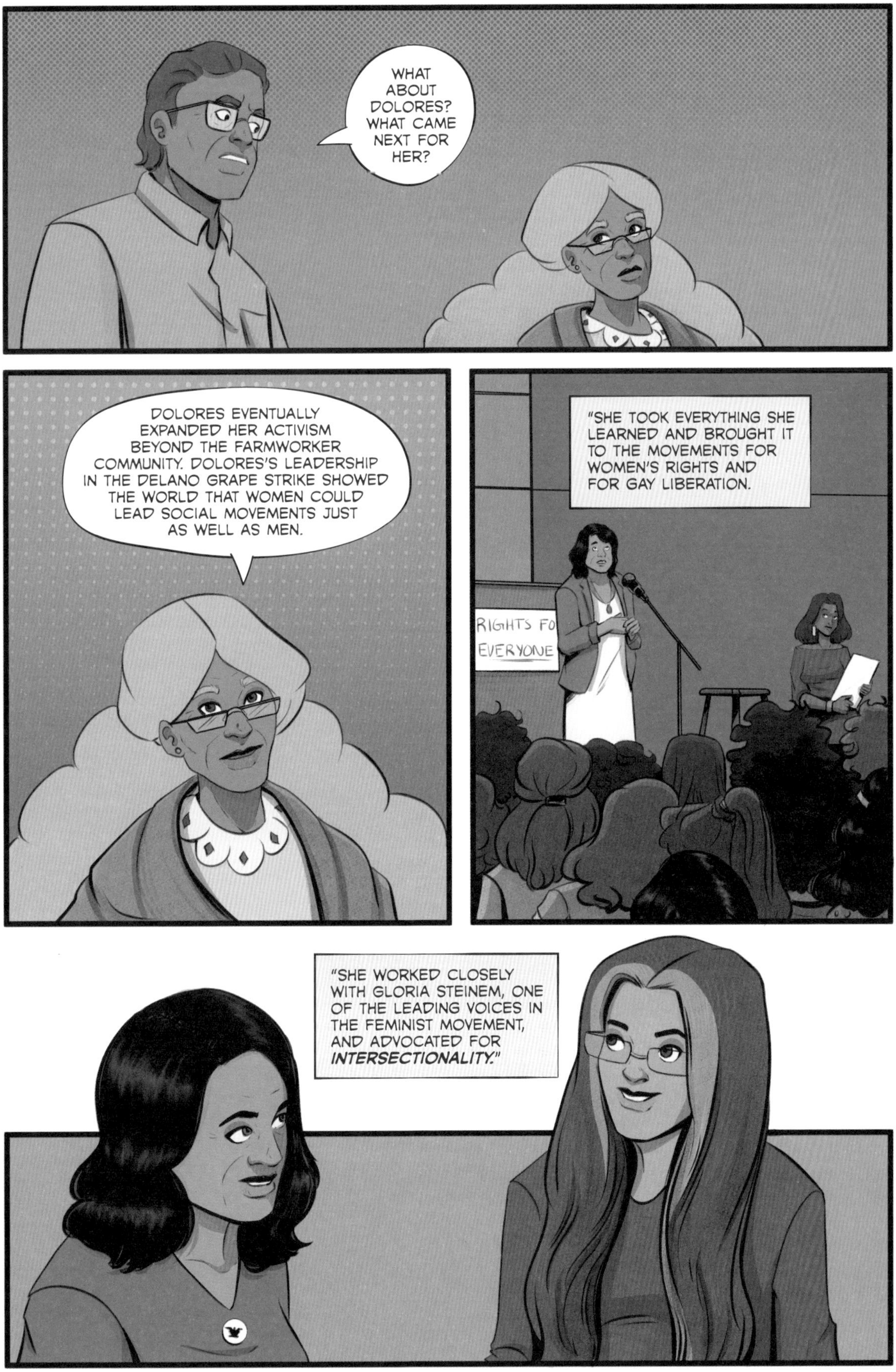
WHAT ABOUT DOLORES? WHAT CAME NEXT FOR HER?
DOLORES EVENTUALLY EXPANDED HER ACTIVISM BEYOND THE FARMWORKER COMMUNITY. DOLORES'S LEADERSHIP IN THE DELANO GRAPE STRIKE SHOWED THE WORLD THAT WOMEN COULD LEAD SOCIAL MOVEMENTS JUST AS WELL AS MEN.
"SHE TOOK EVERYTHING SHE LEARNED AND BROUGHT IT TO THE MOVEMENTS FOR WOMEN'S RIGHTS AND FOR GAY LIBERATION.
RIGHTS FO
EVERYONE
"SHE WORKED CLOSELY WITH GLORIA STEINEM, ONE OF THE LEADING VOICES IN THE FEMINIST MOVEMENT, AND ADVOCATED FOR ***INTERSECTIONALITY.***"

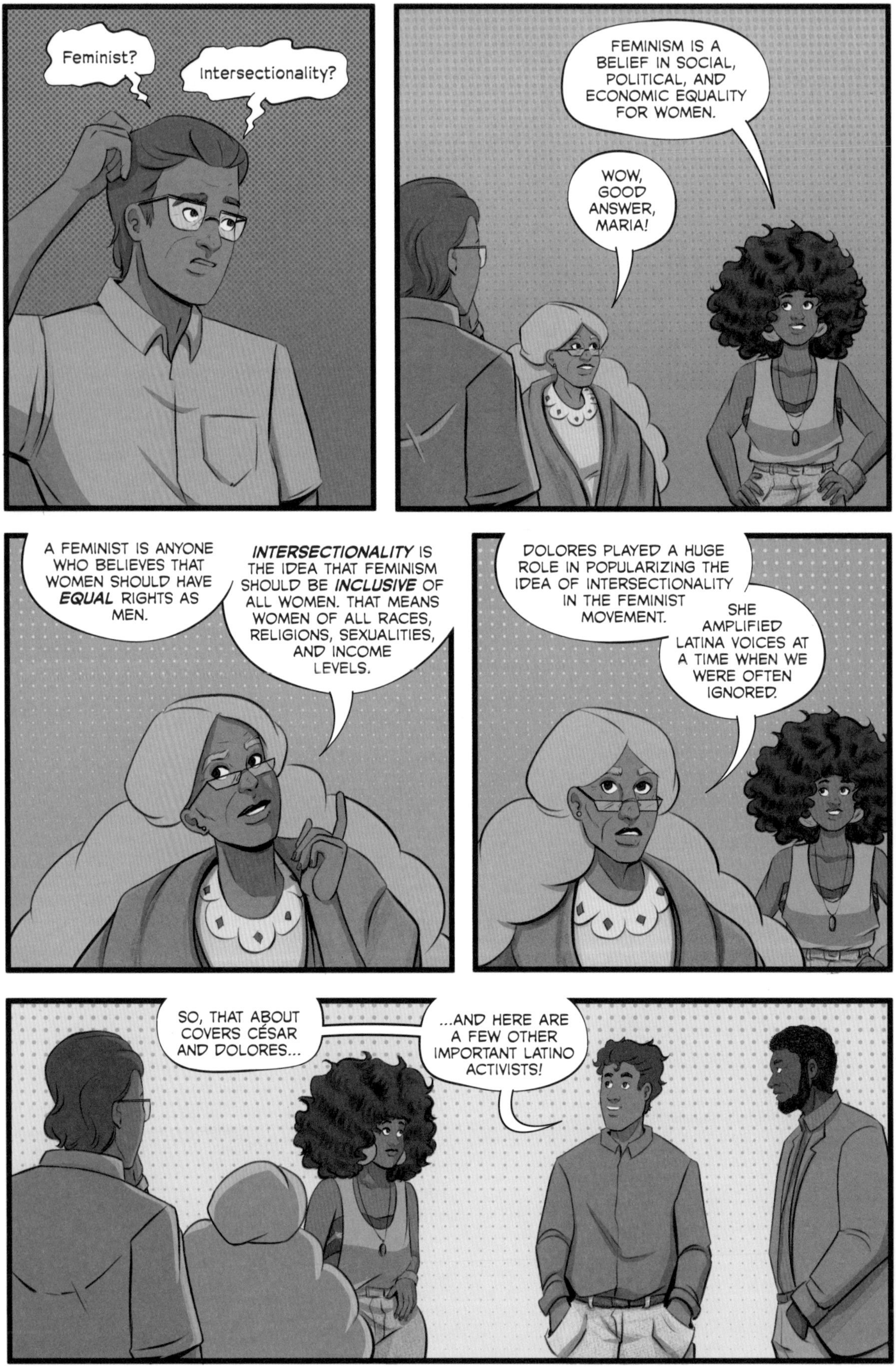
Feminist?
Intersectionality?
FEMINISM IS A BELIEF IN SOCIAL, POLITICAL, AND ECONOMIC EQUALITY FOR WOMEN.
WOW, GOOD ANSWER, MARIA!
A FEMINIST IS ANYONE WHO BELIEVES THAT WOMEN SHOULD HAVE EQUAL RIGHTS AS MEN.
INTERSECTIONALITY IS THE IDEA THAT FEMINISM SHOULD BE INCLUSIVE OF ALL WOMEN. THAT MEANS WOMEN OF ALL RACES, RELIGIONS, SEXUALITIES, AND INCOME LEVELS.
DOLORES PLAYED A HUGE ROLE IN POPULARIZING THE IDEA OF INTERSECTIONALITY IN THE FEMINIST MOVEMENT.
SHE AMPLIFIED LATINA VOICES AT A TIME WHEN WE WERE OFTEN IGNORED.
SO, THAT ABOUT COVERS CÉSAR AND DOLORES...
...AND HERE ARE A FEW OTHER IMPORTANT LATINO ACTIVISTS!

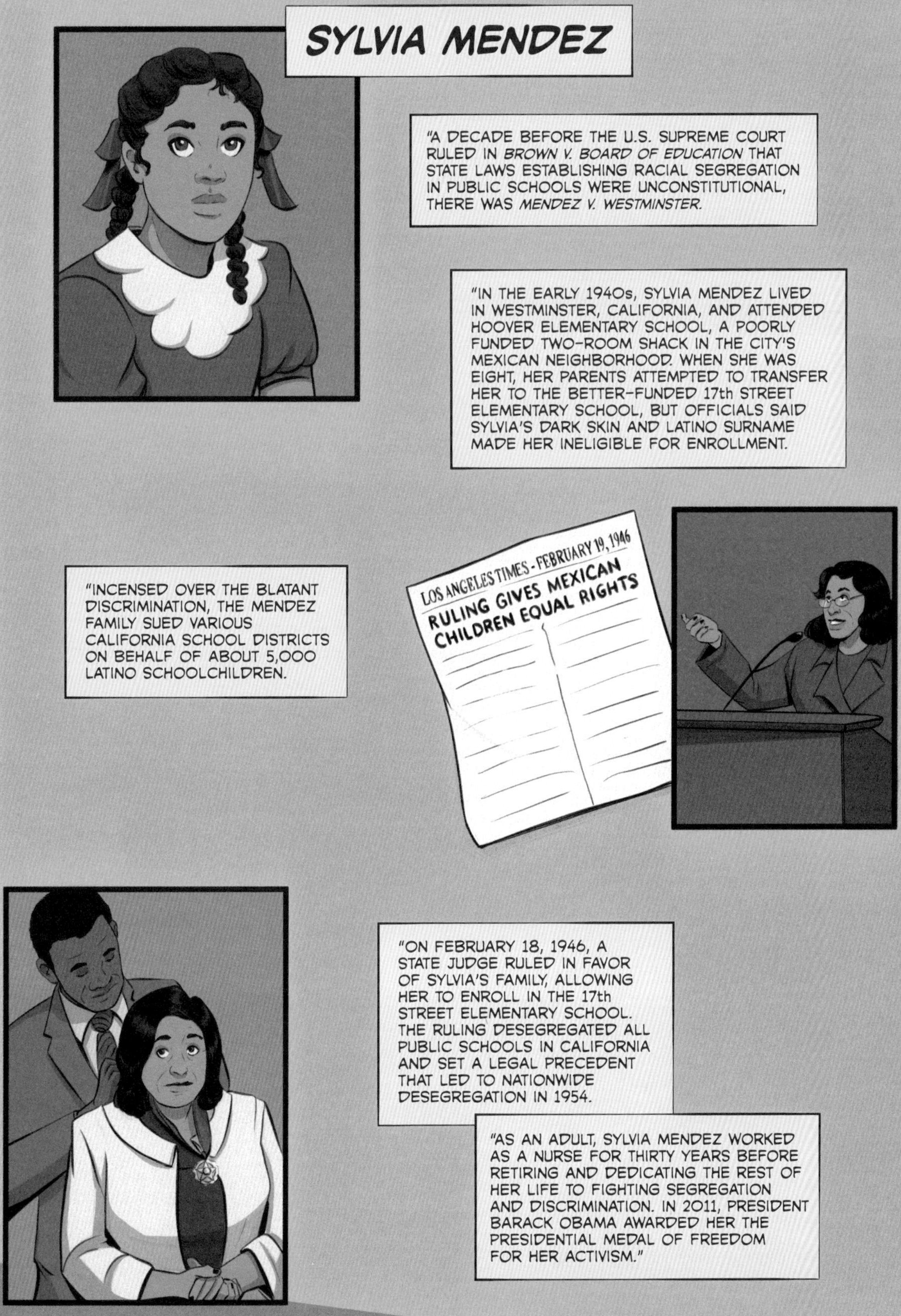
SYLVIA MENDEZ
"A DECADE BEFORE THE U.S. SUPREME COURT RULED IN *BROWN V. BOARD OF EDUCATION* THAT STATE LAWS ESTABLISHING RACIAL SEGREGATION IN PUBLIC SCHOOLS WERE UNCONSTITUTIONAL, THERE WAS *MENDEZ V. WESTMINSTER.*
"IN THE EARLY 1940s, SYLVIA MENDEZ LIVED IN WESTMINSTER, CALIFORNIA, AND ATTENDED HOOVER ELEMENTARY SCHOOL, A POORLY FUNDED TWO-ROOM SHACK IN THE CITY'S MEXICAN NEIGHBORHOOD. WHEN SHE WAS EIGHT, HER PARENTS ATTEMPTED TO TRANSFER HER TO THE BETTER-FUNDED 17th STREET ELEMENTARY SCHOOL, BUT OFFICIALS SAID SYLVIA'S DARK SKIN AND LATINO SURNAME MADE HER INELIGIBLE FOR ENROLLMENT.
"INCENSED OVER THE BLATANT DISCRIMINATION, THE MENDEZ FAMILY SUED VARIOUS CALIFORNIA SCHOOL DISTRICTS ON BEHALF OF ABOUT 5,000 LATINO SCHOOLCHILDREN.
LOS ANGELES TIMES - FEBRUARY 19, 1946
RULING GIVES MEXICAN CHILDREN EQUAL RIGHTS
"ON FEBRUARY 18, 1946, A STATE JUDGE RULED IN FAVOR OF SYLVIA'S FAMILY, ALLOWING HER TO ENROLL IN THE 17th STREET ELEMENTARY SCHOOL. THE RULING DESEGREGATED ALL PUBLIC SCHOOLS IN CALIFORNIA AND SET A LEGAL PRECEDENT THAT LED TO NATIONWIDE DESEGREGATION IN 1954.
"AS AN ADULT, SYLVIA MENDEZ WORKED AS A NURSE FOR THIRTY YEARS BEFORE RETIRING AND DEDICATING THE REST OF HER LIFE TO FIGHTING SEGREGATION AND DISCRIMINATION. IN 2011, PRESIDENT BARACK OBAMA AWARDED HER THE PRESIDENTIAL MEDAL OF FREEDOM FOR HER ACTIVISM."

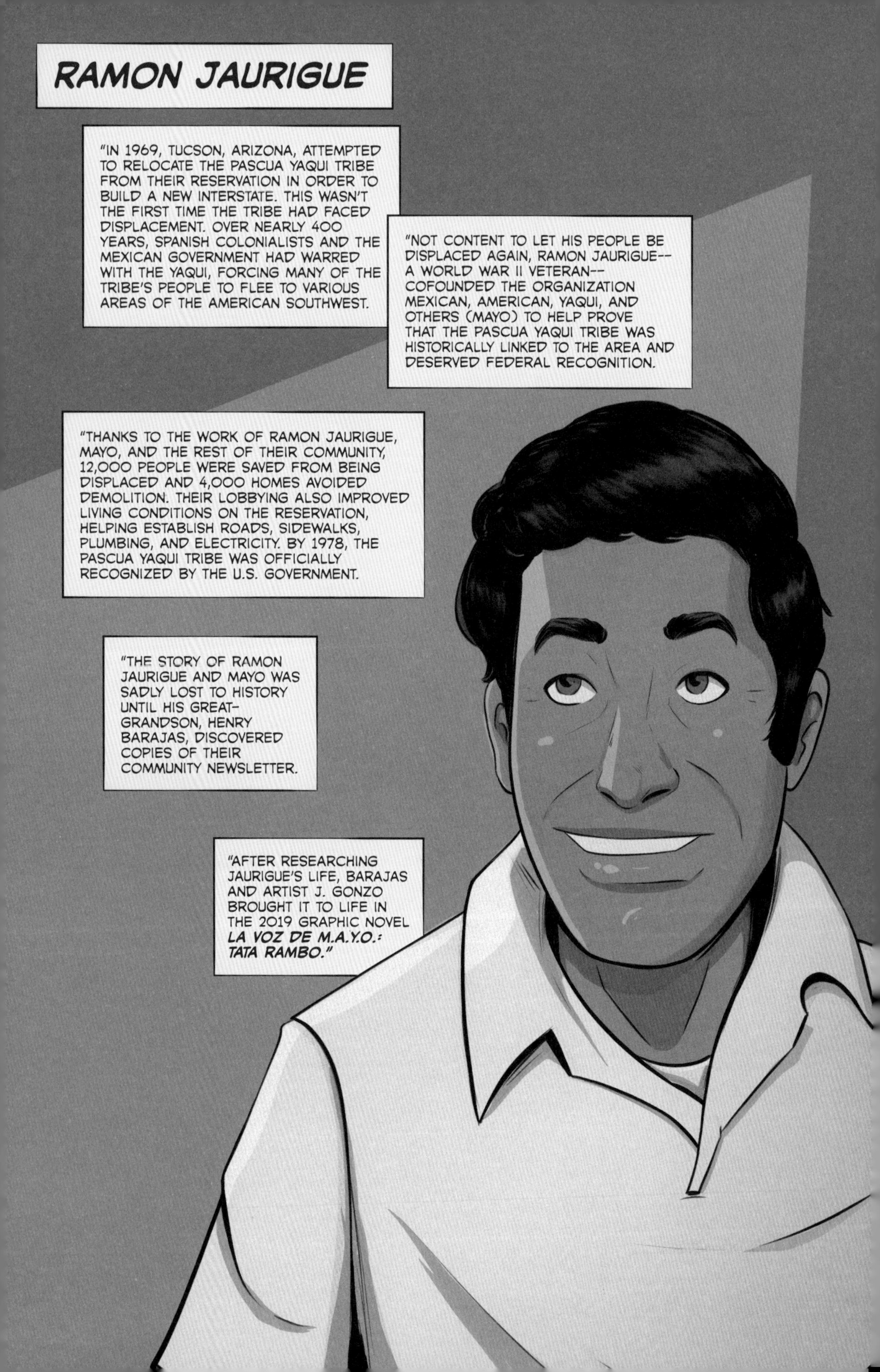
RAMON JAURIGUE
"IN 1969, TUCSON, ARIZONA, ATTEMPTED TO RELOCATE THE PASCUA YAQUI TRIBE FROM THEIR RESERVATION IN ORDER TO BUILD A NEW INTERSTATE. THIS WASN'T THE FIRST TIME THE TRIBE HAD FACED DISPLACEMENT. OVER NEARLY 400 YEARS, SPANISH COLONIALISTS AND THE MEXICAN GOVERNMENT HAD WARRED WITH THE YAQUI, FORCING MANY OF THE TRIBE'S PEOPLE TO FLEE TO VARIOUS AREAS OF THE AMERICAN SOUTHWEST.
"NOT CONTENT TO LET HIS PEOPLE BE DISPLACED AGAIN, RAMON JAURIGUE--A WORLD WAR II VETERAN--COFOUNDED THE ORGANIZATION MEXICAN, AMERICAN, YAQUI, AND OTHERS (MAYO) TO HELP PROVE THAT THE PASCUA YAQUI TRIBE WAS HISTORICALLY LINKED TO THE AREA AND DESERVED FEDERAL RECOGNITION.
"THANKS TO THE WORK OF RAMON JAURIGUE, MAYO, AND THE REST OF THEIR COMMUNITY, 12,000 PEOPLE WERE SAVED FROM BEING DISPLACED AND 4,000 HOMES AVOIDED DEMOLITION. THEIR LOBBYING ALSO IMPROVED LIVING CONDITIONS ON THE RESERVATION, HELPING ESTABLISH ROADS, SIDEWALKS, PLUMBING, AND ELECTRICITY. BY 1978, THE PASCUA YAQUI TRIBE WAS OFFICIALLY RECOGNIZED BY THE U.S. GOVERNMENT.
"THE STORY OF RAMON JAURIGUE AND MAYO WAS SADLY LOST TO HISTORY UNTIL HIS GREAT-GRANDSON, HENRY BARAJAS, DISCOVERED COPIES OF THEIR COMMUNITY NEWSLETTER.
"AFTER RESEARCHING JAURIGUE'S LIFE, BARAJAS AND ARTIST J. GONZO BROUGHT IT TO LIFE IN THE 2019 GRAPHIC NOVEL ***LA VOZ DE M.A.Y.O.: TATA RAMBO."***

# SYLVIA RIVERA

"AT JUST THREE YEARS OLD, **SYLVIA RIVERA** WAS ORPHANED. BY THE 1960s, AT AGE ELEVEN, SHE WAS LIVING ON THE STREETS OF NEW YORK CITY AND LEARNING ABOUT HER TRANSGENDER IDENTITY IN THE MOST DIFFICULT OF CIRCUMSTANCES.

"IN 1970, AFTER ALMOST A DECADE OF SPORADIC HOMELESSNESS, SYLVIA AND HER FRIEND MARSHA P. JOHNSON COFOUNDED THE ORGANIZATION STREET TRANSVESTITE ACTION REVOLUTIONARIES *(STAR)*.

"THE GROUP HAD TWO PILLARS. ONE, TO PROVIDE SERVICES FOR HOMELESS QUEER YOUTH-- THE VAST MAJORITY AT THE TIME WERE QUEER PEOPLE OF COLOR LIKE SYLVIA. TWO, TO ADVOCATE FOR THE PASSAGE OF NEW YORK'S SEXUAL ORIENTATION NON-DISCRIMINATION ACT. THIS LEGISLATION, WHICH WAS FIRST INTRODUCED IN 1971 BUT NOT PASSED UNTIL 2002, BANS DISCRIMINATION IN EMPLOYMENT, HOUSING, EDUCATION, AND MORE.

"SYLVIA ADVOCATED FOR TRANSGENDER RIGHTS THROUGHOUT HER LIFE AND WAS OFTEN ANGERED AT THE LACK OF TRANSGENDER INCLUSION IN THE BROADER LGBTQ+ AGENDA. WHEN MAINSTREAM GAY RIGHTS ORGANIZATIONS PUSHED FOR ASSIMILATION, SYLVIA CALLED FOR ***LIBERATION.***

"SYLVIA RIVERA IS NOW REMEMBERED AS ONE OF MOST IMPORTANT LGBTQ+ ACTIVISTS IN AMERICAN HISTORY-- A PUERTO RICAN AND VENEZUELAN AMERICAN HERO WHO PAVED THE WAY FOR THE MODERN TRANSGENDER RIGHTS MOVEMENT."

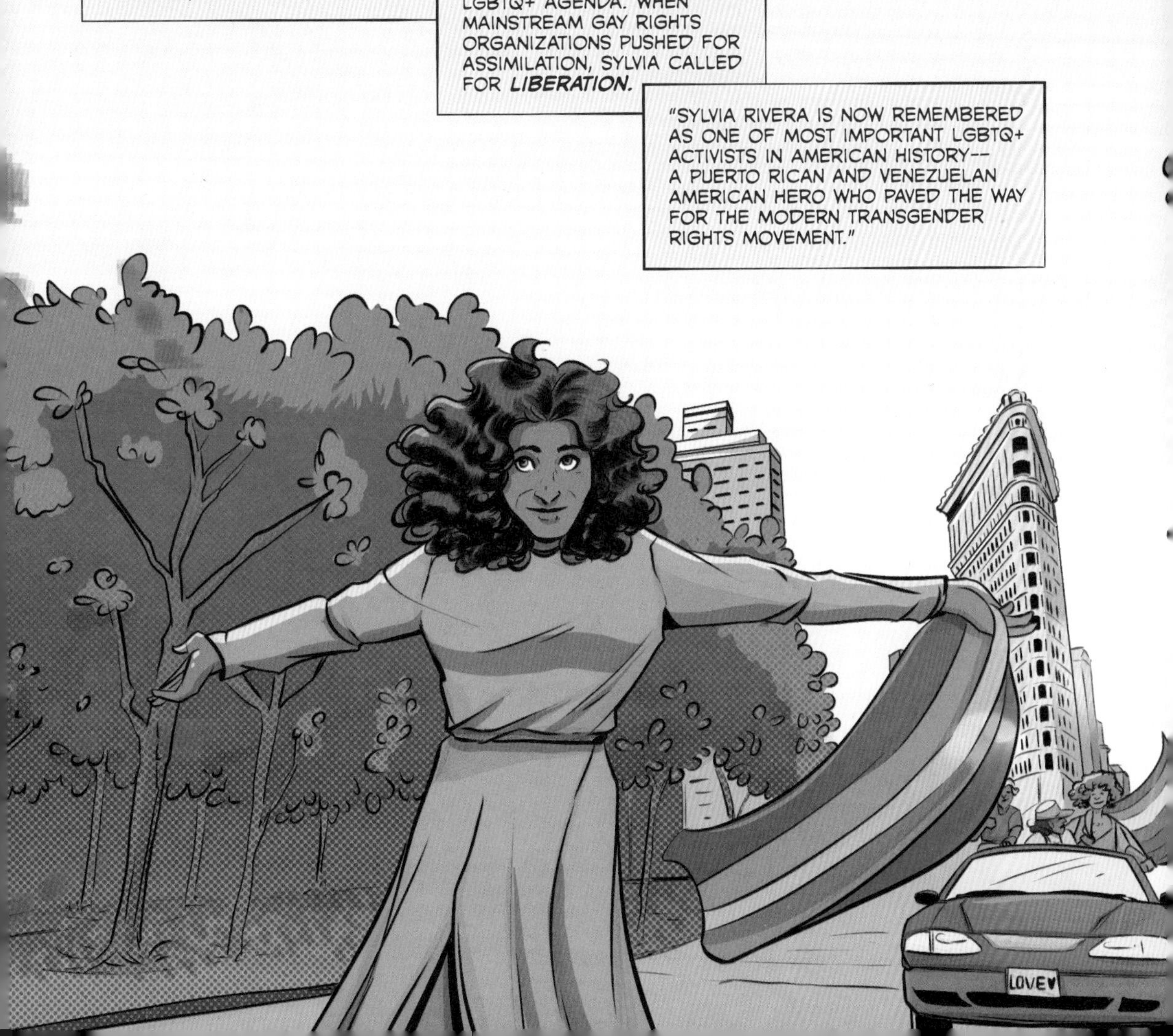

LOVE♥

# FELIPE LUCIANO

"THE LATE 1960s WERE A TIME OF REVOLUTION. WHILE THE BLACK PANTHER PARTY RECEIVED MOST OF THE NATIONWIDE HEADLINES--AND SCORN--ITS REVOLUTIONARY POLITICS WERE INSPIRING A SIMILAR GROUP IN NEW YORK CITY.

"THEY CALLED THEMSELVES THE ***YOUNG LORDS PARTY,*** AND THEY BELIEVED IT WAS THEIR DUTY TO CONFRONT THE RACISM AND CLASSISM INHERENT IN MODERN SOCIETY.

"AT THE PARTY'S HEAD WAS A YOUNG AFRO-PUERTO RICAN POET NAMED ***FELIPE LUCIANO.***

"BORN IN EAST HARLEM, FELIPE FOUND POLITICS AND POETRY WHILE SERVING A TWO-YEAR PRISON SENTENCE. HE EMERGED FROM INCARCERATION WITH A SENSE OF ENLIGHTENMENT AND A HUNGER FOR JUSTICE. FELIPE FORMED THE YOUNG LORDS PARTY AS A STUDENT GROUP AT QUEENS COLLEGE. THE PARTY ORGANIZED IRREVERENT PROTESTS THAT LEAD TO SUBSTANTIAL CHANGE IN THE AREAS OF EDUCATION, SANITATION AND HEALTH CARE, AND SERVED THEIR LOW-INCOME COMMUNITIES THROUGH FREE BREAKFAST PROGRAMS AND CHILDCARE.

TENGO PUERTO RICO
EN MI,
CORAZÓN
YLO

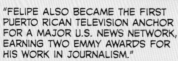

"WHILE THE YOUNG LORDS PARTY WOULD DISSIPATE WITHIN A FEW YEARS OF THEIR INITIAL FORMATION, THEY ARE OFTEN CREDITED FOR JUMP-STARTING A GENERATION OF PUERTO RICAN ACTIVISTS CONCERNED WITH LIBERATION AND SOCIAL JUSTICE.

"AFTER HIS DEPARTURE FROM THE YOUNG LORDS PARTY, FELIPE SOMETIMES WORKED ALONGSIDE THE VERY INSTITUTIONS HE ONCE FOUGHT AGAINST. FOR INSTANCE, EVEN THOUGH HE'D BEEN A VICTIM OF POLICE BRUTALITY, FELIPE CHOSE TO PARTICIPATE IN A NEW YORK CITY TASK FORCE ON CIVILIAN AND POLICE RELATIONS AIMED AT CURBING POLICE VIOLENCE.

"FELIPE CONSIDERED THIS MERELY AN EVOLUTION IN HIS ACTIVISM, SAYING, '*I'M STILL A WARRIOR, BUT I HAVE CHOSEN OTHER WEAPONS. WHEN I TALK, PEOPLE LISTEN.*'

"FELIPE ALSO BECAME THE FIRST PUERTO RICAN TELEVISION ANCHOR FOR A MAJOR U.S. NEWS NETWORK, EARNING TWO EMMY AWARDS FOR HIS WORK IN JOURNALISM."

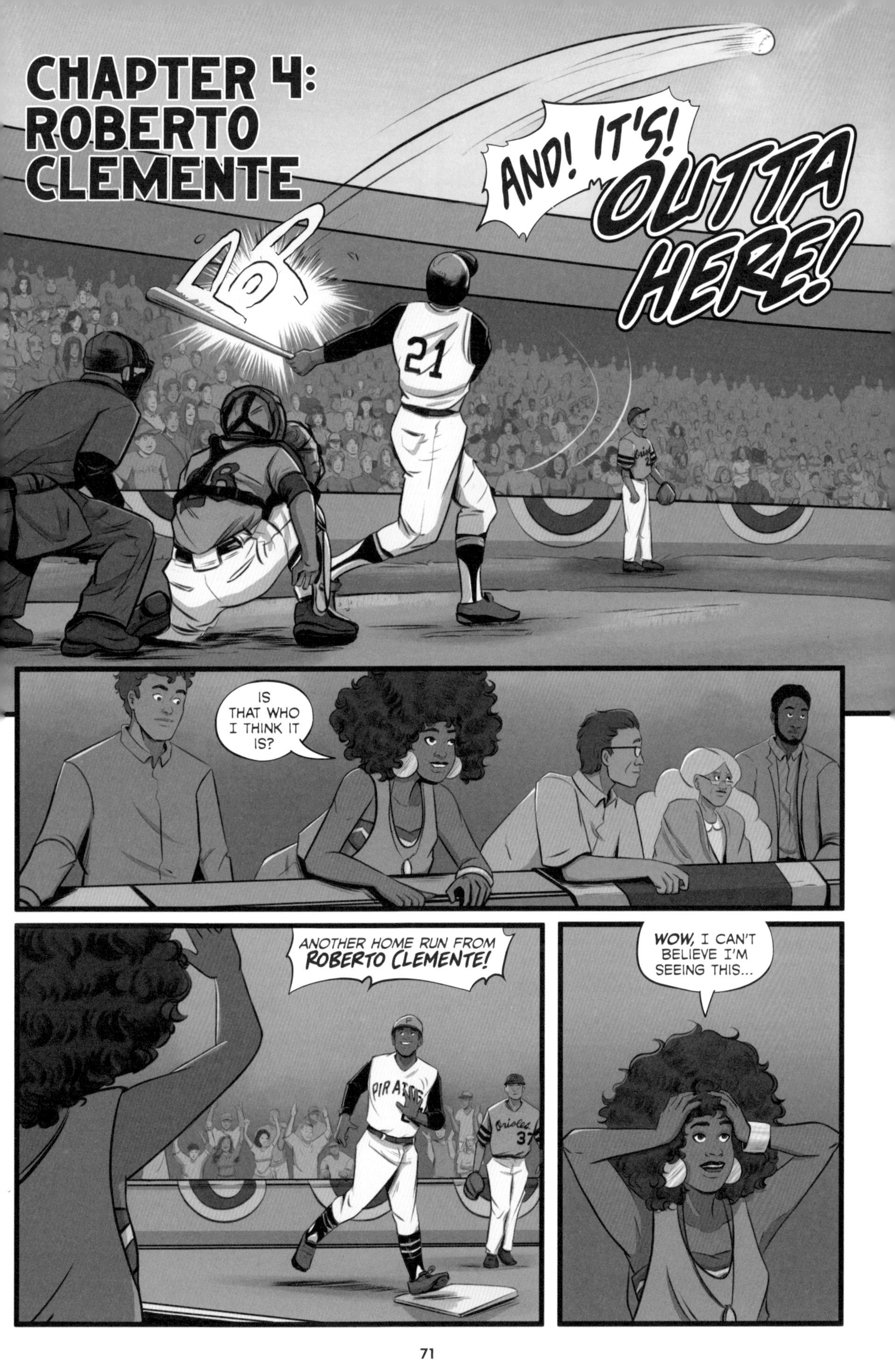
CHAPTER 4: ROBERTO CLEMENTE
AND! IT'S!
OUTTA HERE!
21
IS THAT WHO I THINK IT IS?
ANOTHER HOME RUN FROM ROBERTO CLEMENTE!
PIRATES
Orioles 37
WOW, I CAN'T BELIEVE I'M SEEING THIS...

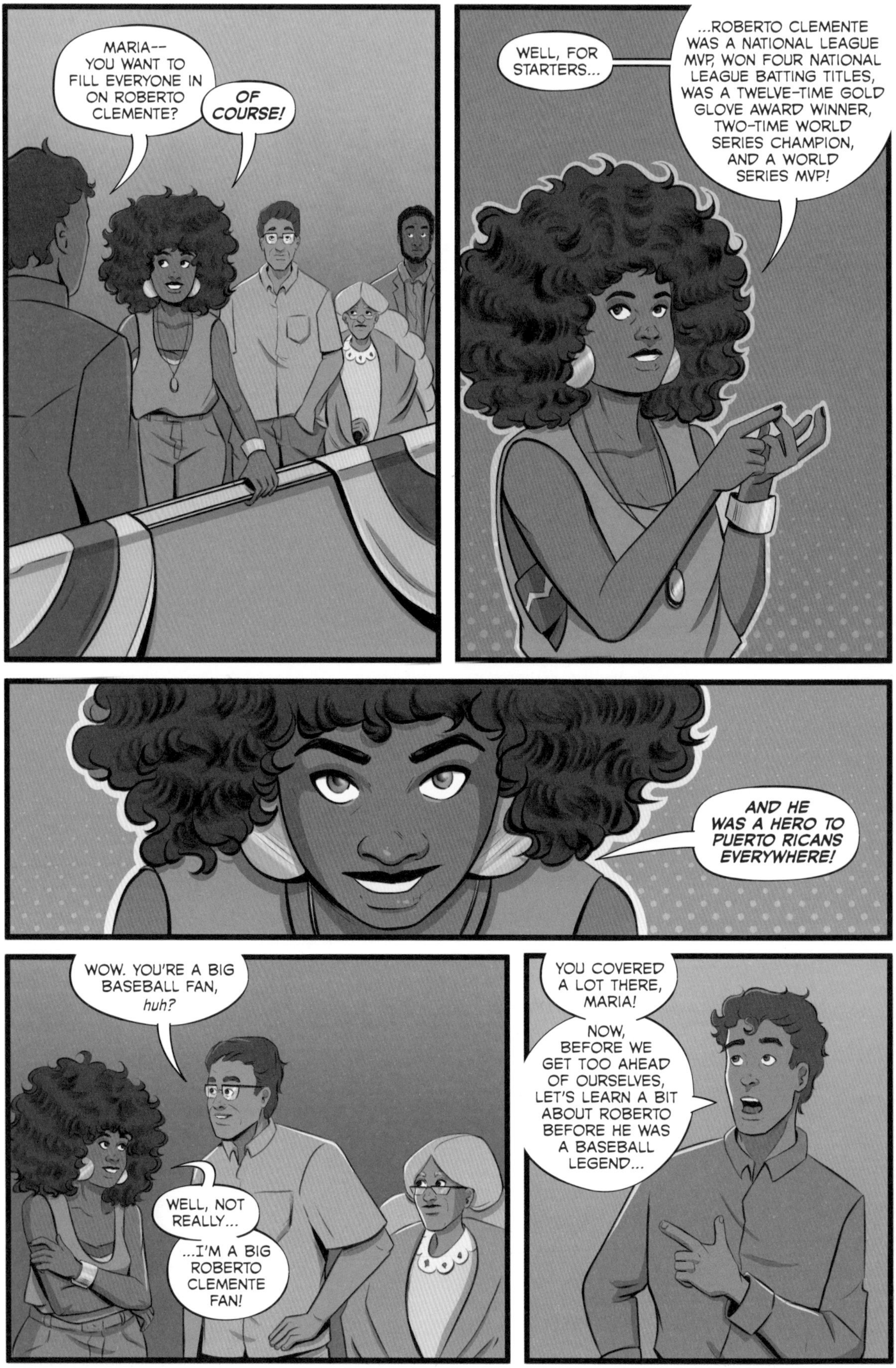
MARIA-- YOU WANT TO FILL EVERYONE IN ON ROBERTO CLEMENTE?
OF COURSE!
WELL, FOR STARTERS...
...ROBERTO CLEMENTE WAS A NATIONAL LEAGUE MVP, WON FOUR NATIONAL LEAGUE BATTING TITLES, WAS A TWELVE-TIME GOLD GLOVE AWARD WINNER, TWO-TIME WORLD SERIES CHAMPION, AND A WORLD SERIES MVP!
AND HE WAS A HERO TO PUERTO RICANS EVERYWHERE!
WOW. YOU'RE A BIG BASEBALL FAN, huh?
WELL, NOT REALLY...
...I'M A BIG ROBERTO CLEMENTE FAN!
YOU COVERED A LOT THERE, MARIA!
NOW, BEFORE WE GET TOO AHEAD OF OURSELVES, LET'S LEARN A BIT ABOUT ROBERTO BEFORE HE WAS A BASEBALL LEGEND...

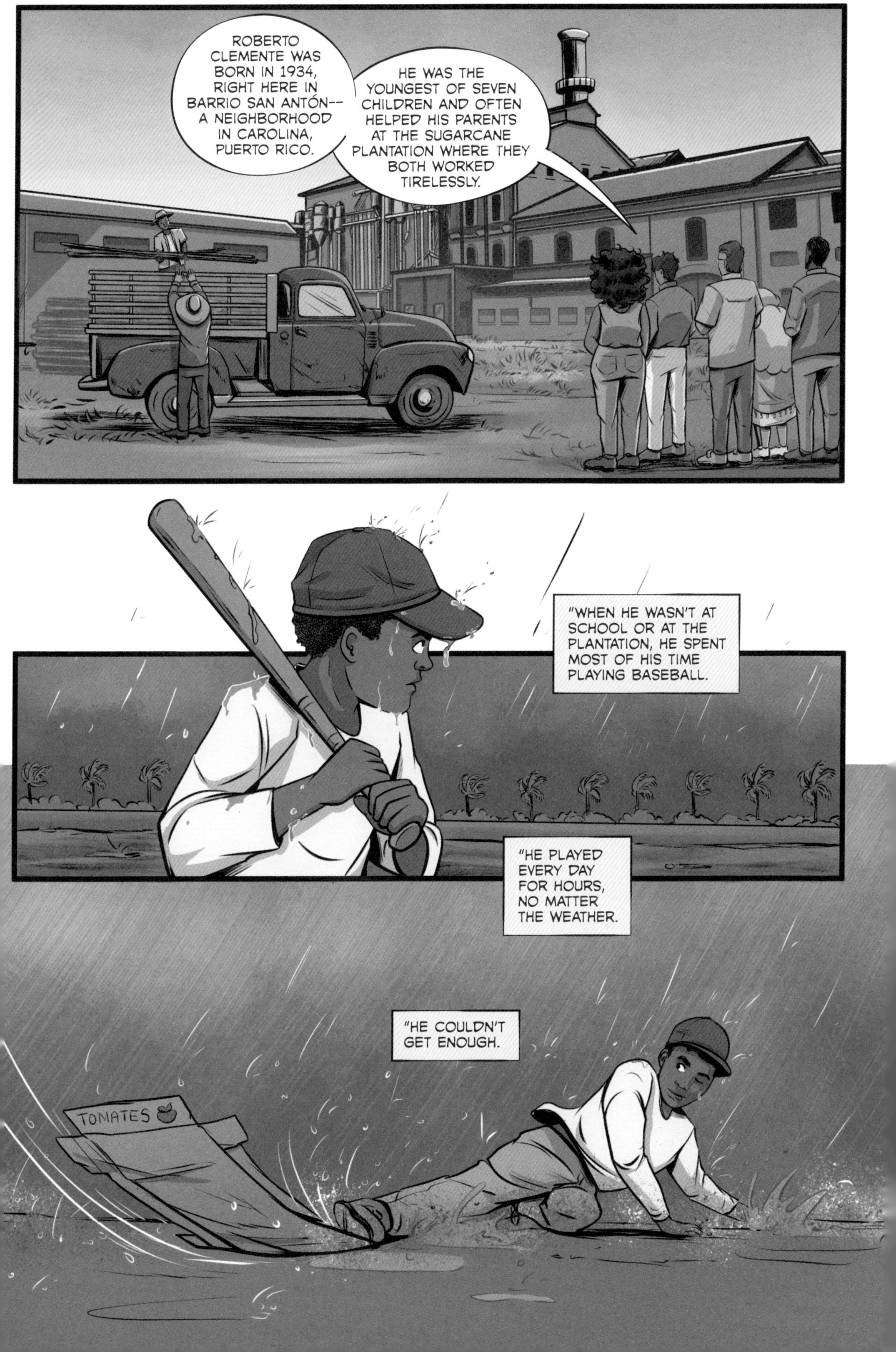
ROBERTO CLEMENTE WAS BORN IN 1934, RIGHT HERE IN BARRIO SAN ANTÓN-- A NEIGHBORHOOD IN CAROLINA, PUERTO RICO.
HE WAS THE YOUNGEST OF SEVEN CHILDREN AND OFTEN HELPED HIS PARENTS AT THE SUGARCANE PLANTATION WHERE THEY BOTH WORKED TIRELESSLY.
"WHEN HE WASN'T AT SCHOOL OR AT THE PLANTATION, HE SPENT MOST OF HIS TIME PLAYING BASEBALL.
"HE PLAYED EVERY DAY FOR HOURS, NO MATTER THE WEATHER.
"HE COULDN'T GET ENOUGH.
TOMATES

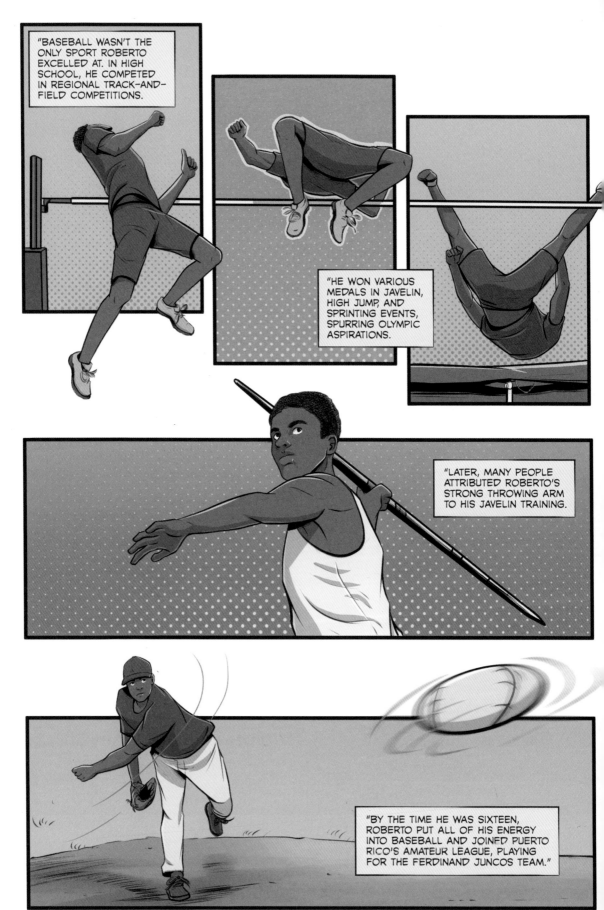

"BASEBALL WASN'T THE ONLY SPORT ROBERTO EXCELLED AT. IN HIGH SCHOOL, HE COMPETED IN REGIONAL TRACK-AND-FIELD COMPETITIONS.

"HE WON VARIOUS MEDALS IN JAVELIN, HIGH JUMP, AND SPRINTING EVENTS, SPURRING OLYMPIC ASPIRATIONS.

"LATER, MANY PEOPLE ATTRIBUTED ROBERTO'S STRONG THROWING ARM TO HIS JAVELIN TRAINING.

"BY THE TIME HE WAS SIXTEEN, ROBERTO PUT ALL OF HIS ENERGY INTO BASEBALL AND JOINED PUERTO RICO'S AMATEUR LEAGUE, PLAYING FOR THE FERDINAND JUNCOS TEAM."

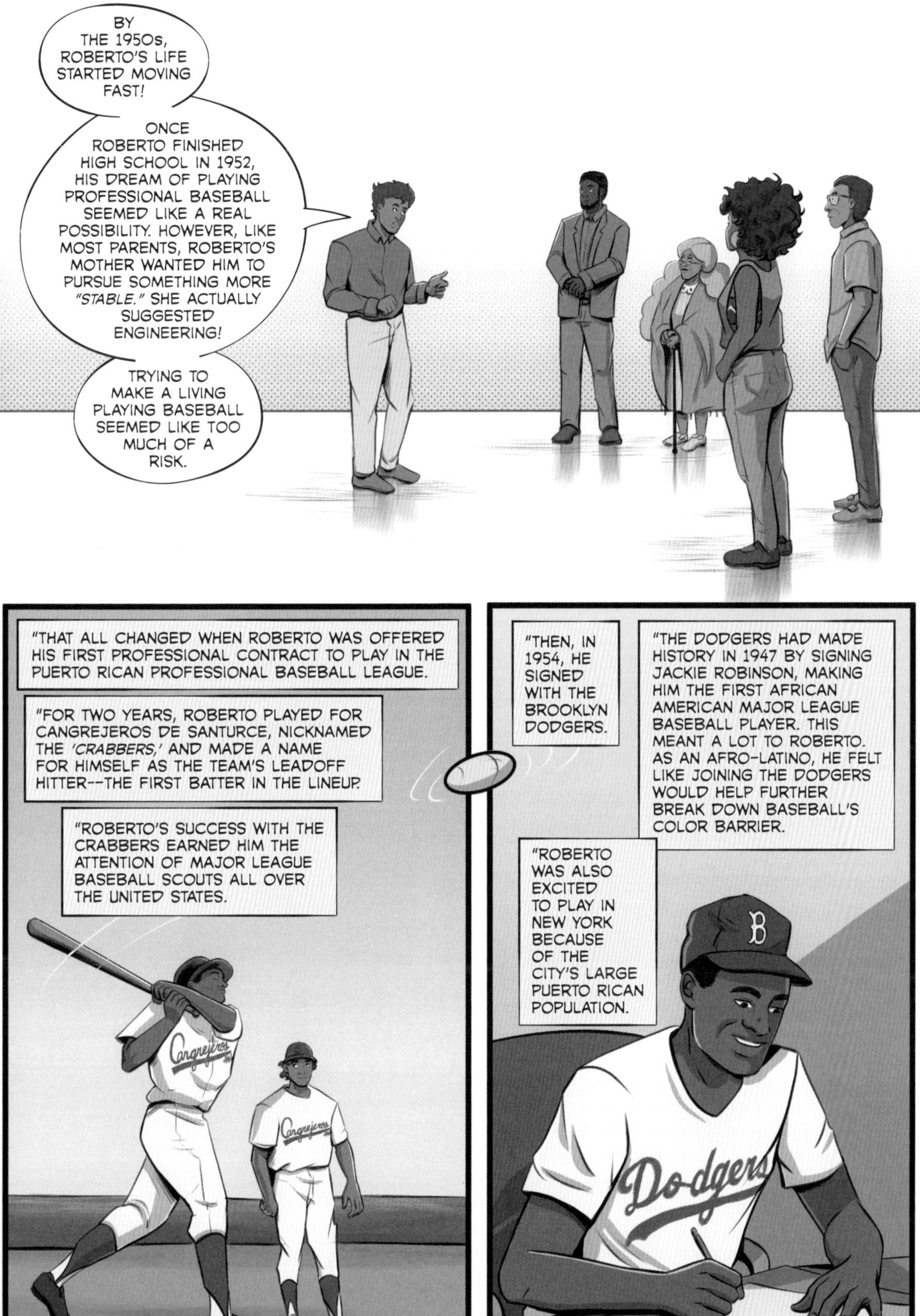

BY THE 1950s, ROBERTO'S LIFE STARTED MOVING FAST!
ONCE ROBERTO FINISHED HIGH SCHOOL IN 1952, HIS DREAM OF PLAYING PROFESSIONAL BASEBALL SEEMED LIKE A REAL POSSIBILITY. HOWEVER, LIKE MOST PARENTS, ROBERTO'S MOTHER WANTED HIM TO PURSUE SOMETHING MORE *"STABLE."* SHE ACTUALLY SUGGESTED ENGINEERING!
TRYING TO MAKE A LIVING PLAYING BASEBALL SEEMED LIKE TOO MUCH OF A RISK.
"THAT ALL CHANGED WHEN ROBERTO WAS OFFERED HIS FIRST PROFESSIONAL CONTRACT TO PLAY IN THE PUERTO RICAN PROFESSIONAL BASEBALL LEAGUE.
"FOR TWO YEARS, ROBERTO PLAYED FOR CANGREJEROS DE SANTURCE, NICKNAMED THE *'CRABBERS,'* AND MADE A NAME FOR HIMSELF AS THE TEAM'S LEADOFF HITTER--THE FIRST BATTER IN THE LINEUP.
"ROBERTO'S SUCCESS WITH THE CRABBERS EARNED HIM THE ATTENTION OF MAJOR LEAGUE BASEBALL SCOUTS ALL OVER THE UNITED STATES.
Cangrejeros
Cangrejeros
"THEN, IN 1954, HE SIGNED WITH THE BROOKLYN DODGERS.
"THE DODGERS HAD MADE HISTORY IN 1947 BY SIGNING JACKIE ROBINSON, MAKING HIM THE FIRST AFRICAN AMERICAN MAJOR LEAGUE BASEBALL PLAYER. THIS MEANT A LOT TO ROBERTO. AS AN AFRO-LATINO, HE FELT LIKE JOINING THE DODGERS WOULD HELP FURTHER BREAK DOWN BASEBALL'S COLOR BARRIER.
"ROBERTO WAS ALSO EXCITED TO PLAY IN NEW YORK BECAUSE OF THE CITY'S LARGE PUERTO RICAN POPULATION.
B
Dodgers

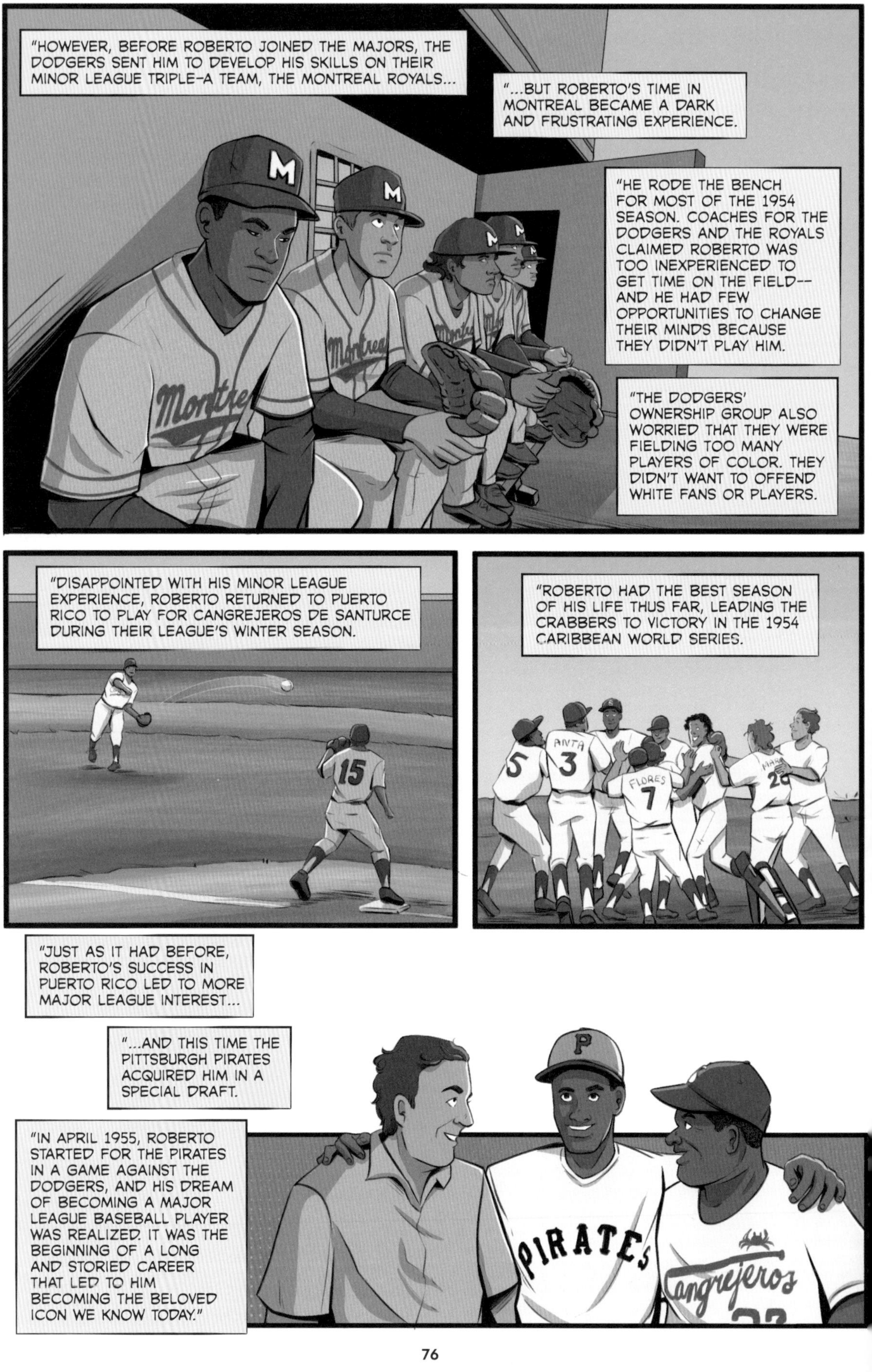
"HOWEVER, BEFORE ROBERTO JOINED THE MAJORS, THE DODGERS SENT HIM TO DEVELOP HIS SKILLS ON THEIR MINOR LEAGUE TRIPLE-A TEAM, THE MONTREAL ROYALS...
"...BUT ROBERTO'S TIME IN MONTREAL BECAME A DARK AND FRUSTRATING EXPERIENCE.
"HE RODE THE BENCH FOR MOST OF THE 1954 SEASON. COACHES FOR THE DODGERS AND THE ROYALS CLAIMED ROBERTO WAS TOO INEXPERIENCED TO GET TIME ON THE FIELD-- AND HE HAD FEW OPPORTUNITIES TO CHANGE THEIR MINDS BECAUSE THEY DIDN'T PLAY HIM.
"THE DODGERS' OWNERSHIP GROUP ALSO WORRIED THAT THEY WERE FIELDING TOO MANY PLAYERS OF COLOR. THEY DIDN'T WANT TO OFFEND WHITE FANS OR PLAYERS.
"DISAPPOINTED WITH HIS MINOR LEAGUE EXPERIENCE, ROBERTO RETURNED TO PUERTO RICO TO PLAY FOR CANGREJEROS DE SANTURCE DURING THEIR LEAGUE'S WINTER SEASON.
"ROBERTO HAD THE BEST SEASON OF HIS LIFE THUS FAR, LEADING THE CRABBERS TO VICTORY IN THE 1954 CARIBBEAN WORLD SERIES.
"JUST AS IT HAD BEFORE, ROBERTO'S SUCCESS IN PUERTO RICO LED TO MORE MAJOR LEAGUE INTEREST...
"...AND THIS TIME THE PITTSBURGH PIRATES ACQUIRED HIM IN A SPECIAL DRAFT.
"IN APRIL 1955, ROBERTO STARTED FOR THE PIRATES IN A GAME AGAINST THE DODGERS, AND HIS DREAM OF BECOMING A MAJOR LEAGUE BASEBALL PLAYER WAS REALIZED. IT WAS THE BEGINNING OF A LONG AND STORIED CAREER THAT LED TO HIM BECOMING THE BELOVED ICON WE KNOW TODAY."
PIRATES
Cangrejeros

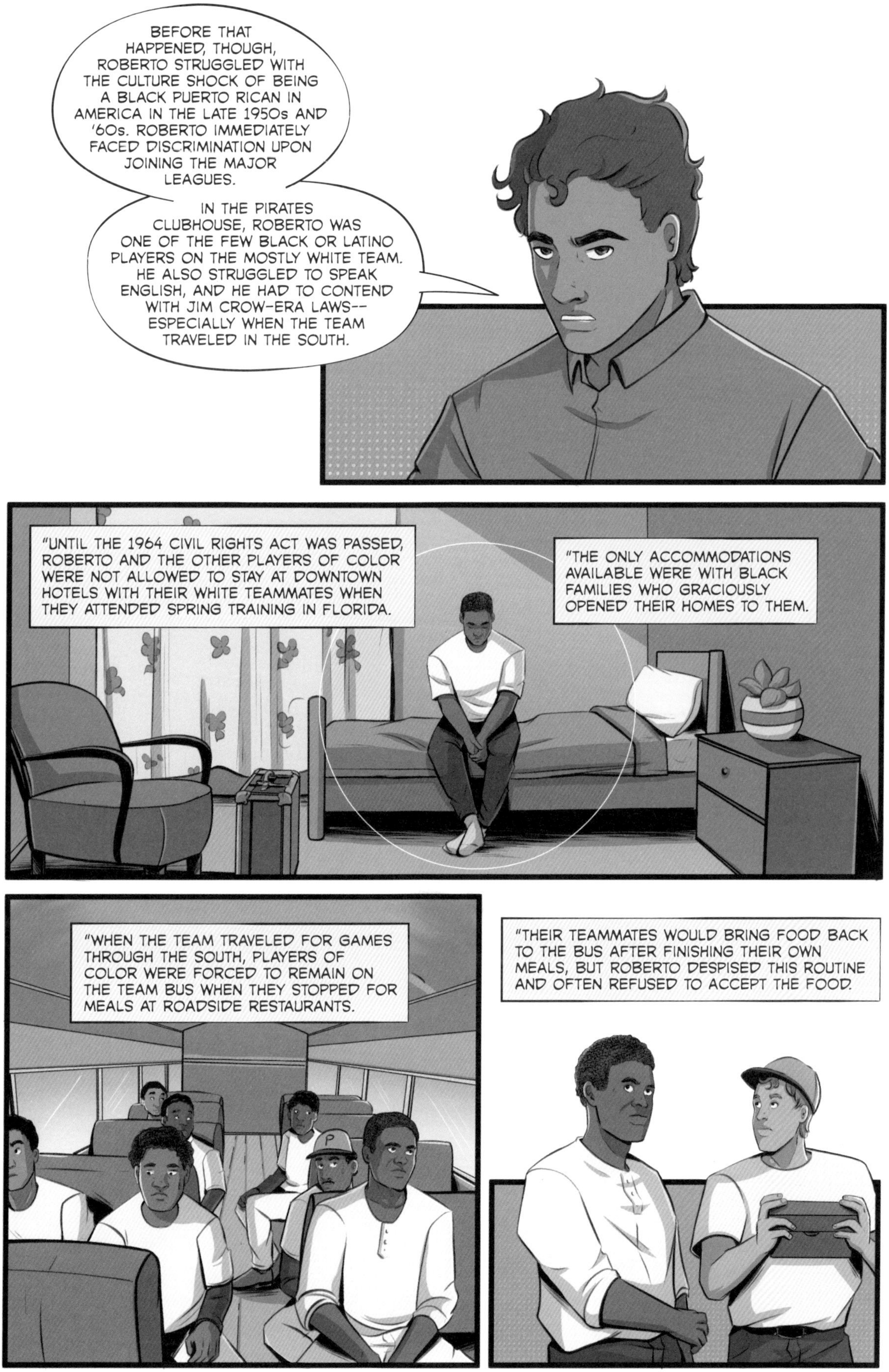
BEFORE THAT HAPPENED, THOUGH, ROBERTO STRUGGLED WITH THE CULTURE SHOCK OF BEING A BLACK PUERTO RICAN IN AMERICA IN THE LATE 1950s AND '60s. ROBERTO IMMEDIATELY FACED DISCRIMINATION UPON JOINING THE MAJOR LEAGUES.
IN THE PIRATES CLUBHOUSE, ROBERTO WAS ONE OF THE FEW BLACK OR LATINO PLAYERS ON THE MOSTLY WHITE TEAM. HE ALSO STRUGGLED TO SPEAK ENGLISH, AND HE HAD TO CONTEND WITH JIM CROW-ERA LAWS--ESPECIALLY WHEN THE TEAM TRAVELED IN THE SOUTH.
"UNTIL THE 1964 CIVIL RIGHTS ACT WAS PASSED, ROBERTO AND THE OTHER PLAYERS OF COLOR WERE NOT ALLOWED TO STAY AT DOWNTOWN HOTELS WITH THEIR WHITE TEAMMATES WHEN THEY ATTENDED SPRING TRAINING IN FLORIDA.
"THE ONLY ACCOMMODATIONS AVAILABLE WERE WITH BLACK FAMILIES WHO GRACIOUSLY OPENED THEIR HOMES TO THEM.
"WHEN THE TEAM TRAVELED FOR GAMES THROUGH THE SOUTH, PLAYERS OF COLOR WERE FORCED TO REMAIN ON THE TEAM BUS WHEN THEY STOPPED FOR MEALS AT ROADSIDE RESTAURANTS.
P
"THEIR TEAMMATES WOULD BRING FOOD BACK TO THE BUS AFTER FINISHING THEIR OWN MEALS, BUT ROBERTO DESPISED THIS ROUTINE AND OFTEN REFUSED TO ACCEPT THE FOOD.

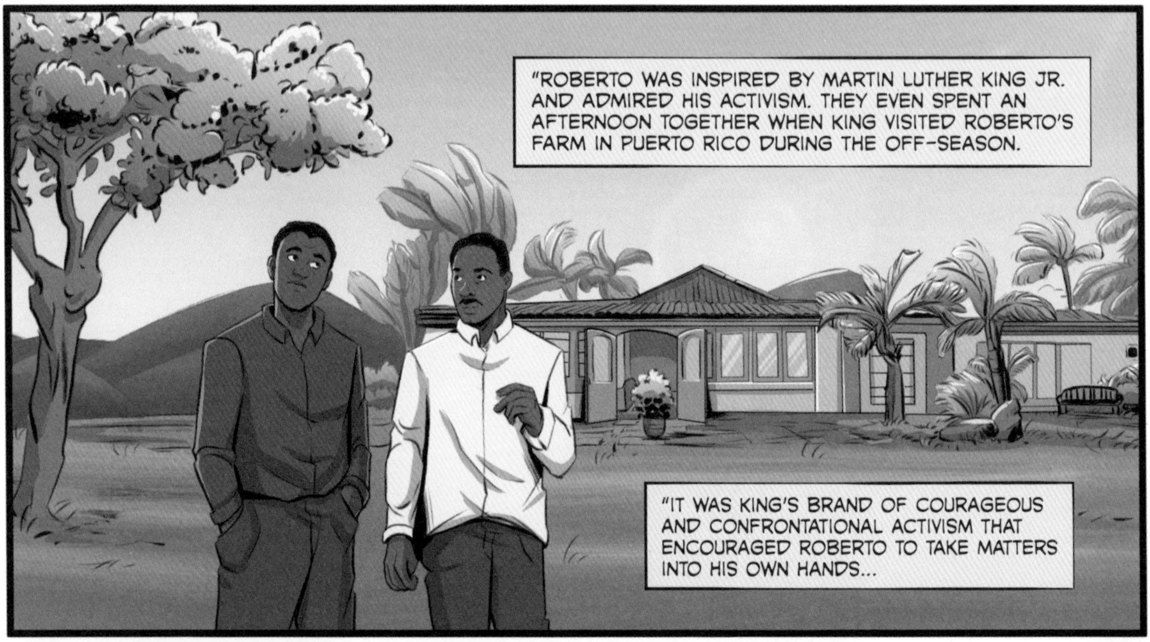
"ROBERTO WAS INSPIRED BY MARTIN LUTHER KING JR. AND ADMIRED HIS ACTIVISM. THEY EVEN SPENT AN AFTERNOON TOGETHER WHEN KING VISITED ROBERTO'S FARM IN PUERTO RICO DURING THE OFF-SEASON.
"IT WAS KING'S BRAND OF COURAGEOUS AND CONFRONTATIONAL ACTIVISM THAT ENCOURAGED ROBERTO TO TAKE MATTERS INTO HIS OWN HANDS...

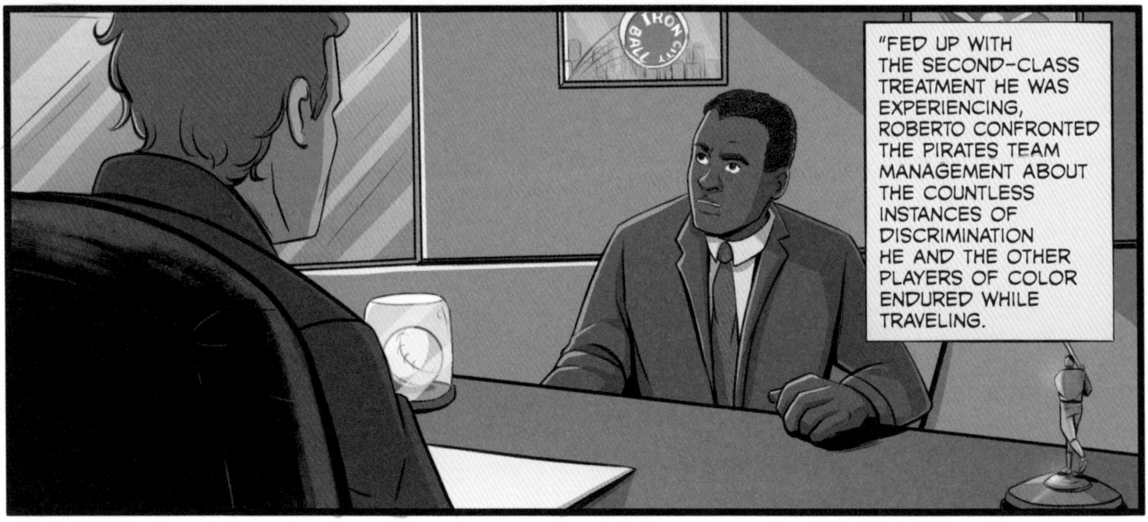
IRON CITY BALL
"FED UP WITH THE SECOND-CLASS TREATMENT HE WAS EXPERIENCING, ROBERTO CONFRONTED THE PIRATES TEAM MANAGEMENT ABOUT THE COUNTLESS INSTANCES OF DISCRIMINATION HE AND THE OTHER PLAYERS OF COLOR ENDURED WHILE TRAVELING.

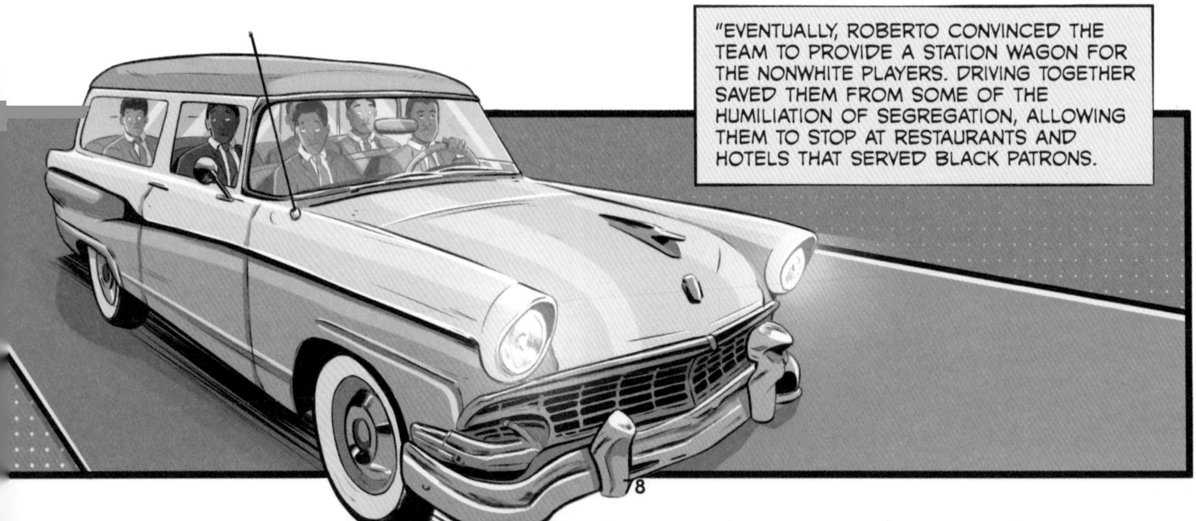
"EVENTUALLY, ROBERTO CONVINCED THE TEAM TO PROVIDE A STATION WAGON FOR THE NONWHITE PLAYERS. DRIVING TOGETHER SAVED THEM FROM SOME OF THE HUMILIATION OF SEGREGATION, ALLOWING THEM TO STOP AT RESTAURANTS AND HOTELS THAT SERVED BLACK PATRONS.

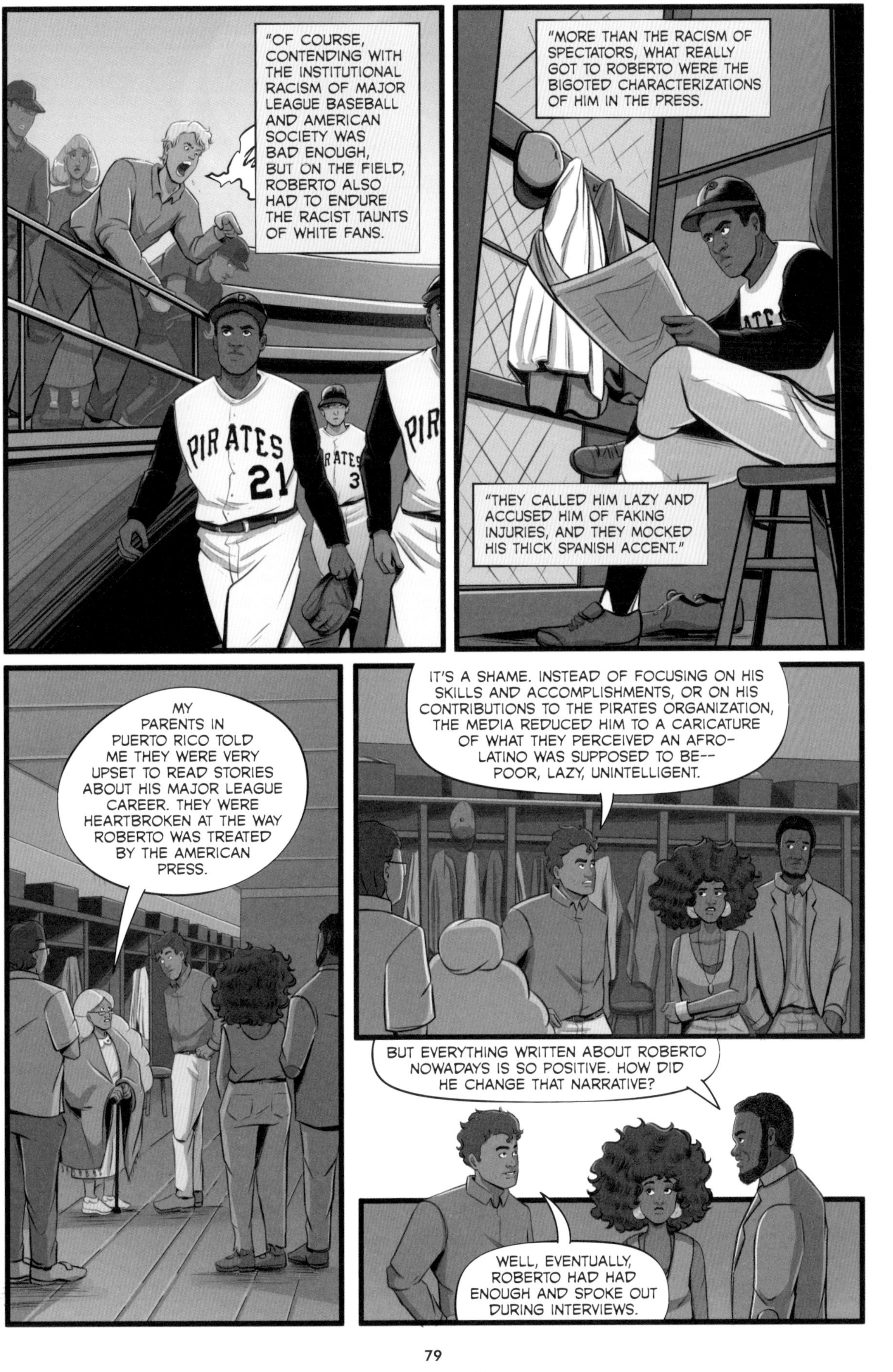
"OF COURSE, CONTENDING WITH THE INSTITUTIONAL RACISM OF MAJOR LEAGUE BASEBALL AND AMERICAN SOCIETY WAS BAD ENOUGH, BUT ON THE FIELD, ROBERTO ALSO HAD TO ENDURE THE RACIST TAUNTS OF WHITE FANS.
PIRATES 21
"MORE THAN THE RACISM OF SPECTATORS, WHAT REALLY GOT TO ROBERTO WERE THE BIGOTED CHARACTERIZATIONS OF HIM IN THE PRESS.
"THEY CALLED HIM LAZY AND ACCUSED HIM OF FAKING INJURIES, AND THEY MOCKED HIS THICK SPANISH ACCENT."
MY PARENTS IN PUERTO RICO TOLD ME THEY WERE VERY UPSET TO READ STORIES ABOUT HIS MAJOR LEAGUE CAREER. THEY WERE HEARTBROKEN AT THE WAY ROBERTO WAS TREATED BY THE AMERICAN PRESS.
IT'S A SHAME. INSTEAD OF FOCUSING ON HIS SKILLS AND ACCOMPLISHMENTS, OR ON HIS CONTRIBUTIONS TO THE PIRATES ORGANIZATION, THE MEDIA REDUCED HIM TO A CARICATURE OF WHAT THEY PERCEIVED AN AFRO-LATINO WAS SUPPOSED TO BE-- POOR, LAZY, UNINTELLIGENT.
BUT EVERYTHING WRITTEN ABOUT ROBERTO NOWADAYS IS SO POSITIVE. HOW DID HE CHANGE THAT NARRATIVE?
WELL, EVENTUALLY, ROBERTO HAD HAD ENOUGH AND SPOKE OUT DURING INTERVIEWS.

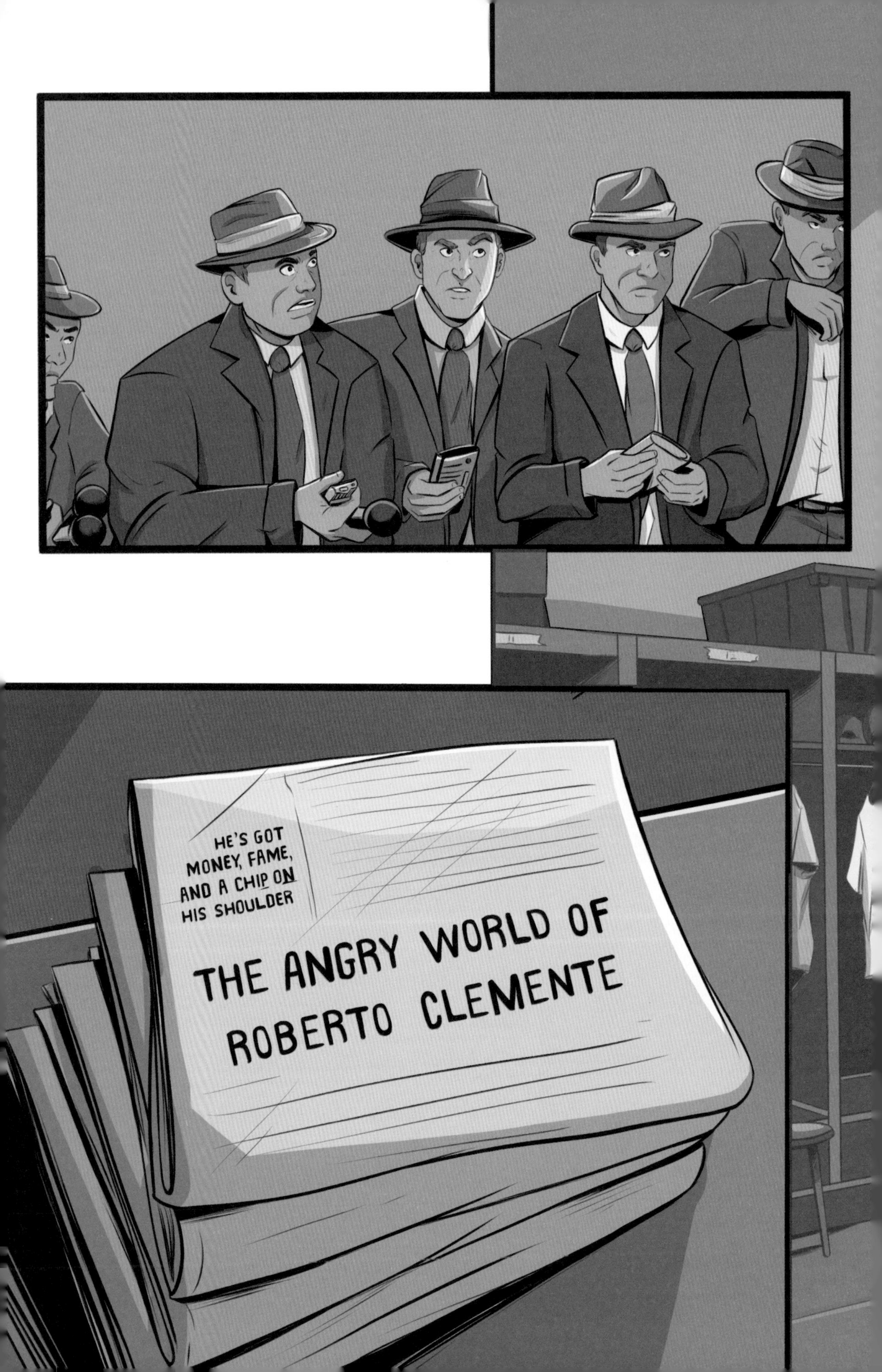
HE'S GOT MONEY, FAME, AND A CHIP ON HIS SHOULDER
THE ANGRY WORLD OF ROBERTO CLEMENTE

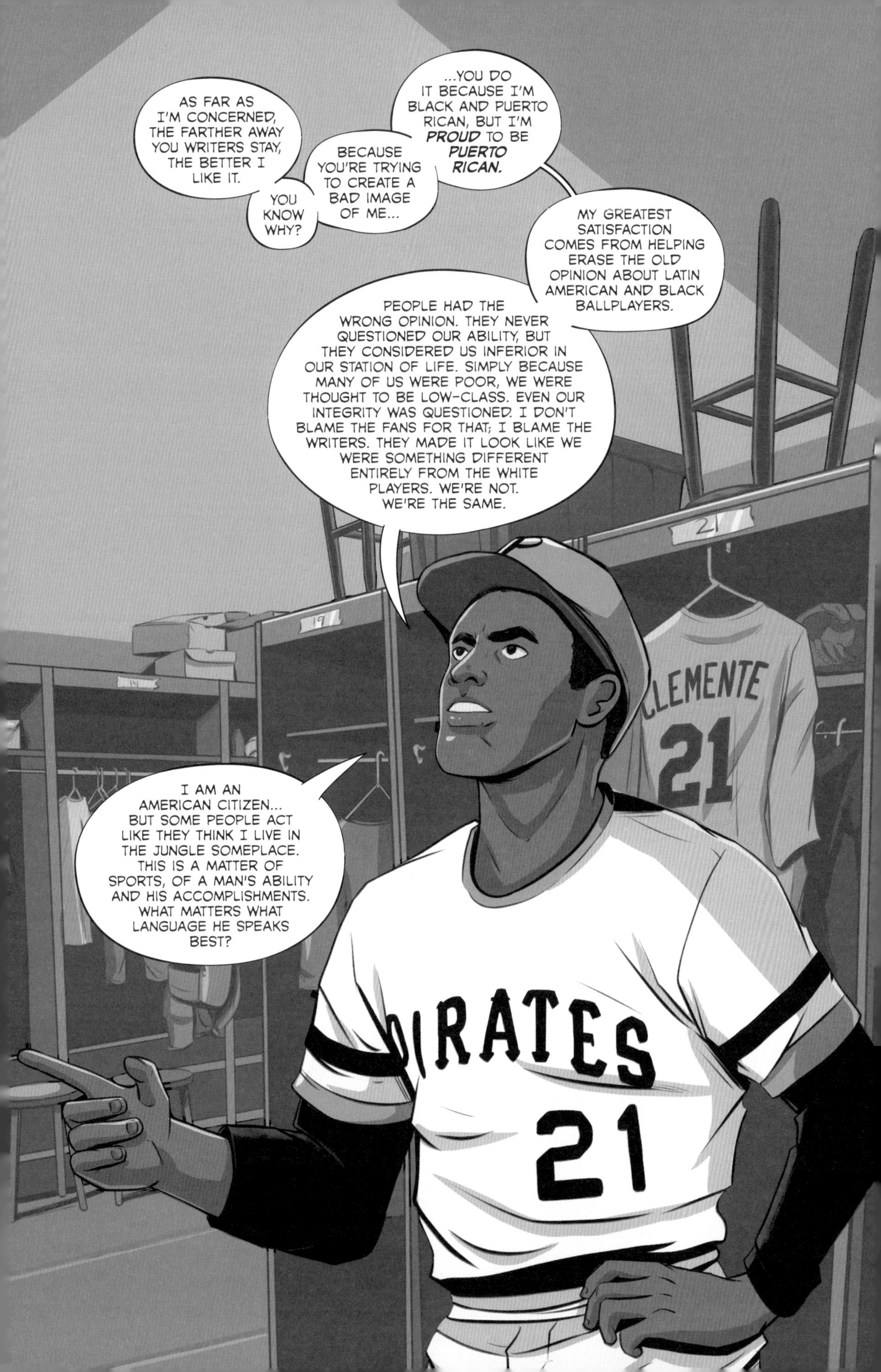
AS FAR AS I'M CONCERNED, THE FARTHER AWAY YOU WRITERS STAY, THE BETTER I LIKE IT.
YOU KNOW WHY?
BECAUSE YOU'RE TRYING TO CREATE A BAD IMAGE OF ME...
...YOU DO IT BECAUSE I'M BLACK AND PUERTO RICAN, BUT I'M *PROUD* TO BE *PUERTO RICAN.*
MY GREATEST SATISFACTION COMES FROM HELPING ERASE THE OLD OPINION ABOUT LATIN AMERICAN AND BLACK BALLPLAYERS.
PEOPLE HAD THE WRONG OPINION. THEY NEVER QUESTIONED OUR ABILITY, BUT THEY CONSIDERED US INFERIOR IN OUR STATION OF LIFE. SIMPLY BECAUSE MANY OF US WERE POOR, WE WERE THOUGHT TO BE LOW-CLASS. EVEN OUR INTEGRITY WAS QUESTIONED. I DON'T BLAME THE FANS FOR THAT; I BLAME THE WRITERS. THEY MADE IT LOOK LIKE WE WERE SOMETHING DIFFERENT ENTIRELY FROM THE WHITE PLAYERS. WE'RE NOT. WE'RE THE SAME.
I AM AN AMERICAN CITIZEN... BUT SOME PEOPLE ACT LIKE THEY THINK I LIVE IN THE JUNGLE SOMEPLACE. THIS IS A MATTER OF SPORTS, OF A MAN'S ABILITY AND HIS ACCOMPLISHMENTS. WHAT MATTERS WHAT LANGUAGE HE SPEAKS BEST?
CLEMENTE
21
PIRATES
21

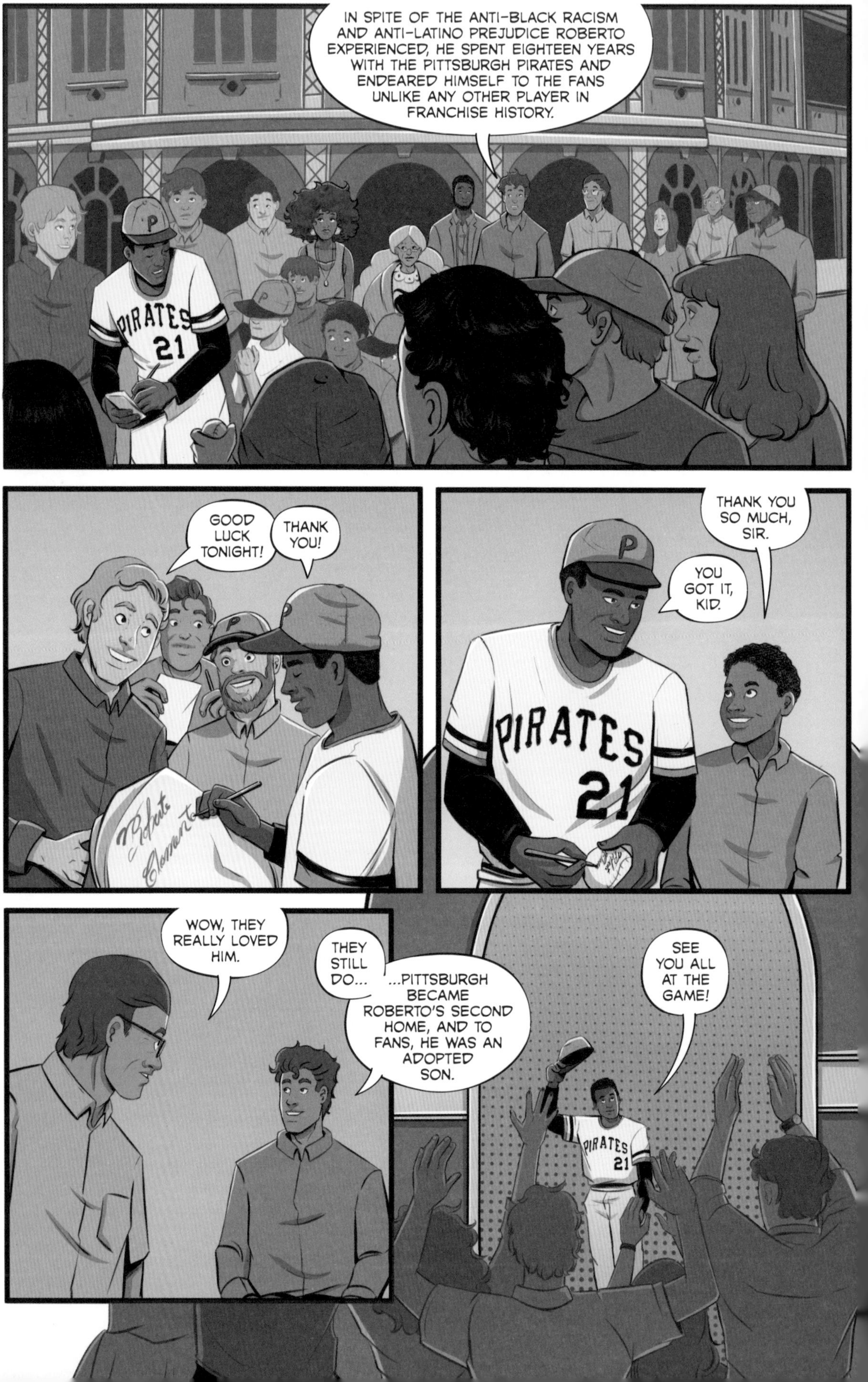
IN SPITE OF THE ANTI-BLACK RACISM AND ANTI-LATINO PREJUDICE ROBERTO EXPERIENCED, HE SPENT EIGHTEEN YEARS WITH THE PITTSBURGH PIRATES AND ENDEARED HIMSELF TO THE FANS UNLIKE ANY OTHER PLAYER IN FRANCHISE HISTORY.
PIRATES 21
GOOD LUCK TONIGHT!
THANK YOU!
Roberto Clemente
THANK YOU SO MUCH, SIR.
YOU GOT IT, KID.
PIRATES 21
WOW, THEY REALLY LOVED HIM.
THEY STILL DO...
...PITTSBURGH BECAME ROBERTO'S SECOND HOME, AND TO FANS, HE WAS AN ADOPTED SON.
SEE YOU ALL AT THE GAME!
PIRATES 21

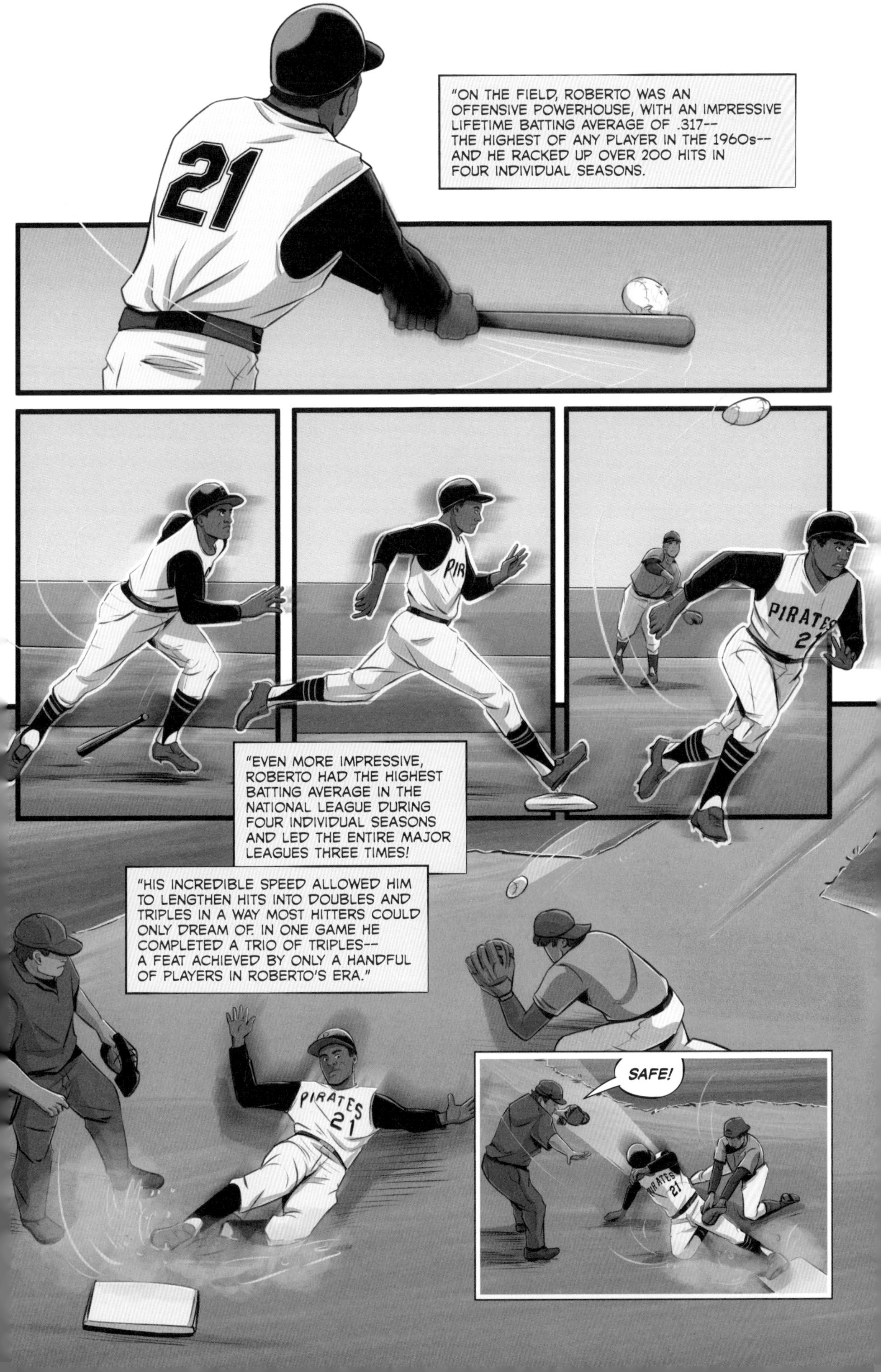
"ON THE FIELD, ROBERTO WAS AN OFFENSIVE POWERHOUSE, WITH AN IMPRESSIVE LIFETIME BATTING AVERAGE OF .317-- THE HIGHEST OF ANY PLAYER IN THE 1960s-- AND HE RACKED UP OVER 200 HITS IN FOUR INDIVIDUAL SEASONS.
"EVEN MORE IMPRESSIVE, ROBERTO HAD THE HIGHEST BATTING AVERAGE IN THE NATIONAL LEAGUE DURING FOUR INDIVIDUAL SEASONS AND LED THE ENTIRE MAJOR LEAGUES THREE TIMES!
"HIS INCREDIBLE SPEED ALLOWED HIM TO LENGTHEN HITS INTO DOUBLES AND TRIPLES IN A WAY MOST HITTERS COULD ONLY DREAM OF. IN ONE GAME HE COMPLETED A TRIO OF TRIPLES-- A FEAT ACHIEVED BY ONLY A HANDFUL OF PLAYERS IN ROBERTO'S ERA."
SAFE!

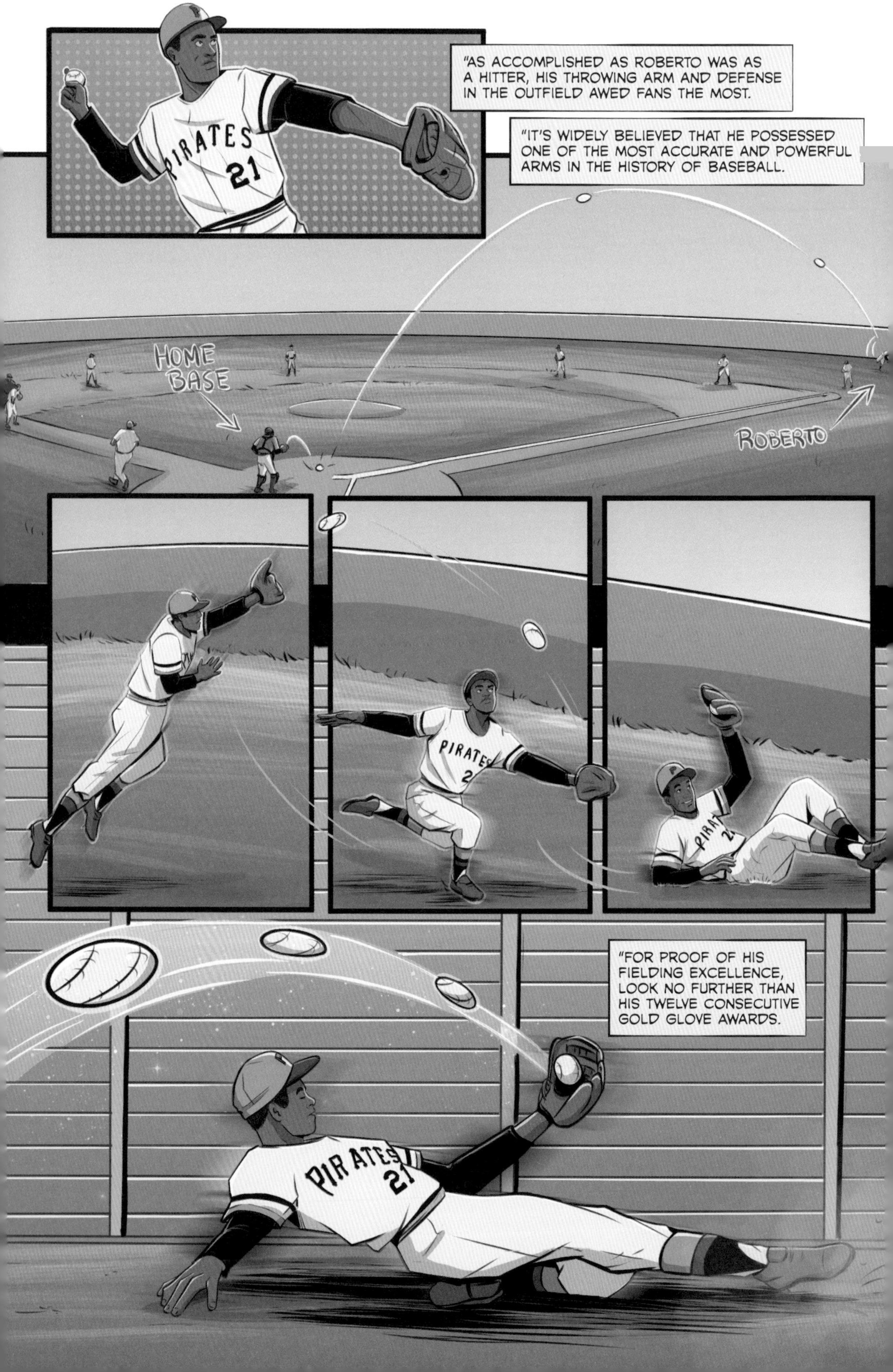
"AS ACCOMPLISHED AS ROBERTO WAS AS A HITTER, HIS THROWING ARM AND DEFENSE IN THE OUTFIELD AWED FANS THE MOST.
"IT'S WIDELY BELIEVED THAT HE POSSESSED ONE OF THE MOST ACCURATE AND POWERFUL ARMS IN THE HISTORY OF BASEBALL.
HOME BASE
ROBERTO
"FOR PROOF OF HIS FIELDING EXCELLENCE, LOOK NO FURTHER THAN HIS TWELVE CONSECUTIVE GOLD GLOVE AWARDS.

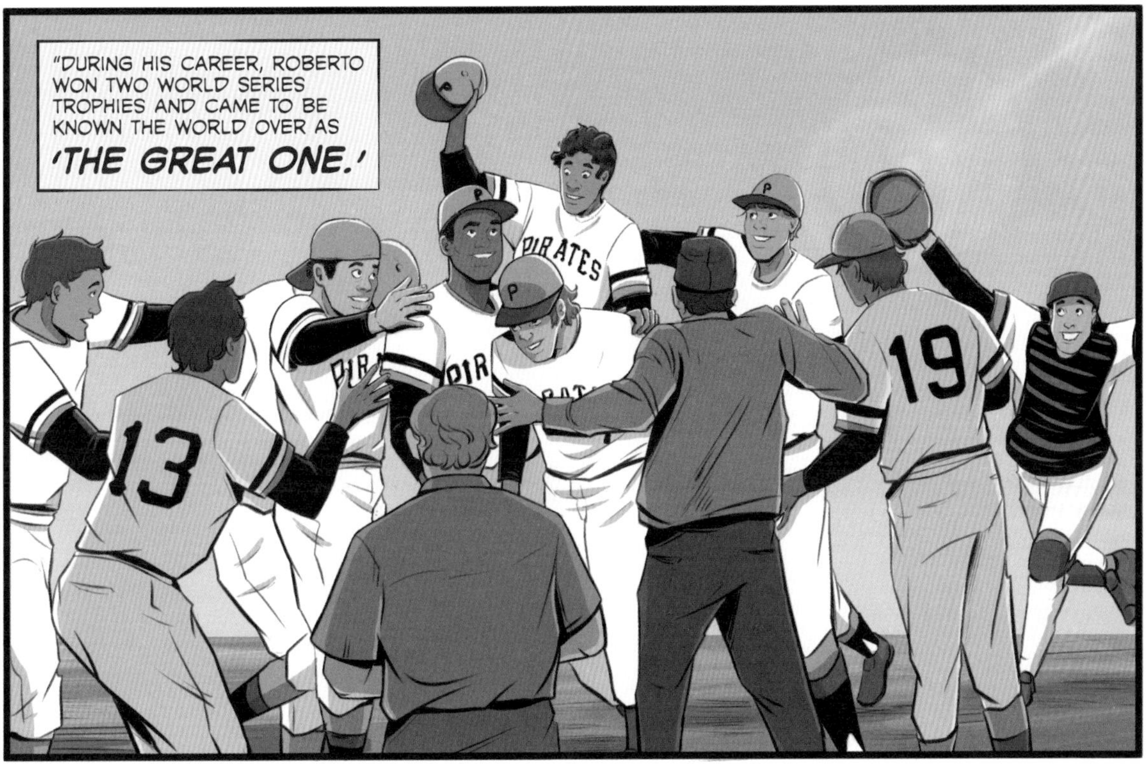
"DURING HIS CAREER, ROBERTO WON TWO WORLD SERIES TROPHIES AND CAME TO BE KNOWN THE WORLD OVER AS 'THE GREAT ONE.'

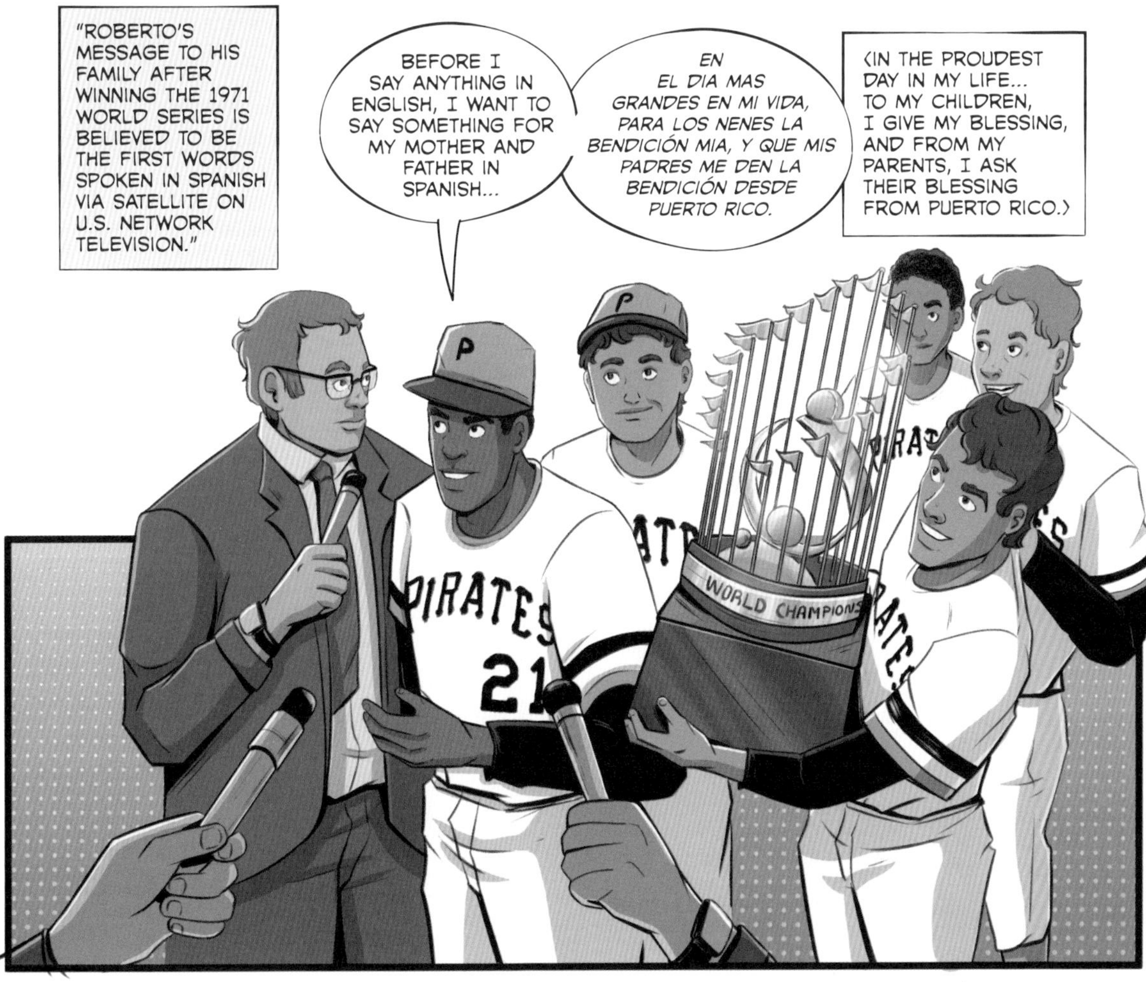
"ROBERTO'S MESSAGE TO HIS FAMILY AFTER WINNING THE 1971 WORLD SERIES IS BELIEVED TO BE THE FIRST WORDS SPOKEN IN SPANISH VIA SATELLITE ON U.S. NETWORK TELEVISION."
BEFORE I SAY ANYTHING IN ENGLISH, I WANT TO SAY SOMETHING FOR MY MOTHER AND FATHER IN SPANISH...
EN EL DIA MAS GRANDES EN MI VIDA, PARA LOS NENES LA BENDICIÓN MIA, Y QUE MIS PADRES ME DEN LA BENDICIÓN DESDE PUERTO RICO.
(IN THE PROUDEST DAY IN MY LIFE... TO MY CHILDREN, I GIVE MY BLESSING, AND FROM MY PARENTS, I ASK THEIR BLESSING FROM PUERTO RICO.)
WORLD CHAMPIONS

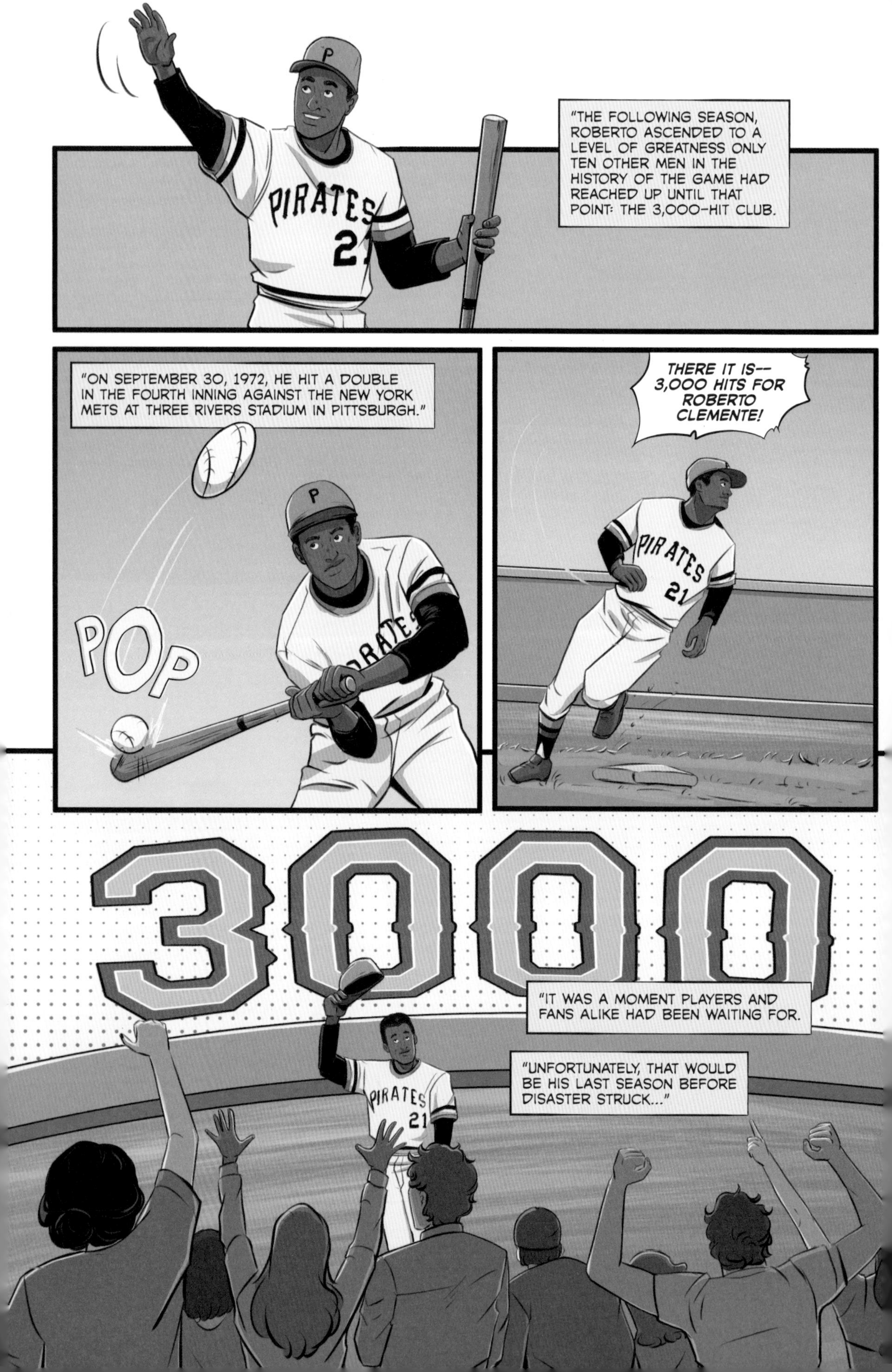
"THE FOLLOWING SEASON, ROBERTO ASCENDED TO A LEVEL OF GREATNESS ONLY TEN OTHER MEN IN THE HISTORY OF THE GAME HAD REACHED UP UNTIL THAT POINT: THE 3,000-HIT CLUB.
PIRATES
21
"ON SEPTEMBER 30, 1972, HE HIT A DOUBLE IN THE FOURTH INNING AGAINST THE NEW YORK METS AT THREE RIVERS STADIUM IN PITTSBURGH."
POP
THERE IT IS-- 3,000 HITS FOR ROBERTO CLEMENTE!
PIRATES
21
3000
"IT WAS A MOMENT PLAYERS AND FANS ALIKE HAD BEEN WAITING FOR.
"UNFORTUNATELY, THAT WOULD BE HIS LAST SEASON BEFORE DISASTER STRUCK..."
PIRATES
21

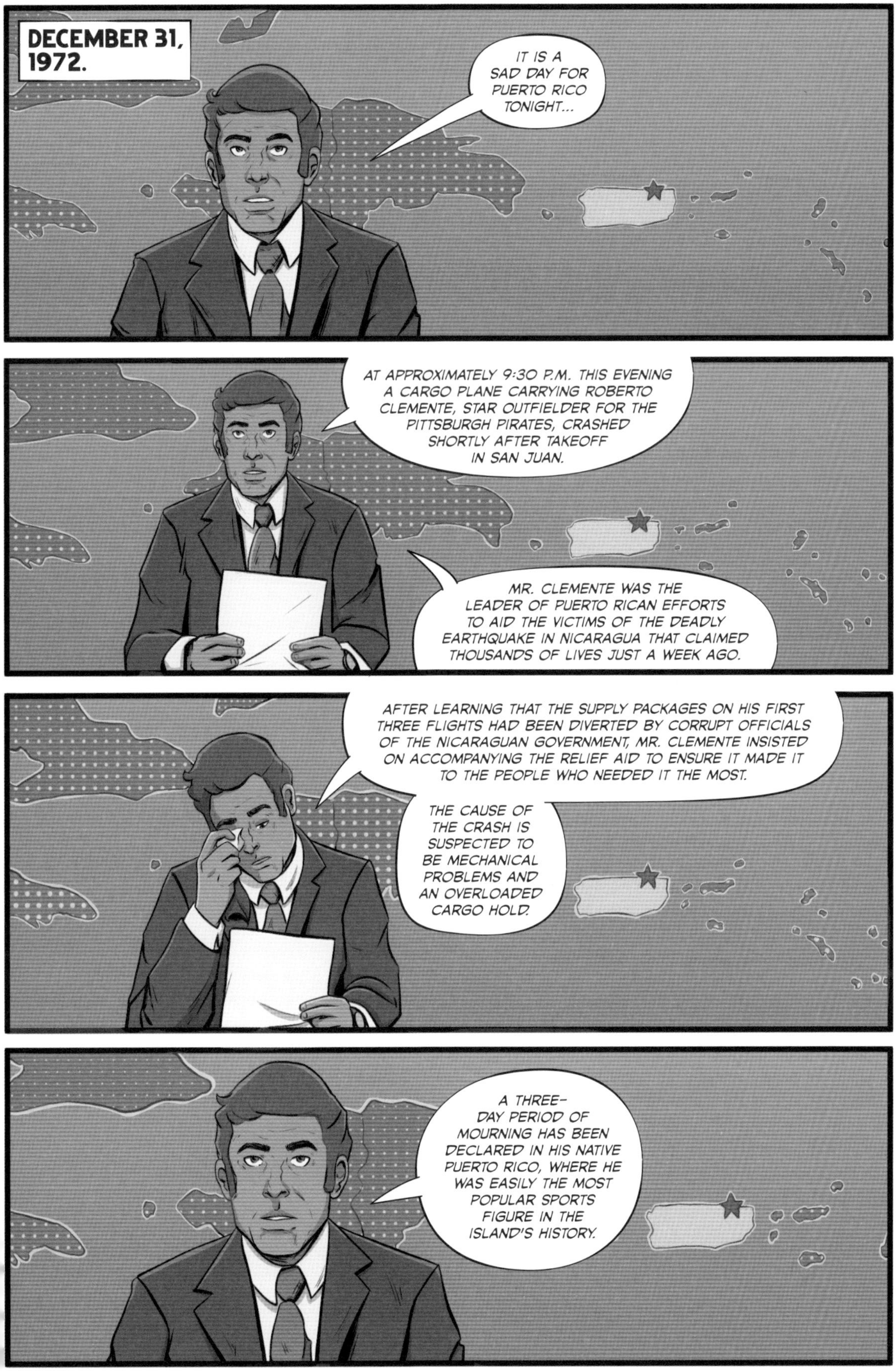

DECEMBER 31, 1972.
IT IS A SAD DAY FOR PUERTO RICO TONIGHT...
AT APPROXIMATELY 9:30 P.M. THIS EVENING A CARGO PLANE CARRYING ROBERTO CLEMENTE, STAR OUTFIELDER FOR THE PITTSBURGH PIRATES, CRASHED SHORTLY AFTER TAKEOFF IN SAN JUAN.
MR. CLEMENTE WAS THE LEADER OF PUERTO RICAN EFFORTS TO AID THE VICTIMS OF THE DEADLY EARTHQUAKE IN NICARAGUA THAT CLAIMED THOUSANDS OF LIVES JUST A WEEK AGO.
AFTER LEARNING THAT THE SUPPLY PACKAGES ON HIS FIRST THREE FLIGHTS HAD BEEN DIVERTED BY CORRUPT OFFICIALS OF THE NICARAGUAN GOVERNMENT, MR. CLEMENTE INSISTED ON ACCOMPANYING THE RELIEF AID TO ENSURE IT MADE IT TO THE PEOPLE WHO NEEDED IT THE MOST.
THE CAUSE OF THE CRASH IS SUSPECTED TO BE MECHANICAL PROBLEMS AND AN OVERLOADED CARGO HOLD.
A THREE-DAY PERIOD OF MOURNING HAS BEEN DECLARED IN HIS NATIVE PUERTO RICO, WHERE HE WAS EASILY THE MOST POPULAR SPORTS FIGURE IN THE ISLAND'S HISTORY.

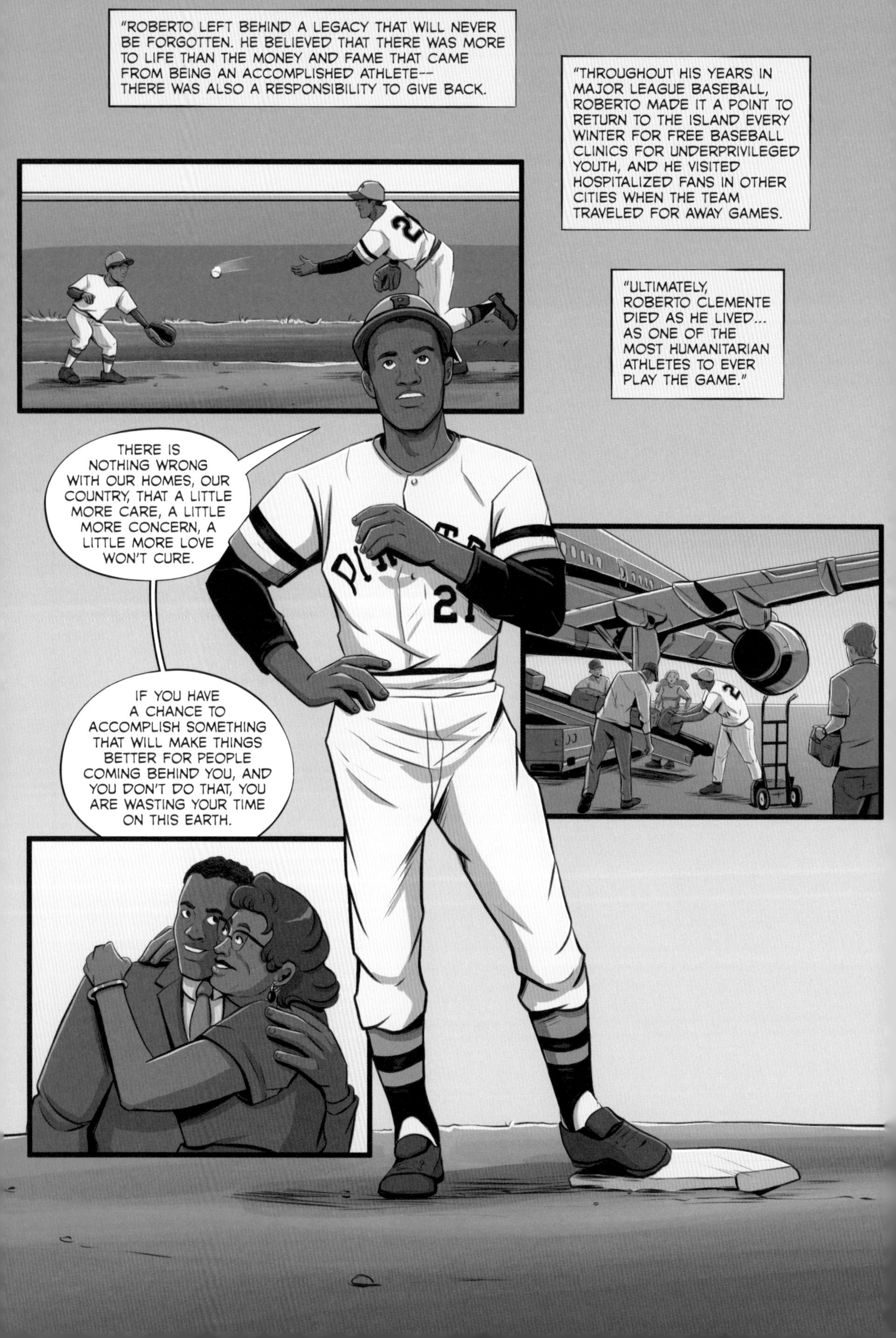
"ROBERTO LEFT BEHIND A LEGACY THAT WILL NEVER BE FORGOTTEN. HE BELIEVED THAT THERE WAS MORE TO LIFE THAN THE MONEY AND FAME THAT CAME FROM BEING AN ACCOMPLISHED ATHLETE-- THERE WAS ALSO A RESPONSIBILITY TO GIVE BACK.
"THROUGHOUT HIS YEARS IN MAJOR LEAGUE BASEBALL, ROBERTO MADE IT A POINT TO RETURN TO THE ISLAND EVERY WINTER FOR FREE BASEBALL CLINICS FOR UNDERPRIVILEGED YOUTH, AND HE VISITED HOSPITALIZED FANS IN OTHER CITIES WHEN THE TEAM TRAVELED FOR AWAY GAMES.
"ULTIMATELY, ROBERTO CLEMENTE DIED AS HE LIVED... AS ONE OF THE MOST HUMANITARIAN ATHLETES TO EVER PLAY THE GAME."
THERE IS NOTHING WRONG WITH OUR HOMES, OUR COUNTRY, THAT A LITTLE MORE CARE, A LITTLE MORE CONCERN, A LITTLE MORE LOVE WON'T CURE.
IF YOU HAVE A CHANCE TO ACCOMPLISH SOMETHING THAT WILL MAKE THINGS BETTER FOR PEOPLE COMING BEHIND YOU, AND YOU DON'T DO THAT, YOU ARE WASTING YOUR TIME ON THIS EARTH.

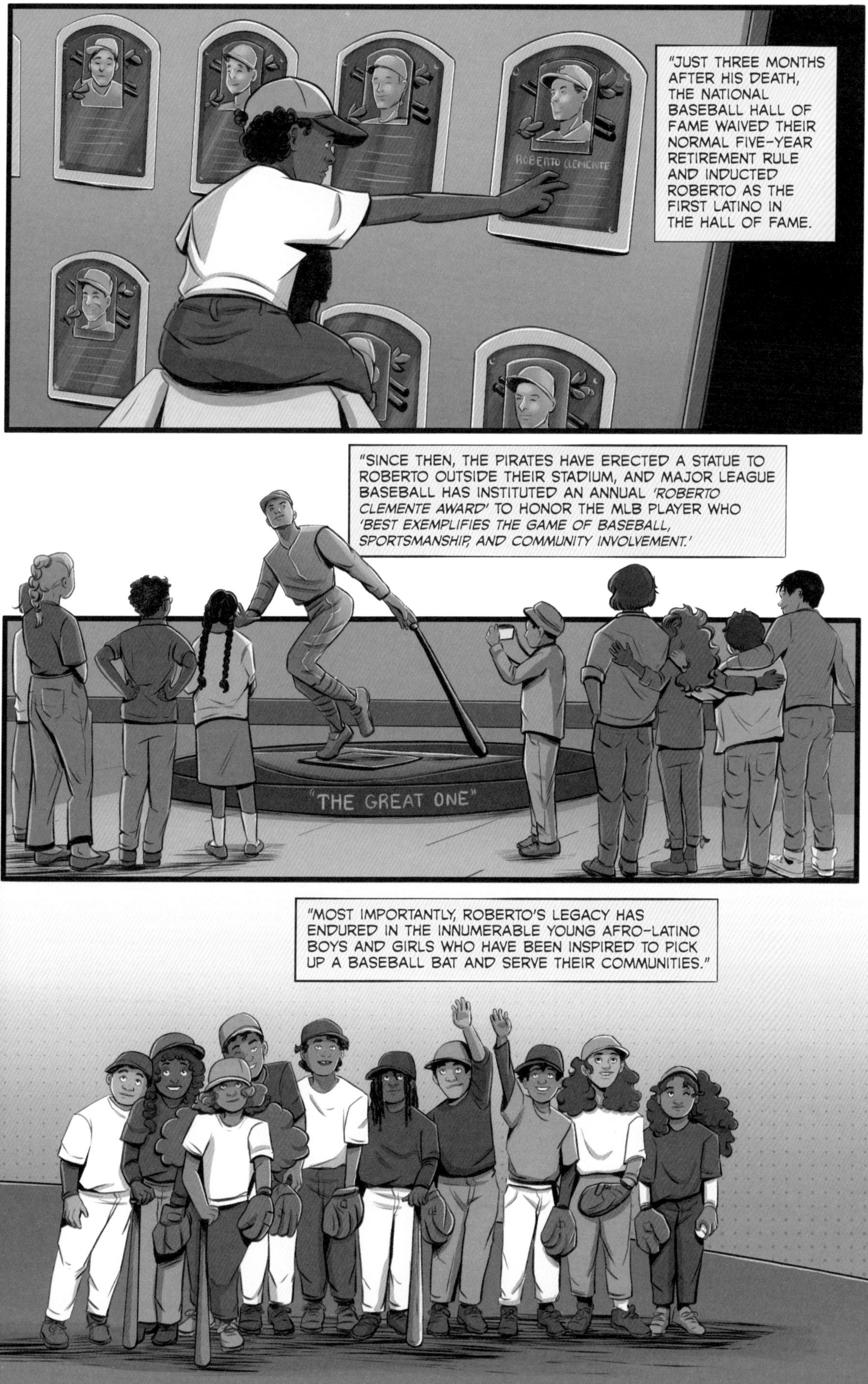
"JUST THREE MONTHS AFTER HIS DEATH, THE NATIONAL BASEBALL HALL OF FAME WAIVED THEIR NORMAL FIVE-YEAR RETIREMENT RULE AND INDUCTED ROBERTO AS THE FIRST LATINO IN THE HALL OF FAME.
ROBERTO CLEMENTE
"SINCE THEN, THE PIRATES HAVE ERECTED A STATUE TO ROBERTO OUTSIDE THEIR STADIUM, AND MAJOR LEAGUE BASEBALL HAS INSTITUTED AN ANNUAL *'ROBERTO CLEMENTE AWARD'* TO HONOR THE MLB PLAYER WHO *'BEST EXEMPLIFIES THE GAME OF BASEBALL, SPORTSMANSHIP, AND COMMUNITY INVOLVEMENT.'*
"THE GREAT ONE"
"MOST IMPORTANTLY, ROBERTO'S LEGACY HAS ENDURED IN THE INNUMERABLE YOUNG AFRO-LATINO BOYS AND GIRLS WHO HAVE BEEN INSPIRED TO PICK UP A BASEBALL BAT AND SERVE THEIR COMMUNITIES."

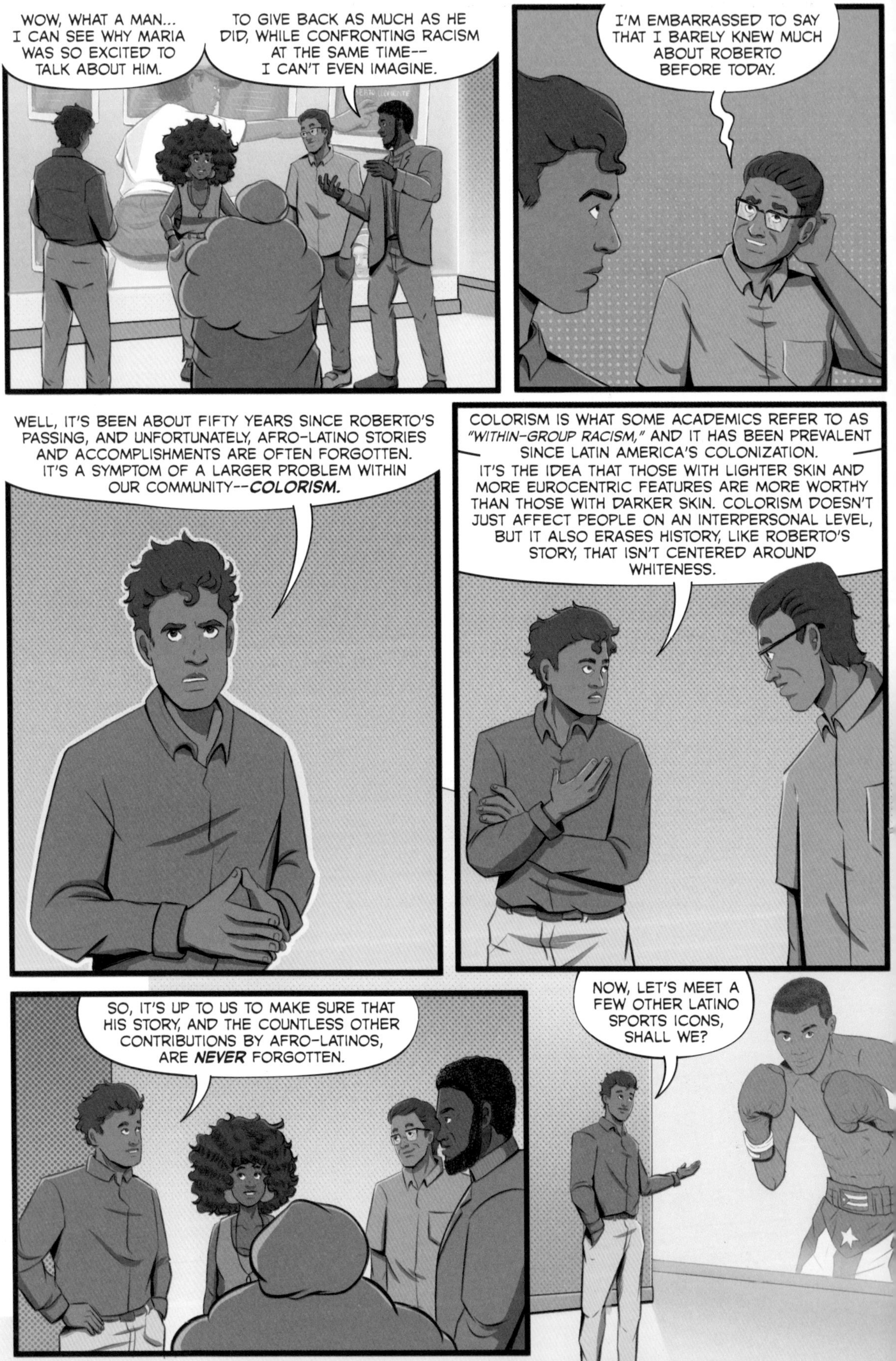
WOW, WHAT A MAN... I CAN SEE WHY MARIA WAS SO EXCITED TO TALK ABOUT HIM.
TO GIVE BACK AS MUCH AS HE DID, WHILE CONFRONTING RACISM AT THE SAME TIME-- I CAN'T EVEN IMAGINE.
I'M EMBARRASSED TO SAY THAT I BARELY KNEW MUCH ABOUT ROBERTO BEFORE TODAY.
WELL, IT'S BEEN ABOUT FIFTY YEARS SINCE ROBERTO'S PASSING, AND UNFORTUNATELY, AFRO-LATINO STORIES AND ACCOMPLISHMENTS ARE OFTEN FORGOTTEN. IT'S A SYMPTOM OF A LARGER PROBLEM WITHIN OUR COMMUNITY--***COLORISM.***
COLORISM IS WHAT SOME ACADEMICS REFER TO AS *"WITHIN-GROUP RACISM,"* AND IT HAS BEEN PREVALENT SINCE LATIN AMERICA'S COLONIZATION. IT'S THE IDEA THAT THOSE WITH LIGHTER SKIN AND MORE EUROCENTRIC FEATURES ARE MORE WORTHY THAN THOSE WITH DARKER SKIN. COLORISM DOESN'T JUST AFFECT PEOPLE ON AN INTERPERSONAL LEVEL, BUT IT ALSO ERASES HISTORY, LIKE ROBERTO'S STORY, THAT ISN'T CENTERED AROUND WHITENESS.
SO, IT'S UP TO US TO MAKE SURE THAT HIS STORY, AND THE COUNTLESS OTHER CONTRIBUTIONS BY AFRO-LATINOS, ARE ***NEVER*** FORGOTTEN.
NOW, LET'S MEET A FEW OTHER LATINO SPORTS ICONS, SHALL WE?

# FÉLIX TRINIDAD

"FÉLIX *'TITO'* TRINIDAD IS KNOWN AS ONE OF THE BEST PUERTO RICAN BOXERS OF ALL TIME. HIS CAREER BEGAN AS A TEENAGER--HE WON FIVE AMATEUR CHAMPIONSHIPS IN PUERTO RICO BEFORE MAKING HIS PROFESSIONAL DEBUT IN 1990 AT JUST SEVENTEEN YEARS OLD.

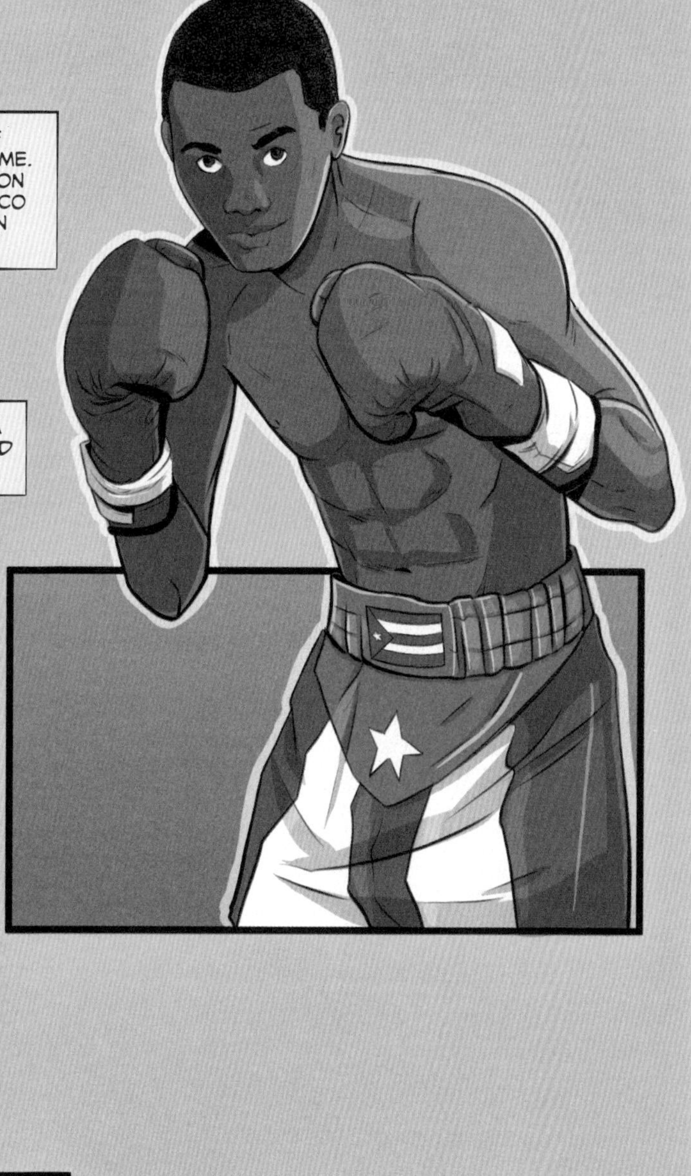

"HE WON HIS FIRST FORTY BOUTS AS A PROFESSIONAL FIGHTER AND REMAINED UNDEFEATED FOR OVER A DECADE.

"AFTER ONE PARTICULARLY IMPRESSIVE WIN AGAINST MEXICAN AMERICAN OSCAR DE LA HOYA IN 1999, TITO RECEIVED A HERO'S WELCOME WHEN HE RETURNED HOME TO PUERTO RICO. OVER 100,000 FANS GATHERED AT THE AIRPORT AND MANY MORE CROWDED THE HIGHWAYS TO CATCH A GLIMPSE OF THE CHAMPION. THE GOVERNOR OF PUERTO RICO EVEN GAVE GOVERNMENT EMPLOYEES THE AFTERNOON OFF TO CELEBRATE TITO'S WIN.

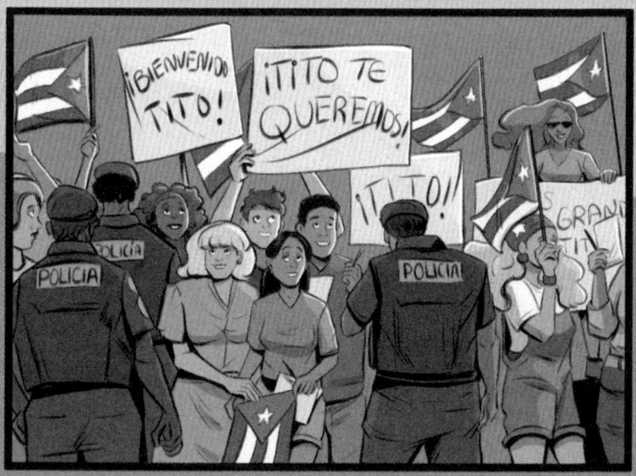
¡BIENVENIDO TITO!
¡TITO TE QUEREMOS!
¡TITO!
POLICIA
POLICIA
POLICIA

"KNOWN AS ***'THE PRIDE OF PUERTO RICO,'*** TITO BECAME A ROLE MODEL TO CHILDREN ACROSS THE ISLAND AND AN ICON FOR HIS COUNTRY."

# DARA TORRES

"BORN INTO A CUBAN AMERICAN HOME IN LOS ANGELES, CALIFORNIA, DARA TORRES IS ONE OF THE MOST DECORATED U.S. FEMALE OLYMPIC ATHLETES OF ALL TIME. SHE WAS THE FIRST SWIMMER TO REPRESENT THE UNITED STATES IN FIVE SEPARATE OLYMPIC GAMES, AND AT FORTY-ONE, SHE BECAME THE OLDEST SWIMMER TO EARN A PLACE ON THE U.S. OLYMPIC TEAM.

"DARA TORRES WAS ONLY SEVEN YEARS OLD WHEN SHE BEGAN SWIMMING COMPETITIVELY. BY THE TIME SHE WAS FIFTEEN YEARS OLD, SHE BROKE HER FIRST WORLD RECORD BY COMPLETING A FIFTY-METER FREESTYLE RACE IN 25.69 SECONDS--A RECORD SHE LATER BROKE TWO MORE TIMES.

"OVER A TWENTY-SIX-YEAR CAREER, DARA EARNED FOUR GOLD, FOUR SILVER, AND FOUR BRONZE OLYMPIC MEDALS FOR THE UNITED STATES. HER DRIVE TO COMPETE AT THE HIGHEST LEVEL INSPIRED WOMEN OF ALL AGES, RACES, AND ETHNICITIES TO SWIM COMPETITIVELY.

"SHE PARTICIPATED IN HER FINAL OLYMPIC GAMES IN 2008 BEFORE RETIRING FROM THE SPORT TO WRITE A SERIES OF BEST-SELLING BOOKS ABOUT HER LIFE."

# ANTHONY MUÑOZ

"ANTHONY MUÑOZ IS AN IMPOSING FIGURE. STANDING AT A HULKING SIX-FOOT-SIX, ANTHONY, A MEXICAN AMERICAN FROM ONTARIO, CALIFORNIA, IS BEST KNOWN AS ONE OF THE GREATEST OFFENSIVE LINEMEN IN NFL HISTORY.

"AFTER THIRTEEN SEASONS AND TWO SUPER BOWL APPEARANCES WITH THE CINCINNATI BENGALS, ANTHONY WAS INDUCTED INTO THE PRO FOOTBALL HALL OF FAME IN 1998-- ONLY THE SECOND LATINO HONORED AT THE TIME.

"DESPITE HIS MANY ACHIEVEMENTS ON THE FIELD, THE LEGACY ANTHONY IS MOST PROUD OF IS HIS FOUNDATION'S FOOTBALL ACADEMY. DESIGNED TO ENCOURAGE LATINO PARTICIPATION IN THE SPORT AND DEVELOP THE NEXT GENERATION OF FOOT-BALL LEADERS, ANTHONY'S 'CHARACTER CAMPS' SHOW THAT FOOTBALL CAN BE MUCH MORE THAN A SPORT-- IT CAN BE LIFE CHANGING."

# LAURIE HERNÁNDEZ

"LAUREN 'LAURIE' HERNÁNDEZ WAS BORN IN NEW BRUNSWICK, NEW JERSEY, AND AT SIXTEEN YEARS OLD BECAME ONE OF ONLY FOUR LATINA GYMNASTS TO EVER REPRESENT TEAM USA AT THE OLYMPICS UP UNTIL THAT POINT.

"LAURIE WAS A MEMBER OF THE 'FINAL FIVE'-- THE WOMEN'S GYMNASTICS TEAM THAT REPRESENTED THE UNITED STATES IN THE 2016 OLYMPICS. NOT ONLY DID THE FINAL FIVE EARN A GOLD MEDAL IN THE TEAM EVENT, BUT THEY CAPTURED THE WORLD'S ATTENTION AS A TALENTED GROUP OF DIVERSE YOUNG WOMEN.

"IN ADDITION TO HER GOLD MEDAL, LAURIE ALSO WON A SILVER MEDAL ON BALANCE BEAM.

"WHEN ASKED WHAT IT WAS LIKE TO BE A LATINA REPRESENTING THE UNITED STATES, LAURIE SAID, 'I THINK IT'S AMAZING THAT I CAN JUST GO OUT THERE AND BE MYSELF, AND THE FACT THAT I'M CARRYING PUERTO RICO ON MY BACK A LITTLE BIT, I THINK THAT'S AN HONOR.'"

# CHAPTER 5: LATINO SCIENTISTS

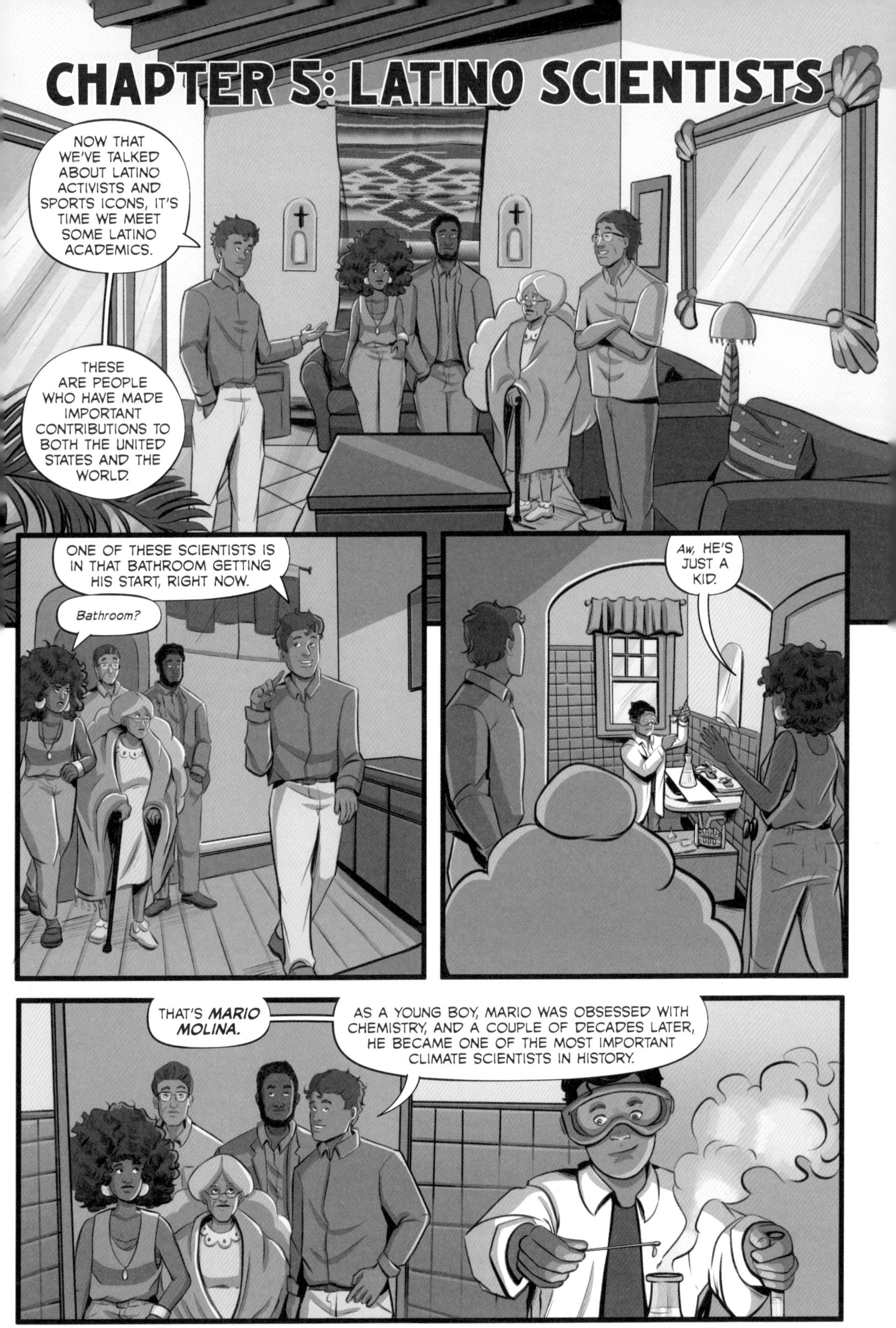

NOW THAT WE'VE TALKED ABOUT LATINO ACTIVISTS AND SPORTS ICONS, IT'S TIME WE MEET SOME LATINO ACADEMICS.
THESE ARE PEOPLE WHO HAVE MADE IMPORTANT CONTRIBUTIONS TO BOTH THE UNITED STATES AND THE WORLD.
ONE OF THESE SCIENTISTS IS IN THAT BATHROOM GETTING HIS START, RIGHT NOW.
*Bathroom?*
*Aw,* HE'S JUST A KID.
THAT'S ***MARIO MOLINA.***
AS A YOUNG BOY, MARIO WAS OBSESSED WITH CHEMISTRY, AND A COUPLE OF DECADES LATER, HE BECAME ONE OF THE MOST IMPORTANT CLIMATE SCIENTISTS IN HISTORY.

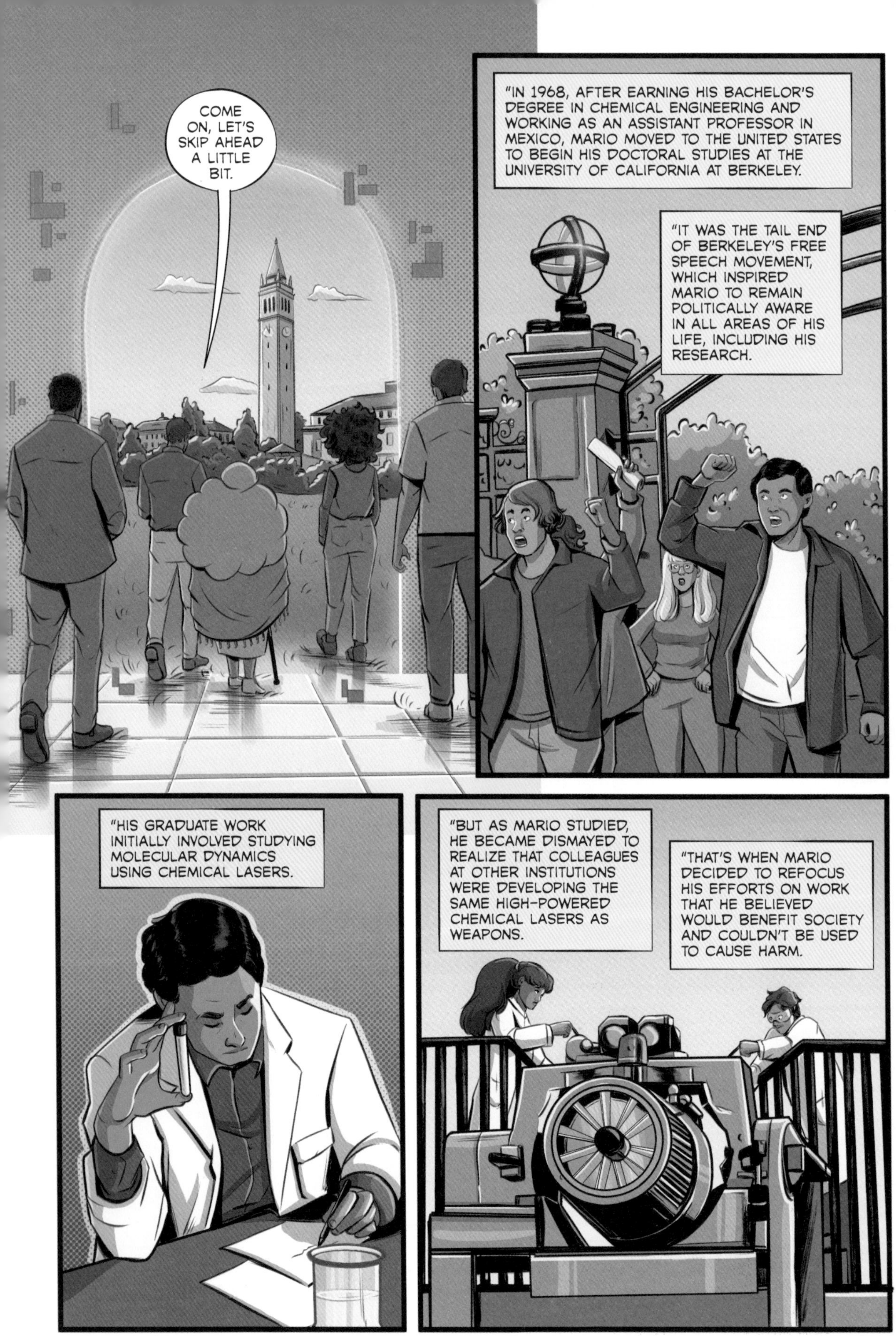
COME ON, LET'S SKIP AHEAD A LITTLE BIT.
"IN 1968, AFTER EARNING HIS BACHELOR'S DEGREE IN CHEMICAL ENGINEERING AND WORKING AS AN ASSISTANT PROFESSOR IN MEXICO, MARIO MOVED TO THE UNITED STATES TO BEGIN HIS DOCTORAL STUDIES AT THE UNIVERSITY OF CALIFORNIA AT BERKELEY.
"IT WAS THE TAIL END OF BERKELEY'S FREE SPEECH MOVEMENT, WHICH INSPIRED MARIO TO REMAIN POLITICALLY AWARE IN ALL AREAS OF HIS LIFE, INCLUDING HIS RESEARCH.
"HIS GRADUATE WORK INITIALLY INVOLVED STUDYING MOLECULAR DYNAMICS USING CHEMICAL LASERS.
"BUT AS MARIO STUDIED, HE BECAME DISMAYED TO REALIZE THAT COLLEAGUES AT OTHER INSTITUTIONS WERE DEVELOPING THE SAME HIGH-POWERED CHEMICAL LASERS AS WEAPONS.
"THAT'S WHEN MARIO DECIDED TO REFOCUS HIS EFFORTS ON WORK THAT HE BELIEVED WOULD BENEFIT SOCIETY AND COULDN'T BE USED TO CAUSE HARM.

"AFTER COMPLETING HIS PhD IN 1972, DR. MOLINA MOVED TO IRVINE, CALIFORNIA, TO WORK WITH DR. F. SHERWOOD ROWLAND-- A DISTINGUISHED PROFESSOR WHO PIONEERED RESEARCH ON *'HOT ATOM'* CHEMISTRY.

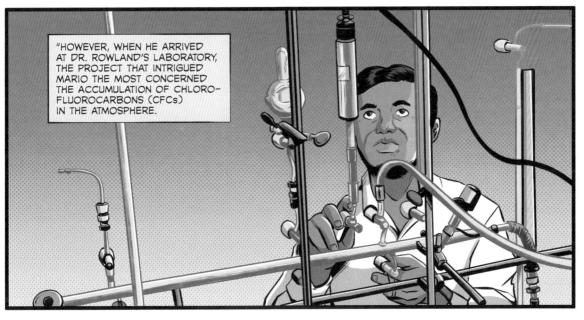

"HOWEVER, WHEN HE ARRIVED AT DR. ROWLAND'S LABORATORY, THE PROJECT THAT INTRIGUED MARIO THE MOST CONCERNED THE ACCUMULATION OF CHLORO-FLUOROCARBONS (CFCs) IN THE ATMOSPHERE.

"AT THE TIME, PEOPLE BELIEVED THAT THESE INDUSTRIAL CHEMICALS, WIDELY USED IN AEROSOL CANS LIKE HAIR SPRAY, WERE HARMLESS AND HAD LITTLE EFFECT ON THE ENVIRONMENT...

"...BUT MARIO HAD ANOTHER THEORY, WHICH HE AND DR. ROWLAND CALLED THE *'CFC-OZONE DEPLETION THEORY.'*

"JUST THREE MONTHS AFTER ARRIVING AT IRVINE, THE IMPLICATIONS OF THEIR FINDINGS WERE DIRE: MARIO REALIZED THAT THE ATOMS PRODUCED BY THE DECOMPOSITION OF CFCs IN THE ATMOSPHERE WERE ACTUALLY *DESTROYING* THE OZONE LAYER.

"THE OZONE LAYER ACTS LIKE SUNSCREEN, BLOCKING SIGNIFICANT AMOUNTS OF HARMFUL ULTRAVIOLET RADIATION FROM REACHING EARTH'S SURFACE."

I DON'T THINK ANYONE UNDERSTANDS HOW MUCH UNFILTERED UV RADIATION WE'RE ALLOWING TO PENETRATE INTO THE EARTH'S SURFACE...

...IF THE OZONE LAYER IS TRULY DEPLETING THIS QUICKLY, THAT MEANS SKIN CANCER, EYE DAMAGE, AND WHO KNOWS WHAT ELSE...

"ON JUNE 28, 1974, THEY PUBLISHED THEIR FINDINGS IN *NATURE,* ONE OF THE WORLD'S LEADING SCIENCE JOURNALS.

"MANY YEARS LATER, THE *NEW YORK TIMES* CALLED THEIR DISCOVERY 'A WATERSHED IN ENVIRONMENTAL THINKING... IT SHOWED FOR THE FIRST TIME THAT HUMAN ACTIVITIES COULD UNDERMINE GLOBAL LIFE SUPPORT PROCESSES AND THAT THE FABRIC OF NATURE WAS NOT INFINITELY RESILIENT TO INSULT.'

"BUT AT THE TIME, MARIO KNEW THE GENERAL PUBLIC WASN'T GOING TO READ THEIR SCIENTIFIC ARTICLE AND UNDERSTAND THE URGENCY OF THIS ENVIRONMENTAL DANGER. SO HE DECIDED TO GET THE WORD OUT HIMSELF.

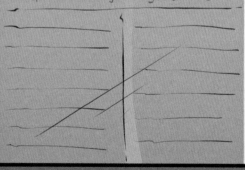

Stratospheric sink for chlorofluoromethanes : chlorine atomc-atalysed destruction of ozone

Mario J. Molina & F. S. Rowland
Department of Chemistry University of California

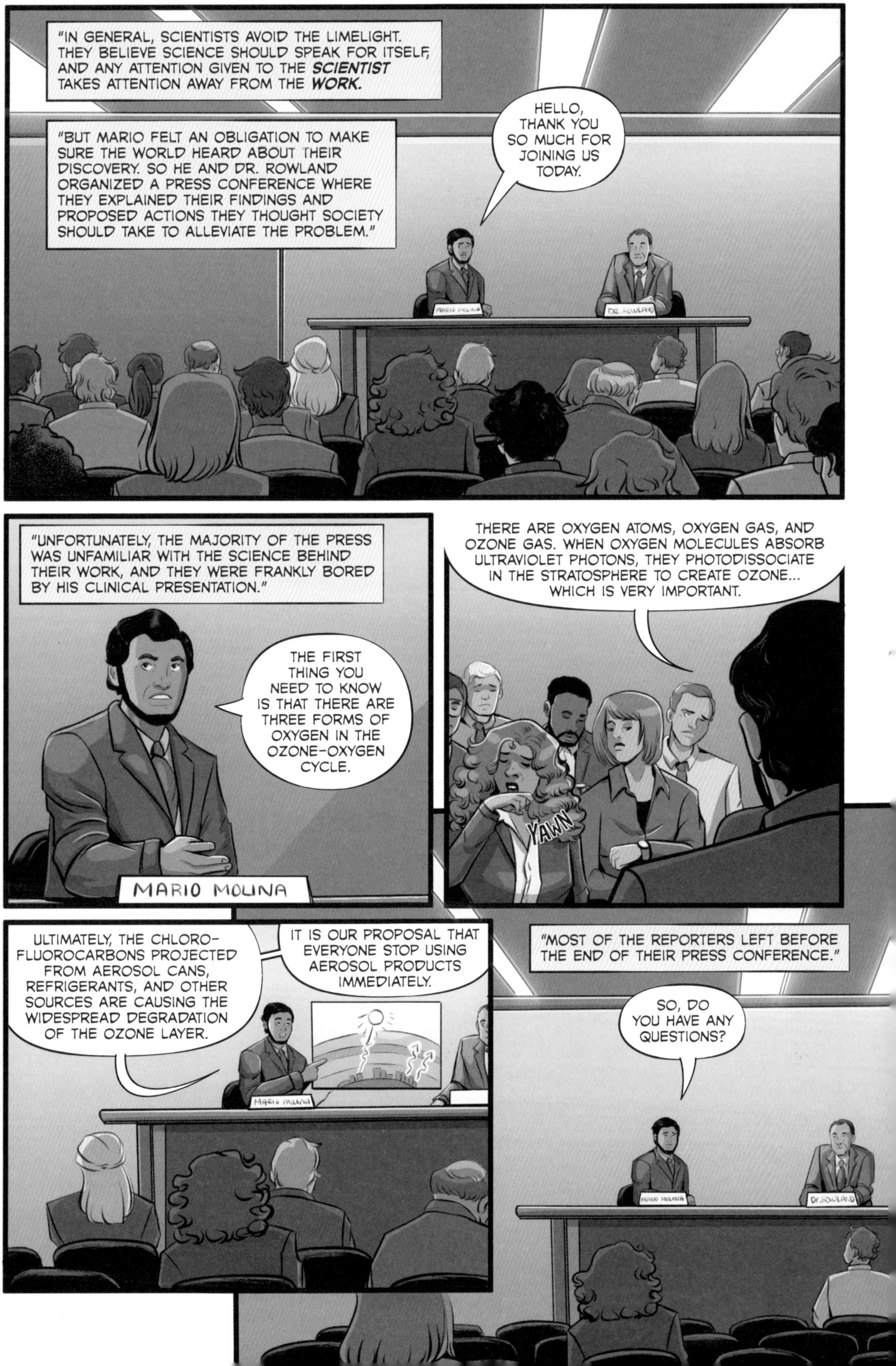
"IN GENERAL, SCIENTISTS AVOID THE LIMELIGHT. THEY BELIEVE SCIENCE SHOULD SPEAK FOR ITSELF, AND ANY ATTENTION GIVEN TO THE ***SCIENTIST*** TAKES ATTENTION AWAY FROM THE ***WORK.***
"BUT MARIO FELT AN OBLIGATION TO MAKE SURE THE WORLD HEARD ABOUT THEIR DISCOVERY. SO HE AND DR. ROWLAND ORGANIZED A PRESS CONFERENCE WHERE THEY EXPLAINED THEIR FINDINGS AND PROPOSED ACTIONS THEY THOUGHT SOCIETY SHOULD TAKE TO ALLEVIATE THE PROBLEM."
HELLO, THANK YOU SO MUCH FOR JOINING US TODAY.
MARIO MOLINA
DR. ROWLAND
"UNFORTUNATELY, THE MAJORITY OF THE PRESS WAS UNFAMILIAR WITH THE SCIENCE BEHIND THEIR WORK, AND THEY WERE FRANKLY BORED BY HIS CLINICAL PRESENTATION."
THE FIRST THING YOU NEED TO KNOW IS THAT THERE ARE THREE FORMS OF OXYGEN IN THE OZONE-OXYGEN CYCLE.
MARIO MOLINA
THERE ARE OXYGEN ATOMS, OXYGEN GAS, AND OZONE GAS. WHEN OXYGEN MOLECULES ABSORB ULTRAVIOLET PHOTONS, THEY PHOTODISSOCIATE IN THE STRATOSPHERE TO CREATE OZONE... WHICH IS VERY IMPORTANT.
YAWN
ULTIMATELY, THE CHLOROFLUOROCARBONS PROJECTED FROM AEROSOL CANS, REFRIGERANTS, AND OTHER SOURCES ARE CAUSING THE WIDESPREAD DEGRADATION OF THE OZONE LAYER.
IT IS OUR PROPOSAL THAT EVERYONE STOP USING AEROSOL PRODUCTS IMMEDIATELY.
MARIO MOLINA
"MOST OF THE REPORTERS LEFT BEFORE THE END OF THEIR PRESS CONFERENCE."
SO, DO YOU HAVE ANY QUESTIONS?
MARIO MOLINA
DR. ROWLAND

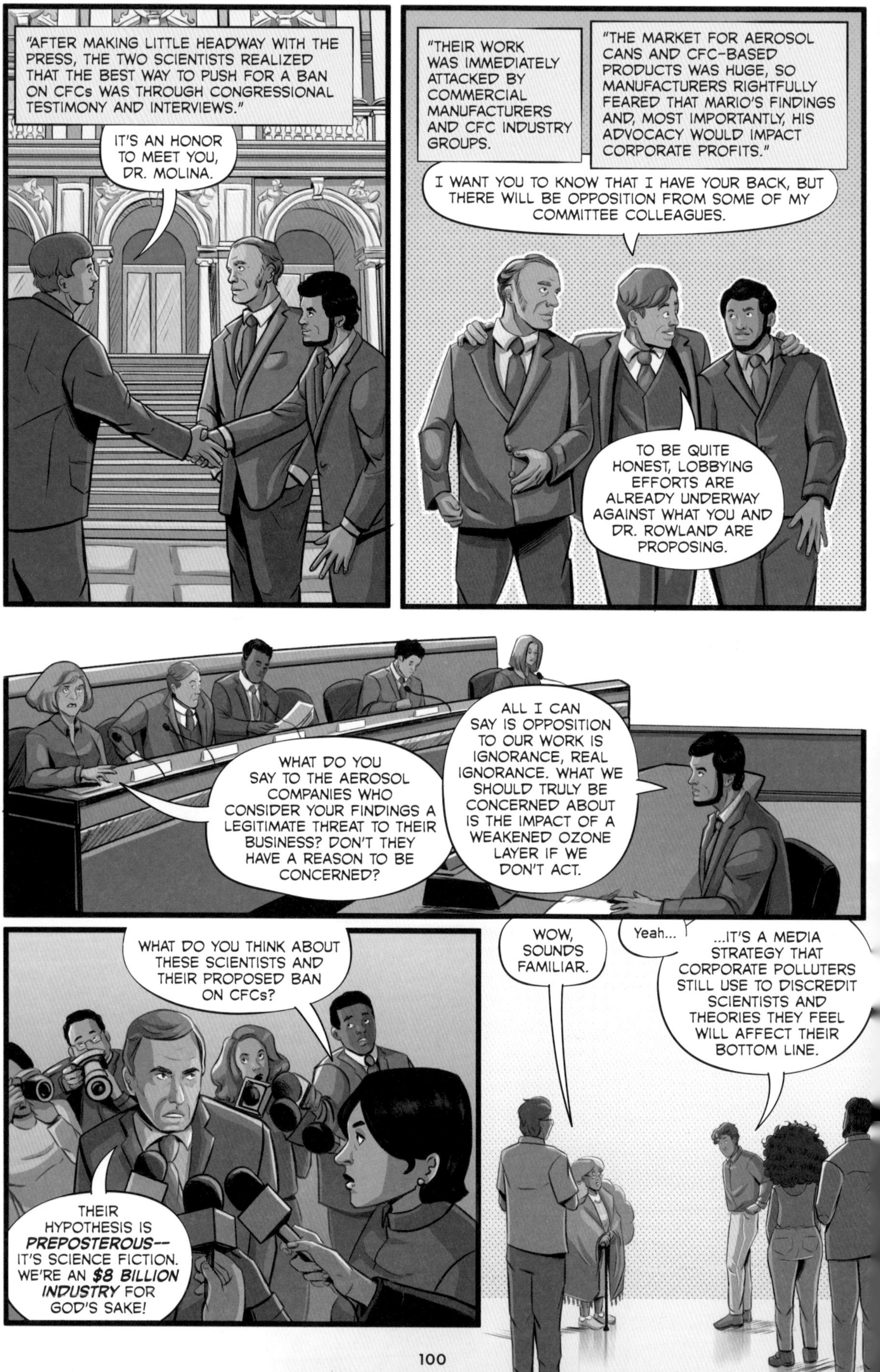
"AFTER MAKING LITTLE HEADWAY WITH THE PRESS, THE TWO SCIENTISTS REALIZED THAT THE BEST WAY TO PUSH FOR A BAN ON CFCs WAS THROUGH CONGRESSIONAL TESTIMONY AND INTERVIEWS."
IT'S AN HONOR TO MEET YOU, DR. MOLINA.
"THEIR WORK WAS IMMEDIATELY ATTACKED BY COMMERCIAL MANUFACTURERS AND CFC INDUSTRY GROUPS.
"THE MARKET FOR AEROSOL CANS AND CFC-BASED PRODUCTS WAS HUGE, SO MANUFACTURERS RIGHTFULLY FEARED THAT MARIO'S FINDINGS AND, MOST IMPORTANTLY, HIS ADVOCACY WOULD IMPACT CORPORATE PROFITS."
I WANT YOU TO KNOW THAT I HAVE YOUR BACK, BUT THERE WILL BE OPPOSITION FROM SOME OF MY COMMITTEE COLLEAGUES.
TO BE QUITE HONEST, LOBBYING EFFORTS ARE ALREADY UNDERWAY AGAINST WHAT YOU AND DR. ROWLAND ARE PROPOSING.
WHAT DO YOU SAY TO THE AEROSOL COMPANIES WHO CONSIDER YOUR FINDINGS A LEGITIMATE THREAT TO THEIR BUSINESS? DON'T THEY HAVE A REASON TO BE CONCERNED?
ALL I CAN SAY IS OPPOSITION TO OUR WORK IS IGNORANCE, REAL IGNORANCE. WHAT WE SHOULD TRULY BE CONCERNED ABOUT IS THE IMPACT OF A WEAKENED OZONE LAYER IF WE DON'T ACT.
WHAT DO YOU THINK ABOUT THESE SCIENTISTS AND THEIR PROPOSED BAN ON CFCs?
THEIR HYPOTHESIS IS ***PREPOSTEROUS***--IT'S SCIENCE FICTION. WE'RE AN ***$8 BILLION INDUSTRY*** FOR GOD'S SAKE!
WOW, SOUNDS FAMILIAR.
Yeah...
...IT'S A MEDIA STRATEGY THAT CORPORATE POLLUTERS STILL USE TO DISCREDIT SCIENTISTS AND THEORIES THEY FEEL WILL AFFECT THEIR BOTTOM LINE.

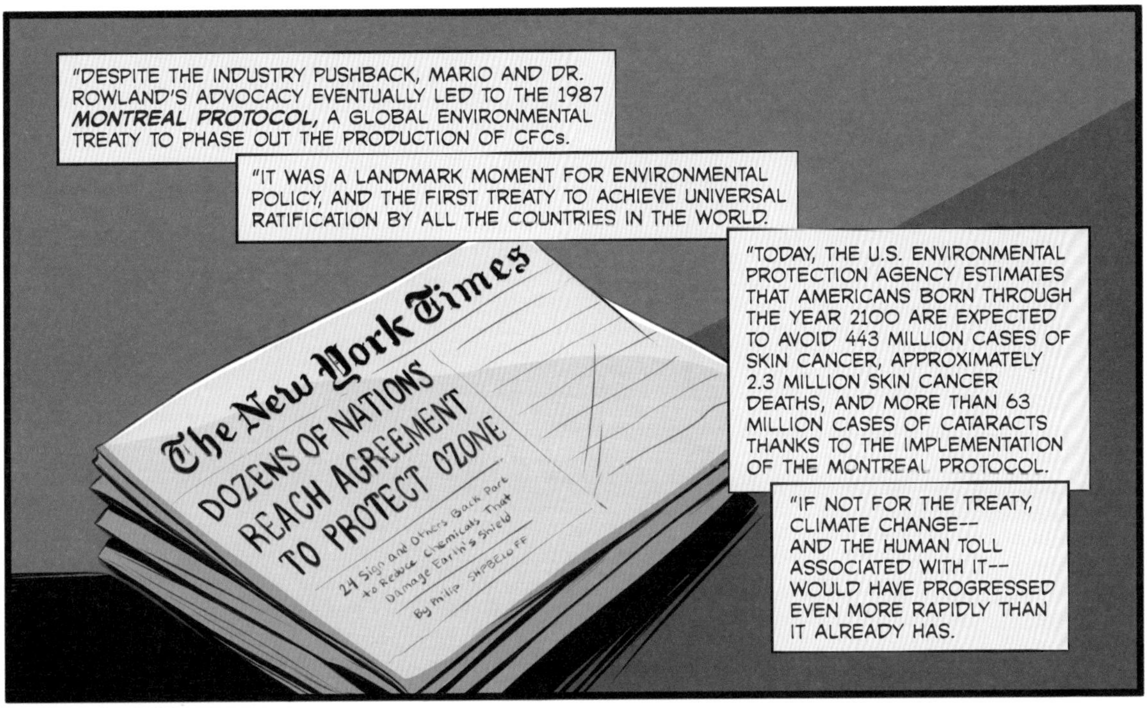
"DESPITE THE INDUSTRY PUSHBACK, MARIO AND DR. ROWLAND'S ADVOCACY EVENTUALLY LED TO THE 1987 ***MONTREAL PROTOCOL,*** A GLOBAL ENVIRONMENTAL TREATY TO PHASE OUT THE PRODUCTION OF CFCs.
"IT WAS A LANDMARK MOMENT FOR ENVIRONMENTAL POLICY, AND THE FIRST TREATY TO ACHIEVE UNIVERSAL RATIFICATION BY ALL THE COUNTRIES IN THE WORLD.
The New York Times
DOZENS OF NATIONS REACH AGREEMENT TO PROTECT OZONE
24 Sign and Others Back Part to Reduce Chemicals That Damage Earth's Shield
By Philip SHPBELOFF
"TODAY, THE U.S. ENVIRONMENTAL PROTECTION AGENCY ESTIMATES THAT AMERICANS BORN THROUGH THE YEAR 2100 ARE EXPECTED TO AVOID 443 MILLION CASES OF SKIN CANCER, APPROXIMATELY 2.3 MILLION SKIN CANCER DEATHS, AND MORE THAN 63 MILLION CASES OF CATARACTS THANKS TO THE IMPLEMENTATION OF THE MONTREAL PROTOCOL.
"IF NOT FOR THE TREATY, CLIMATE CHANGE-- AND THE HUMAN TOLL ASSOCIATED WITH IT-- WOULD HAVE PROGRESSED EVEN MORE RAPIDLY THAN IT ALREADY HAS.

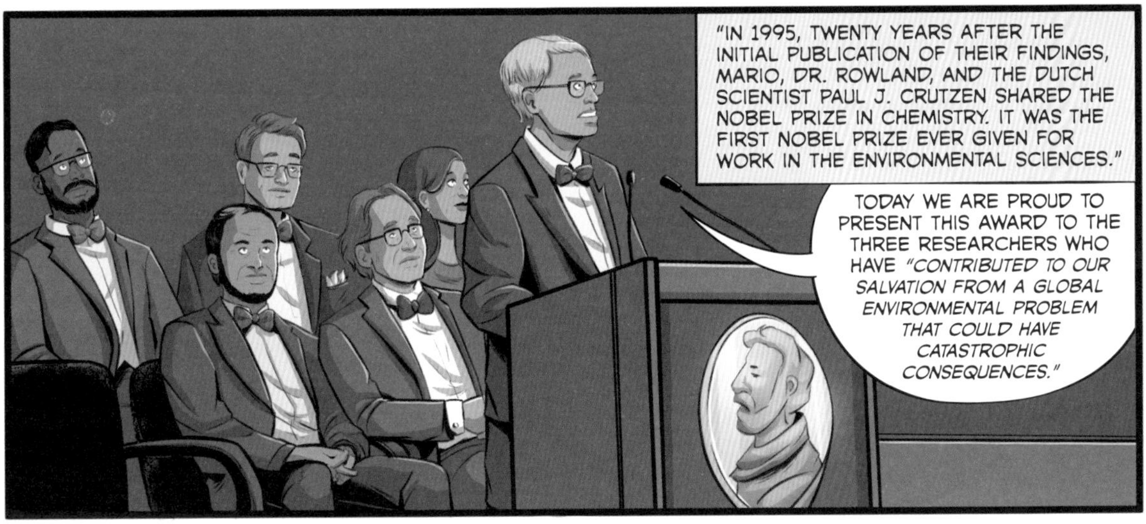
"IN 1995, TWENTY YEARS AFTER THE INITIAL PUBLICATION OF THEIR FINDINGS, MARIO, DR. ROWLAND, AND THE DUTCH SCIENTIST PAUL J. CRUTZEN SHARED THE NOBEL PRIZE IN CHEMISTRY. IT WAS THE FIRST NOBEL PRIZE EVER GIVEN FOR WORK IN THE ENVIRONMENTAL SCIENCES."
TODAY WE ARE PROUD TO PRESENT THIS AWARD TO THE THREE RESEARCHERS WHO HAVE *"CONTRIBUTED TO OUR SALVATION FROM A GLOBAL ENVIRONMENTAL PROBLEM THAT COULD HAVE CATASTROPHIC CONSEQUENCES."*

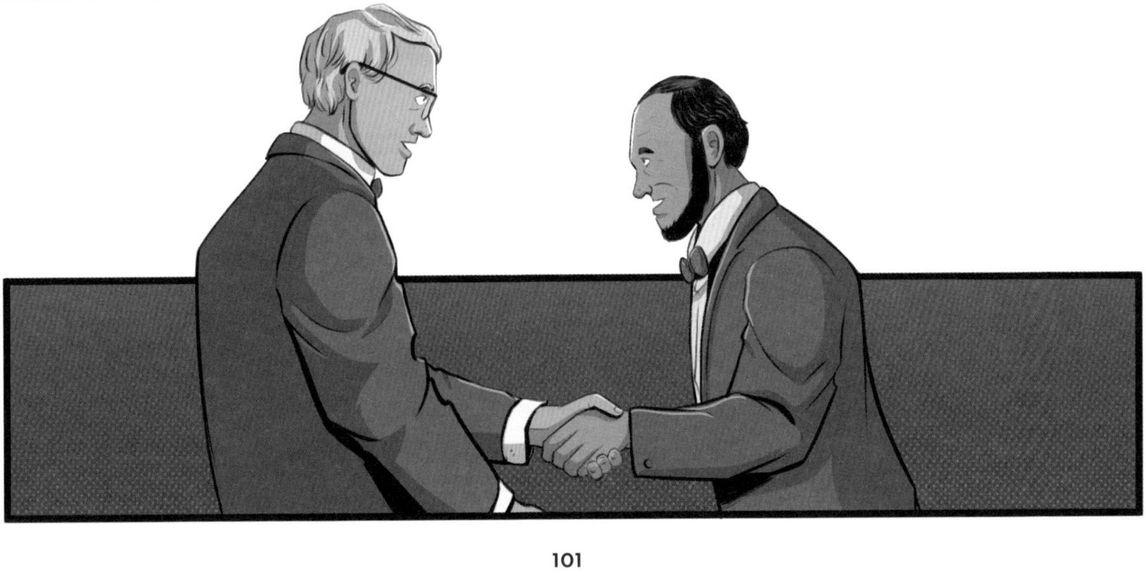

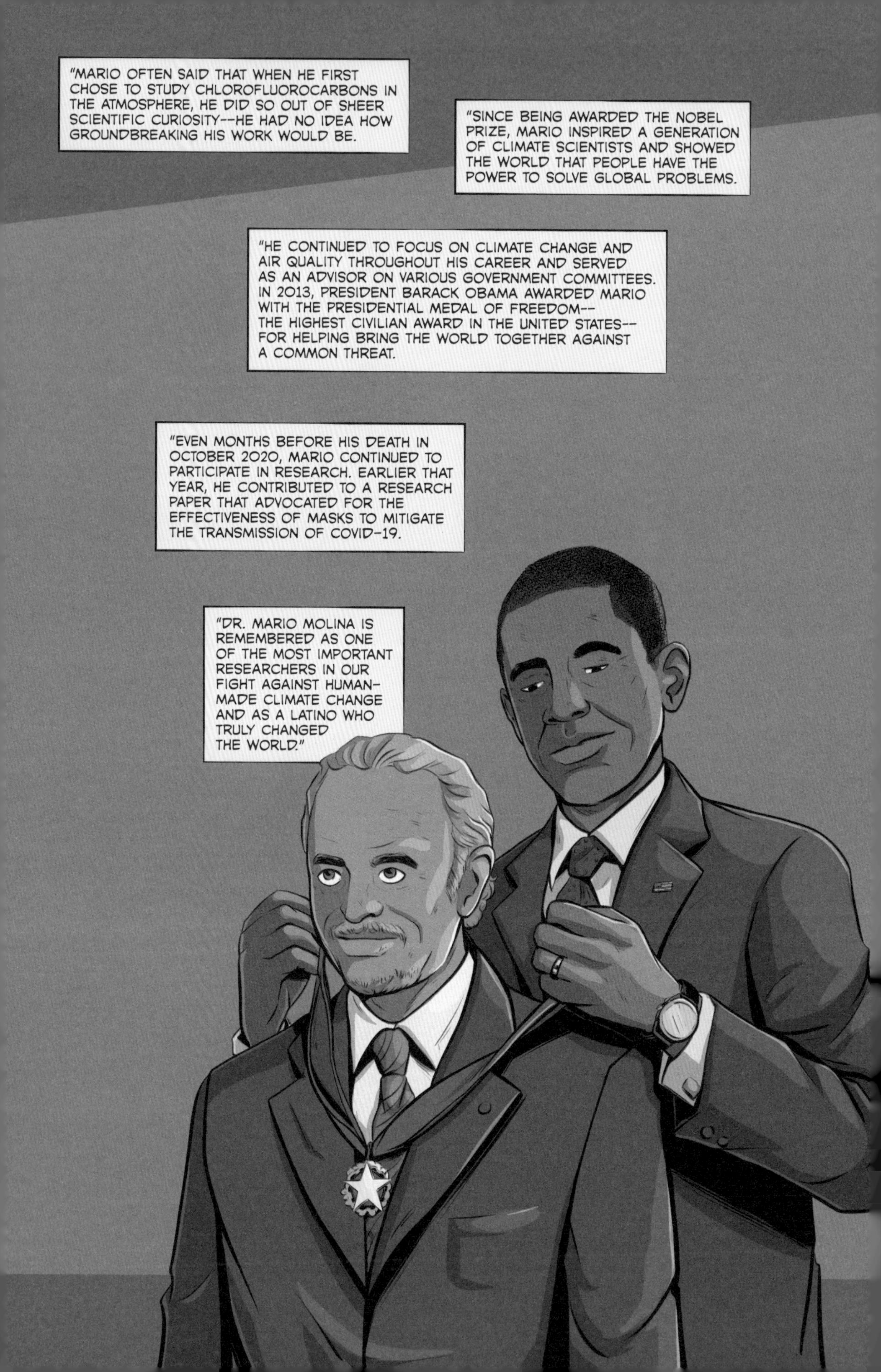
"MARIO OFTEN SAID THAT WHEN HE FIRST CHOSE TO STUDY CHLOROFLUOROCARBONS IN THE ATMOSPHERE, HE DID SO OUT OF SHEER SCIENTIFIC CURIOSITY--HE HAD NO IDEA HOW GROUNDBREAKING HIS WORK WOULD BE.
"SINCE BEING AWARDED THE NOBEL PRIZE, MARIO INSPIRED A GENERATION OF CLIMATE SCIENTISTS AND SHOWED THE WORLD THAT PEOPLE HAVE THE POWER TO SOLVE GLOBAL PROBLEMS.
"HE CONTINUED TO FOCUS ON CLIMATE CHANGE AND AIR QUALITY THROUGHOUT HIS CAREER AND SERVED AS AN ADVISOR ON VARIOUS GOVERNMENT COMMITTEES. IN 2013, PRESIDENT BARACK OBAMA AWARDED MARIO WITH THE PRESIDENTIAL MEDAL OF FREEDOM-- THE HIGHEST CIVILIAN AWARD IN THE UNITED STATES-- FOR HELPING BRING THE WORLD TOGETHER AGAINST A COMMON THREAT.
"EVEN MONTHS BEFORE HIS DEATH IN OCTOBER 2020, MARIO CONTINUED TO PARTICIPATE IN RESEARCH. EARLIER THAT YEAR, HE CONTRIBUTED TO A RESEARCH PAPER THAT ADVOCATED FOR THE EFFECTIVENESS OF MASKS TO MITIGATE THE TRANSMISSION OF COVID-19.
"DR. MARIO MOLINA IS REMEMBERED AS ONE OF THE MOST IMPORTANT RESEARCHERS IN OUR FIGHT AGAINST HUMAN-MADE CLIMATE CHANGE AND AS A LATINO WHO TRULY CHANGED THE WORLD."

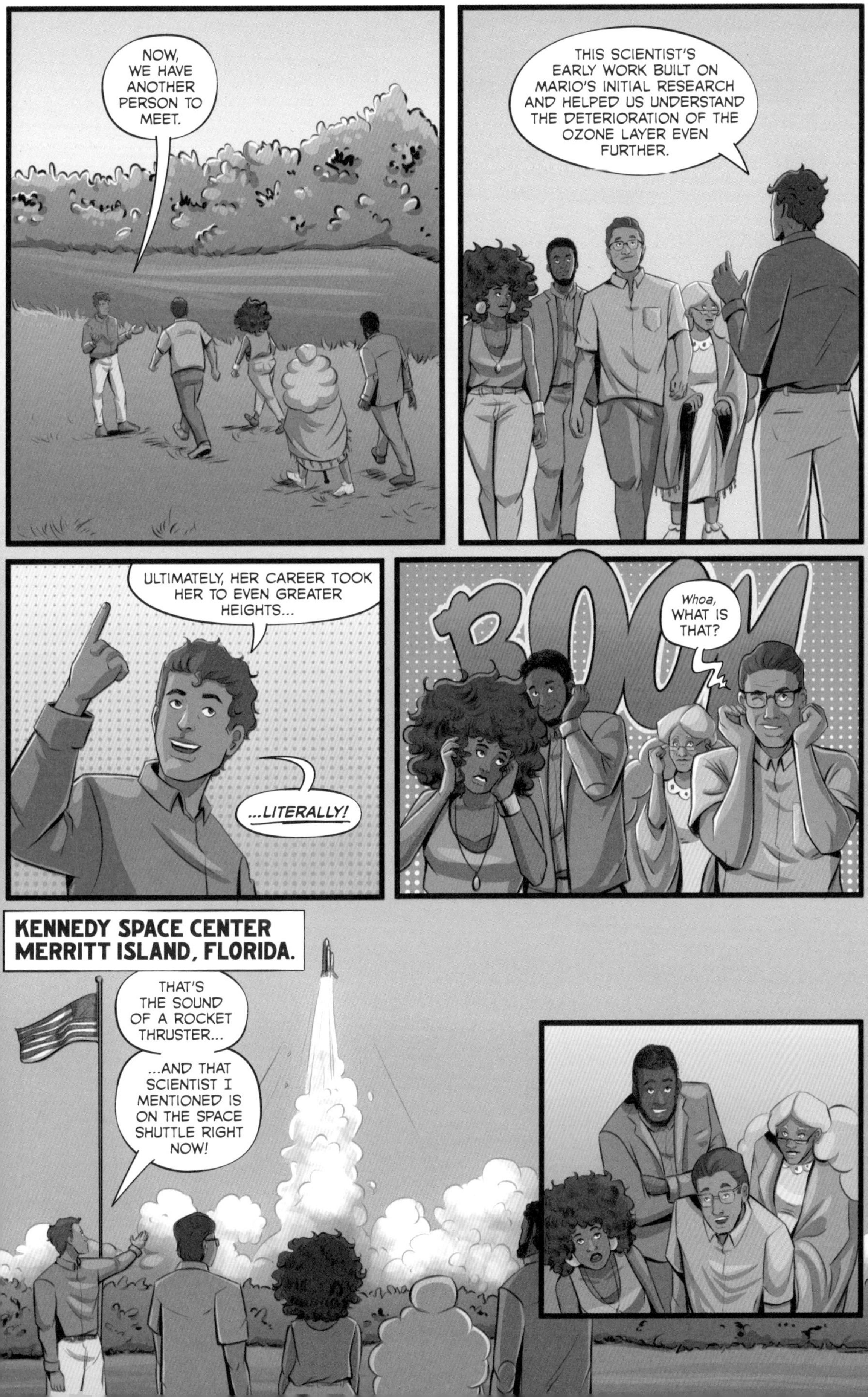

NOW, WE HAVE ANOTHER PERSON TO MEET.
THIS SCIENTIST'S EARLY WORK BUILT ON MARIO'S INITIAL RESEARCH AND HELPED US UNDERSTAND THE DETERIORATION OF THE OZONE LAYER EVEN FURTHER.
ULTIMATELY, HER CAREER TOOK HER TO EVEN GREATER HEIGHTS...
...LITERALLY!
BOOM
Whoa, WHAT IS THAT?
KENNEDY SPACE CENTER
MERRITT ISLAND, FLORIDA.
THAT'S THE SOUND OF A ROCKET THRUSTER...
...AND THAT SCIENTIST I MENTIONED IS ON THE SPACE SHUTTLE RIGHT NOW!

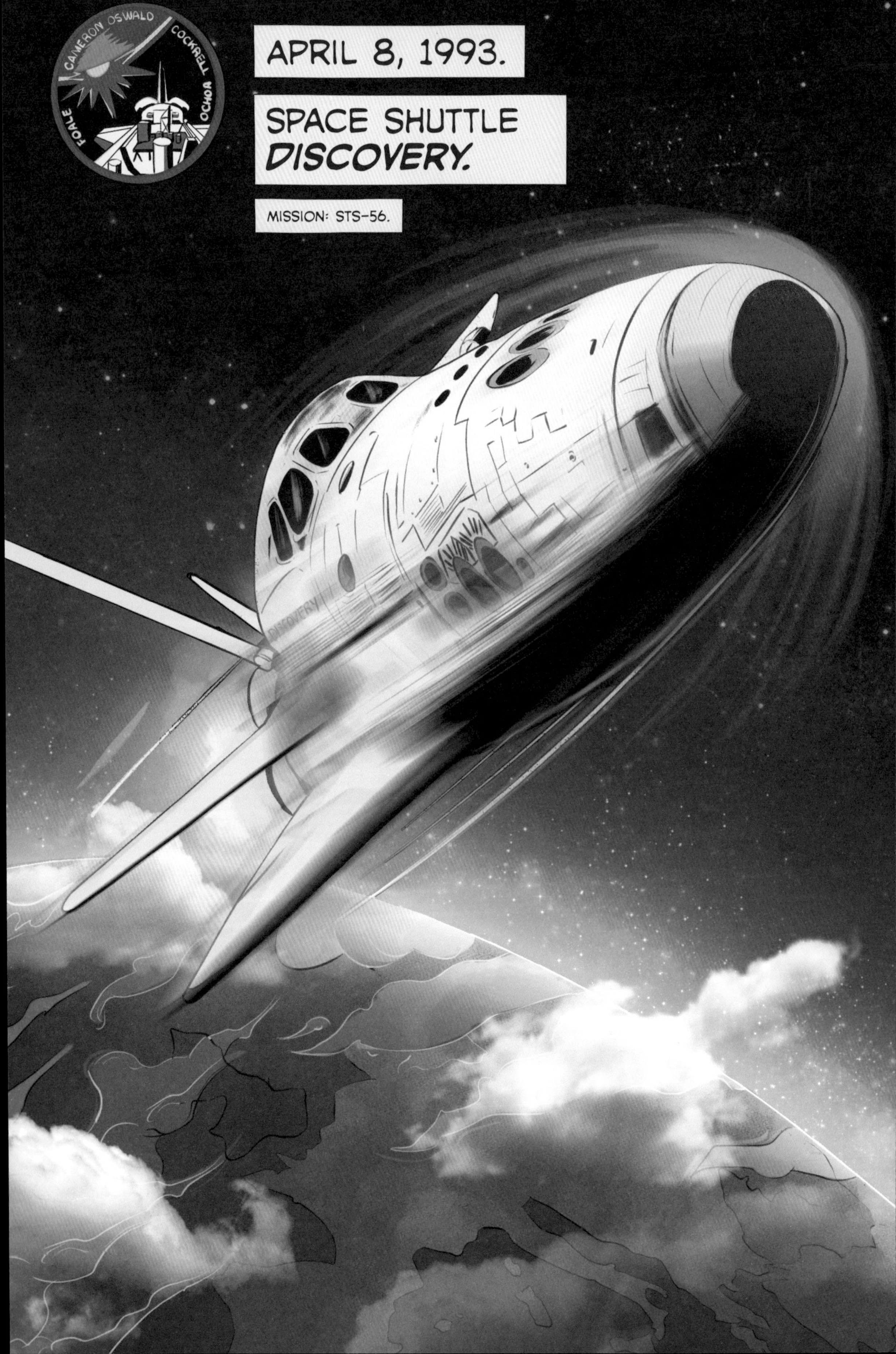
CAMERON OSWALD
COCKRELL
OCHOA
FOALE
APRIL 8, 1993.
SPACE SHUTTLE
*DISCOVERY.*
MISSION: STS-56.
DISCOVERY

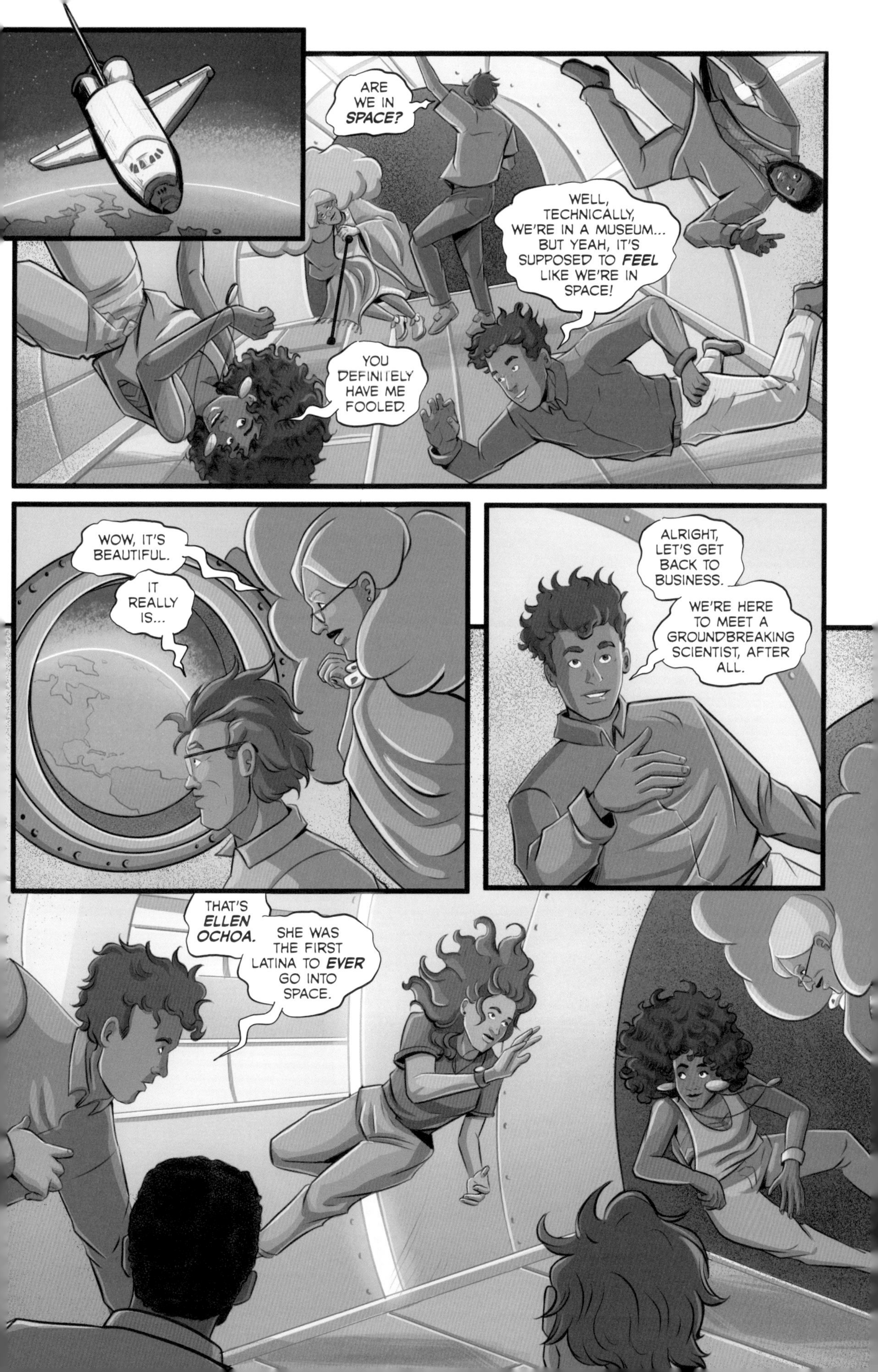
ARE WE IN *SPACE?*
WELL, TECHNICALLY, WE'RE IN A MUSEUM... BUT YEAH, IT'S SUPPOSED TO *FEEL* LIKE WE'RE IN SPACE!
YOU DEFINITELY HAVE ME FOOLED.
WOW, IT'S BEAUTIFUL.
IT REALLY IS...
ALRIGHT, LET'S GET BACK TO BUSINESS.
WE'RE HERE TO MEET A GROUNDBREAKING SCIENTIST, AFTER ALL.
THAT'S *ELLEN OCHOA.*
SHE WAS THE FIRST LATINA TO *EVER* GO INTO SPACE.

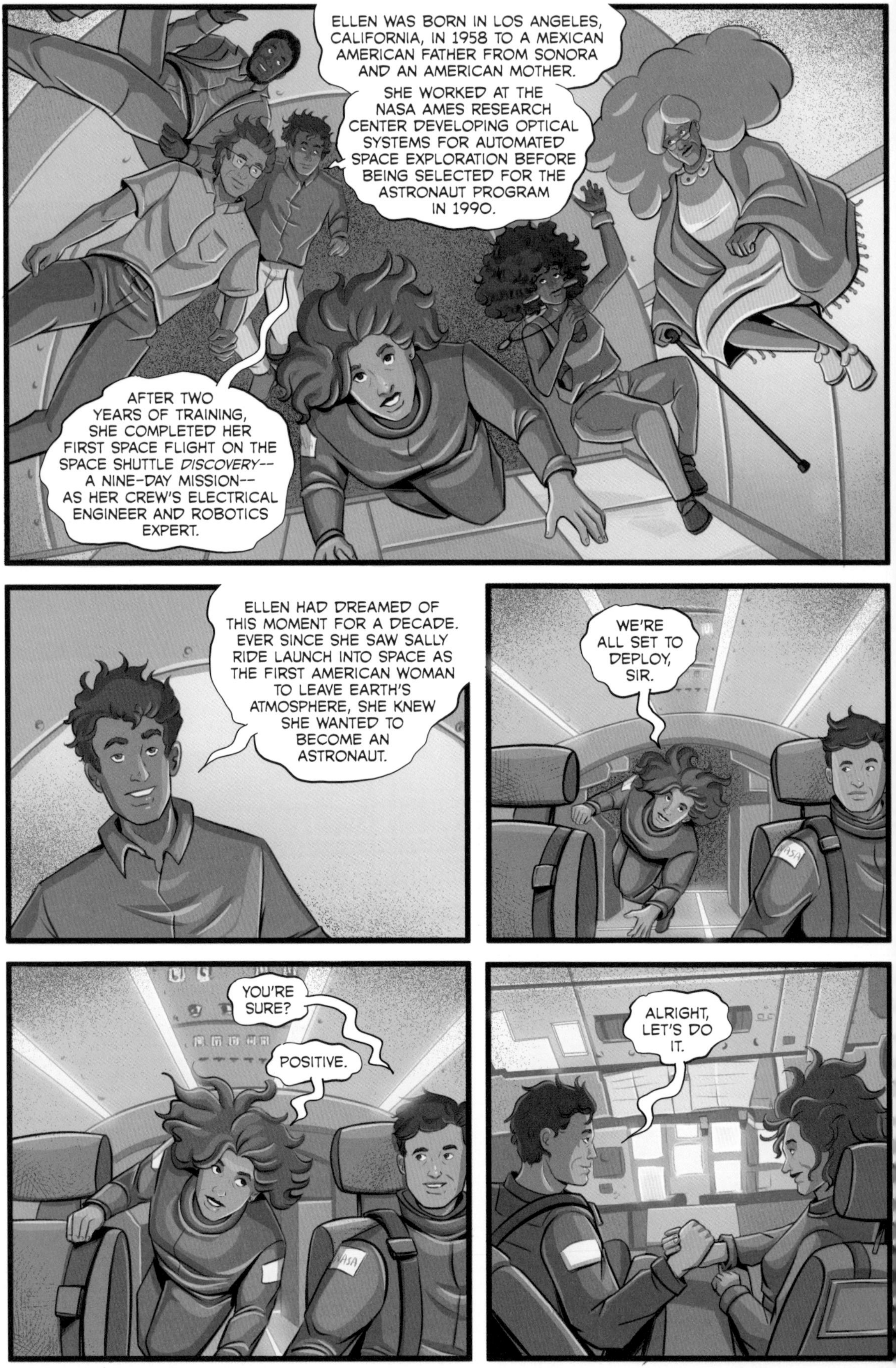
ELLEN WAS BORN IN LOS ANGELES, CALIFORNIA, IN 1958 TO A MEXICAN AMERICAN FATHER FROM SONORA AND AN AMERICAN MOTHER.
SHE WORKED AT THE NASA AMES RESEARCH CENTER DEVELOPING OPTICAL SYSTEMS FOR AUTOMATED SPACE EXPLORATION BEFORE BEING SELECTED FOR THE ASTRONAUT PROGRAM IN 1990.
AFTER TWO YEARS OF TRAINING, SHE COMPLETED HER FIRST SPACE FLIGHT ON THE SPACE SHUTTLE *DISCOVERY*-- A NINE-DAY MISSION-- AS HER CREW'S ELECTRICAL ENGINEER AND ROBOTICS EXPERT.
ELLEN HAD DREAMED OF THIS MOMENT FOR A DECADE. EVER SINCE SHE SAW SALLY RIDE LAUNCH INTO SPACE AS THE FIRST AMERICAN WOMAN TO LEAVE EARTH'S ATMOSPHERE, SHE KNEW SHE WANTED TO BECOME AN ASTRONAUT.
WE'RE ALL SET TO DEPLOY, SIR.
YOU'RE SURE?
POSITIVE.
ALRIGHT, LET'S DO IT.

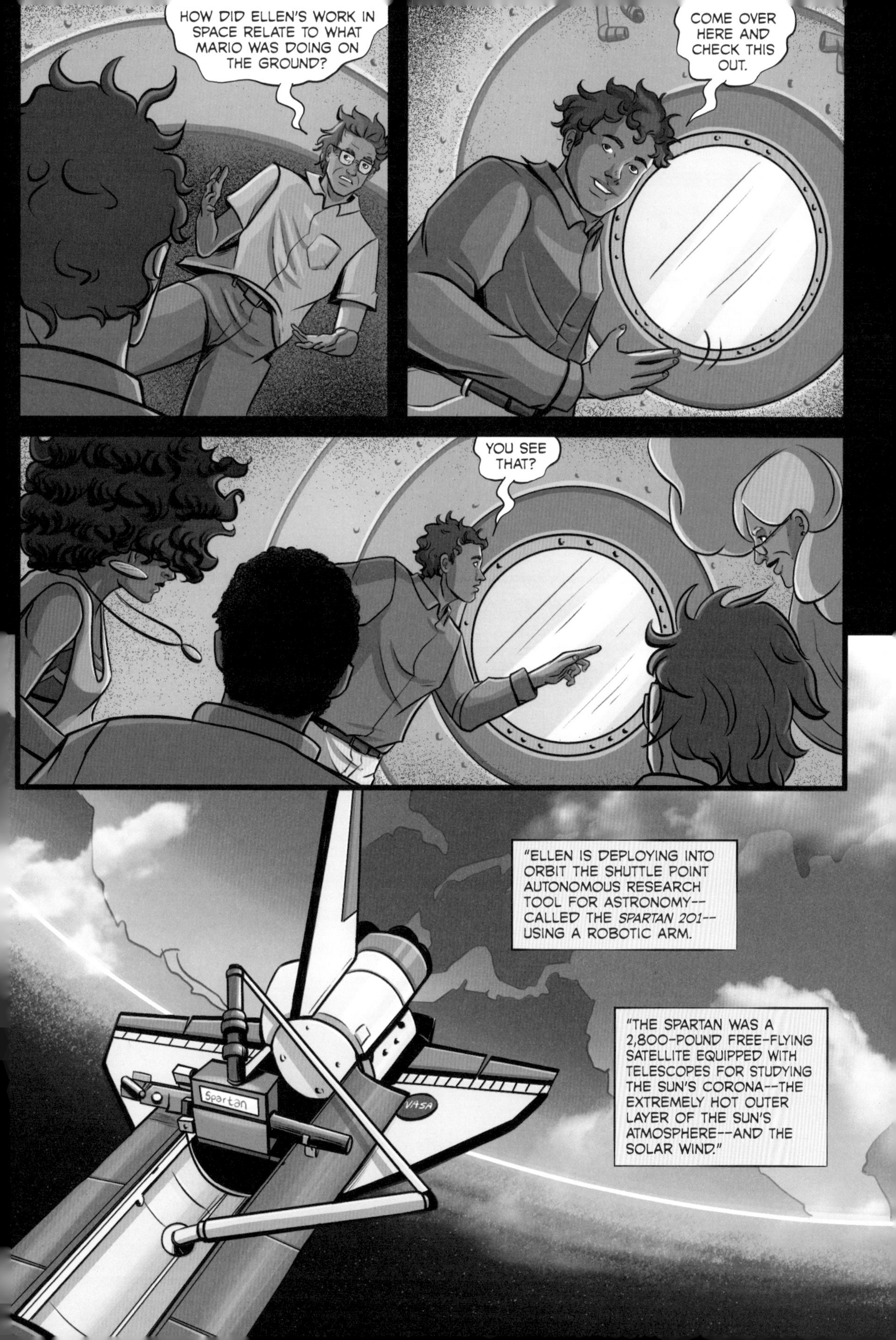
HOW DID ELLEN'S WORK IN SPACE RELATE TO WHAT MARIO WAS DOING ON THE GROUND?
COME OVER HERE AND CHECK THIS OUT.
YOU SEE THAT?
"ELLEN IS DEPLOYING INTO ORBIT THE SHUTTLE POINT AUTONOMOUS RESEARCH TOOL FOR ASTRONOMY-- CALLED THE *SPARTAN 201*-- USING A ROBOTIC ARM.
"THE SPARTAN WAS A 2,800-POUND FREE-FLYING SATELLITE EQUIPPED WITH TELESCOPES FOR STUDYING THE SUN'S CORONA--THE EXTREMELY HOT OUTER LAYER OF THE SUN'S ATMOSPHERE--AND THE SOLAR WIND."
Spartan
NASA

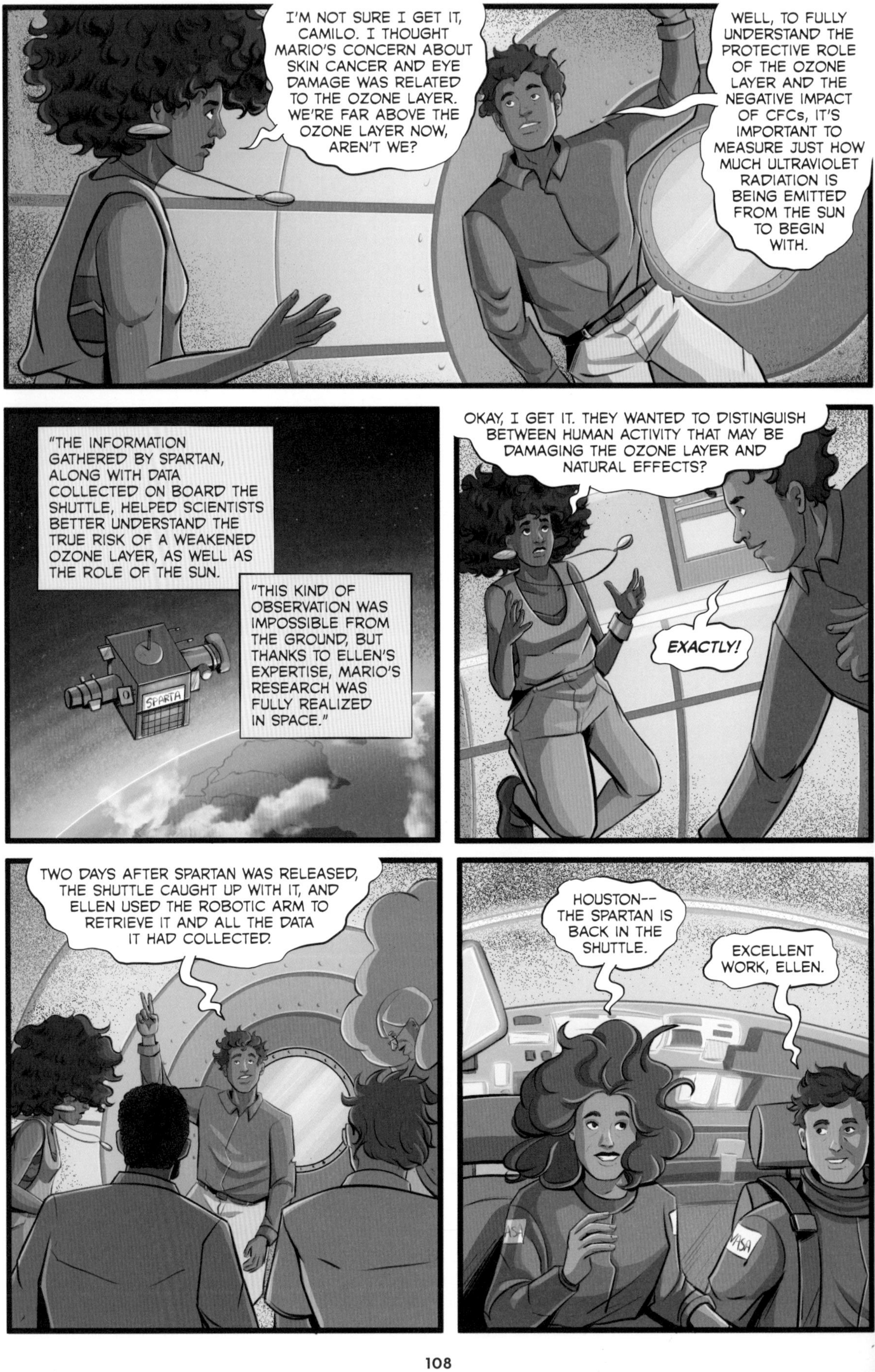
I'M NOT SURE I GET IT, CAMILO. I THOUGHT MARIO'S CONCERN ABOUT SKIN CANCER AND EYE DAMAGE WAS RELATED TO THE OZONE LAYER. WE'RE FAR ABOVE THE OZONE LAYER NOW, AREN'T WE?
WELL, TO FULLY UNDERSTAND THE PROTECTIVE ROLE OF THE OZONE LAYER AND THE NEGATIVE IMPACT OF CFCs, IT'S IMPORTANT TO MEASURE JUST HOW MUCH ULTRAVIOLET RADIATION IS BEING EMITTED FROM THE SUN TO BEGIN WITH.
"THE INFORMATION GATHERED BY SPARTAN, ALONG WITH DATA COLLECTED ON BOARD THE SHUTTLE, HELPED SCIENTISTS BETTER UNDERSTAND THE TRUE RISK OF A WEAKENED OZONE LAYER, AS WELL AS THE ROLE OF THE SUN.
"THIS KIND OF OBSERVATION WAS IMPOSSIBLE FROM THE GROUND, BUT THANKS TO ELLEN'S EXPERTISE, MARIO'S RESEARCH WAS FULLY REALIZED IN SPACE."
SPARTA
OKAY, I GET IT. THEY WANTED TO DISTINGUISH BETWEEN HUMAN ACTIVITY THAT MAY BE DAMAGING THE OZONE LAYER AND NATURAL EFFECTS?
EXACTLY!
TWO DAYS AFTER SPARTAN WAS RELEASED, THE SHUTTLE CAUGHT UP WITH IT, AND ELLEN USED THE ROBOTIC ARM TO RETRIEVE IT AND ALL THE DATA IT HAD COLLECTED.
HOUSTON-- THE SPARTAN IS BACK IN THE SHUTTLE.
EXCELLENT WORK, ELLEN.

"ELLEN WENT ON THREE MORE SPACE FLIGHTS, LOGGING NEARLY 1,000 HOURS IN SPACE.

"FIRST, ON NOVEMBER 3, 1994, ELLEN RETURNED TO SPACE TO CONTINUE STUDYING THE OZONE. ELLEN AND THE REST OF THE CREW WERE ABLE TO COLLECT PRECISE MEASUREMENTS OF THE SUN'S RADIATION AND ENERGY OUTPUT OVER THE COURSE OF THIRTY ORBITS.

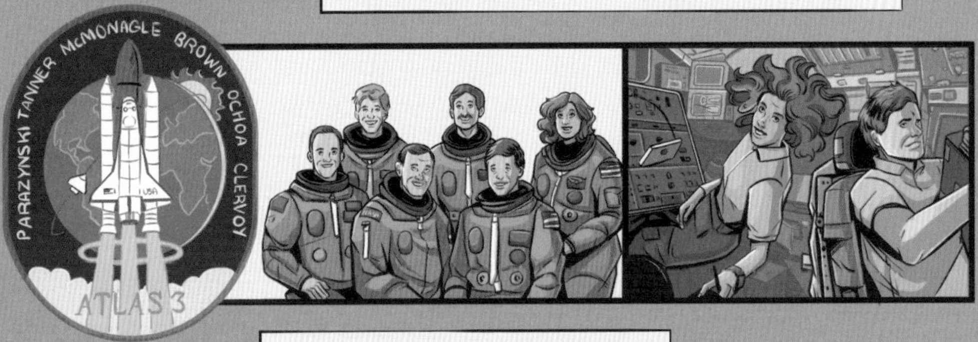
PARAZYNSKI TANNER McMONAGLE BROWN OCHOA CLERVOY
ATLAS 3

"NEXT, IN 1999, ELLEN PARTICIPATED IN THE FIRST EVER SHUTTLE DOCKING AT THE INTERNATIONAL SPACE STATION.

"THE STATION WAS MADE UP OF ONLY TWO MODULES AT THE TIME, SO THIS LOGISTICS AND RESUPPLY MISSION WAS CRITICAL TO THE FUTURE OF THE COMPLEX. THEY DELIVERED A CRANE CALLED THE ORBITAL TRANSFER DEVICE, AS WELL AS 3,567 POUNDS OF MATERIAL TO HELP OUTFIT THE STATION SO THAT ASTRONAUTS COULD EVENTUALLY LIVE AND WORK IN IT.

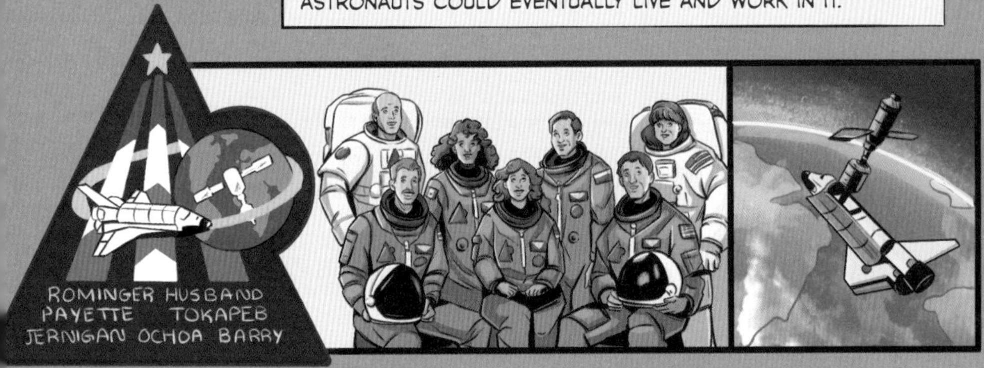
ROMINGER HUSBAND
PAYETTE TOKAPEB
JERNIGAN OCHOA BARRY

"IN 2002, ON HER FINAL MISSION INTO SPACE, ELLEN AND HER CREW INSTALLED THE LARGE SØ TRUSS SEGMENT, WHICH FORMED THE CENTRAL BACKBONE OF THE INTERNATIONAL SPACE STATION. THE TRUSS CONTAINED NAVIGATIONAL DEVICES, COMPUTERS, AND COOLING AND POWER SYSTEMS THAT WERE LATER ATTACHED TO ADDITIONAL LABORATORIES IN THE STATION."

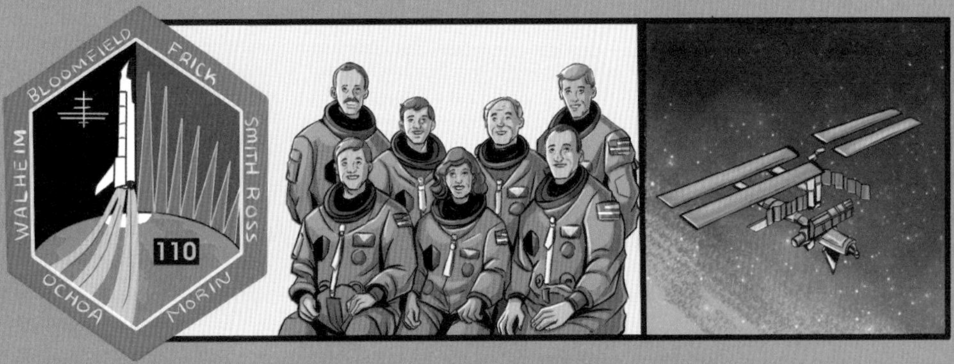
BLOOMFIELD FRICK SMITH ROSS MORIN OCHOA WALHEIM
110

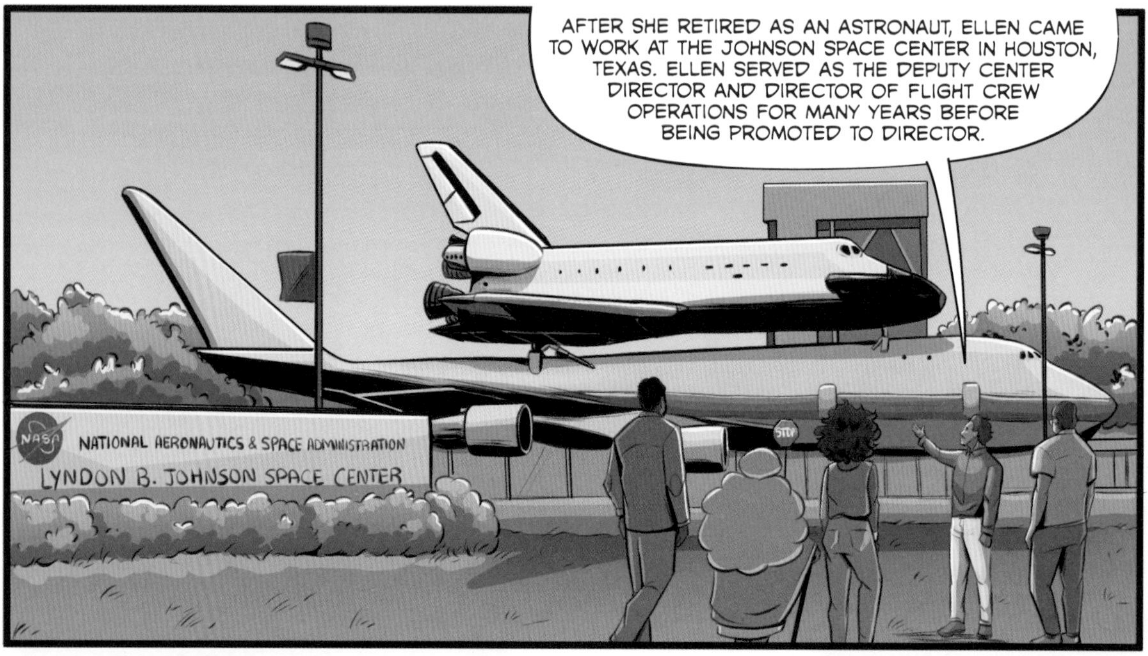
AFTER SHE RETIRED AS AN ASTRONAUT, ELLEN CAME TO WORK AT THE JOHNSON SPACE CENTER IN HOUSTON, TEXAS. ELLEN SERVED AS THE DEPUTY CENTER DIRECTOR AND DIRECTOR OF FLIGHT CREW OPERATIONS FOR MANY YEARS BEFORE BEING PROMOTED TO DIRECTOR.
NASA
NATIONAL AERONAUTICS & SPACE ADMINISTRATION
LYNDON B. JOHNSON SPACE CENTER
STOP

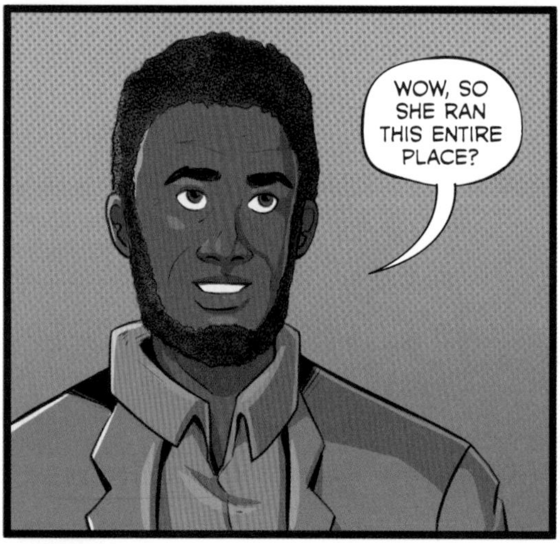
WOW, SO SHE RAN THIS ENTIRE PLACE?

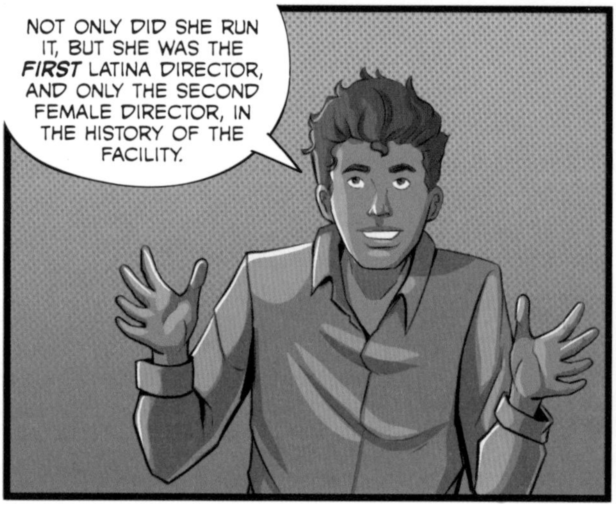
NOT ONLY DID SHE RUN IT, BUT SHE WAS THE *FIRST* LATINA DIRECTOR, AND ONLY THE SECOND FEMALE DIRECTOR, IN THE HISTORY OF THE FACILITY.

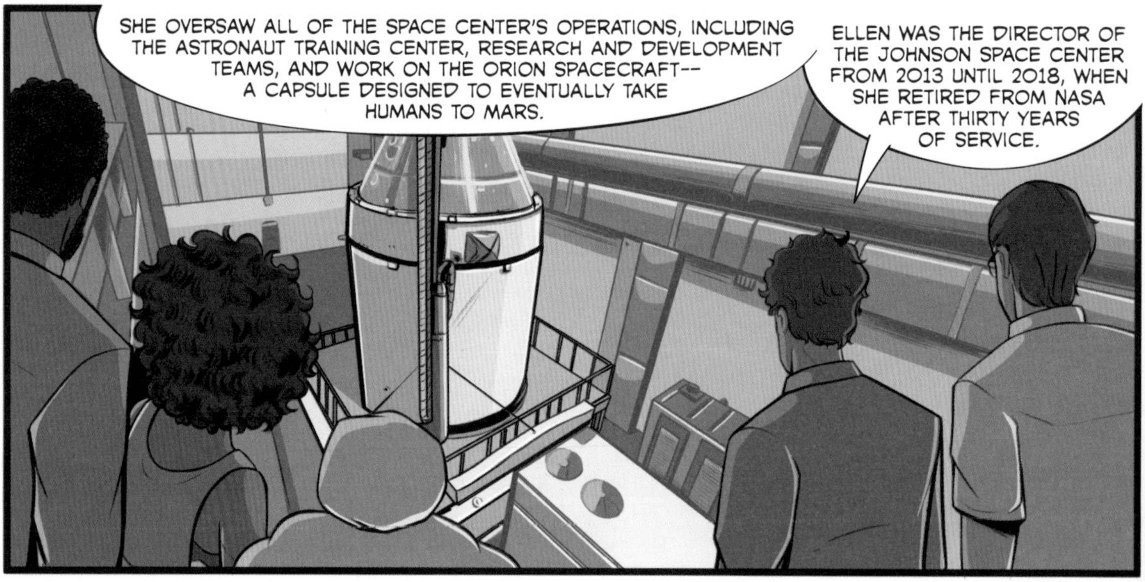
SHE OVERSAW ALL OF THE SPACE CENTER'S OPERATIONS, INCLUDING THE ASTRONAUT TRAINING CENTER, RESEARCH AND DEVELOPMENT TEAMS, AND WORK ON THE ORION SPACECRAFT-- A CAPSULE DESIGNED TO EVENTUALLY TAKE HUMANS TO MARS.
ELLEN WAS THE DIRECTOR OF THE JOHNSON SPACE CENTER FROM 2013 UNTIL 2018, WHEN SHE RETIRED FROM NASA AFTER THIRTY YEARS OF SERVICE.

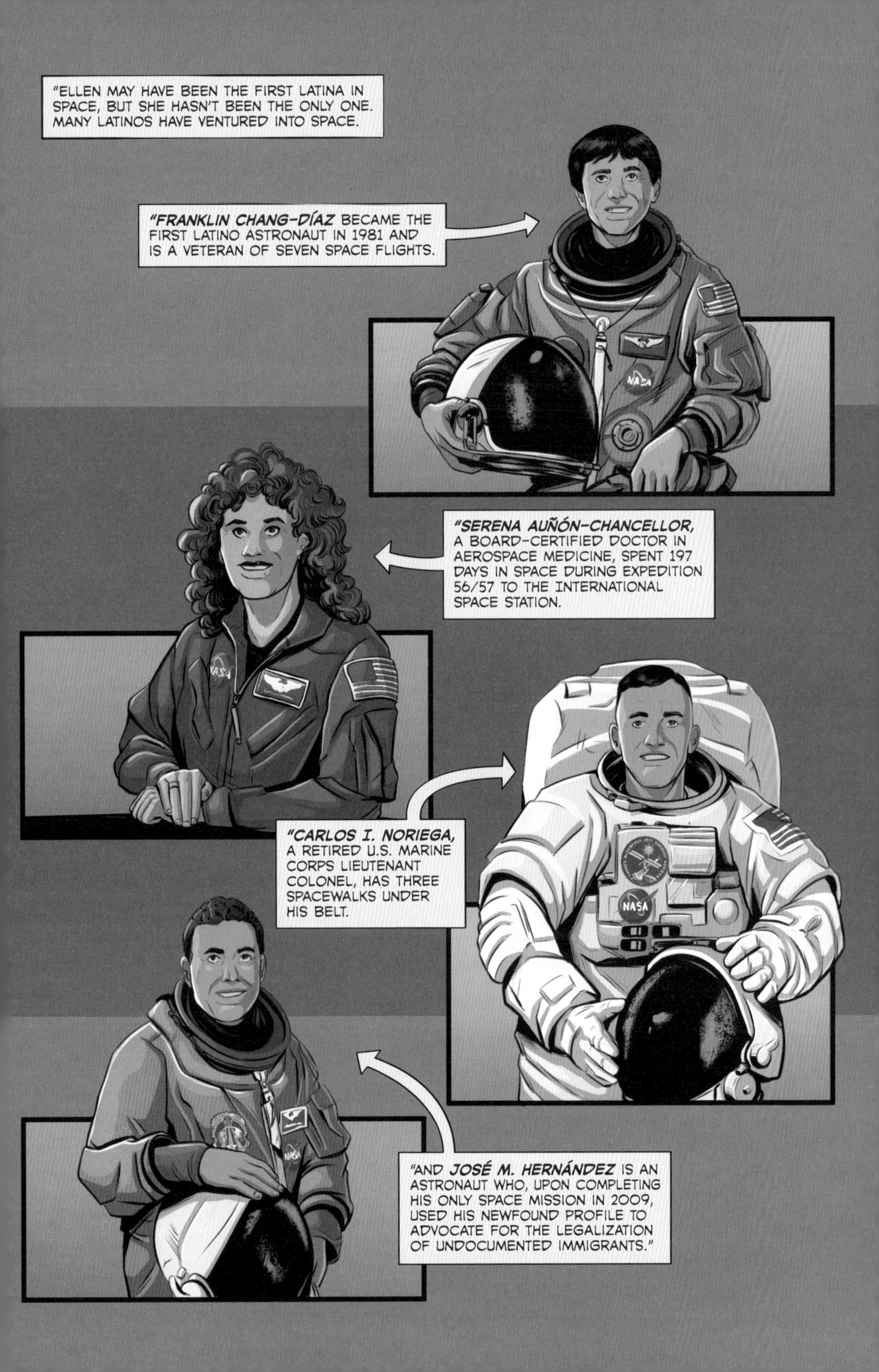
"ELLEN MAY HAVE BEEN THE FIRST LATINA IN SPACE, BUT SHE HASN'T BEEN THE ONLY ONE. MANY LATINOS HAVE VENTURED INTO SPACE.
"FRANKLIN CHANG-DÍAZ BECAME THE FIRST LATINO ASTRONAUT IN 1981 AND IS A VETERAN OF SEVEN SPACE FLIGHTS.
"SERENA AUÑÓN-CHANCELLOR, A BOARD-CERTIFIED DOCTOR IN AEROSPACE MEDICINE, SPENT 197 DAYS IN SPACE DURING EXPEDITION 56/57 TO THE INTERNATIONAL SPACE STATION.
"CARLOS I. NORIEGA, A RETIRED U.S. MARINE CORPS LIEUTENANT COLONEL, HAS THREE SPACEWALKS UNDER HIS BELT.
"AND JOSÉ M. HERNÁNDEZ IS AN ASTRONAUT WHO, UPON COMPLETING HIS ONLY SPACE MISSION IN 2009, USED HIS NEWFOUND PROFILE TO ADVOCATE FOR THE LEGALIZATION OF UNDOCUMENTED IMMIGRANTS."

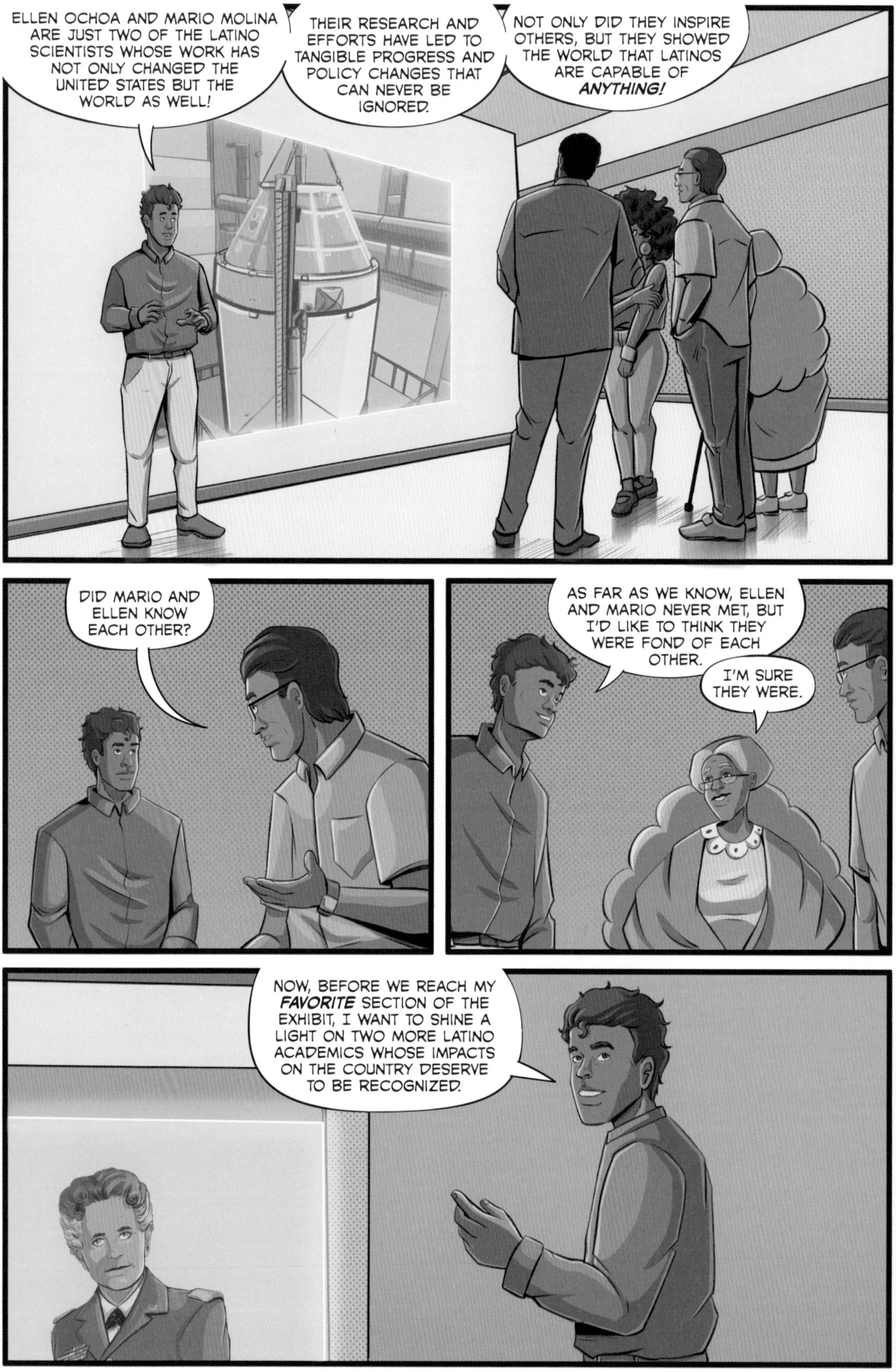
ELLEN OCHOA AND MARIO MOLINA ARE JUST TWO OF THE LATINO SCIENTISTS WHOSE WORK HAS NOT ONLY CHANGED THE UNITED STATES BUT THE WORLD AS WELL!
THEIR RESEARCH AND EFFORTS HAVE LED TO TANGIBLE PROGRESS AND POLICY CHANGES THAT CAN NEVER BE IGNORED.
NOT ONLY DID THEY INSPIRE OTHERS, BUT THEY SHOWED THE WORLD THAT LATINOS ARE CAPABLE OF ***ANYTHING!***
DID MARIO AND ELLEN KNOW EACH OTHER?
AS FAR AS WE KNOW, ELLEN AND MARIO NEVER MET, BUT I'D LIKE TO THINK THEY WERE FOND OF EACH OTHER.
I'M SURE THEY WERE.
NOW, BEFORE WE REACH MY ***FAVORITE*** SECTION OF THE EXHIBIT, I WANT TO SHINE A LIGHT ON TWO MORE LATINO ACADEMICS WHOSE IMPACTS ON THE COUNTRY DESERVE TO BE RECOGNIZED.

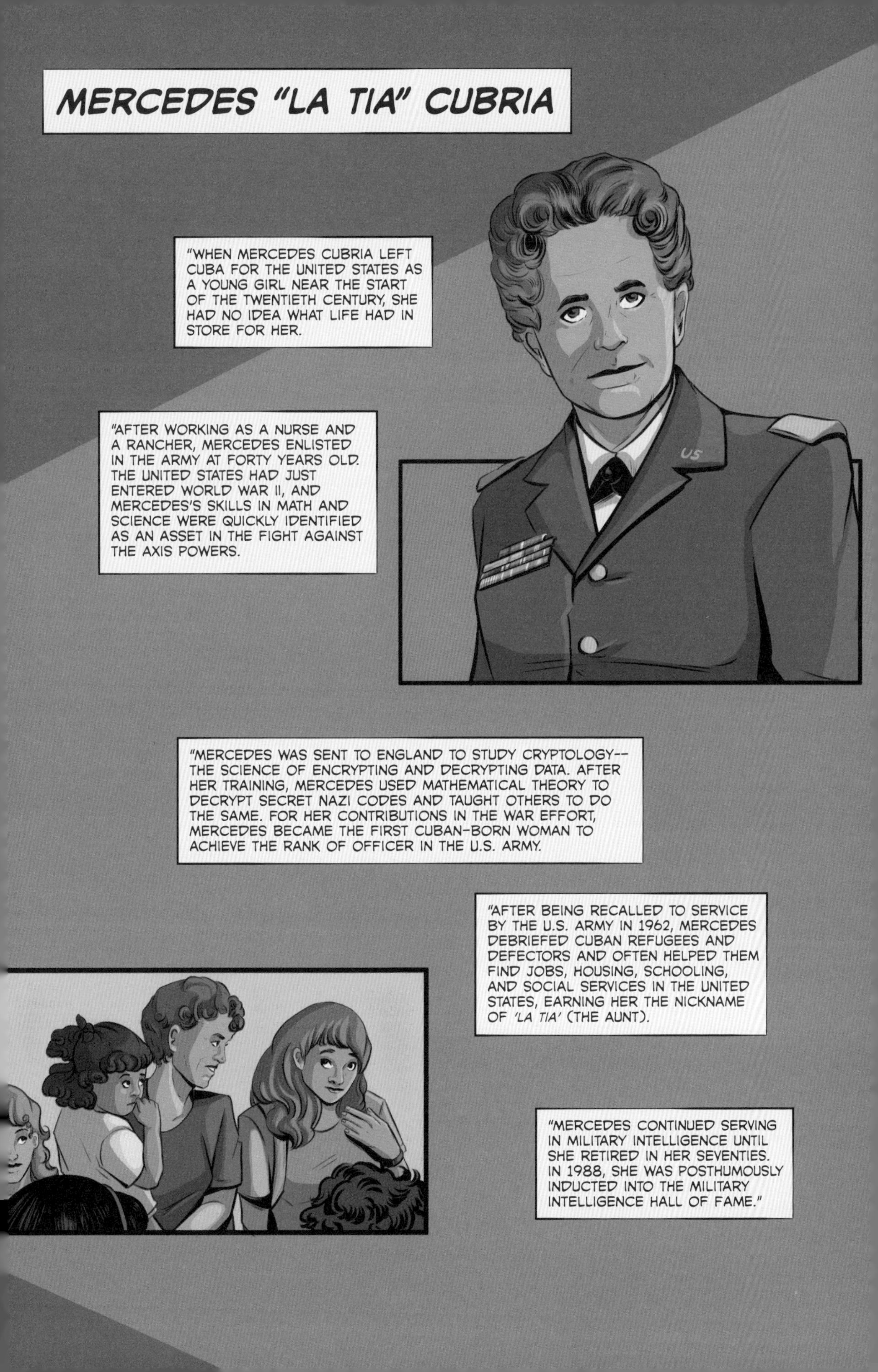
MERCEDES "LA TIA" CUBRIA
"WHEN MERCEDES CUBRIA LEFT CUBA FOR THE UNITED STATES AS A YOUNG GIRL NEAR THE START OF THE TWENTIETH CENTURY, SHE HAD NO IDEA WHAT LIFE HAD IN STORE FOR HER.
"AFTER WORKING AS A NURSE AND A RANCHER, MERCEDES ENLISTED IN THE ARMY AT FORTY YEARS OLD. THE UNITED STATES HAD JUST ENTERED WORLD WAR II, AND MERCEDES'S SKILLS IN MATH AND SCIENCE WERE QUICKLY IDENTIFIED AS AN ASSET IN THE FIGHT AGAINST THE AXIS POWERS.
US
"MERCEDES WAS SENT TO ENGLAND TO STUDY CRYPTOLOGY--THE SCIENCE OF ENCRYPTING AND DECRYPTING DATA. AFTER HER TRAINING, MERCEDES USED MATHEMATICAL THEORY TO DECRYPT SECRET NAZI CODES AND TAUGHT OTHERS TO DO THE SAME. FOR HER CONTRIBUTIONS IN THE WAR EFFORT, MERCEDES BECAME THE FIRST CUBAN-BORN WOMAN TO ACHIEVE THE RANK OF OFFICER IN THE U.S. ARMY.
"AFTER BEING RECALLED TO SERVICE BY THE U.S. ARMY IN 1962, MERCEDES DEBRIEFED CUBAN REFUGEES AND DEFECTORS AND OFTEN HELPED THEM FIND JOBS, HOUSING, SCHOOLING, AND SOCIAL SERVICES IN THE UNITED STATES, EARNING HER THE NICKNAME OF *'LA TIA'* (THE AUNT).
"MERCEDES CONTINUED SERVING IN MILITARY INTELLIGENCE UNTIL SHE RETIRED IN HER SEVENTIES. IN 1988, SHE WAS POSTHUMOUSLY INDUCTED INTO THE MILITARY INTELLIGENCE HALL OF FAME."

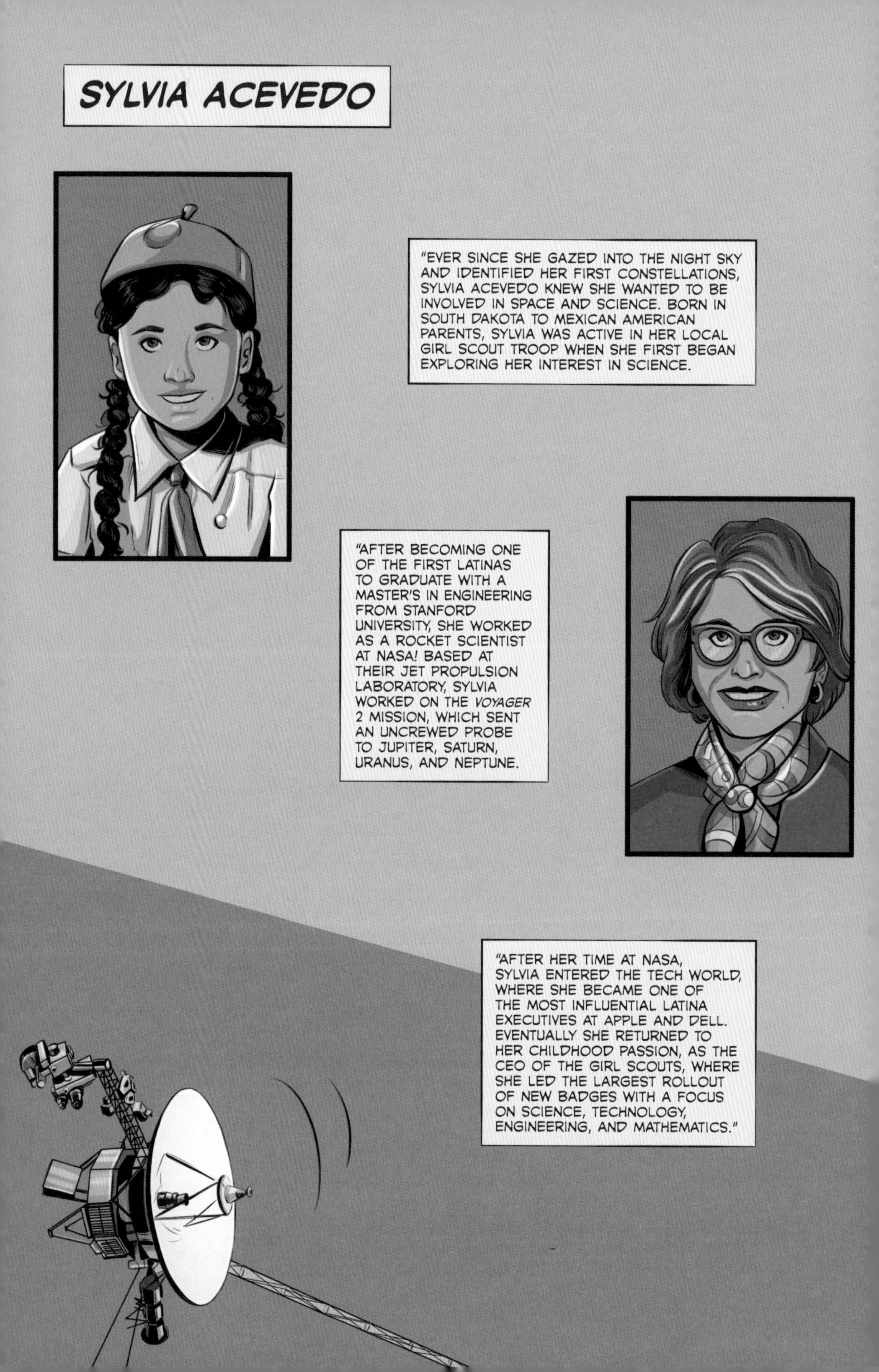
SYLVIA ACEVEDO
"EVER SINCE SHE GAZED INTO THE NIGHT SKY AND IDENTIFIED HER FIRST CONSTELLATIONS, SYLVIA ACEVEDO KNEW SHE WANTED TO BE INVOLVED IN SPACE AND SCIENCE. BORN IN SOUTH DAKOTA TO MEXICAN AMERICAN PARENTS, SYLVIA WAS ACTIVE IN HER LOCAL GIRL SCOUT TROOP WHEN SHE FIRST BEGAN EXPLORING HER INTEREST IN SCIENCE.
"AFTER BECOMING ONE OF THE FIRST LATINAS TO GRADUATE WITH A MASTER'S IN ENGINEERING FROM STANFORD UNIVERSITY, SHE WORKED AS A ROCKET SCIENTIST AT NASA! BASED AT THEIR JET PROPULSION LABORATORY, SYLVIA WORKED ON THE *VOYAGER* 2 MISSION, WHICH SENT AN UNCREWED PROBE TO JUPITER, SATURN, URANUS, AND NEPTUNE.
"AFTER HER TIME AT NASA, SYLVIA ENTERED THE TECH WORLD, WHERE SHE BECAME ONE OF THE MOST INFLUENTIAL LATINA EXECUTIVES AT APPLE AND DELL. EVENTUALLY SHE RETURNED TO HER CHILDHOOD PASSION, AS THE CEO OF THE GIRL SCOUTS, WHERE SHE LED THE LARGEST ROLLOUT OF NEW BADGES WITH A FOCUS ON SCIENCE, TECHNOLOGY, ENGINEERING, AND MATHEMATICS."

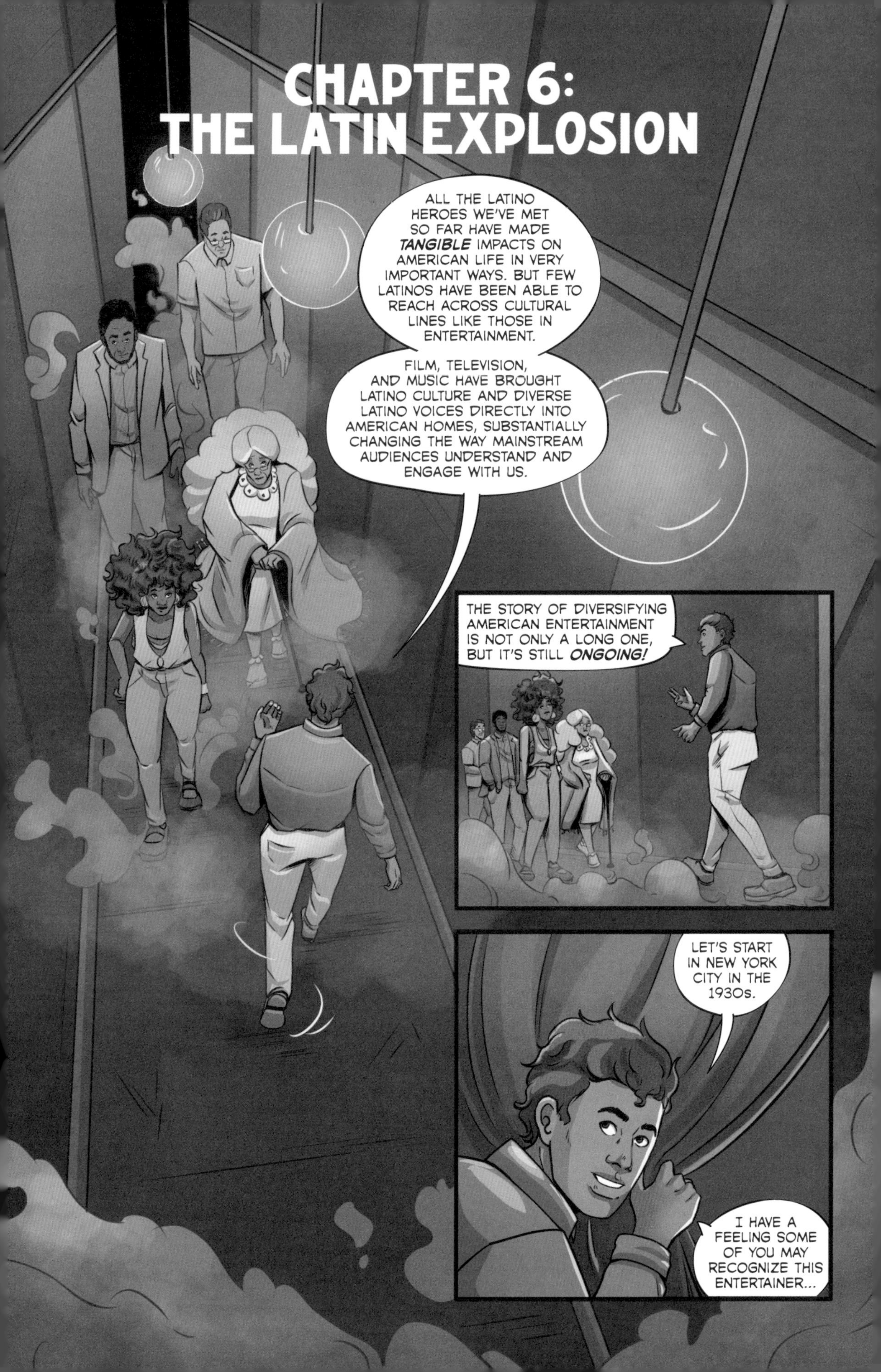
CHAPTER 6:
THE LATIN EXPLOSION
ALL THE LATINO HEROES WE'VE MET SO FAR HAVE MADE *TANGIBLE* IMPACTS ON AMERICAN LIFE IN VERY IMPORTANT WAYS. BUT FEW LATINOS HAVE BEEN ABLE TO REACH ACROSS CULTURAL LINES LIKE THOSE IN ENTERTAINMENT.
FILM, TELEVISION, AND MUSIC HAVE BROUGHT LATINO CULTURE AND DIVERSE LATINO VOICES DIRECTLY INTO AMERICAN HOMES, SUBSTANTIALLY CHANGING THE WAY MAINSTREAM AUDIENCES UNDERSTAND AND ENGAGE WITH US.
THE STORY OF DIVERSIFYING AMERICAN ENTERTAINMENT IS NOT ONLY A LONG ONE, BUT IT'S STILL *ONGOING!*
LET'S START IN NEW YORK CITY IN THE 1930s.
I HAVE A FEELING SOME OF YOU MAY RECOGNIZE THIS ENTERTAINER...

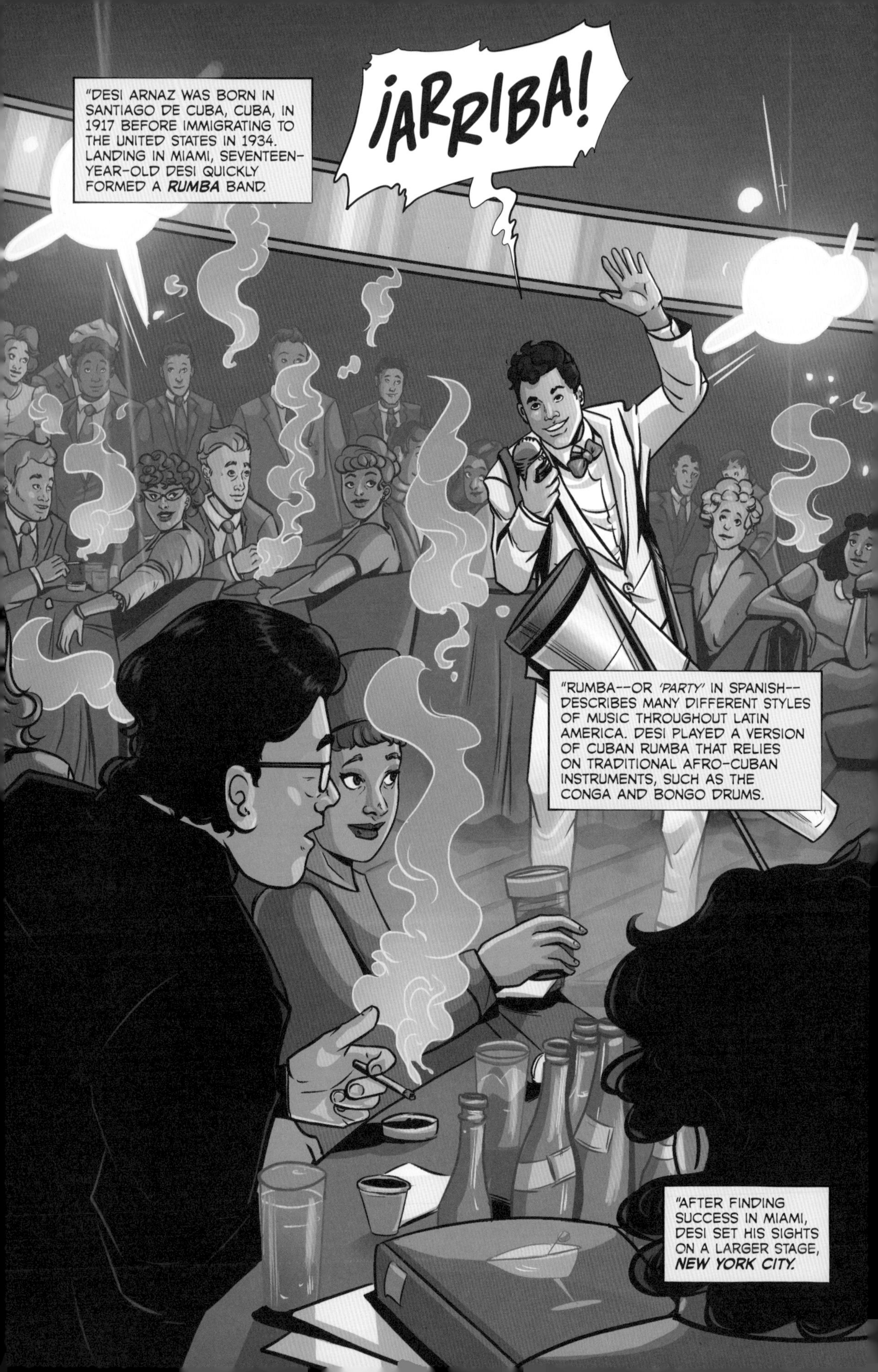
"DESI ARNAZ WAS BORN IN SANTIAGO DE CUBA, CUBA, IN 1917 BEFORE IMMIGRATING TO THE UNITED STATES IN 1934. LANDING IN MIAMI, SEVENTEEN-YEAR-OLD DESI QUICKLY FORMED A **RUMBA** BAND.
¡ARRIBA!
"RUMBA--OR *'PARTY'* IN SPANISH--DESCRIBES MANY DIFFERENT STYLES OF MUSIC THROUGHOUT LATIN AMERICA. DESI PLAYED A VERSION OF CUBAN RUMBA THAT RELIES ON TRADITIONAL AFRO-CUBAN INSTRUMENTS, SUCH AS THE CONGA AND BONGO DRUMS.
"AFTER FINDING SUCCESS IN MIAMI, DESI SET HIS SIGHTS ON A LARGER STAGE, ***NEW YORK CITY.***

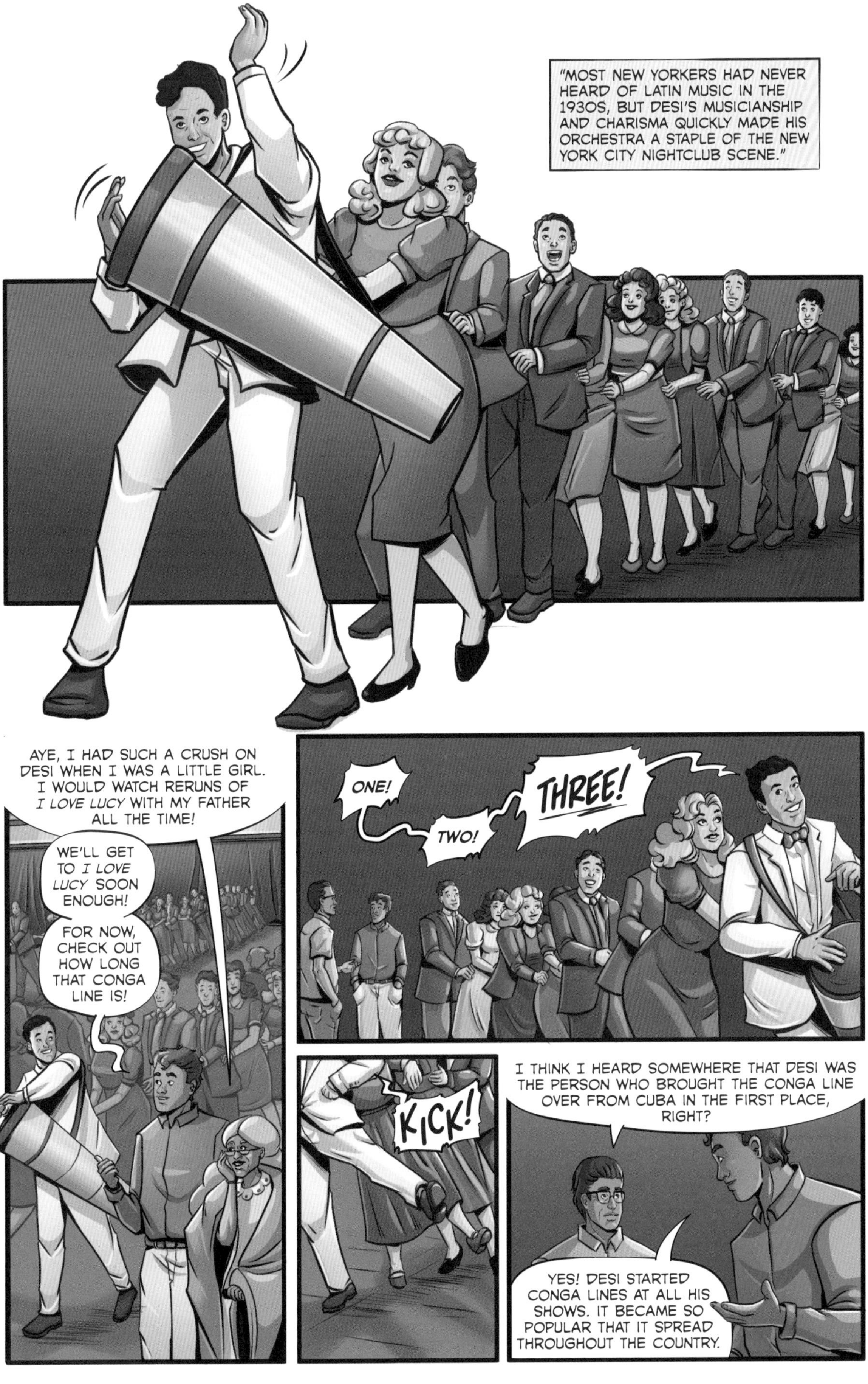
"MOST NEW YORKERS HAD NEVER HEARD OF LATIN MUSIC IN THE 1930S, BUT DESI'S MUSICIANSHIP AND CHARISMA QUICKLY MADE HIS ORCHESTRA A STAPLE OF THE NEW YORK CITY NIGHTCLUB SCENE."
AYE, I HAD SUCH A CRUSH ON DESI WHEN I WAS A LITTLE GIRL. I WOULD WATCH RERUNS OF *I LOVE LUCY* WITH MY FATHER ALL THE TIME!
WE'LL GET TO *I LOVE LUCY* SOON ENOUGH!
FOR NOW, CHECK OUT HOW LONG THAT CONGA LINE IS!
ONE!
TWO!
THREE!
KICK!
I THINK I HEARD SOMEWHERE THAT DESI WAS THE PERSON WHO BROUGHT THE CONGA LINE OVER FROM CUBA IN THE FIRST PLACE, RIGHT?
YES! DESI STARTED CONGA LINES AT ALL HIS SHOWS. IT BECAME SO POPULAR THAT IT SPREAD THROUGHOUT THE COUNTRY.

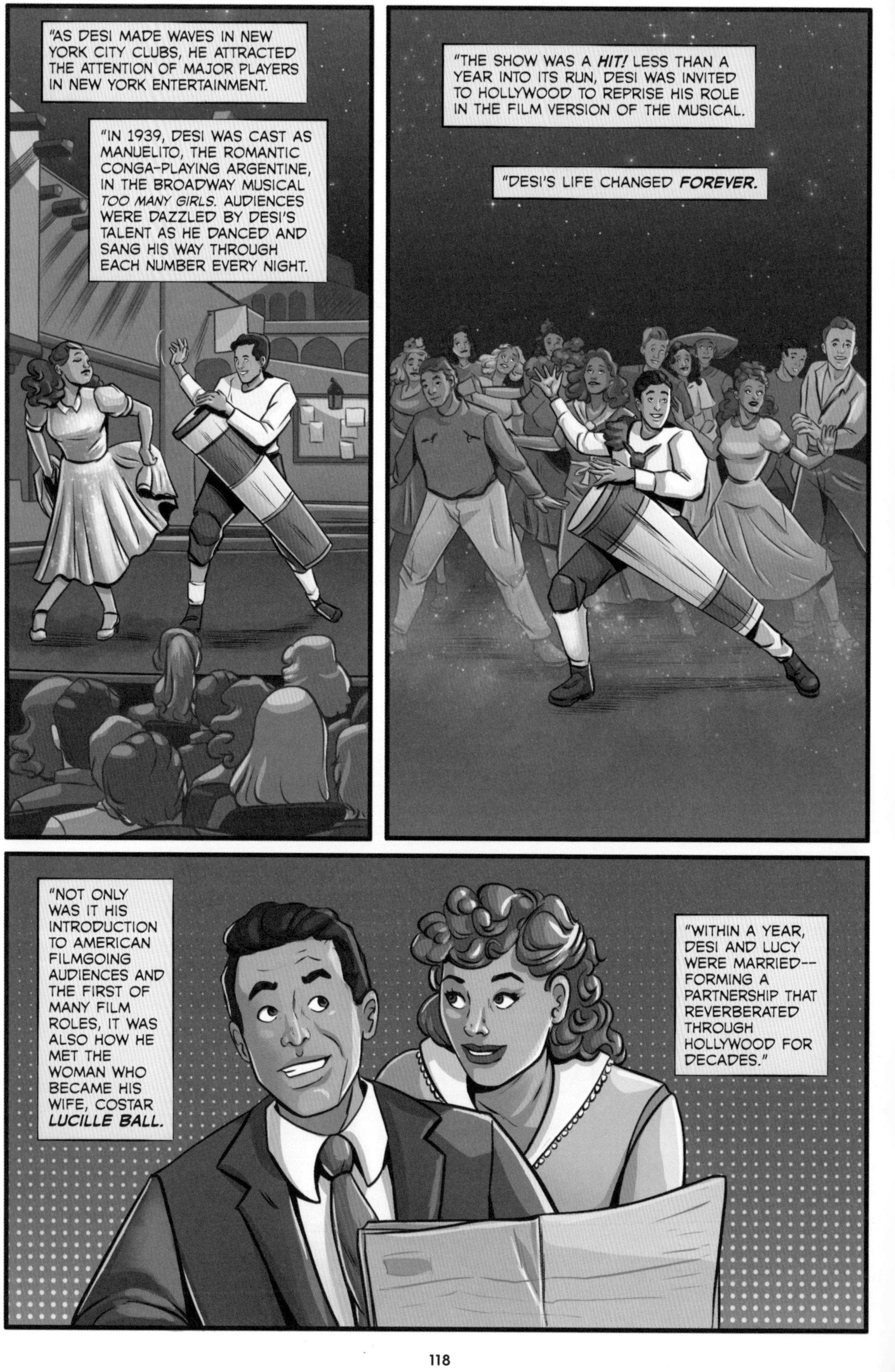
"AS DESI MADE WAVES IN NEW YORK CITY CLUBS, HE ATTRACTED THE ATTENTION OF MAJOR PLAYERS IN NEW YORK ENTERTAINMENT.
"IN 1939, DESI WAS CAST AS MANUELITO, THE ROMANTIC CONGA-PLAYING ARGENTINE, IN THE BROADWAY MUSICAL *TOO MANY GIRLS.* AUDIENCES WERE DAZZLED BY DESI'S TALENT AS HE DANCED AND SANG HIS WAY THROUGH EACH NUMBER EVERY NIGHT.
"THE SHOW WAS A ***HIT!*** LESS THAN A YEAR INTO ITS RUN, DESI WAS INVITED TO HOLLYWOOD TO REPRISE HIS ROLE IN THE FILM VERSION OF THE MUSICAL.
"DESI'S LIFE CHANGED ***FOREVER.***
"NOT ONLY WAS IT HIS INTRODUCTION TO AMERICAN FILMGOING AUDIENCES AND THE FIRST OF MANY FILM ROLES, IT WAS ALSO HOW HE MET THE WOMAN WHO BECAME HIS WIFE, COSTAR ***LUCILLE BALL.***
"WITHIN A YEAR, DESI AND LUCY WERE MARRIED--FORMING A PARTNERSHIP THAT REVERBERATED THROUGH HOLLYWOOD FOR DECADES."

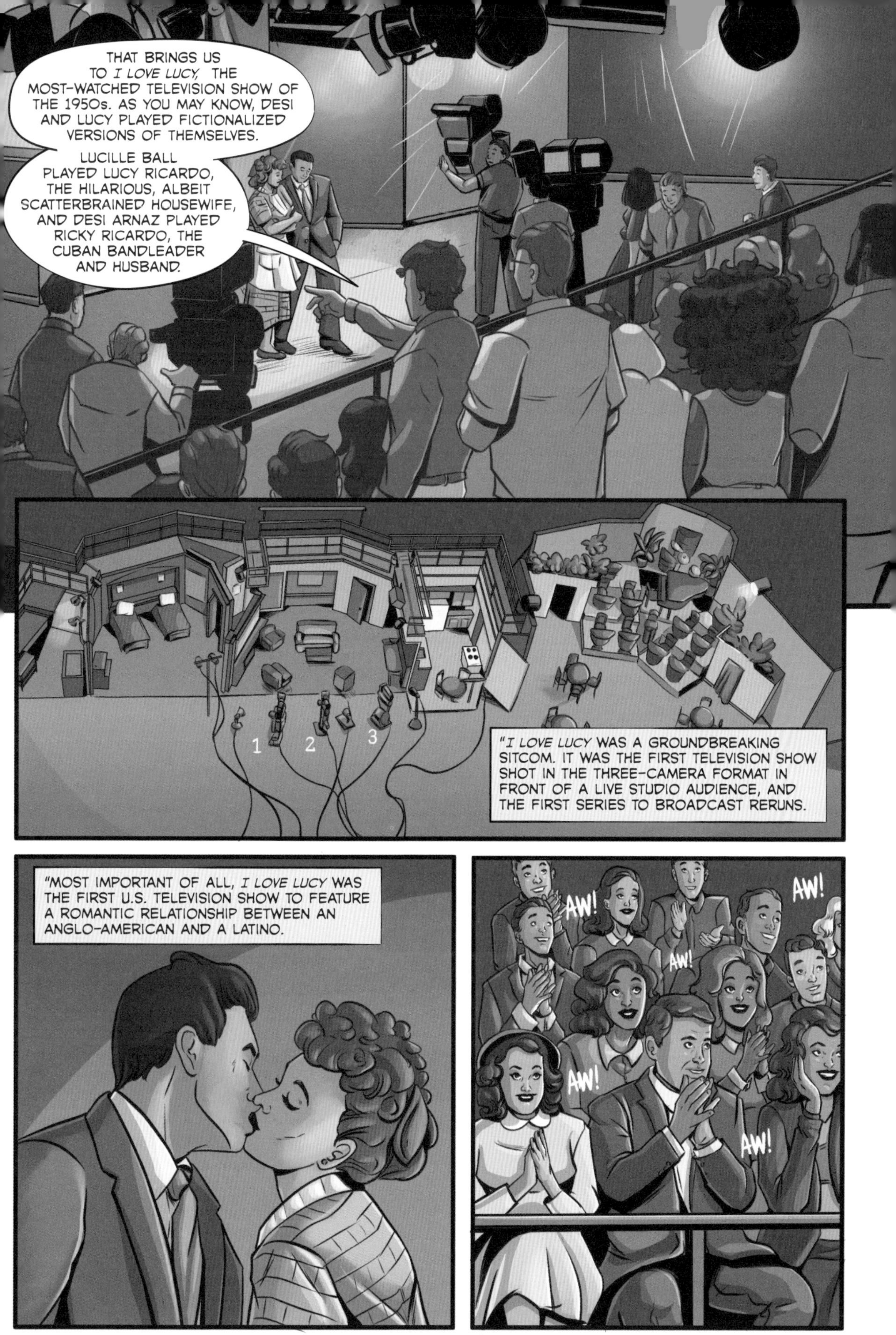
THAT BRINGS US TO *I LOVE LUCY*, THE MOST-WATCHED TELEVISION SHOW OF THE 1950s. AS YOU MAY KNOW, DESI AND LUCY PLAYED FICTIONALIZED VERSIONS OF THEMSELVES.
LUCILLE BALL PLAYED LUCY RICARDO, THE HILARIOUS, ALBEIT SCATTERBRAINED HOUSEWIFE, AND DESI ARNAZ PLAYED RICKY RICARDO, THE CUBAN BANDLEADER AND HUSBAND.
1
2
3
"*I LOVE LUCY* WAS A GROUNDBREAKING SITCOM. IT WAS THE FIRST TELEVISION SHOW SHOT IN THE THREE-CAMERA FORMAT IN FRONT OF A LIVE STUDIO AUDIENCE, AND THE FIRST SERIES TO BROADCAST RERUNS.
"MOST IMPORTANT OF ALL, *I LOVE LUCY* WAS THE FIRST U.S. TELEVISION SHOW TO FEATURE A ROMANTIC RELATIONSHIP BETWEEN AN ANGLO-AMERICAN AND A LATINO.
AW!
AW!
AW!
AW!
AW!

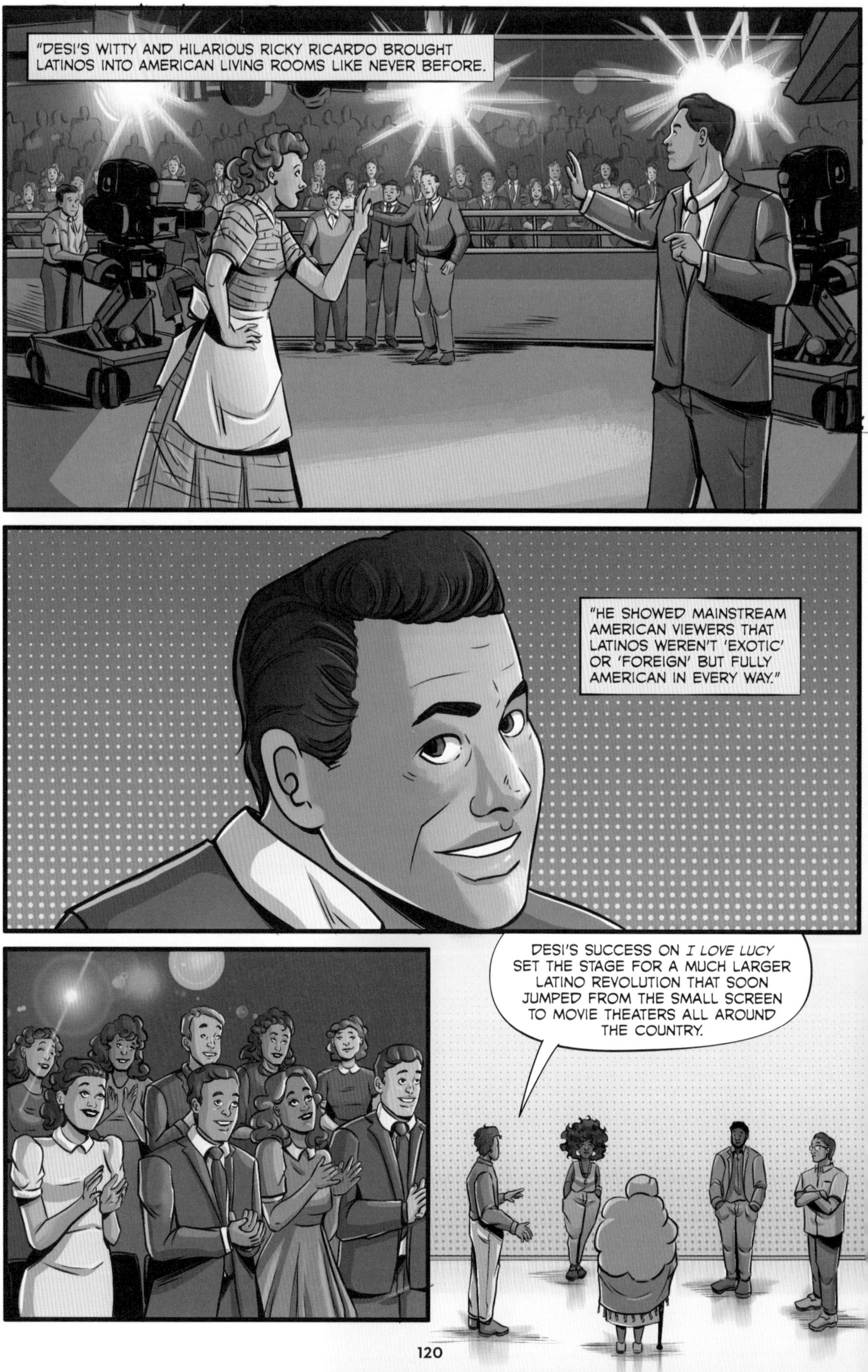
"DESI'S WITTY AND HILARIOUS RICKY RICARDO BROUGHT LATINOS INTO AMERICAN LIVING ROOMS LIKE NEVER BEFORE.
"HE SHOWED MAINSTREAM AMERICAN VIEWERS THAT LATINOS WEREN'T 'EXOTIC' OR 'FOREIGN' BUT FULLY AMERICAN IN EVERY WAY."
DESI'S SUCCESS ON *I LOVE LUCY* SET THE STAGE FOR A MUCH LARGER LATINO REVOLUTION THAT SOON JUMPED FROM THE SMALL SCREEN TO MOVIE THEATERS ALL AROUND THE COUNTRY.

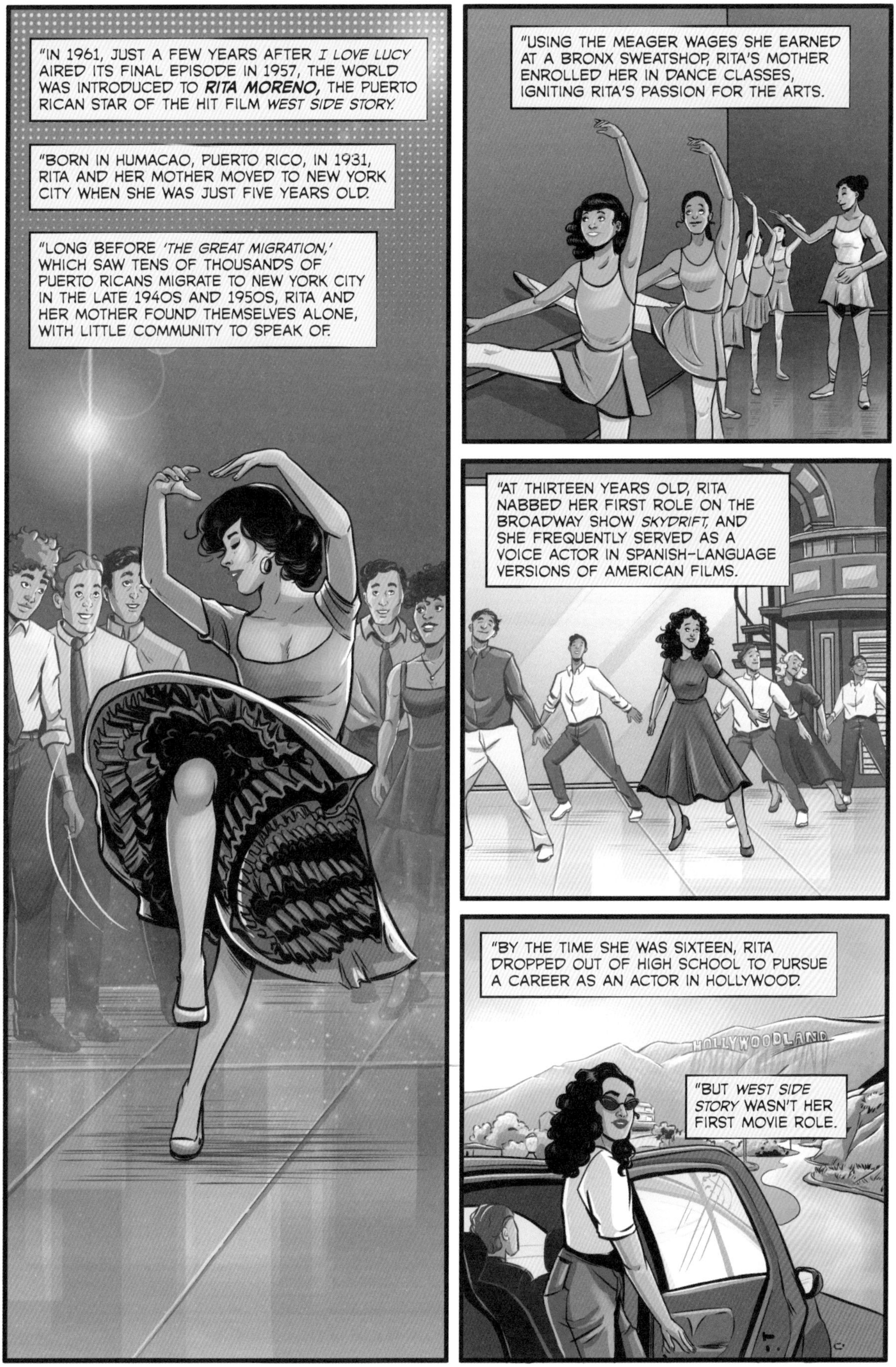
"IN 1961, JUST A FEW YEARS AFTER *I LOVE LUCY* AIRED ITS FINAL EPISODE IN 1957, THE WORLD WAS INTRODUCED TO ***RITA MORENO,*** THE PUERTO RICAN STAR OF THE HIT FILM *WEST SIDE STORY.*
"BORN IN HUMACAO, PUERTO RICO, IN 1931, RITA AND HER MOTHER MOVED TO NEW YORK CITY WHEN SHE WAS JUST FIVE YEARS OLD.
"LONG BEFORE *'THE GREAT MIGRATION,'* WHICH SAW TENS OF THOUSANDS OF PUERTO RICANS MIGRATE TO NEW YORK CITY IN THE LATE 1940S AND 1950S, RITA AND HER MOTHER FOUND THEMSELVES ALONE, WITH LITTLE COMMUNITY TO SPEAK OF.
"USING THE MEAGER WAGES SHE EARNED AT A BRONX SWEATSHOP, RITA'S MOTHER ENROLLED HER IN DANCE CLASSES, IGNITING RITA'S PASSION FOR THE ARTS.
"AT THIRTEEN YEARS OLD, RITA NABBED HER FIRST ROLE ON THE BROADWAY SHOW *SKYDRIFT,* AND SHE FREQUENTLY SERVED AS A VOICE ACTOR IN SPANISH-LANGUAGE VERSIONS OF AMERICAN FILMS.
"BY THE TIME SHE WAS SIXTEEN, RITA DROPPED OUT OF HIGH SCHOOL TO PURSUE A CAREER AS AN ACTOR IN HOLLYWOOD.
HOLLYWOODLAND
"BUT *WEST SIDE STORY* WASN'T HER FIRST MOVIE ROLE.

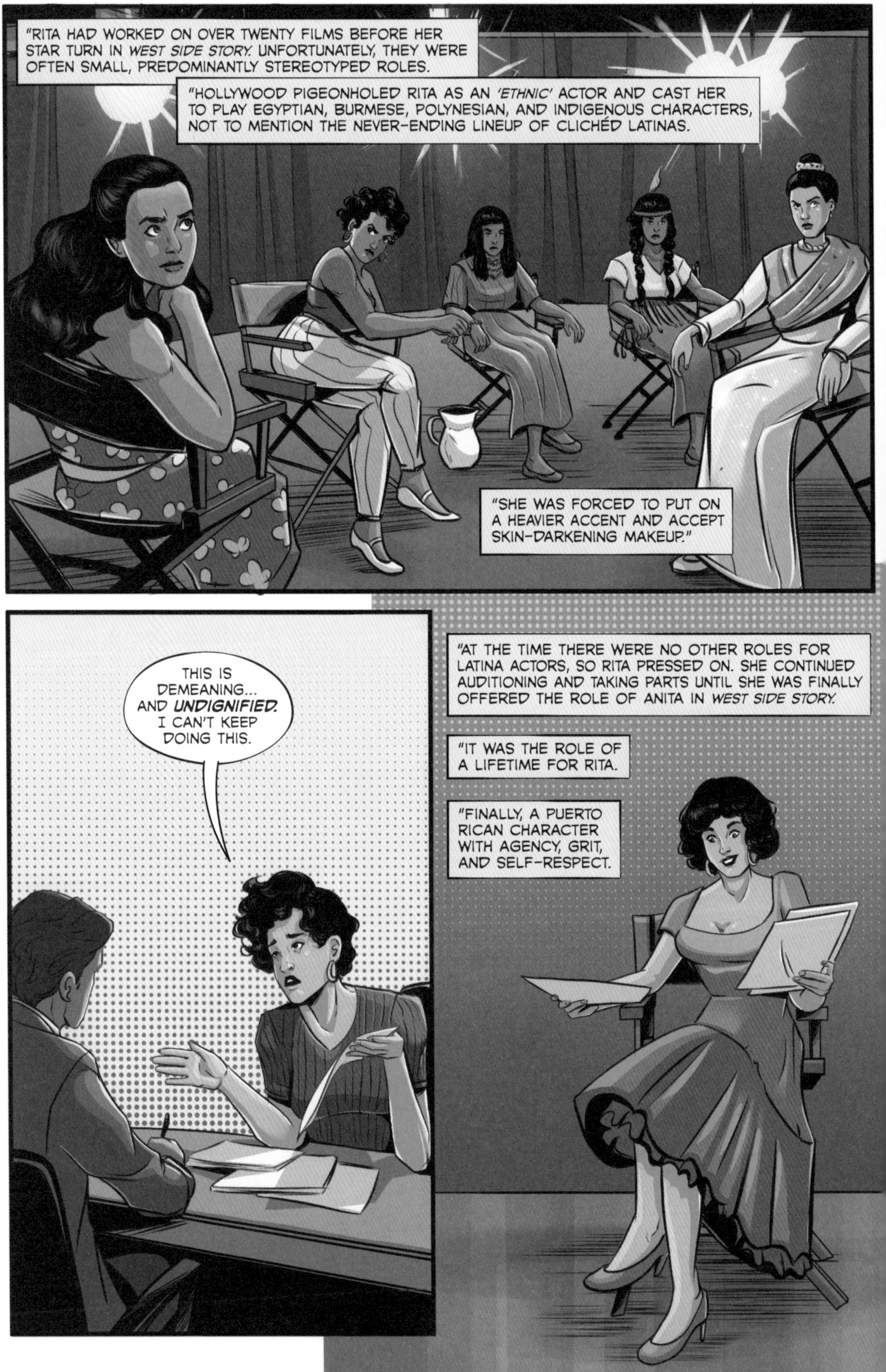
"RITA HAD WORKED ON OVER TWENTY FILMS BEFORE HER STAR TURN IN *WEST SIDE STORY.* UNFORTUNATELY, THEY WERE OFTEN SMALL, PREDOMINANTLY STEREOTYPED ROLES.
"HOLLYWOOD PIGEONHOLED RITA AS AN *'ETHNIC'* ACTOR AND CAST HER TO PLAY EGYPTIAN, BURMESE, POLYNESIAN, AND INDIGENOUS CHARACTERS, NOT TO MENTION THE NEVER-ENDING LINEUP OF CLICHÉD LATINAS.
"SHE WAS FORCED TO PUT ON A HEAVIER ACCENT AND ACCEPT SKIN-DARKENING MAKEUP."
THIS IS DEMEANING... AND ***UNDIGNIFIED.*** I CAN'T KEEP DOING THIS.
"AT THE TIME THERE WERE NO OTHER ROLES FOR LATINA ACTORS, SO RITA PRESSED ON. SHE CONTINUED AUDITIONING AND TAKING PARTS UNTIL SHE WAS FINALLY OFFERED THE ROLE OF ANITA IN *WEST SIDE STORY.*
"IT WAS THE ROLE OF A LIFETIME FOR RITA.
"FINALLY, A PUERTO RICAN CHARACTER WITH AGENCY, GRIT, AND SELF-RESPECT.

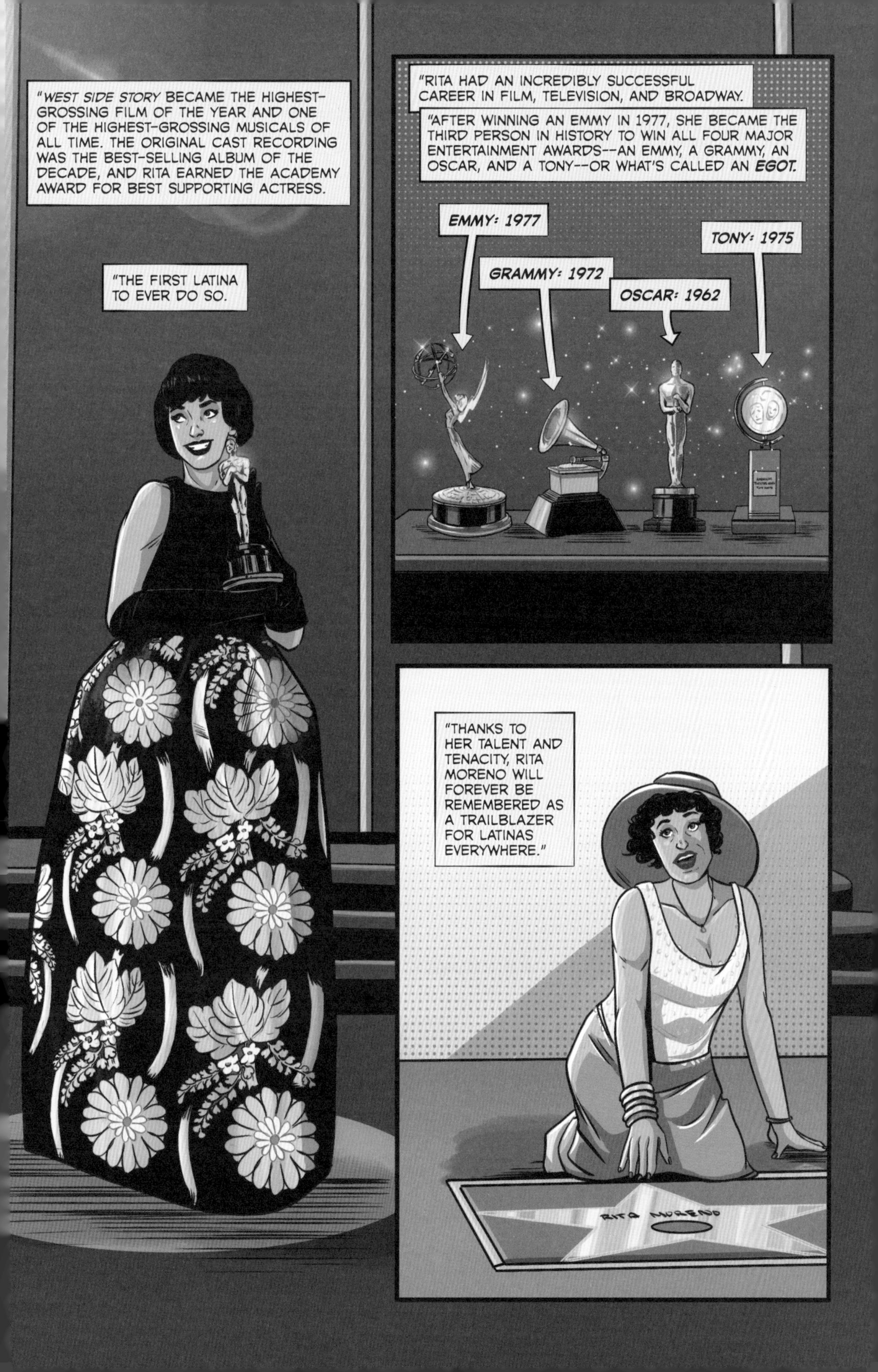
"WEST SIDE STORY BECAME THE HIGHEST-GROSSING FILM OF THE YEAR AND ONE OF THE HIGHEST-GROSSING MUSICALS OF ALL TIME. THE ORIGINAL CAST RECORDING WAS THE BEST-SELLING ALBUM OF THE DECADE, AND RITA EARNED THE ACADEMY AWARD FOR BEST SUPPORTING ACTRESS.
"THE FIRST LATINA TO EVER DO SO.
"RITA HAD AN INCREDIBLY SUCCESSFUL CAREER IN FILM, TELEVISION, AND BROADWAY.
"AFTER WINNING AN EMMY IN 1977, SHE BECAME THE THIRD PERSON IN HISTORY TO WIN ALL FOUR MAJOR ENTERTAINMENT AWARDS--AN EMMY, A GRAMMY, AN OSCAR, AND A TONY--OR WHAT'S CALLED AN EGOT.
EMMY: 1977
GRAMMY: 1972
OSCAR: 1962
TONY: 1975
"THANKS TO HER TALENT AND TENACITY, RITA MORENO WILL FOREVER BE REMEMBERED AS A TRAILBLAZER FOR LATINAS EVERYWHERE."
RITA MORENO

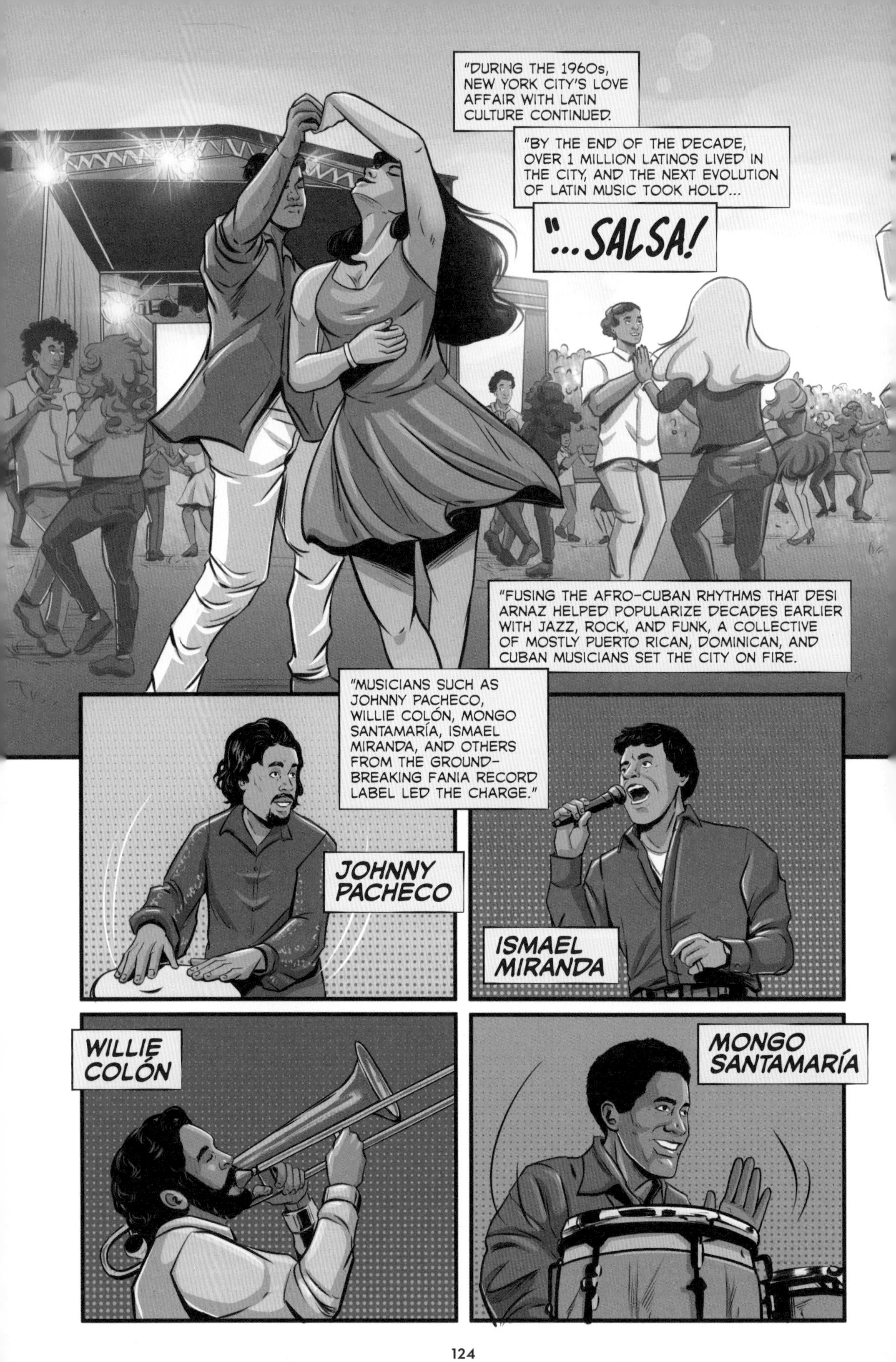
"DURING THE 1960s, NEW YORK CITY'S LOVE AFFAIR WITH LATIN CULTURE CONTINUED.
"BY THE END OF THE DECADE, OVER 1 MILLION LATINOS LIVED IN THE CITY, AND THE NEXT EVOLUTION OF LATIN MUSIC TOOK HOLD...
"...SALSA!
"FUSING THE AFRO-CUBAN RHYTHMS THAT DESI ARNAZ HELPED POPULARIZE DECADES EARLIER WITH JAZZ, ROCK, AND FUNK, A COLLECTIVE OF MOSTLY PUERTO RICAN, DOMINICAN, AND CUBAN MUSICIANS SET THE CITY ON FIRE.
"MUSICIANS SUCH AS JOHNNY PACHECO, WILLIE COLÓN, MONGO SANTAMARÍA, ISMAEL MIRANDA, AND OTHERS FROM THE GROUND-BREAKING FANIA RECORD LABEL LED THE CHARGE."
JOHNNY PACHECO
ISMAEL MIRANDA
WILLIE COLÓN
MONGO SANTAMARÍA

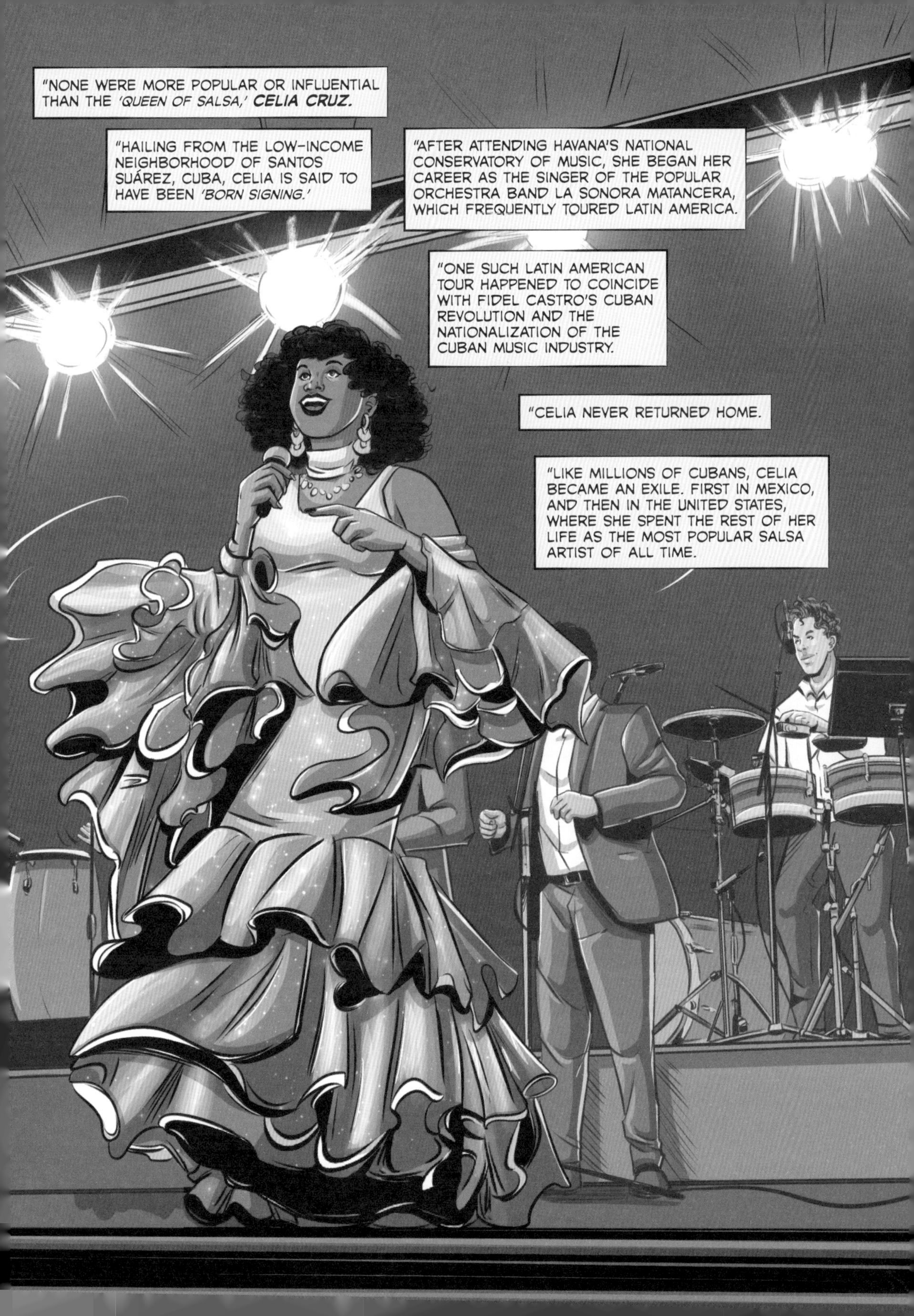
"NONE WERE MORE POPULAR OR INFLUENTIAL THAN THE *'QUEEN OF SALSA,'* ***CELIA CRUZ.***
"HAILING FROM THE LOW-INCOME NEIGHBORHOOD OF SANTOS SUÁREZ, CUBA, CELIA IS SAID TO HAVE BEEN *'BORN SIGNING.'*
"AFTER ATTENDING HAVANA'S NATIONAL CONSERVATORY OF MUSIC, SHE BEGAN HER CAREER AS THE SINGER OF THE POPULAR ORCHESTRA BAND LA SONORA MATANCERA, WHICH FREQUENTLY TOURED LATIN AMERICA.
"ONE SUCH LATIN AMERICAN TOUR HAPPENED TO COINCIDE WITH FIDEL CASTRO'S CUBAN REVOLUTION AND THE NATIONALIZATION OF THE CUBAN MUSIC INDUSTRY.
"CELIA NEVER RETURNED HOME.
"LIKE MILLIONS OF CUBANS, CELIA BECAME AN EXILE. FIRST IN MEXICO, AND THEN IN THE UNITED STATES, WHERE SHE SPENT THE REST OF HER LIFE AS THE MOST POPULAR SALSA ARTIST OF ALL TIME.

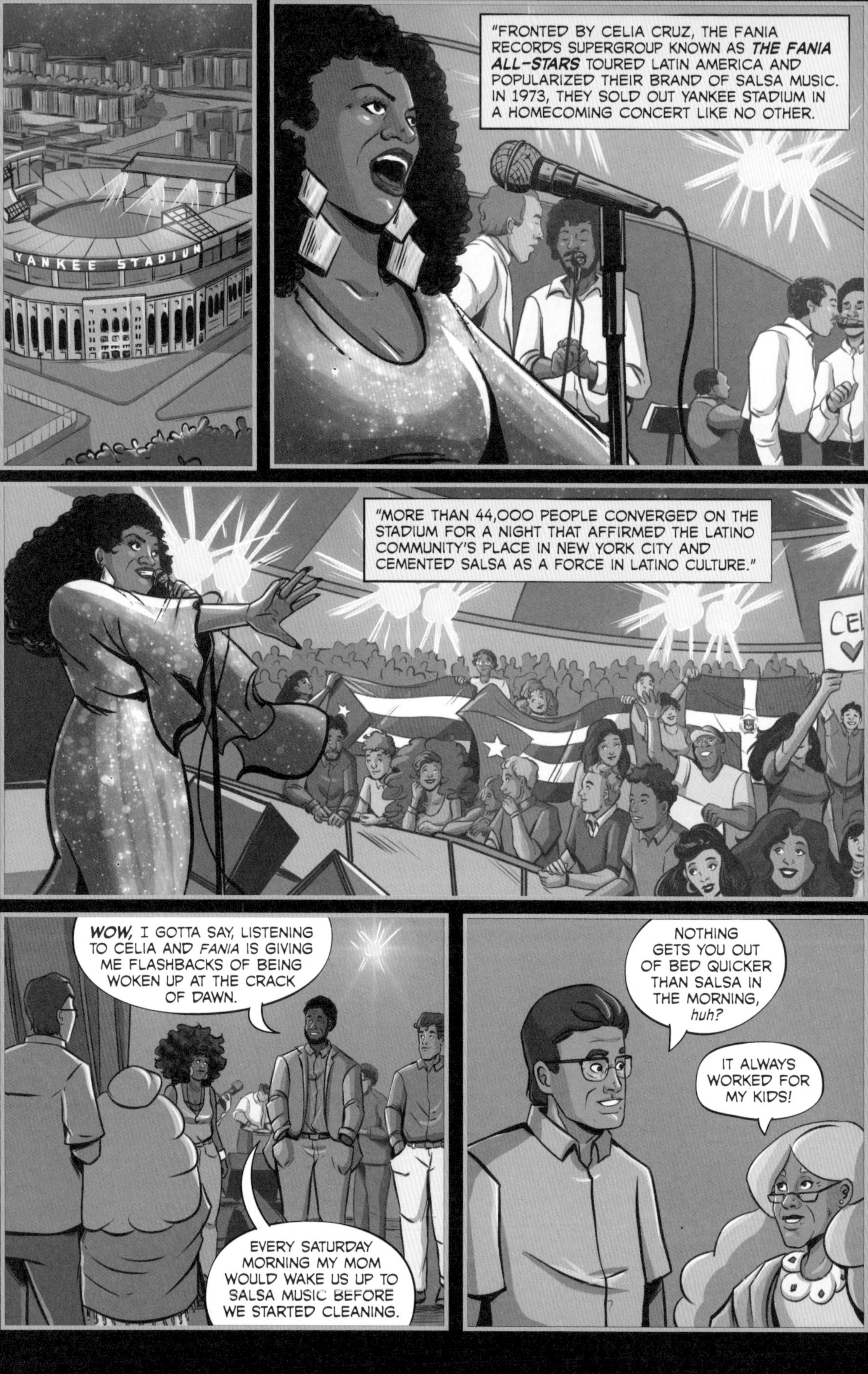
YANKEE STADIUM
"FRONTED BY CELIA CRUZ, THE FANIA RECORDS SUPERGROUP KNOWN AS ***THE FANIA ALL-STARS*** TOURED LATIN AMERICA AND POPULARIZED THEIR BRAND OF SALSA MUSIC. IN 1973, THEY SOLD OUT YANKEE STADIUM IN A HOMECOMING CONCERT LIKE NO OTHER.
"MORE THAN 44,000 PEOPLE CONVERGED ON THE STADIUM FOR A NIGHT THAT AFFIRMED THE LATINO COMMUNITY'S PLACE IN NEW YORK CITY AND CEMENTED SALSA AS A FORCE IN LATINO CULTURE."
***WOW,*** I GOTTA SAY, LISTENING TO CELIA AND *FANIA* IS GIVING ME FLASHBACKS OF BEING WOKEN UP AT THE CRACK OF DAWN.
EVERY SATURDAY MORNING MY MOM WOULD WAKE US UP TO SALSA MUSIC BEFORE WE STARTED CLEANING.
NOTHING GETS YOU OUT OF BED QUICKER THAN SALSA IN THE MORNING, *huh?*
IT ALWAYS WORKED FOR MY KIDS!

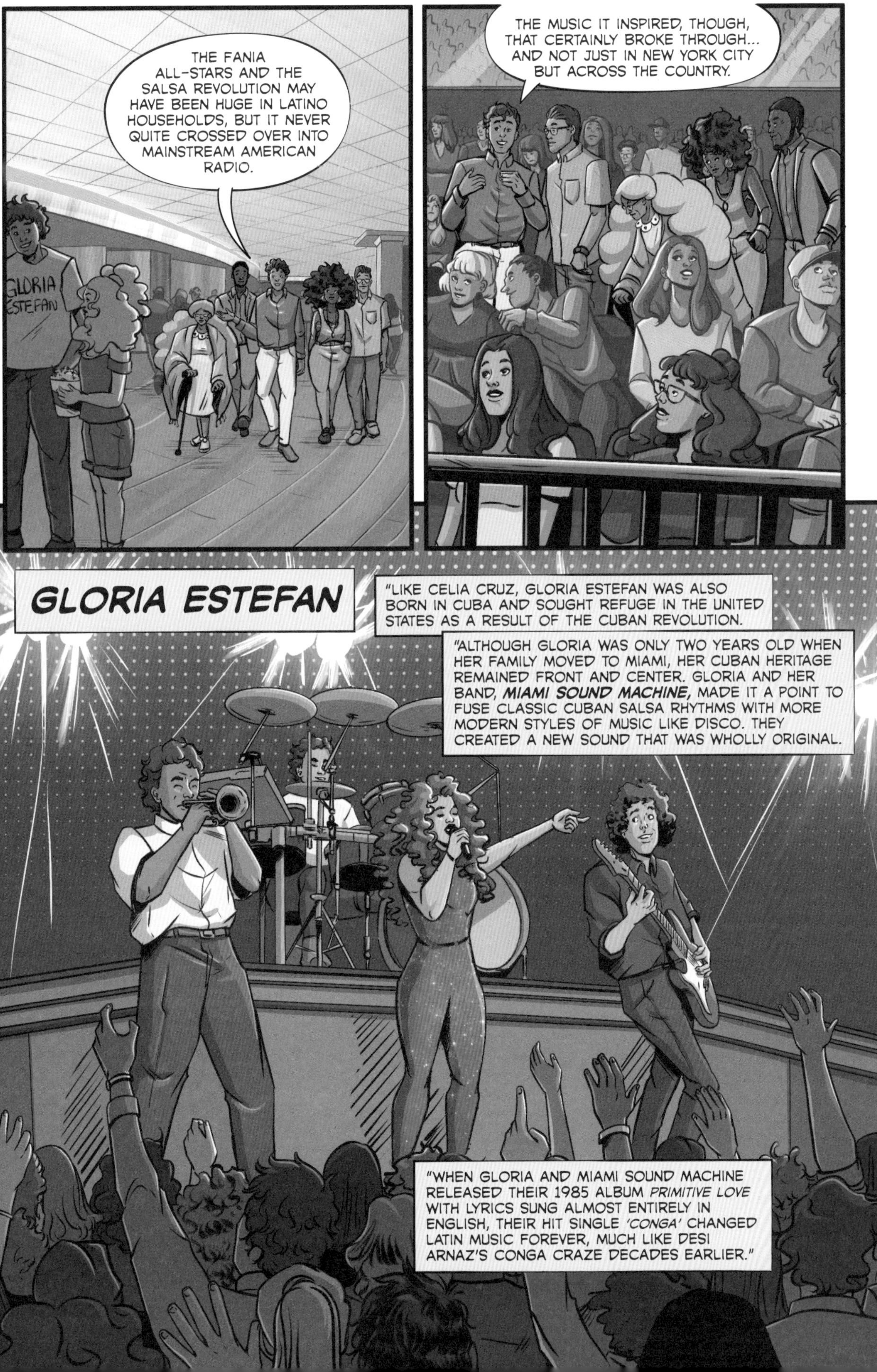
THE FANIA ALL-STARS AND THE SALSA REVOLUTION MAY HAVE BEEN HUGE IN LATINO HOUSEHOLDS, BUT IT NEVER QUITE CROSSED OVER INTO MAINSTREAM AMERICAN RADIO.
GLORIA ESTEFAN
THE MUSIC IT INSPIRED, THOUGH, THAT CERTAINLY BROKE THROUGH... AND NOT JUST IN NEW YORK CITY BUT ACROSS THE COUNTRY.
GLORIA ESTEFAN
"LIKE CELIA CRUZ, GLORIA ESTEFAN WAS ALSO BORN IN CUBA AND SOUGHT REFUGE IN THE UNITED STATES AS A RESULT OF THE CUBAN REVOLUTION.
"ALTHOUGH GLORIA WAS ONLY TWO YEARS OLD WHEN HER FAMILY MOVED TO MIAMI, HER CUBAN HERITAGE REMAINED FRONT AND CENTER. GLORIA AND HER BAND, MIAMI SOUND MACHINE, MADE IT A POINT TO FUSE CLASSIC CUBAN SALSA RHYTHMS WITH MORE MODERN STYLES OF MUSIC LIKE DISCO. THEY CREATED A NEW SOUND THAT WAS WHOLLY ORIGINAL.
"WHEN GLORIA AND MIAMI SOUND MACHINE RELEASED THEIR 1985 ALBUM PRIMITIVE LOVE WITH LYRICS SUNG ALMOST ENTIRELY IN ENGLISH, THEIR HIT SINGLE 'CONGA' CHANGED LATIN MUSIC FOREVER, MUCH LIKE DESI ARNAZ'S CONGA CRAZE DECADES EARLIER."

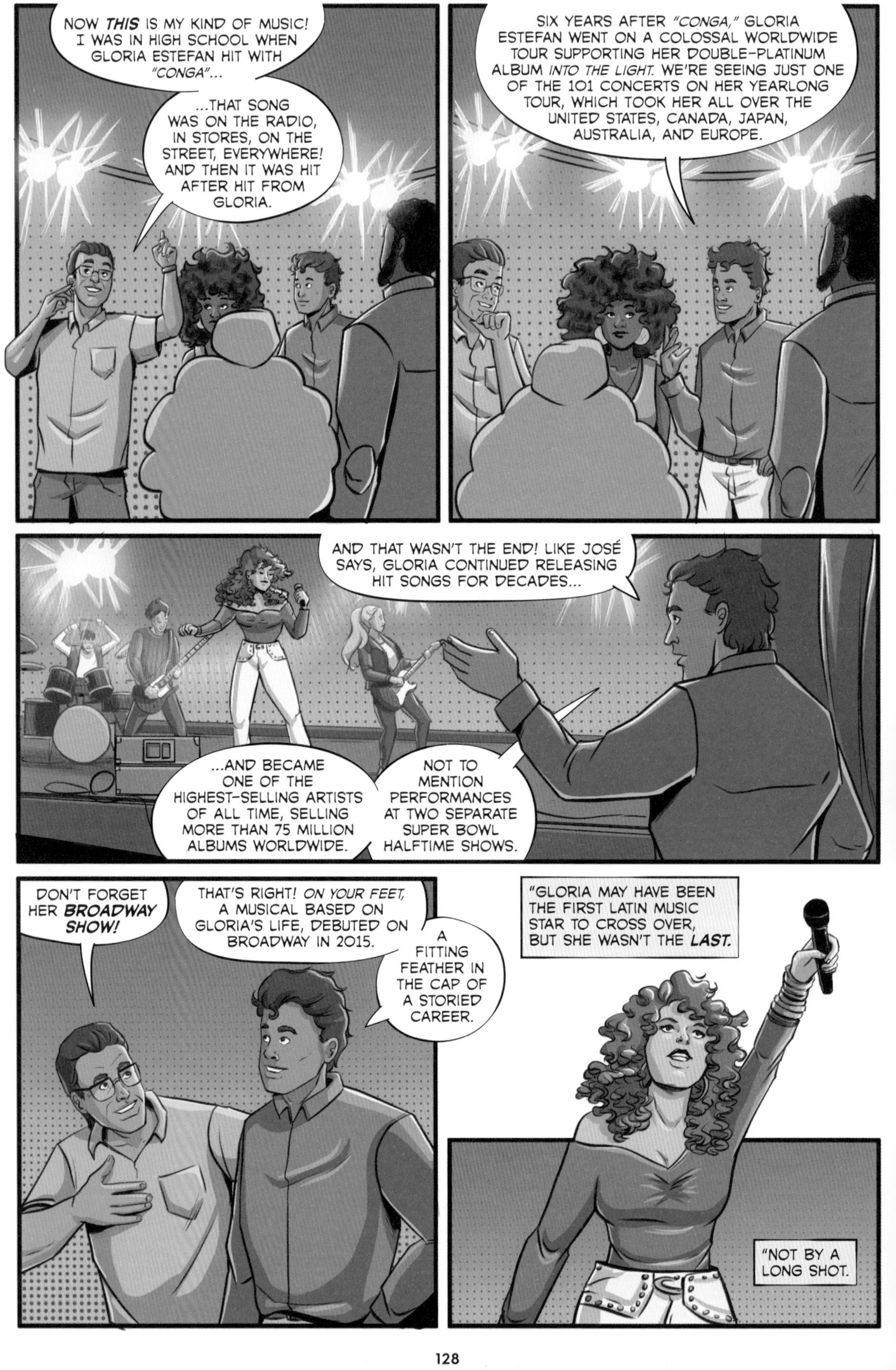
NOW *THIS* IS MY KIND OF MUSIC! I WAS IN HIGH SCHOOL WHEN GLORIA ESTEFAN HIT WITH *"CONGA"*...
...THAT SONG WAS ON THE RADIO, IN STORES, ON THE STREET, EVERYWHERE! AND THEN IT WAS HIT AFTER HIT FROM GLORIA.
SIX YEARS AFTER *"CONGA,"* GLORIA ESTEFAN WENT ON A COLOSSAL WORLDWIDE TOUR SUPPORTING HER DOUBLE-PLATINUM ALBUM *INTO THE LIGHT.* WE'RE SEEING JUST ONE OF THE 101 CONCERTS ON HER YEARLONG TOUR, WHICH TOOK HER ALL OVER THE UNITED STATES, CANADA, JAPAN, AUSTRALIA, AND EUROPE.
AND THAT WASN'T THE END! LIKE JOSÉ SAYS, GLORIA CONTINUED RELEASING HIT SONGS FOR DECADES...
...AND BECAME ONE OF THE HIGHEST-SELLING ARTISTS OF ALL TIME, SELLING MORE THAN 75 MILLION ALBUMS WORLDWIDE.
NOT TO MENTION PERFORMANCES AT TWO SEPARATE SUPER BOWL HALFTIME SHOWS.
DON'T FORGET HER **BROADWAY SHOW!**
THAT'S RIGHT! *ON YOUR FEET,* A MUSICAL BASED ON GLORIA'S LIFE, DEBUTED ON BROADWAY IN 2015.
A FITTING FEATHER IN THE CAP OF A STORIED CAREER.
"GLORIA MAY HAVE BEEN THE FIRST LATIN MUSIC STAR TO CROSS OVER, BUT SHE WASN'T THE ***LAST.***
"NOT BY A LONG SHOT.

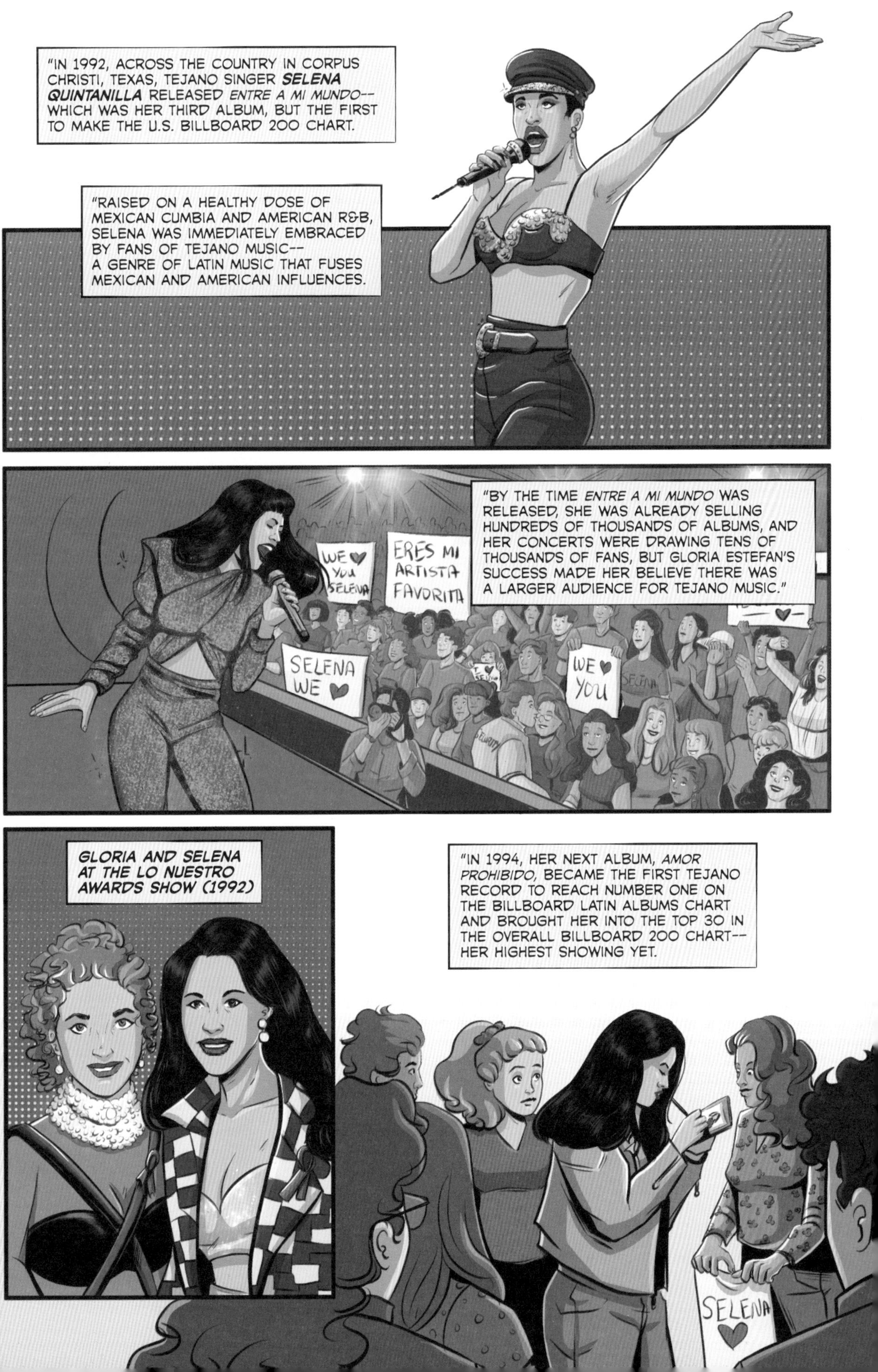
"IN 1992, ACROSS THE COUNTRY IN CORPUS CHRISTI, TEXAS, TEJANO SINGER ***SELENA QUINTANILLA*** RELEASED *ENTRE A MI MUNDO*-- WHICH WAS HER THIRD ALBUM, BUT THE FIRST TO MAKE THE U.S. BILLBOARD 200 CHART.
"RAISED ON A HEALTHY DOSE OF MEXICAN CUMBIA AND AMERICAN R&B, SELENA WAS IMMEDIATELY EMBRACED BY FANS OF TEJANO MUSIC-- A GENRE OF LATIN MUSIC THAT FUSES MEXICAN AND AMERICAN INFLUENCES.
"BY THE TIME *ENTRE A MI MUNDO* WAS RELEASED, SHE WAS ALREADY SELLING HUNDREDS OF THOUSANDS OF ALBUMS, AND HER CONCERTS WERE DRAWING TENS OF THOUSANDS OF FANS, BUT GLORIA ESTEFAN'S SUCCESS MADE HER BELIEVE THERE WAS A LARGER AUDIENCE FOR TEJANO MUSIC."
WE ♥ YOU SELENA
ERES MI ARTISTA FAVORITA
SELENA WE ♥
WE ♥ YOU
***GLORIA AND SELENA AT THE LO NUESTRO AWARDS SHOW (1992)***
"IN 1994, HER NEXT ALBUM, *AMOR PROHIBIDO*, BECAME THE FIRST TEJANO RECORD TO REACH NUMBER ONE ON THE BILLBOARD LATIN ALBUMS CHART AND BROUGHT HER INTO THE TOP 30 IN THE OVERALL BILLBOARD 200 CHART-- HER HIGHEST SHOWING YET.
SELENA ♥

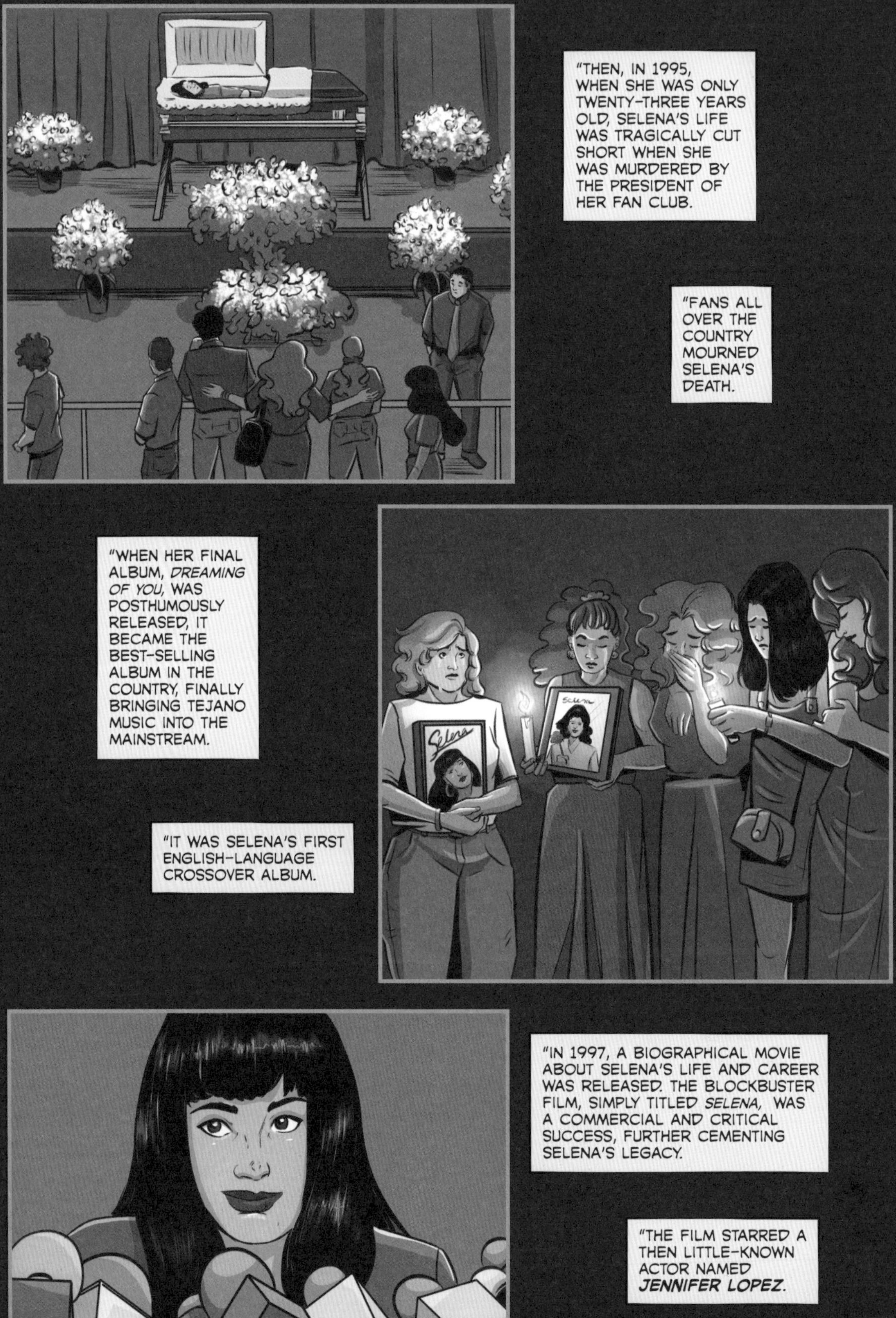
"THEN, IN 1995, WHEN SHE WAS ONLY TWENTY-THREE YEARS OLD, SELENA'S LIFE WAS TRAGICALLY CUT SHORT WHEN SHE WAS MURDERED BY THE PRESIDENT OF HER FAN CLUB.
"FANS ALL OVER THE COUNTRY MOURNED SELENA'S DEATH.
"WHEN HER FINAL ALBUM, *DREAMING OF YOU,* WAS POSTHUMOUSLY RELEASED, IT BECAME THE BEST-SELLING ALBUM IN THE COUNTRY, FINALLY BRINGING TEJANO MUSIC INTO THE MAINSTREAM.
"IT WAS SELENA'S FIRST ENGLISH-LANGUAGE CROSSOVER ALBUM.
Selena
"IN 1997, A BIOGRAPHICAL MOVIE ABOUT SELENA'S LIFE AND CAREER WAS RELEASED. THE BLOCKBUSTER FILM, SIMPLY TITLED *SELENA,* WAS A COMMERCIAL AND CRITICAL SUCCESS, FURTHER CEMENTING SELENA'S LEGACY.
"THE FILM STARRED A THEN LITTLE-KNOWN ACTOR NAMED ***JENNIFER LOPEZ***.

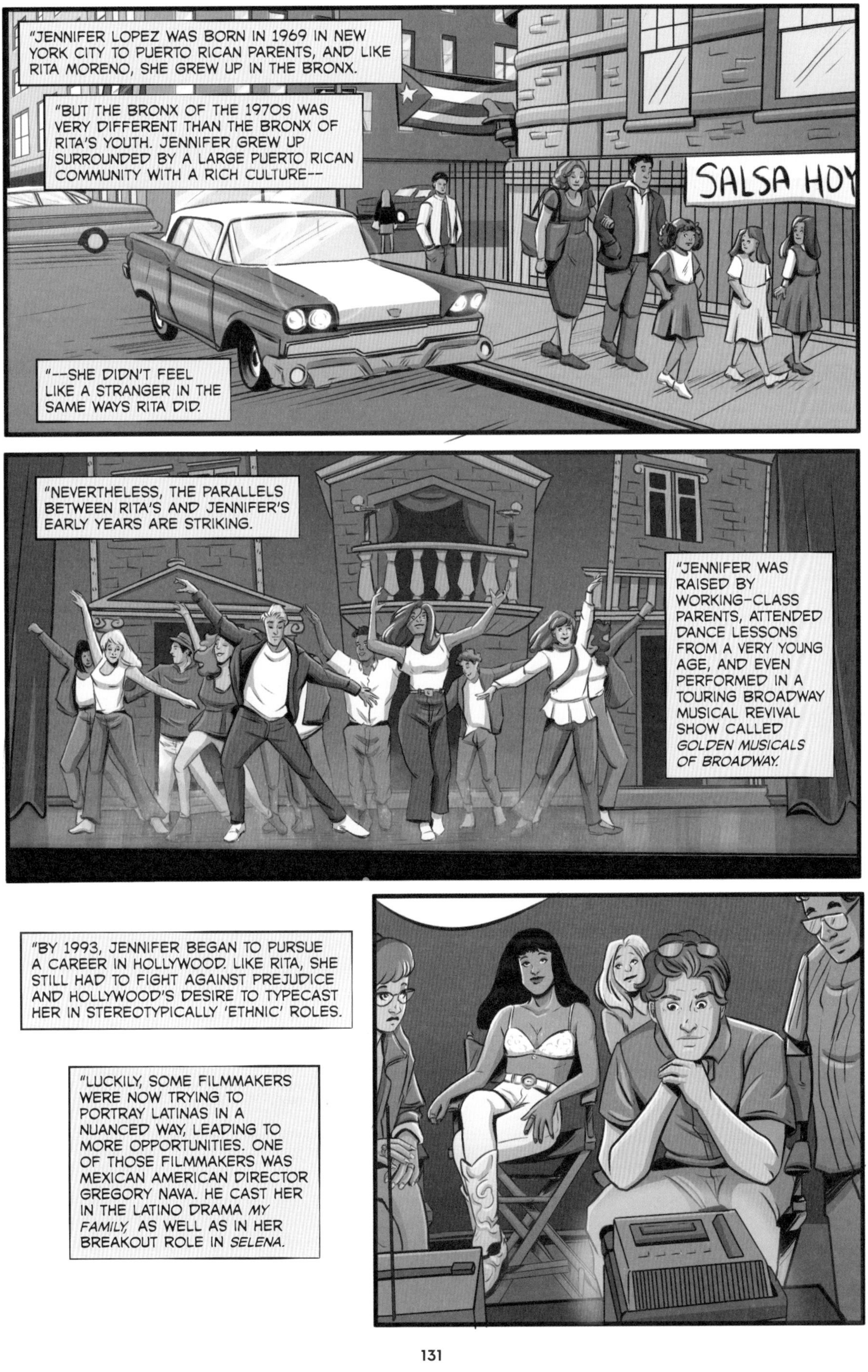
"JENNIFER LOPEZ WAS BORN IN 1969 IN NEW YORK CITY TO PUERTO RICAN PARENTS, AND LIKE RITA MORENO, SHE GREW UP IN THE BRONX.
"BUT THE BRONX OF THE 1970S WAS VERY DIFFERENT THAN THE BRONX OF RITA'S YOUTH. JENNIFER GREW UP SURROUNDED BY A LARGE PUERTO RICAN COMMUNITY WITH A RICH CULTURE--
SALSA HOY
"--SHE DIDN'T FEEL LIKE A STRANGER IN THE SAME WAYS RITA DID.
"NEVERTHELESS, THE PARALLELS BETWEEN RITA'S AND JENNIFER'S EARLY YEARS ARE STRIKING.
"JENNIFER WAS RAISED BY WORKING-CLASS PARENTS, ATTENDED DANCE LESSONS FROM A VERY YOUNG AGE, AND EVEN PERFORMED IN A TOURING BROADWAY MUSICAL REVIVAL SHOW CALLED *GOLDEN MUSICALS OF BROADWAY.*
"BY 1993, JENNIFER BEGAN TO PURSUE A CAREER IN HOLLYWOOD. LIKE RITA, SHE STILL HAD TO FIGHT AGAINST PREJUDICE AND HOLLYWOOD'S DESIRE TO TYPECAST HER IN STEREOTYPICALLY 'ETHNIC' ROLES.
"LUCKILY, SOME FILMMAKERS WERE NOW TRYING TO PORTRAY LATINAS IN A NUANCED WAY, LEADING TO MORE OPPORTUNITIES. ONE OF THOSE FILMMAKERS WAS MEXICAN AMERICAN DIRECTOR GREGORY NAVA. HE CAST HER IN THE LATINO DRAMA *MY FAMILY,* AS WELL AS IN HER BREAKOUT ROLE IN *SELENA.*

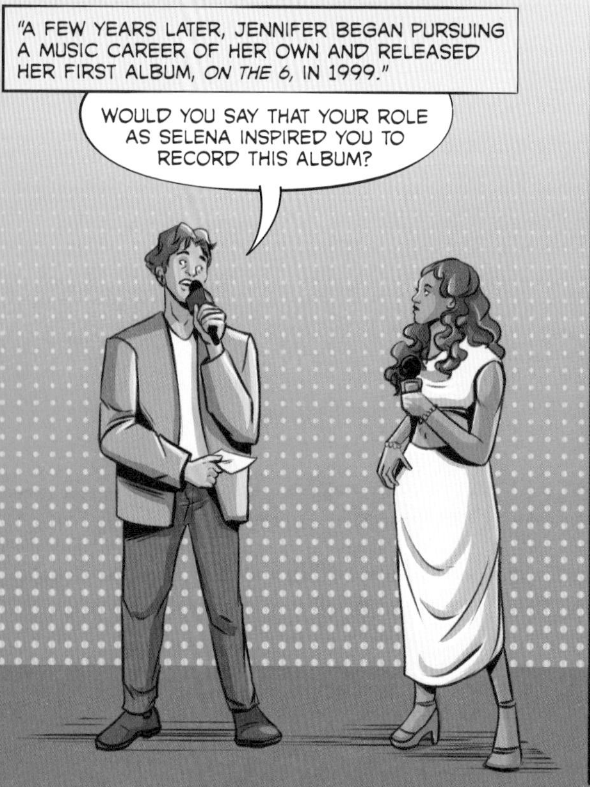
"A FEW YEARS LATER, JENNIFER BEGAN PURSUING A MUSIC CAREER OF HER OWN AND RELEASED HER FIRST ALBUM, *ON THE 6*, IN 1999."
WOULD YOU SAY THAT YOUR ROLE AS SELENA INSPIRED YOU TO RECORD THIS ALBUM?

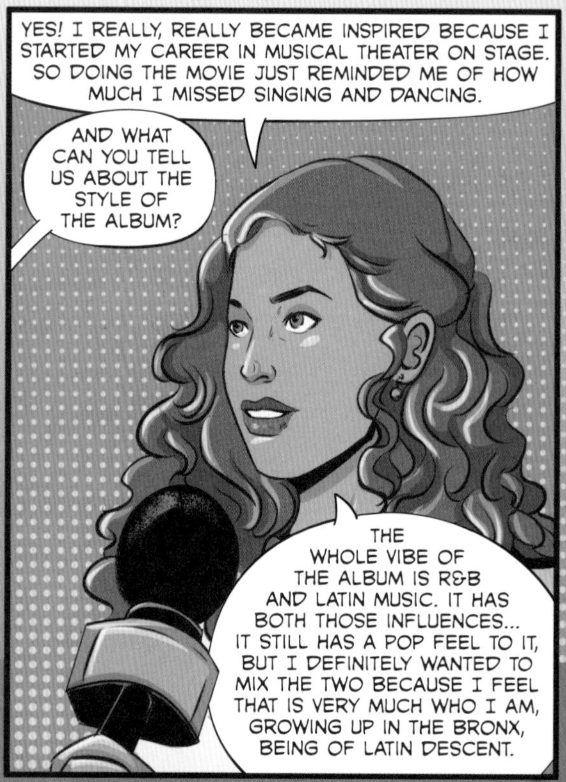
YES! I REALLY, REALLY BECAME INSPIRED BECAUSE I STARTED MY CAREER IN MUSICAL THEATER ON STAGE. SO DOING THE MOVIE JUST REMINDED ME OF HOW MUCH I MISSED SINGING AND DANCING.
AND WHAT CAN YOU TELL US ABOUT THE STYLE OF THE ALBUM?
THE WHOLE VIBE OF THE ALBUM IS R&B AND LATIN MUSIC. IT HAS BOTH THOSE INFLUENCES... IT STILL HAS A POP FEEL TO IT, BUT I DEFINITELY WANTED TO MIX THE TWO BECAUSE I FEEL THAT IS VERY MUCH WHO I AM, GROWING UP IN THE BRONX, BEING OF LATIN DESCENT.

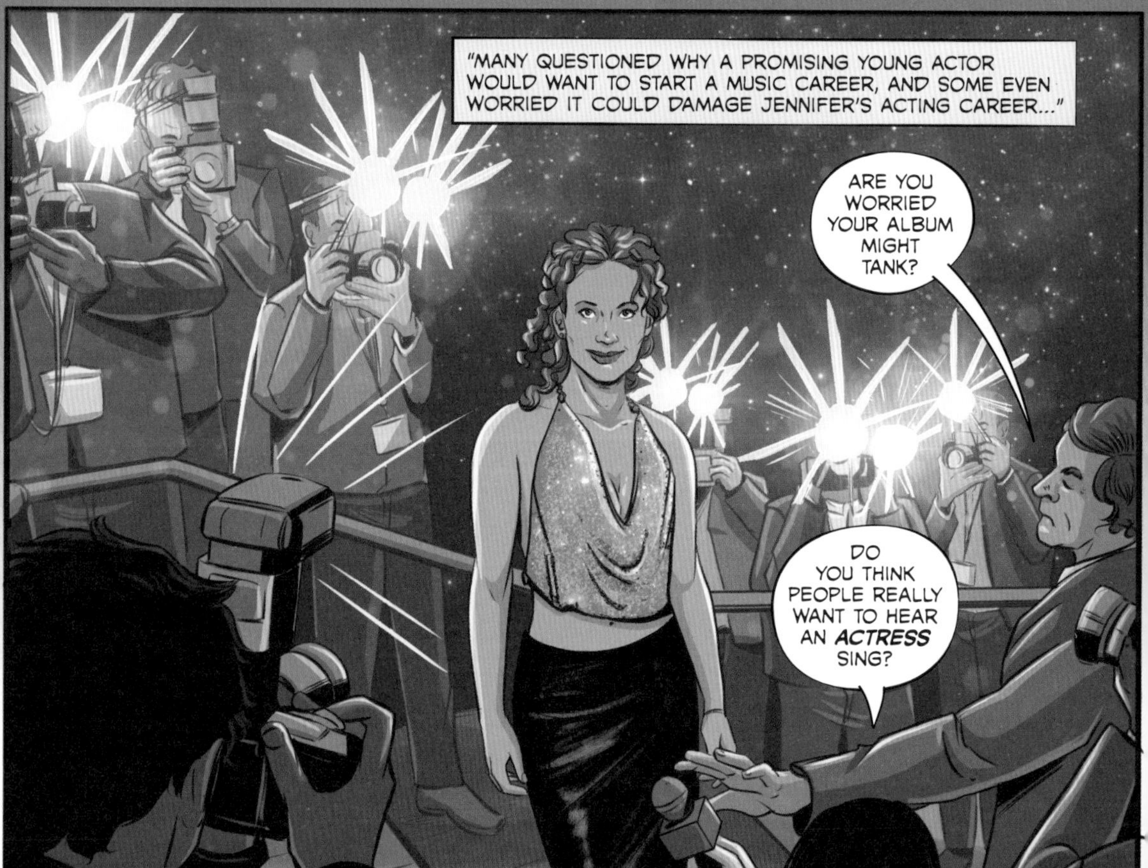
"MANY QUESTIONED WHY A PROMISING YOUNG ACTOR WOULD WANT TO START A MUSIC CAREER, AND SOME EVEN WORRIED IT COULD DAMAGE JENNIFER'S ACTING CAREER..."
ARE YOU WORRIED YOUR ALBUM MIGHT TANK?
DO YOU THINK PEOPLE REALLY WANT TO HEAR AN ***ACTRESS*** SING?

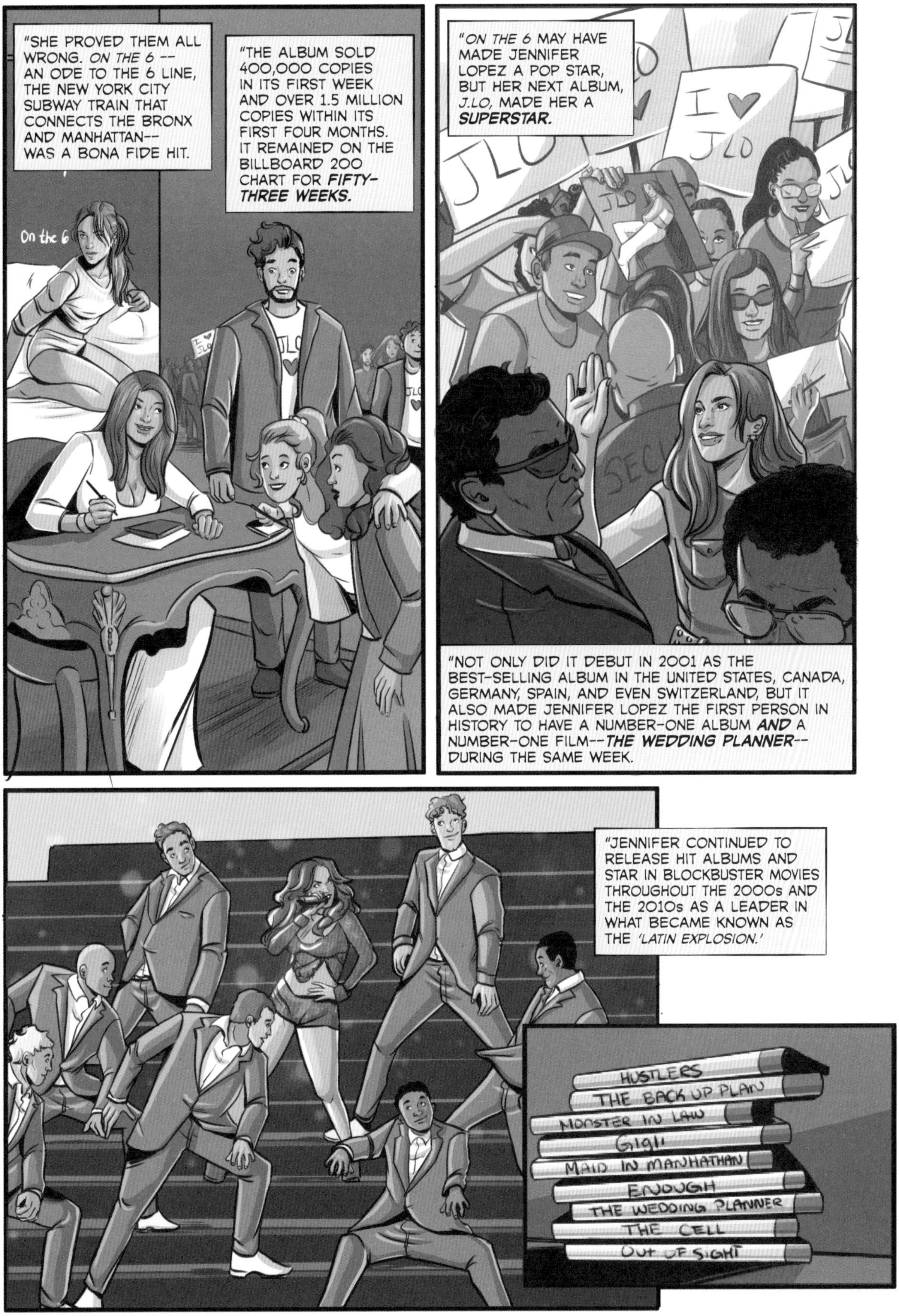
"SHE PROVED THEM ALL WRONG. *ON THE 6* -- AN ODE TO THE 6 LINE, THE NEW YORK CITY SUBWAY TRAIN THAT CONNECTS THE BRONX AND MANHATTAN-- WAS A BONA FIDE HIT.
"THE ALBUM SOLD 400,000 COPIES IN ITS FIRST WEEK AND OVER 1.5 MILLION COPIES WITHIN ITS FIRST FOUR MONTHS. IT REMAINED ON THE BILLBOARD 200 CHART FOR ***FIFTY-THREE WEEKS.***
On the 6
"*ON THE 6* MAY HAVE MADE JENNIFER LOPEZ A POP STAR, BUT HER NEXT ALBUM, *J.LO,* MADE HER A ***SUPERSTAR.***
JLO
I ♥ JLO
"NOT ONLY DID IT DEBUT IN 2001 AS THE BEST-SELLING ALBUM IN THE UNITED STATES, CANADA, GERMANY, SPAIN, AND EVEN SWITZERLAND, BUT IT ALSO MADE JENNIFER LOPEZ THE FIRST PERSON IN HISTORY TO HAVE A NUMBER-ONE ALBUM ***AND*** A NUMBER-ONE FILM--***THE WEDDING PLANNER***-- DURING THE SAME WEEK.
"JENNIFER CONTINUED TO RELEASE HIT ALBUMS AND STAR IN BLOCKBUSTER MOVIES THROUGHOUT THE 2000s AND THE 2010s AS A LEADER IN WHAT BECAME KNOWN AS THE *'LATIN EXPLOSION.'*
HUSTLERS
THE BACK UP PLAN
MONSTER IN LAW
GIGLI
MAID IN MANHATTAN
ENOUGH
THE WEDDING PLANNER
THE CELL
OUT OF SIGHT

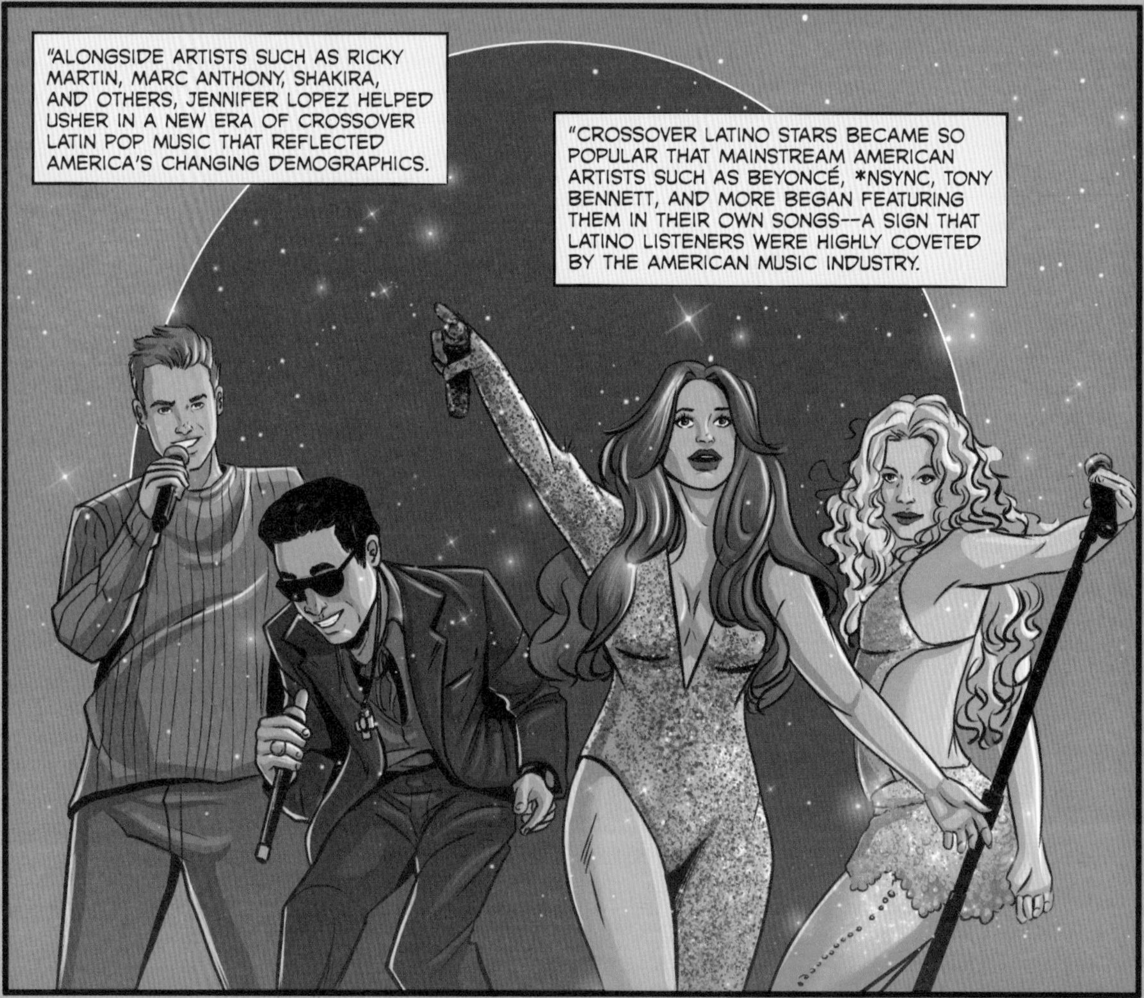
"ALONGSIDE ARTISTS SUCH AS RICKY MARTIN, MARC ANTHONY, SHAKIRA, AND OTHERS, JENNIFER LOPEZ HELPED USHER IN A NEW ERA OF CROSSOVER LATIN POP MUSIC THAT REFLECTED AMERICA'S CHANGING DEMOGRAPHICS.
"CROSSOVER LATINO STARS BECAME SO POPULAR THAT MAINSTREAM AMERICAN ARTISTS SUCH AS BEYONCÉ, *NSYNC, TONY BENNETT, AND MORE BEGAN FEATURING THEM IN THEIR OWN SONGS--A SIGN THAT LATINO LISTENERS WERE HIGHLY COVETED BY THE AMERICAN MUSIC INDUSTRY.

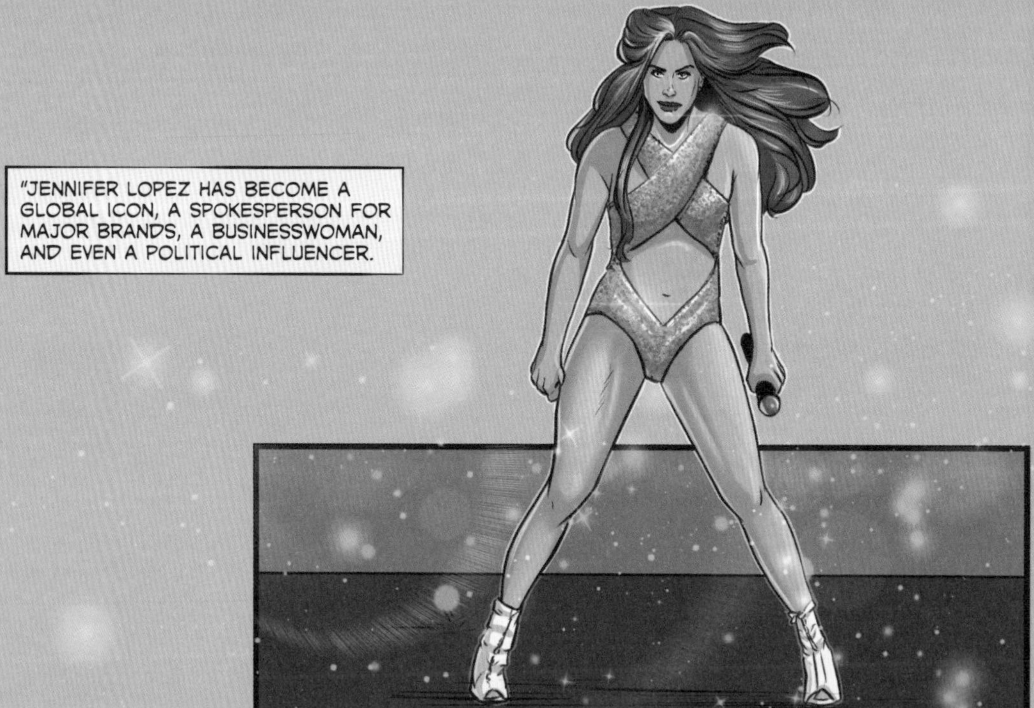
"JENNIFER LOPEZ HAS BECOME A GLOBAL ICON, A SPOKESPERSON FOR MAJOR BRANDS, A BUSINESSWOMAN, AND EVEN A POLITICAL INFLUENCER.

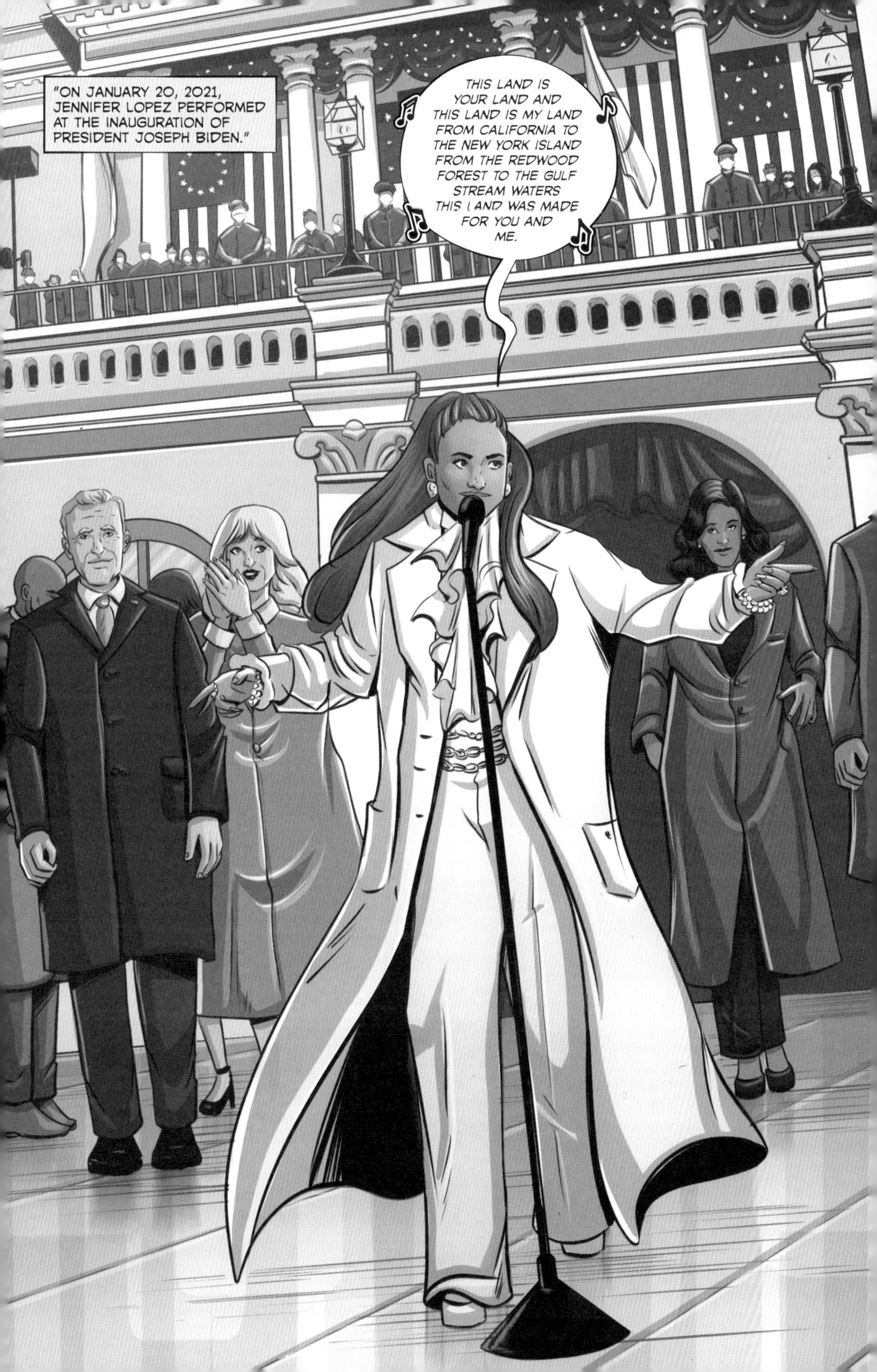
"ON JANUARY 20, 2021, JENNIFER LOPEZ PERFORMED AT THE INAUGURATION OF PRESIDENT JOSEPH BIDEN."
THIS LAND IS YOUR LAND AND THIS LAND IS MY LAND FROM CALIFORNIA TO THE NEW YORK ISLAND FROM THE REDWOOD FOREST TO THE GULF STREAM WATERS THIS LAND WAS MADE FOR YOU AND ME.

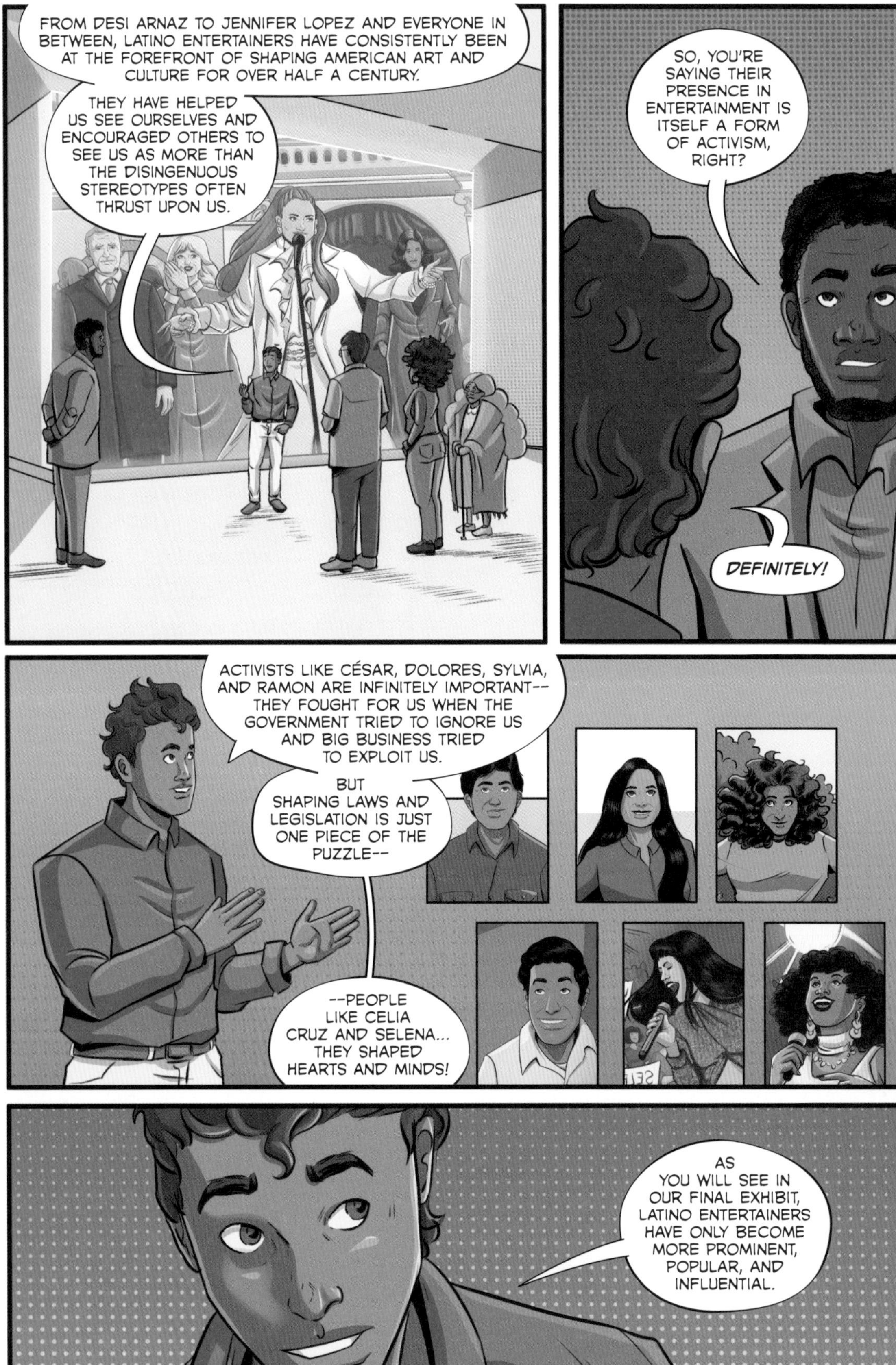
FROM DESI ARNAZ TO JENNIFER LOPEZ AND EVERYONE IN BETWEEN, LATINO ENTERTAINERS HAVE CONSISTENTLY BEEN AT THE FOREFRONT OF SHAPING AMERICAN ART AND CULTURE FOR OVER HALF A CENTURY.
THEY HAVE HELPED US SEE OURSELVES AND ENCOURAGED OTHERS TO SEE US AS MORE THAN THE DISINGENUOUS STEREOTYPES OFTEN THRUST UPON US.
SO, YOU'RE SAYING THEIR PRESENCE IN ENTERTAINMENT IS ITSELF A FORM OF ACTIVISM, RIGHT?
DEFINITELY!
ACTIVISTS LIKE CÉSAR, DOLORES, SYLVIA, AND RAMON ARE INFINITELY IMPORTANT-- THEY FOUGHT FOR US WHEN THE GOVERNMENT TRIED TO IGNORE US AND BIG BUSINESS TRIED TO EXPLOIT US.
BUT SHAPING LAWS AND LEGISLATION IS JUST ONE PIECE OF THE PUZZLE--
--PEOPLE LIKE CELIA CRUZ AND SELENA... THEY SHAPED HEARTS AND MINDS!
AS YOU WILL SEE IN OUR FINAL EXHIBIT, LATINO ENTERTAINERS HAVE ONLY BECOME MORE PROMINENT, POPULAR, AND INFLUENTIAL.

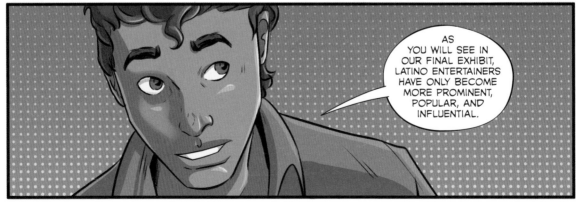

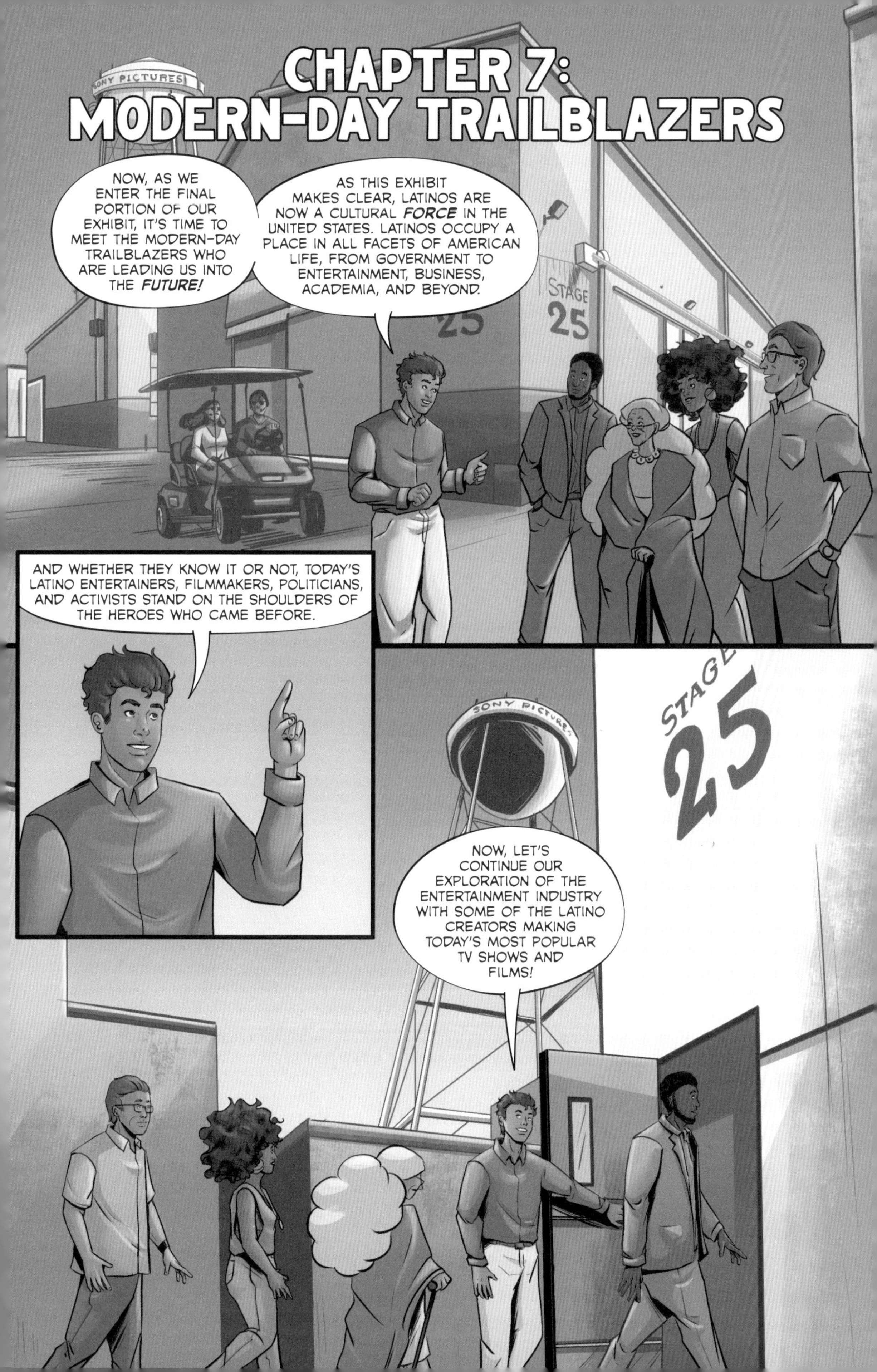
CHAPTER 7: MODERN-DAY TRAILBLAZERS
SONY PICTURES
NOW, AS WE ENTER THE FINAL PORTION OF OUR EXHIBIT, IT'S TIME TO MEET THE MODERN-DAY TRAILBLAZERS WHO ARE LEADING US INTO THE *FUTURE!*
AS THIS EXHIBIT MAKES CLEAR, LATINOS ARE NOW A CULTURAL *FORCE* IN THE UNITED STATES. LATINOS OCCUPY A PLACE IN ALL FACETS OF AMERICAN LIFE, FROM GOVERNMENT TO ENTERTAINMENT, BUSINESS, ACADEMIA, AND BEYOND.
STAGE 25
AND WHETHER THEY KNOW IT OR NOT, TODAY'S LATINO ENTERTAINERS, FILMMAKERS, POLITICIANS, AND ACTIVISTS STAND ON THE SHOULDERS OF THE HEROES WHO CAME BEFORE.
SONY PICTURES
STAGE 25
NOW, LET'S CONTINUE OUR EXPLORATION OF THE ENTERTAINMENT INDUSTRY WITH SOME OF THE LATINO CREATORS MAKING TODAY'S MOST POPULAR TV SHOWS AND FILMS!

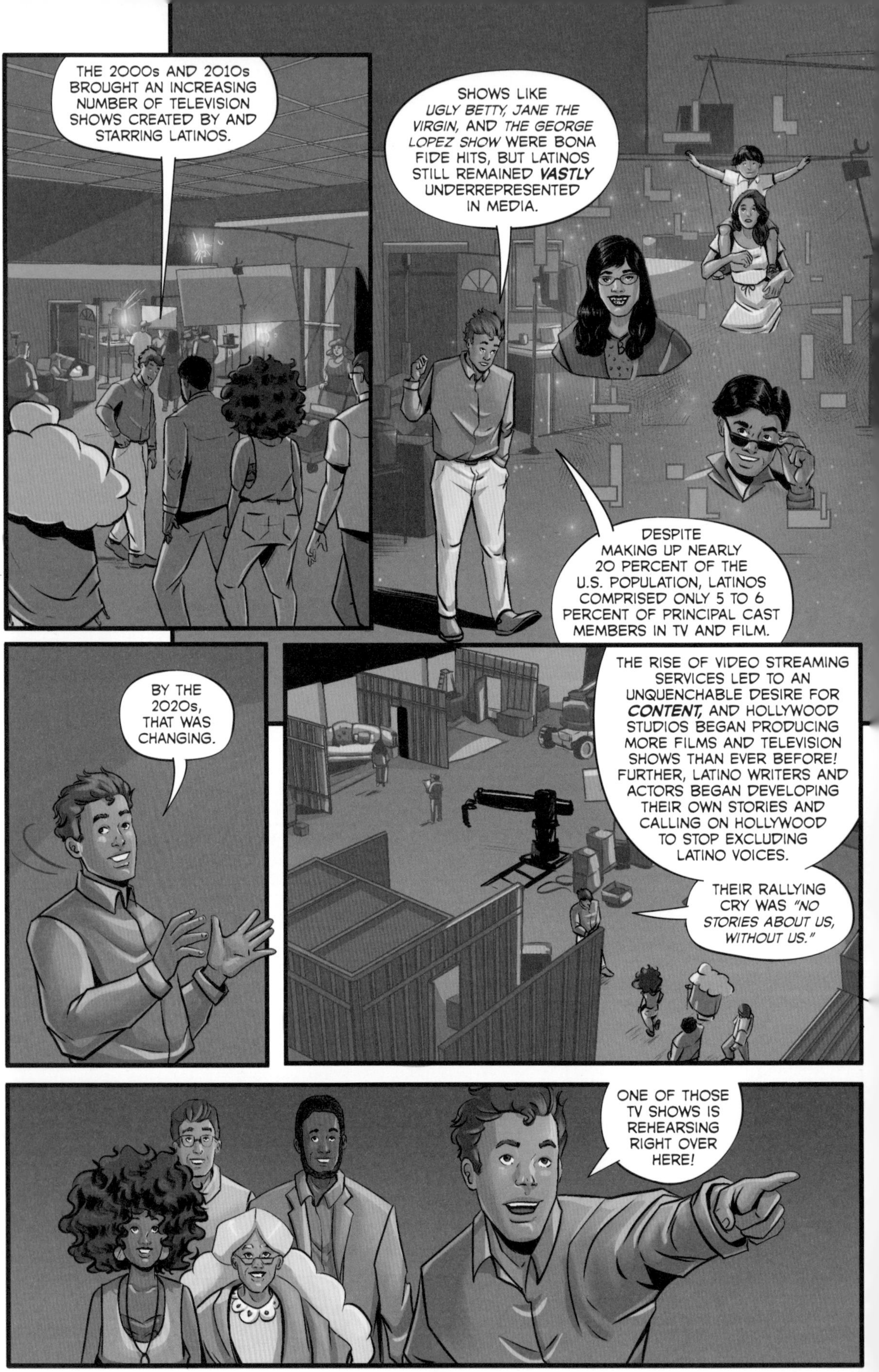
THE 2000s AND 2010s BROUGHT AN INCREASING NUMBER OF TELEVISION SHOWS CREATED BY AND STARRING LATINOS.
SHOWS LIKE *UGLY BETTY, JANE THE VIRGIN,* AND *THE GEORGE LOPEZ SHOW* WERE BONA FIDE HITS, BUT LATINOS STILL REMAINED ***VASTLY*** UNDERREPRESENTED IN MEDIA.
DESPITE MAKING UP NEARLY 20 PERCENT OF THE U.S. POPULATION, LATINOS COMPRISED ONLY 5 TO 6 PERCENT OF PRINCIPAL CAST MEMBERS IN TV AND FILM.
BY THE 2020s, THAT WAS CHANGING.
THE RISE OF VIDEO STREAMING SERVICES LED TO AN UNQUENCHABLE DESIRE FOR ***CONTENT,*** AND HOLLYWOOD STUDIOS BEGAN PRODUCING MORE FILMS AND TELEVISION SHOWS THAN EVER BEFORE! FURTHER, LATINO WRITERS AND ACTORS BEGAN DEVELOPING THEIR OWN STORIES AND CALLING ON HOLLYWOOD TO STOP EXCLUDING LATINO VOICES.
THEIR RALLYING CRY WAS *"NO STORIES ABOUT US, WITHOUT US."*
ONE OF THOSE TV SHOWS IS REHEARSING RIGHT OVER HERE!

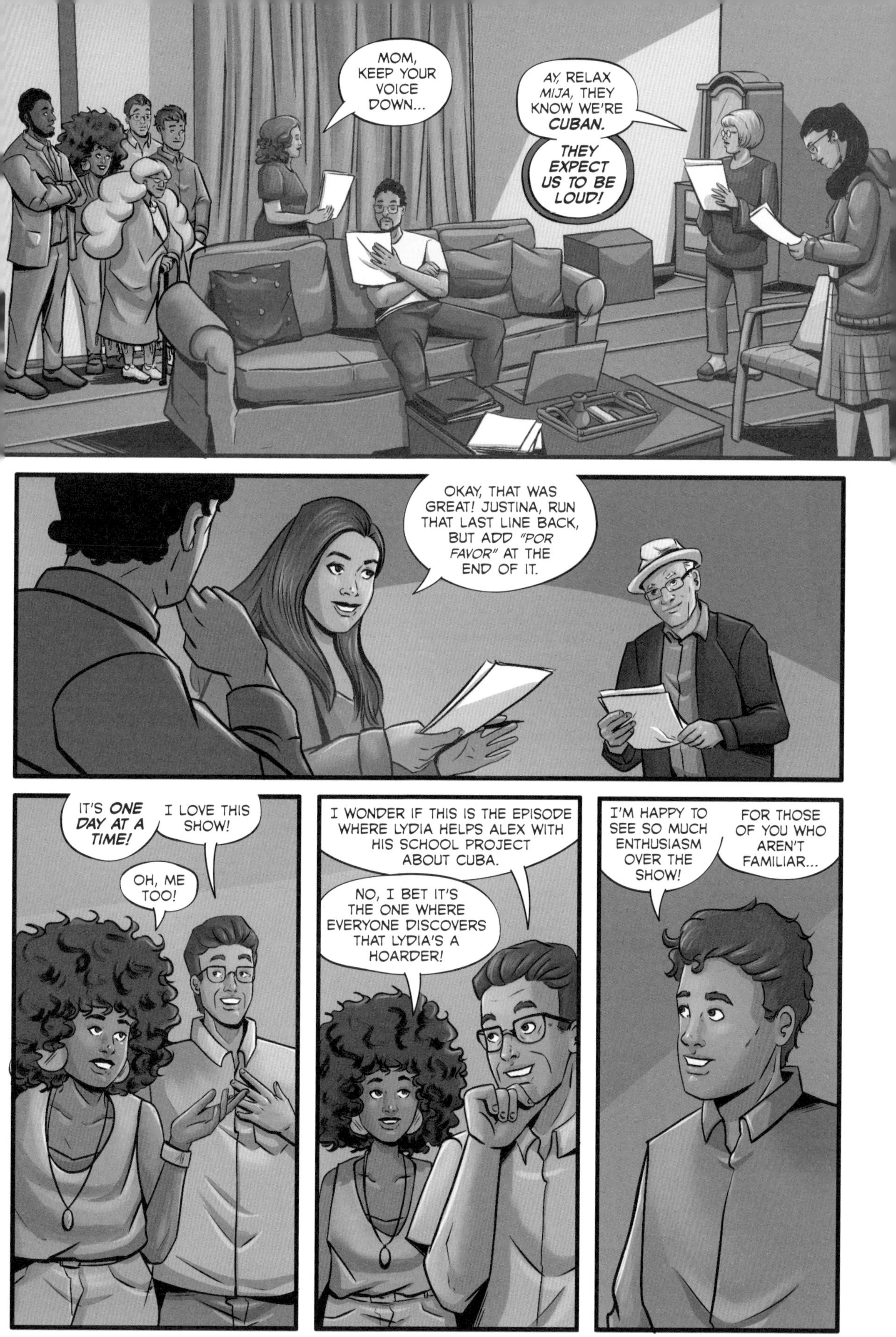
MOM, KEEP YOUR VOICE DOWN...
AY, RELAX *MIJA*, THEY KNOW WE'RE **CUBAN.**
**THEY EXPECT US TO BE LOUD!**
OKAY, THAT WAS GREAT! JUSTINA, RUN THAT LAST LINE BACK, BUT ADD *"POR FAVOR"* AT THE END OF IT.
IT'S ***ONE DAY AT A TIME!***
I LOVE THIS SHOW!
OH, ME TOO!
I WONDER IF THIS IS THE EPISODE WHERE LYDIA HELPS ALEX WITH HIS SCHOOL PROJECT ABOUT CUBA.
NO, I BET IT'S THE ONE WHERE EVERYONE DISCOVERS THAT LYDIA'S A HOARDER!
I'M HAPPY TO SEE SO MUCH ENTHUSIASM OVER THE SHOW!
FOR THOSE OF YOU WHO AREN'T FAMILIAR...

ONE DAY AT A TIME WAS A 2017 REBOOT OF THE HIT 1975 SERIES OF THE SAME TITLE. BUT RATHER THAN CENTERING AROUND AN ANGLO-AMERICAN FAMILY IN INDIANAPOLIS, THE SHOW FOLLOWED A CUBAN AMERICAN FAMILY IN LOS ANGELES.

THE SHOW WAS THE BRAINCHILD OF **GLORIA CALDERÓN KELLETT**, THE AMERICAN-BORN DAUGHTER OF CUBAN EXILES.

AND IT STARRED SOMEONE YOU MAY RECOGNIZE-- **RITA MORENO.**

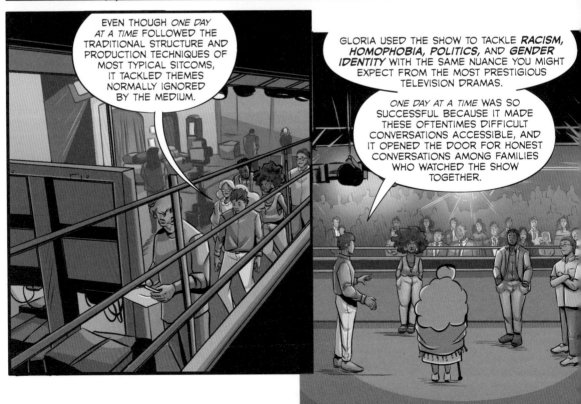

EVEN THOUGH *ONE DAY AT A TIME* FOLLOWED THE TRADITIONAL STRUCTURE AND PRODUCTION TECHNIQUES OF MOST TYPICAL SITCOMS, IT TACKLED THEMES NORMALLY IGNORED BY THE MEDIUM.

GLORIA USED THE SHOW TO TACKLE **RACISM, HOMOPHOBIA, POLITICS,** AND **GENDER IDENTITY** WITH THE SAME NUANCE YOU MIGHT EXPECT FROM THE MOST PRESTIGIOUS TELEVISION DRAMAS.

*ONE DAY AT A TIME* WAS SO SUCCESSFUL BECAUSE IT MADE THESE OFTENTIMES DIFFICULT CONVERSATIONS ACCESSIBLE, AND IT OPENED THE DOOR FOR HONEST CONVERSATIONS AMONG FAMILIES WHO WATCHED THE SHOW TOGETHER.

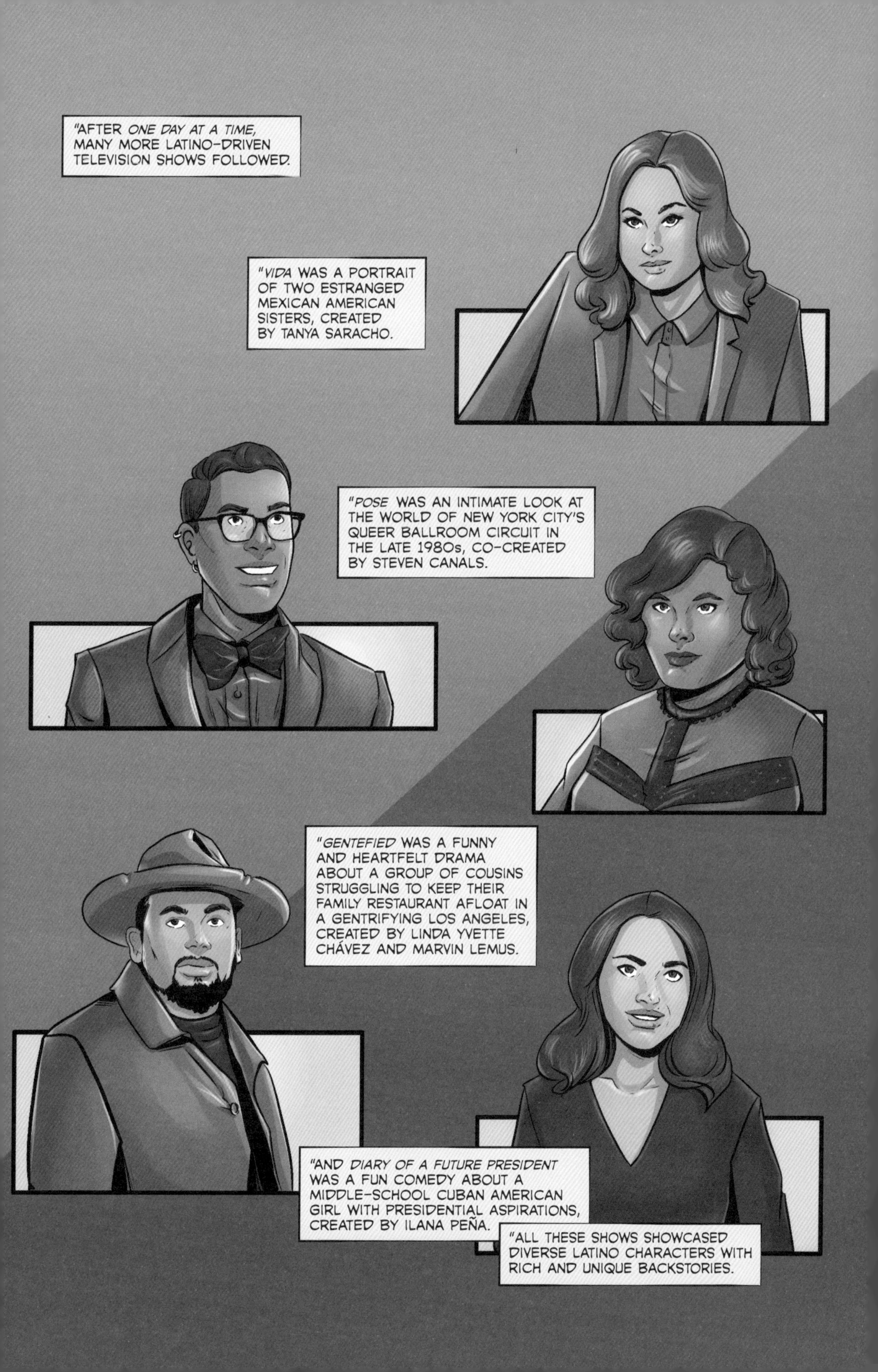
"AFTER *ONE DAY AT A TIME*, MANY MORE LATINO-DRIVEN TELEVISION SHOWS FOLLOWED.
"*VIDA* WAS A PORTRAIT OF TWO ESTRANGED MEXICAN AMERICAN SISTERS, CREATED BY TANYA SARACHO.
"*POSE* WAS AN INTIMATE LOOK AT THE WORLD OF NEW YORK CITY'S QUEER BALLROOM CIRCUIT IN THE LATE 1980s, CO-CREATED BY STEVEN CANALS.
"*GENTEFIED* WAS A FUNNY AND HEARTFELT DRAMA ABOUT A GROUP OF COUSINS STRUGGLING TO KEEP THEIR FAMILY RESTAURANT AFLOAT IN A GENTRIFYING LOS ANGELES, CREATED BY LINDA YVETTE CHÁVEZ AND MARVIN LEMUS.
"AND *DIARY OF A FUTURE PRESIDENT* WAS A FUN COMEDY ABOUT A MIDDLE-SCHOOL CUBAN AMERICAN GIRL WITH PRESIDENTIAL ASPIRATIONS, CREATED BY ILANA PEÑA.
"ALL THESE SHOWS SHOWCASED DIVERSE LATINO CHARACTERS WITH RICH AND UNIQUE BACKSTORIES.

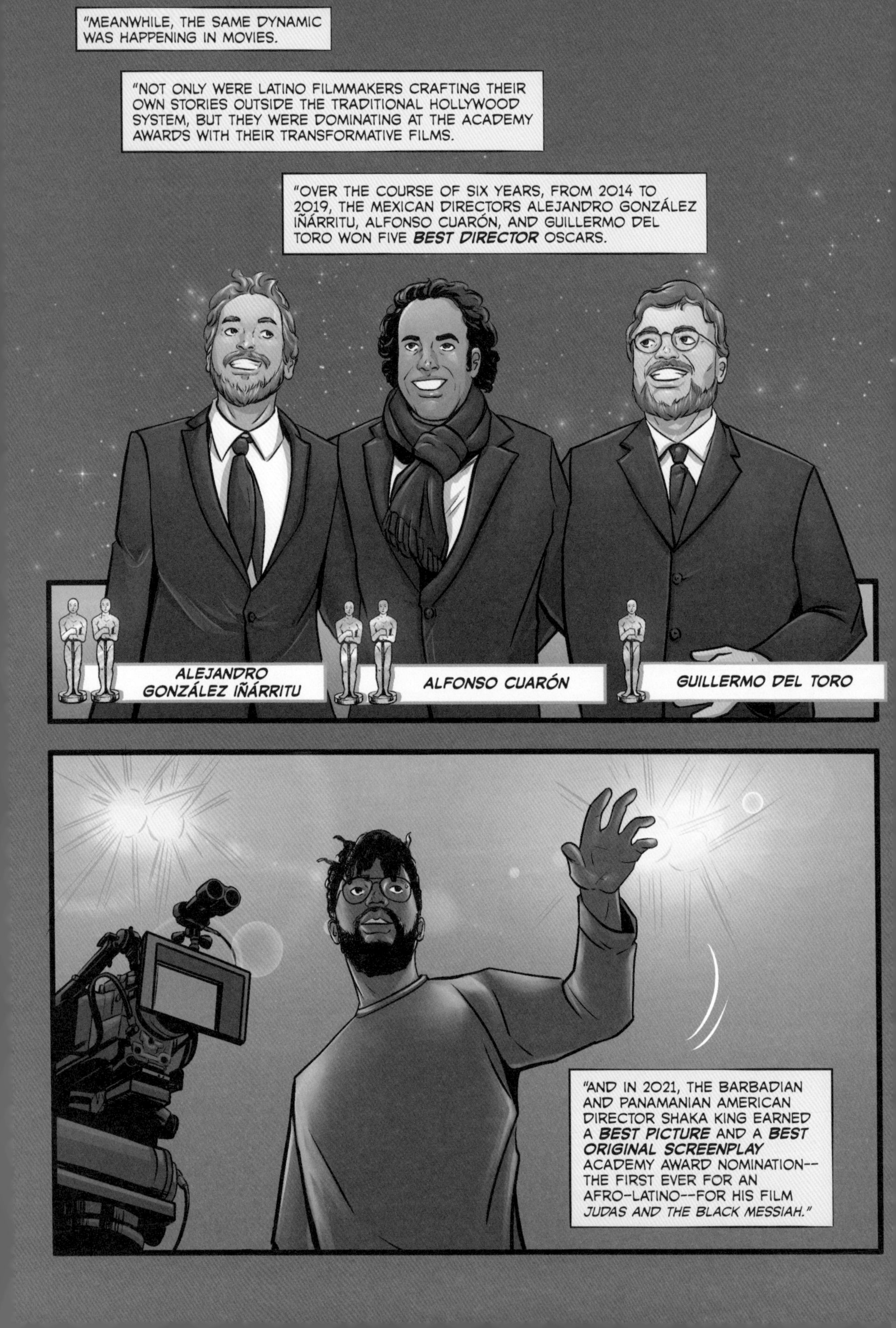
"MEANWHILE, THE SAME DYNAMIC WAS HAPPENING IN MOVIES.
"NOT ONLY WERE LATINO FILMMAKERS CRAFTING THEIR OWN STORIES OUTSIDE THE TRADITIONAL HOLLYWOOD SYSTEM, BUT THEY WERE DOMINATING AT THE ACADEMY AWARDS WITH THEIR TRANSFORMATIVE FILMS.
"OVER THE COURSE OF SIX YEARS, FROM 2014 TO 2019, THE MEXICAN DIRECTORS ALEJANDRO GONZÁLEZ IÑÁRRITU, ALFONSO CUARÓN, AND GUILLERMO DEL TORO WON FIVE ***BEST DIRECTOR*** OSCARS.
ALEJANDRO GONZÁLEZ IÑÁRRITU
ALFONSO CUARÓN
GUILLERMO DEL TORO
"AND IN 2021, THE BARBADIAN AND PANAMANIAN AMERICAN DIRECTOR SHAKA KING EARNED A ***BEST PICTURE*** AND A ***BEST ORIGINAL SCREENPLAY*** ACADEMY AWARD NOMINATION-- THE FIRST EVER FOR AN AFRO-LATINO--FOR HIS FILM *JUDAS AND THE BLACK MESSIAH.*"

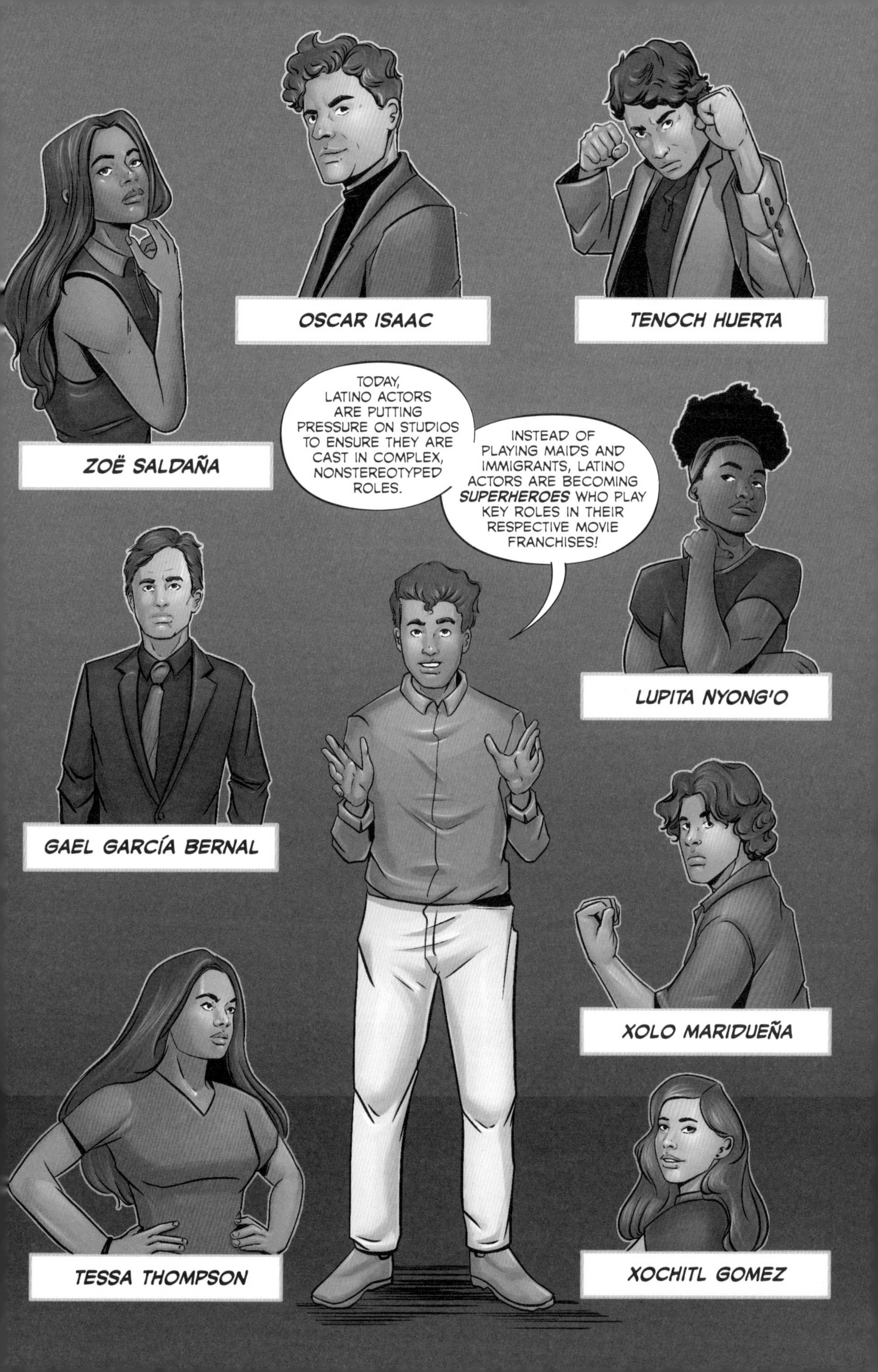
OSCAR ISAAC
TENOCH HUERTA
ZOË SALDAÑA
TODAY, LATINO ACTORS ARE PUTTING PRESSURE ON STUDIOS TO ENSURE THEY ARE CAST IN COMPLEX, NONSTEREOTYPED ROLES.
INSTEAD OF PLAYING MAIDS AND IMMIGRANTS, LATINO ACTORS ARE BECOMING SUPERHEROES WHO PLAY KEY ROLES IN THEIR RESPECTIVE MOVIE FRANCHISES!
LUPITA NYONG'O
GAEL GARCÍA BERNAL
XOLO MARIDUEÑA
TESSA THOMPSON
XOCHITL GOMEZ

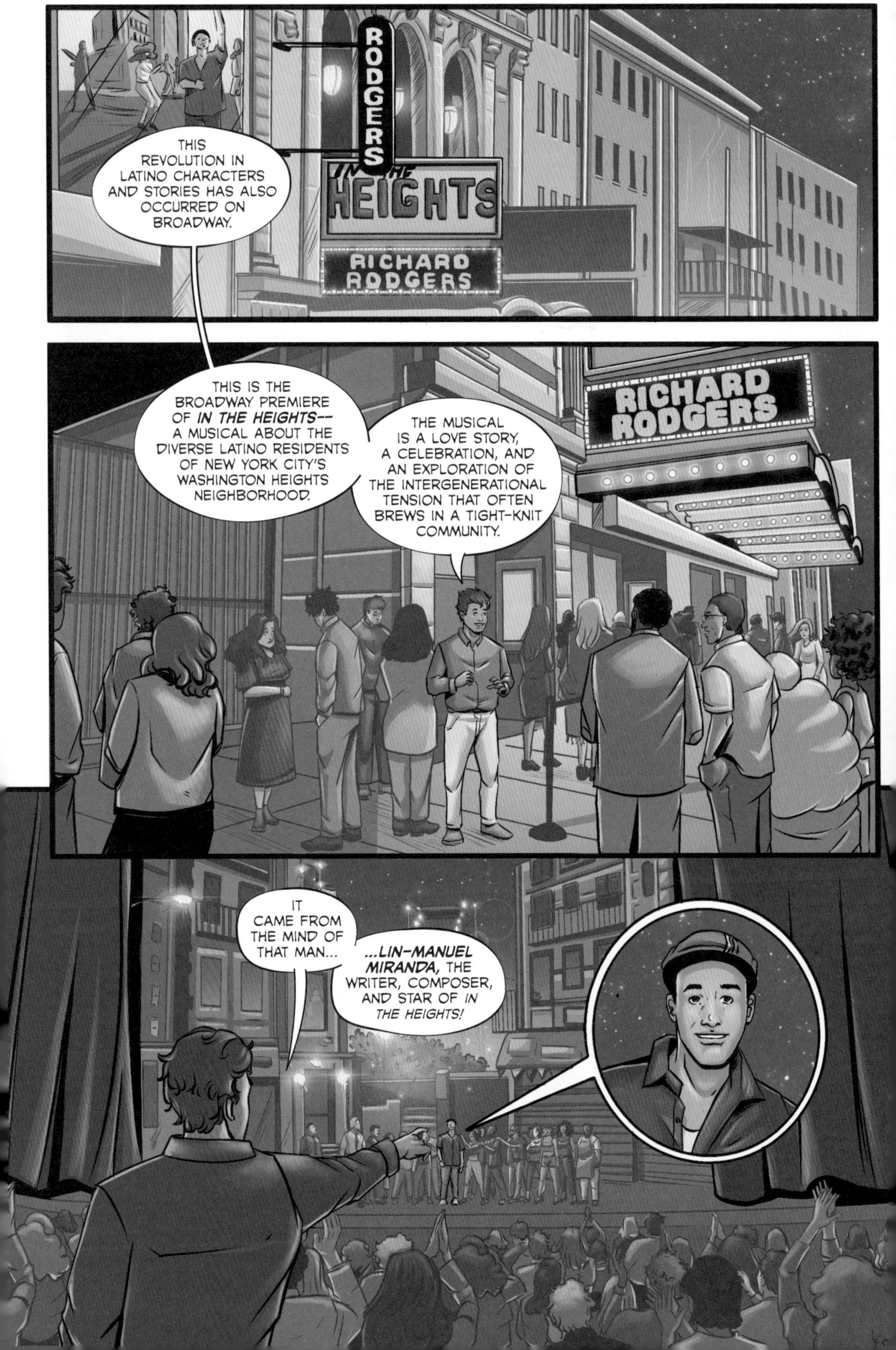
RODGERS
IN THE HEIGHTS
RICHARD RODGERS
THIS REVOLUTION IN LATINO CHARACTERS AND STORIES HAS ALSO OCCURRED ON BROADWAY.
RICHARD RODGERS
THIS IS THE BROADWAY PREMIERE OF *IN THE HEIGHTS*-- A MUSICAL ABOUT THE DIVERSE LATINO RESIDENTS OF NEW YORK CITY'S WASHINGTON HEIGHTS NEIGHBORHOOD.
THE MUSICAL IS A LOVE STORY, A CELEBRATION, AND AN EXPLORATION OF THE INTERGENERATIONAL TENSION THAT OFTEN BREWS IN A TIGHT-KNIT COMMUNITY.
IT CAME FROM THE MIND OF THAT MAN...
***...LIN-MANUEL MIRANDA,*** THE WRITER, COMPOSER, AND STAR OF *IN THE HEIGHTS!*

AS A PUERTO RICAN AMERICAN, LIN FELT A DUTY TO SHOW HIS PEOPLE IN A POSITIVE AND EMPATHETIC LIGHT. HE DREAMED OF TELLING STORIES ABOUT FULLY REALIZED LATINO CHARACTERS.

SO, AFTER A CHILDHOOD SPENT DIGGING THROUGH HIS PARENTS' EXTENSIVE BROADWAY SOUNDTRACK COLLECTION AND WATCHING DISNEY MUSICALS ON REPEAT, LIN WENT OFF TO WESLEYAN UNIVERSITY IN CONNECTICUT TO STUDY THEATER AND FILM.

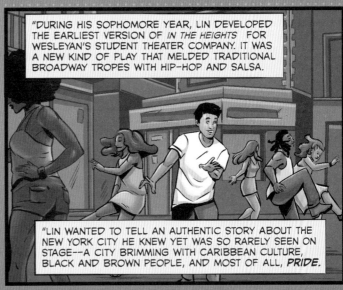

"DURING HIS SOPHOMORE YEAR, LIN DEVELOPED THE EARLIEST VERSION OF *IN THE HEIGHTS* FOR WESLEYAN'S STUDENT THEATER COMPANY. IT WAS A NEW KIND OF PLAY THAT MELDED TRADITIONAL BROADWAY TROPES WITH HIP-HOP AND SALSA.

"LIN WANTED TO TELL AN AUTHENTIC STORY ABOUT THE NEW YORK CITY HE KNEW YET WAS SO RARELY SEEN ON STAGE--A CITY BRIMMING WITH CARIBBEAN CULTURE, BLACK AND BROWN PEOPLE, AND MOST OF ALL, *PRIDE*.

"AFTER REFINING THE SHOW IN SMALLER THEATERS, *IN THE HEIGHTS* DEBUTED ON BROADWAY IN MARCH 2008, NINE YEARS AFTER LIN ORIGINALLY CONCEIVED OF THE IDEA.

"*IN THE HEIGHTS* QUICKLY BECAME THE MOST CELEBRATED PLAY ABOUT LATINO LIFE SINCE *WEST SIDE STORY*.

"IT WAS NOMINATED FOR THIRTEEN TONY AWARDS AND WON FOUR--INCLUDING BEST MUSICAL. IT ALSO WON A GRAMMY FOR BEST MUSICAL SHOW ALBUM AND WAS EVEN NOMINATED FOR A PULITZER PRIZE FOR DRAMA.

"IN 2021, THE FILM ADAPTATION HIT THEATERS AROUND THE WORLD.

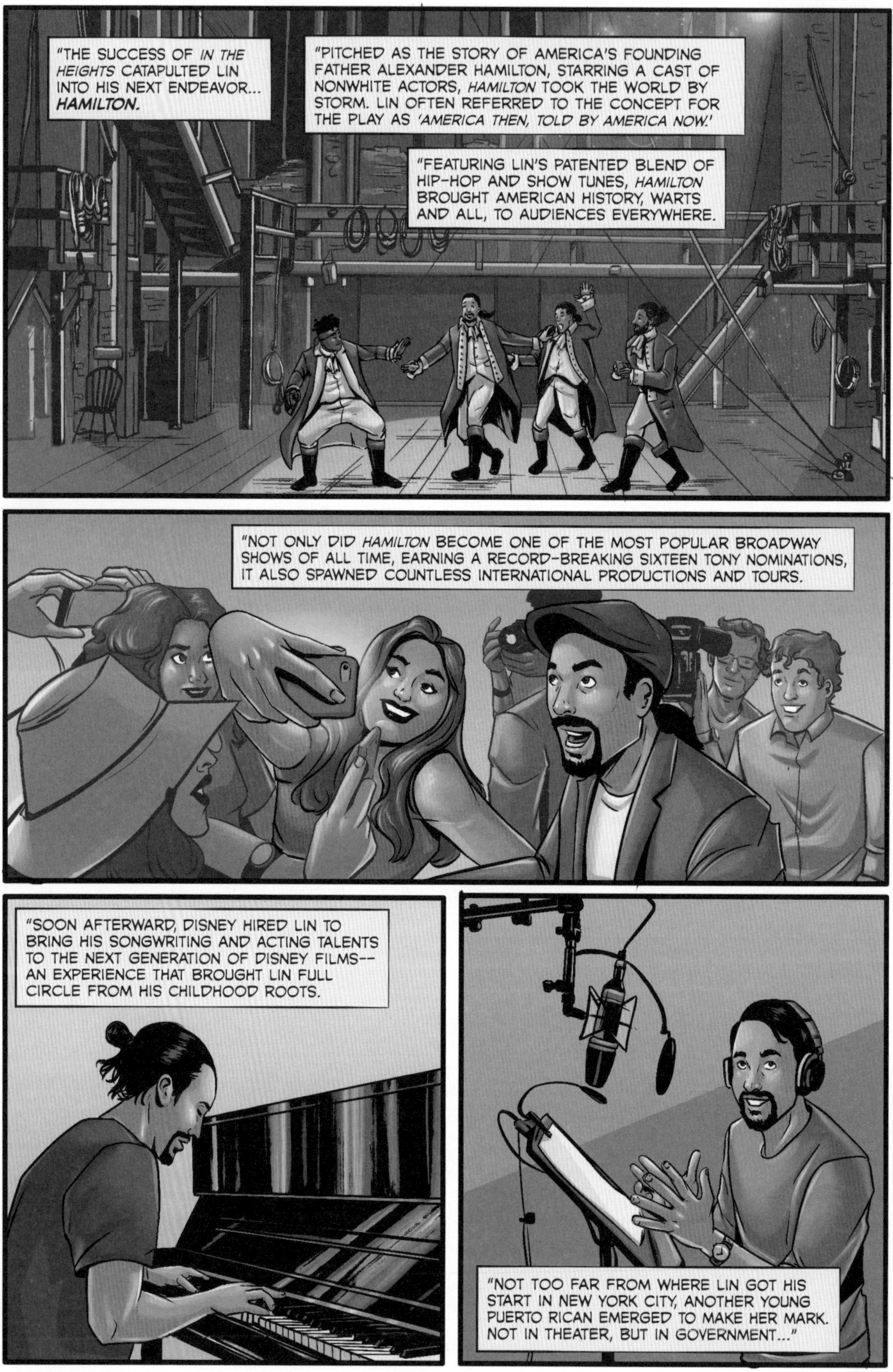
"THE SUCCESS OF *IN THE HEIGHTS* CATAPULTED LIN INTO HIS NEXT ENDEAVOR... ***HAMILTON.***
"PITCHED AS THE STORY OF AMERICA'S FOUNDING FATHER ALEXANDER HAMILTON, STARRING A CAST OF NONWHITE ACTORS, *HAMILTON* TOOK THE WORLD BY STORM. LIN OFTEN REFERRED TO THE CONCEPT FOR THE PLAY AS *'AMERICA THEN, TOLD BY AMERICA NOW.'*
"FEATURING LIN'S PATENTED BLEND OF HIP-HOP AND SHOW TUNES, *HAMILTON* BROUGHT AMERICAN HISTORY, WARTS AND ALL, TO AUDIENCES EVERYWHERE.
"NOT ONLY DID *HAMILTON* BECOME ONE OF THE MOST POPULAR BROADWAY SHOWS OF ALL TIME, EARNING A RECORD-BREAKING SIXTEEN TONY NOMINATIONS, IT ALSO SPAWNED COUNTLESS INTERNATIONAL PRODUCTIONS AND TOURS.
"SOON AFTERWARD, DISNEY HIRED LIN TO BRING HIS SONGWRITING AND ACTING TALENTS TO THE NEXT GENERATION OF DISNEY FILMS-- AN EXPERIENCE THAT BROUGHT LIN FULL CIRCLE FROM HIS CHILDHOOD ROOTS.
"NOT TOO FAR FROM WHERE LIN GOT HIS START IN NEW YORK CITY, ANOTHER YOUNG PUERTO RICAN EMERGED TO MAKE HER MARK. NOT IN THEATER, BUT IN GOVERNMENT..."

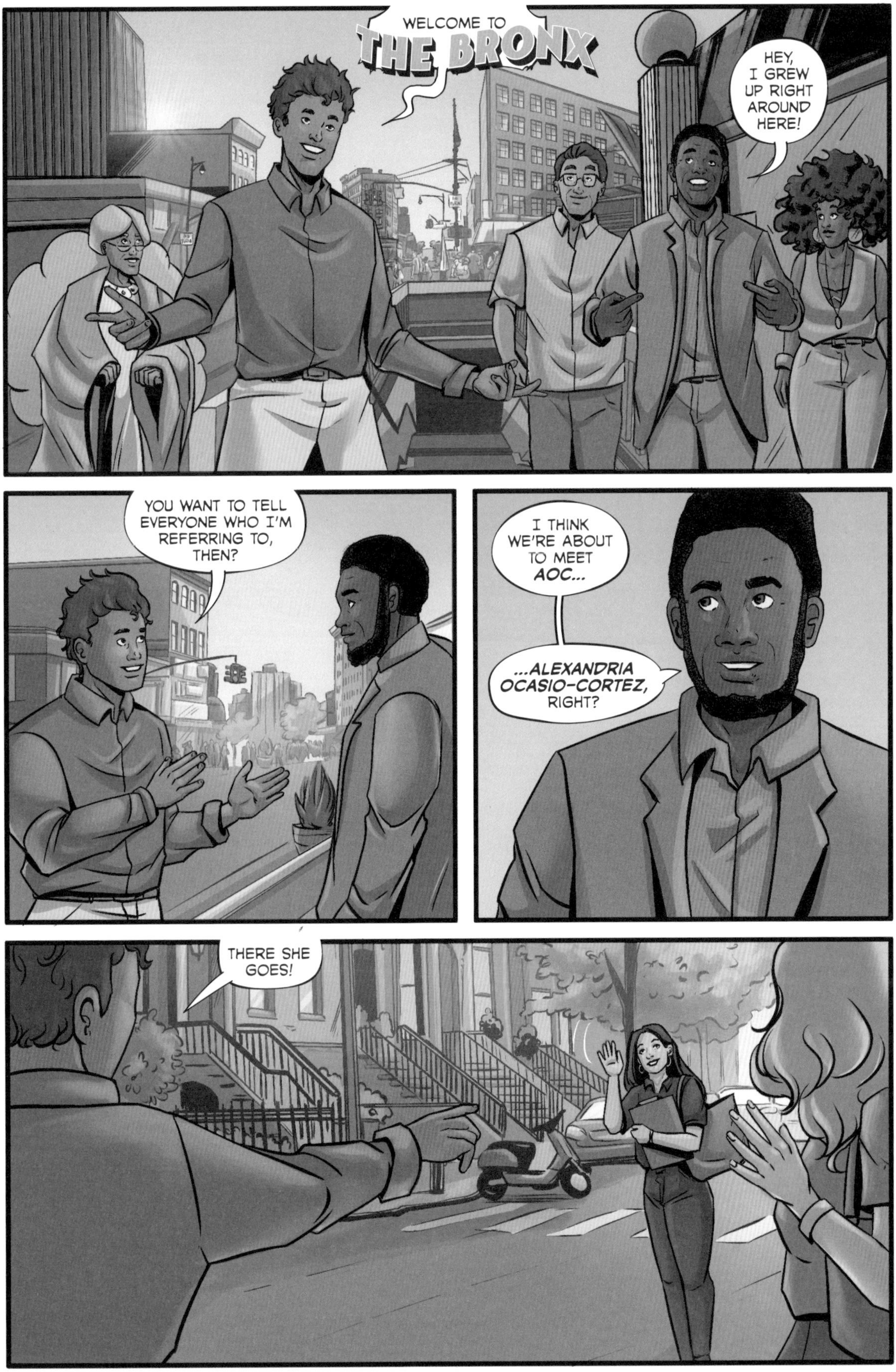
WELCOME TO
THE BRONX
HEY, I GREW UP RIGHT AROUND HERE!
YOU WANT TO TELL EVERYONE WHO I'M REFERRING TO, THEN?
I THINK WE'RE ABOUT TO MEET AOC...
...ALEXANDRIA OCASIO-CORTEZ, RIGHT?
THERE SHE GOES!

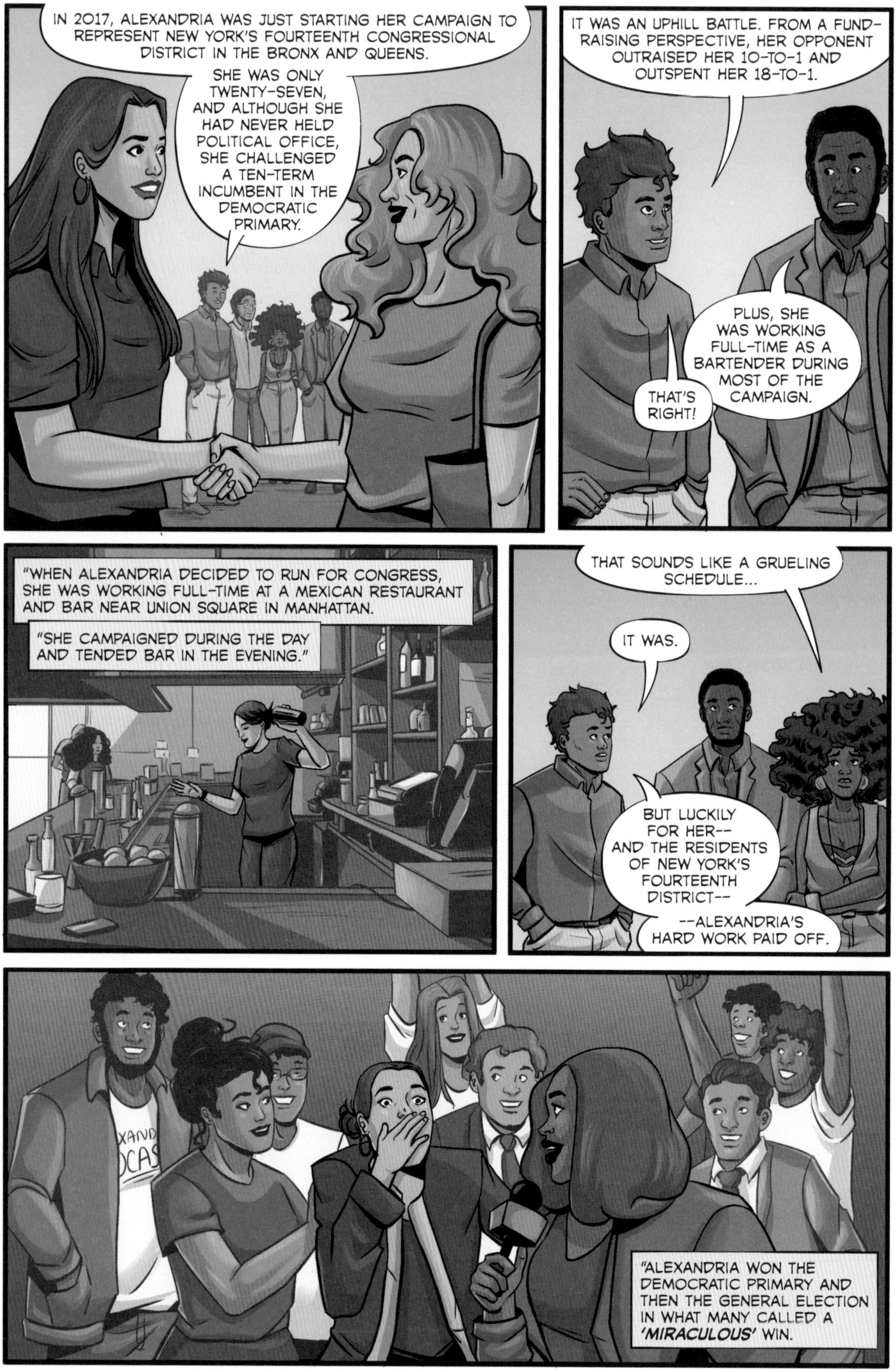
IN 2017, ALEXANDRIA WAS JUST STARTING HER CAMPAIGN TO REPRESENT NEW YORK'S FOURTEENTH CONGRESSIONAL DISTRICT IN THE BRONX AND QUEENS.
SHE WAS ONLY TWENTY-SEVEN, AND ALTHOUGH SHE HAD NEVER HELD POLITICAL OFFICE, SHE CHALLENGED A TEN-TERM INCUMBENT IN THE DEMOCRATIC PRIMARY.
IT WAS AN UPHILL BATTLE. FROM A FUND-RAISING PERSPECTIVE, HER OPPONENT OUTRAISED HER 10-TO-1 AND OUTSPENT HER 18-TO-1.
PLUS, SHE WAS WORKING FULL-TIME AS A BARTENDER DURING MOST OF THE CAMPAIGN.
THAT'S RIGHT!
"WHEN ALEXANDRIA DECIDED TO RUN FOR CONGRESS, SHE WAS WORKING FULL-TIME AT A MEXICAN RESTAURANT AND BAR NEAR UNION SQUARE IN MANHATTAN.
"SHE CAMPAIGNED DURING THE DAY AND TENDED BAR IN THE EVENING."
THAT SOUNDS LIKE A GRUELING SCHEDULE...
IT WAS.
BUT LUCKILY FOR HER-- AND THE RESIDENTS OF NEW YORK'S FOURTEENTH DISTRICT--
--ALEXANDRIA'S HARD WORK PAID OFF.
"ALEXANDRIA WON THE DEMOCRATIC PRIMARY AND THEN THE GENERAL ELECTION IN WHAT MANY CALLED A ***'MIRACULOUS'*** WIN.

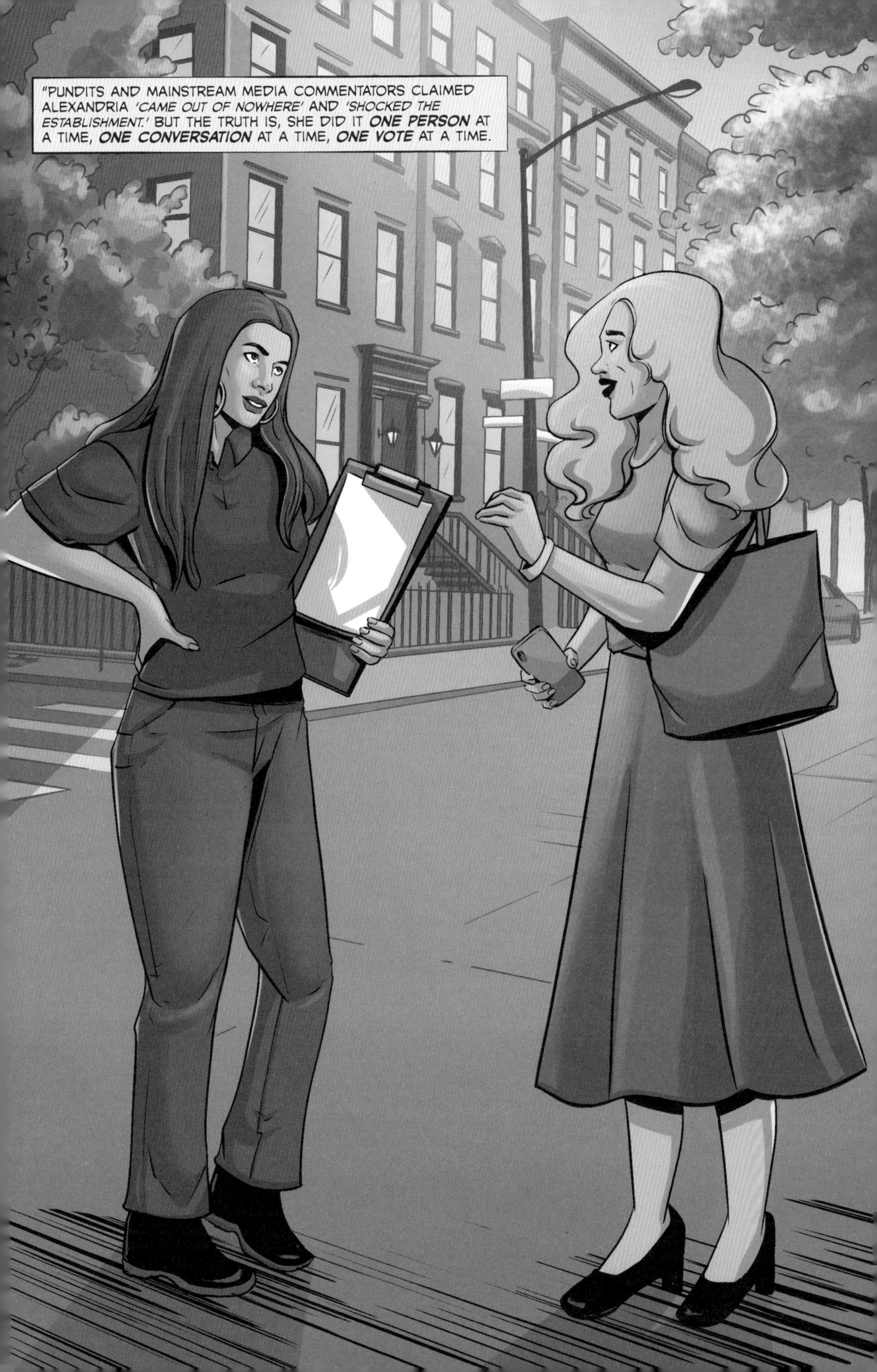
"PUNDITS AND MAINSTREAM MEDIA COMMENTATORS CLAIMED ALEXANDRIA *'CAME OUT OF NOWHERE'* AND *'SHOCKED THE ESTABLISHMENT.'* BUT THE TRUTH IS, SHE DID IT ***ONE PERSON*** AT A TIME, ***ONE CONVERSATION*** AT A TIME, ***ONE VOTE*** AT A TIME.

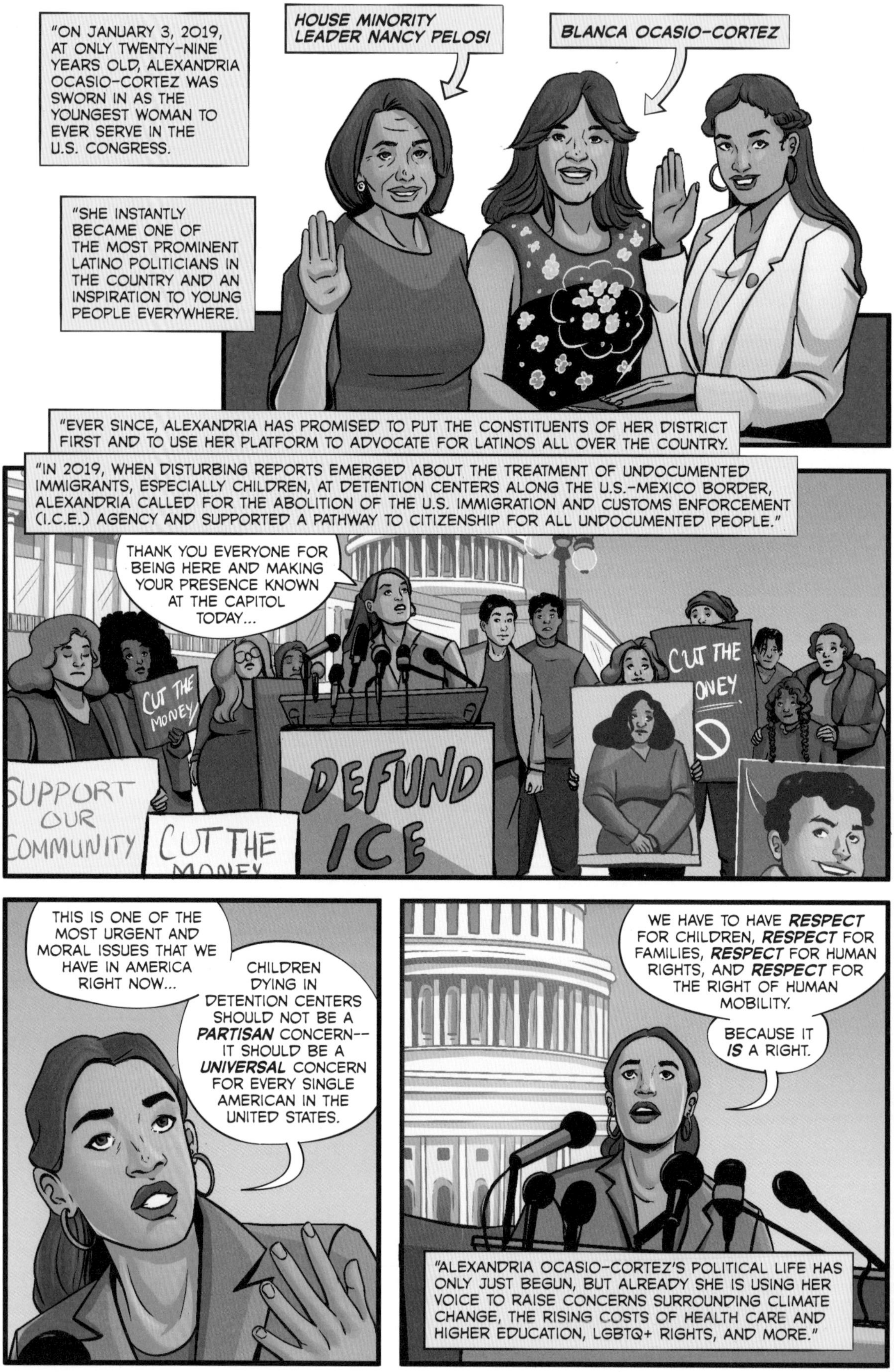
"ON JANUARY 3, 2019, AT ONLY TWENTY-NINE YEARS OLD, ALEXANDRIA OCASIO-CORTEZ WAS SWORN IN AS THE YOUNGEST WOMAN TO EVER SERVE IN THE U.S. CONGRESS.
HOUSE MINORITY LEADER NANCY PELOSI
BLANCA OCASIO-CORTEZ
"SHE INSTANTLY BECAME ONE OF THE MOST PROMINENT LATINO POLITICIANS IN THE COUNTRY AND AN INSPIRATION TO YOUNG PEOPLE EVERYWHERE.
"EVER SINCE, ALEXANDRIA HAS PROMISED TO PUT THE CONSTITUENTS OF HER DISTRICT FIRST AND TO USE HER PLATFORM TO ADVOCATE FOR LATINOS ALL OVER THE COUNTRY.
"IN 2019, WHEN DISTURBING REPORTS EMERGED ABOUT THE TREATMENT OF UNDOCUMENTED IMMIGRANTS, ESPECIALLY CHILDREN, AT DETENTION CENTERS ALONG THE U.S.-MEXICO BORDER, ALEXANDRIA CALLED FOR THE ABOLITION OF THE U.S. IMMIGRATION AND CUSTOMS ENFORCEMENT (I.C.E.) AGENCY AND SUPPORTED A PATHWAY TO CITIZENSHIP FOR ALL UNDOCUMENTED PEOPLE."
THANK YOU EVERYONE FOR BEING HERE AND MAKING YOUR PRESENCE KNOWN AT THE CAPITOL TODAY...
CUT THE MONEY
CUT THE
SUPPORT OUR COMMUNITY
CUT THE
DEFUND ICE
THIS IS ONE OF THE MOST URGENT AND MORAL ISSUES THAT WE HAVE IN AMERICA RIGHT NOW...
CHILDREN DYING IN DETENTION CENTERS SHOULD NOT BE A ***PARTISAN*** CONCERN-- IT SHOULD BE A ***UNIVERSAL*** CONCERN FOR EVERY SINGLE AMERICAN IN THE UNITED STATES.
WE HAVE TO HAVE ***RESPECT*** FOR CHILDREN, ***RESPECT*** FOR FAMILIES, ***RESPECT*** FOR HUMAN RIGHTS, AND ***RESPECT*** FOR THE RIGHT OF HUMAN MOBILITY.
BECAUSE IT ***IS*** A RIGHT.
"ALEXANDRIA OCASIO-CORTEZ'S POLITICAL LIFE HAS ONLY JUST BEGUN, BUT ALREADY SHE IS USING HER VOICE TO RAISE CONCERNS SURROUNDING CLIMATE CHANGE, THE RISING COSTS OF HEALTH CARE AND HIGHER EDUCATION, LGBTQ+ RIGHTS, AND MORE."

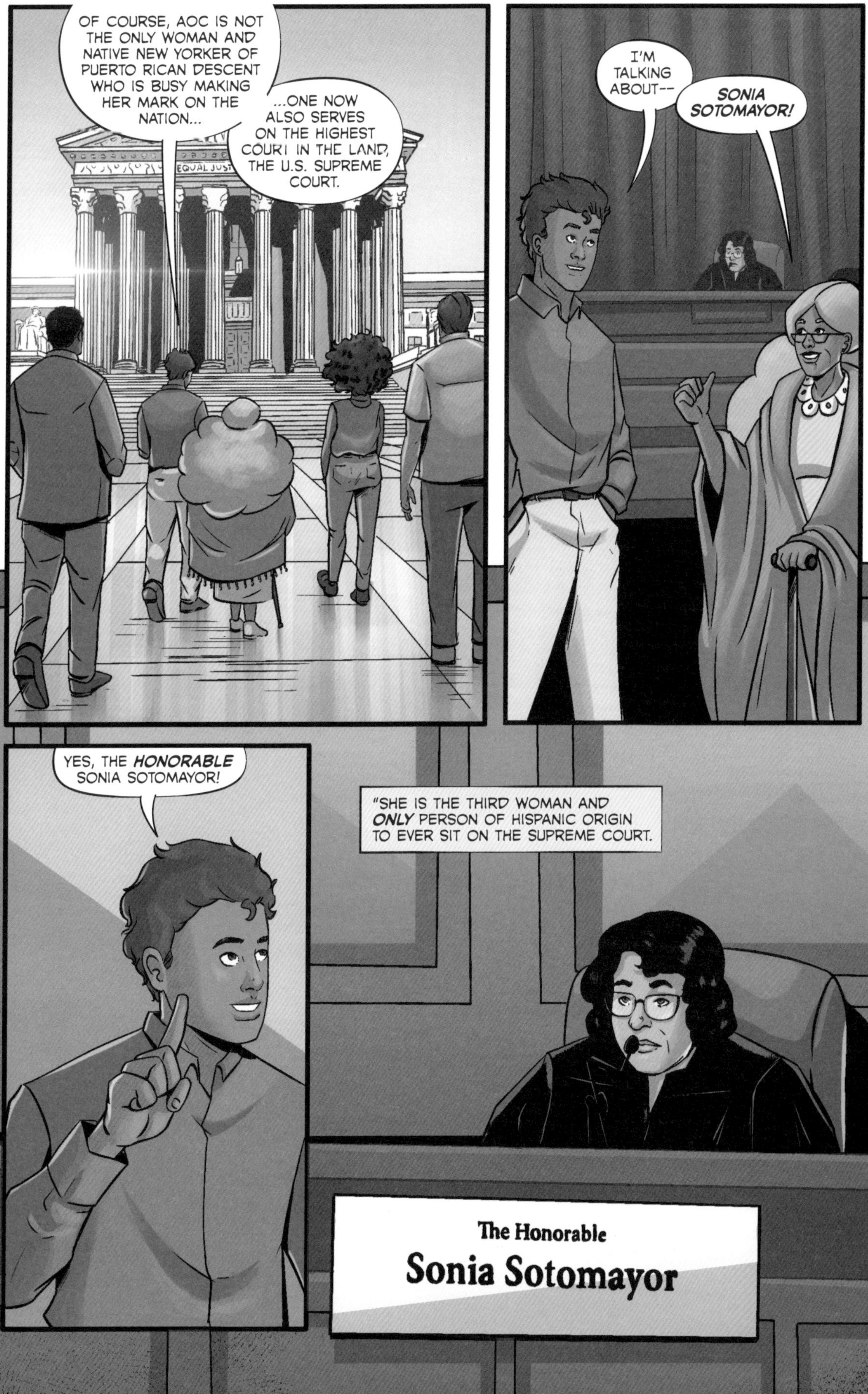
OF COURSE, AOC IS NOT THE ONLY WOMAN AND NATIVE NEW YORKER OF PUERTO RICAN DESCENT WHO IS BUSY MAKING HER MARK ON THE NATION...
...ONE NOW ALSO SERVES ON THE HIGHEST COURT IN THE LAND, THE U.S. SUPREME COURT.
EQUAL JUST
I'M TALKING ABOUT--
SONIA SOTOMAYOR!
YES, THE HONORABLE SONIA SOTOMAYOR!
"SHE IS THE THIRD WOMAN AND ONLY PERSON OF HISPANIC ORIGIN TO EVER SIT ON THE SUPREME COURT.
The Honorable
Sonia Sotomayor

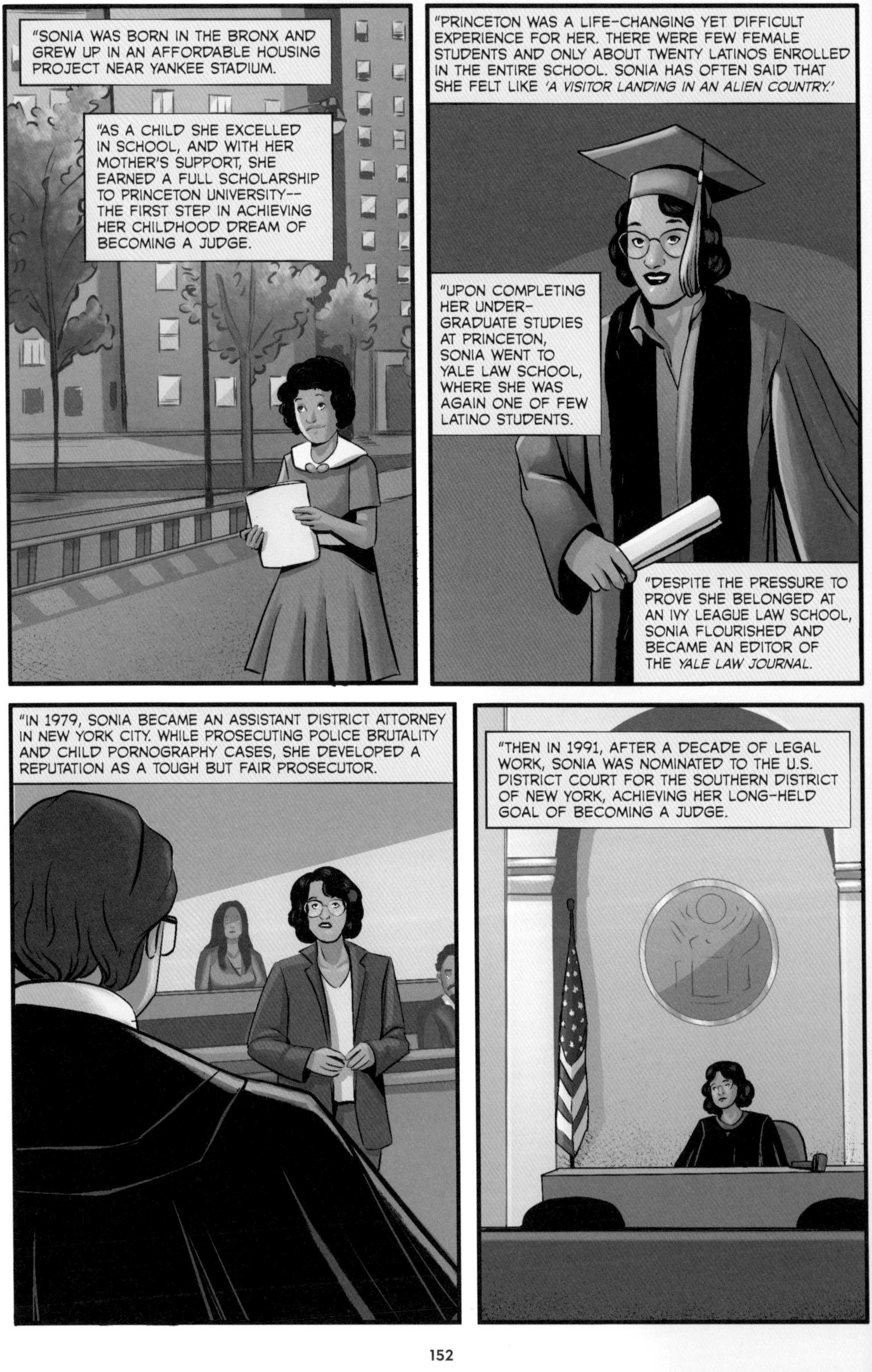
"SONIA WAS BORN IN THE BRONX AND GREW UP IN AN AFFORDABLE HOUSING PROJECT NEAR YANKEE STADIUM.
"AS A CHILD SHE EXCELLED IN SCHOOL, AND WITH HER MOTHER'S SUPPORT, SHE EARNED A FULL SCHOLARSHIP TO PRINCETON UNIVERSITY-- THE FIRST STEP IN ACHIEVING HER CHILDHOOD DREAM OF BECOMING A JUDGE.
"PRINCETON WAS A LIFE-CHANGING YET DIFFICULT EXPERIENCE FOR HER. THERE WERE FEW FEMALE STUDENTS AND ONLY ABOUT TWENTY LATINOS ENROLLED IN THE ENTIRE SCHOOL. SONIA HAS OFTEN SAID THAT SHE FELT LIKE *'A VISITOR LANDING IN AN ALIEN COUNTRY.'*
"UPON COMPLETING HER UNDER-GRADUATE STUDIES AT PRINCETON, SONIA WENT TO YALE LAW SCHOOL, WHERE SHE WAS AGAIN ONE OF FEW LATINO STUDENTS.
"DESPITE THE PRESSURE TO PROVE SHE BELONGED AT AN IVY LEAGUE LAW SCHOOL, SONIA FLOURISHED AND BECAME AN EDITOR OF THE *YALE LAW JOURNAL.*
"IN 1979, SONIA BECAME AN ASSISTANT DISTRICT ATTORNEY IN NEW YORK CITY. WHILE PROSECUTING POLICE BRUTALITY AND CHILD PORNOGRAPHY CASES, SHE DEVELOPED A REPUTATION AS A TOUGH BUT FAIR PROSECUTOR.
"THEN IN 1991, AFTER A DECADE OF LEGAL WORK, SONIA WAS NOMINATED TO THE U.S. DISTRICT COURT FOR THE SOUTHERN DISTRICT OF NEW YORK, ACHIEVING HER LONG-HELD GOAL OF BECOMING A JUDGE.

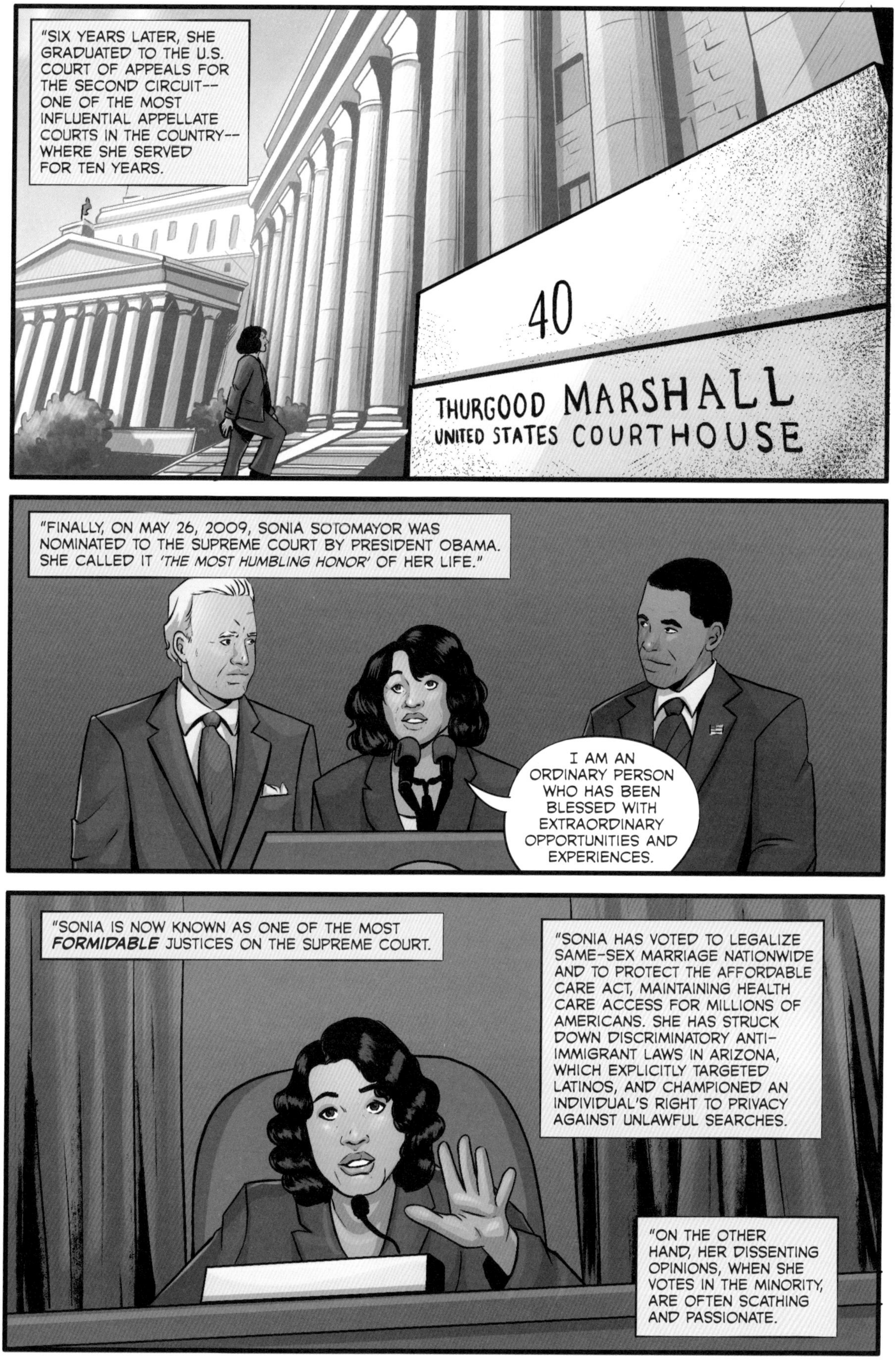
"SIX YEARS LATER, SHE GRADUATED TO THE U.S. COURT OF APPEALS FOR THE SECOND CIRCUIT-- ONE OF THE MOST INFLUENTIAL APPELLATE COURTS IN THE COUNTRY-- WHERE SHE SERVED FOR TEN YEARS.
40
THURGOOD MARSHALL
UNITED STATES COURTHOUSE
"FINALLY, ON MAY 26, 2009, SONIA SOTOMAYOR WAS NOMINATED TO THE SUPREME COURT BY PRESIDENT OBAMA. SHE CALLED IT *'THE MOST HUMBLING HONOR'* OF HER LIFE."
I AM AN ORDINARY PERSON WHO HAS BEEN BLESSED WITH EXTRAORDINARY OPPORTUNITIES AND EXPERIENCES.
"SONIA IS NOW KNOWN AS ONE OF THE MOST ***FORMIDABLE*** JUSTICES ON THE SUPREME COURT.
"SONIA HAS VOTED TO LEGALIZE SAME-SEX MARRIAGE NATIONWIDE AND TO PROTECT THE AFFORDABLE CARE ACT, MAINTAINING HEALTH CARE ACCESS FOR MILLIONS OF AMERICANS. SHE HAS STRUCK DOWN DISCRIMINATORY ANTI-IMMIGRANT LAWS IN ARIZONA, WHICH EXPLICITLY TARGETED LATINOS, AND CHAMPIONED AN INDIVIDUAL'S RIGHT TO PRIVACY AGAINST UNLAWFUL SEARCHES.
"ON THE OTHER HAND, HER DISSENTING OPINIONS, WHEN SHE VOTES IN THE MINORITY, ARE OFTEN SCATHING AND PASSIONATE.

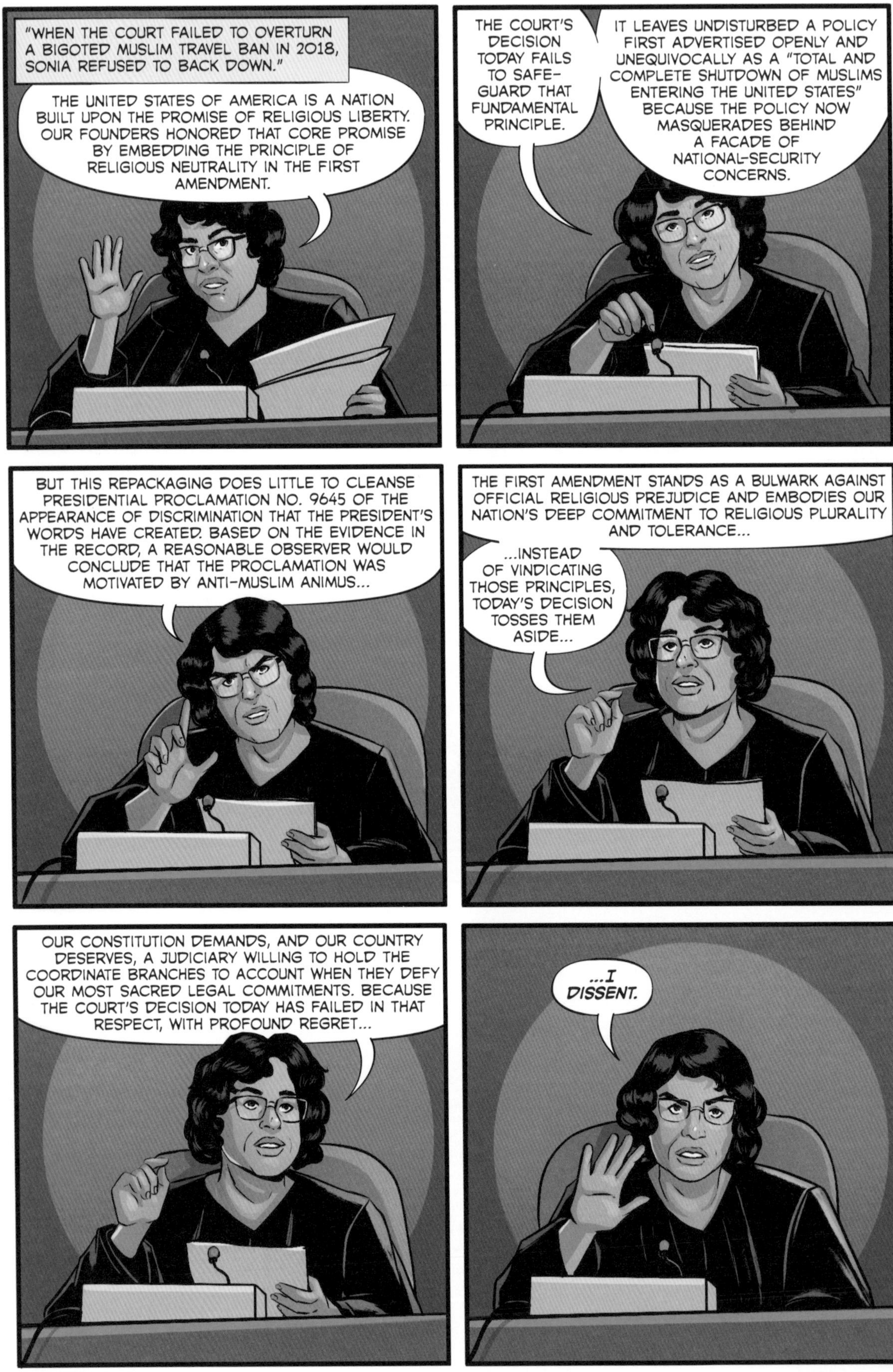
"WHEN THE COURT FAILED TO OVERTURN A BIGOTED MUSLIM TRAVEL BAN IN 2018, SONIA REFUSED TO BACK DOWN."
THE UNITED STATES OF AMERICA IS A NATION BUILT UPON THE PROMISE OF RELIGIOUS LIBERTY. OUR FOUNDERS HONORED THAT CORE PROMISE BY EMBEDDING THE PRINCIPLE OF RELIGIOUS NEUTRALITY IN THE FIRST AMENDMENT.
THE COURT'S DECISION TODAY FAILS TO SAFE-GUARD THAT FUNDAMENTAL PRINCIPLE.
IT LEAVES UNDISTURBED A POLICY FIRST ADVERTISED OPENLY AND UNEQUIVOCALLY AS A "TOTAL AND COMPLETE SHUTDOWN OF MUSLIMS ENTERING THE UNITED STATES" BECAUSE THE POLICY NOW MASQUERADES BEHIND A FACADE OF NATIONAL-SECURITY CONCERNS.
BUT THIS REPACKAGING DOES LITTLE TO CLEANSE PRESIDENTIAL PROCLAMATION NO. 9645 OF THE APPEARANCE OF DISCRIMINATION THAT THE PRESIDENT'S WORDS HAVE CREATED. BASED ON THE EVIDENCE IN THE RECORD, A REASONABLE OBSERVER WOULD CONCLUDE THAT THE PROCLAMATION WAS MOTIVATED BY ANTI-MUSLIM ANIMUS...
THE FIRST AMENDMENT STANDS AS A BULWARK AGAINST OFFICIAL RELIGIOUS PREJUDICE AND EMBODIES OUR NATION'S DEEP COMMITMENT TO RELIGIOUS PLURALITY AND TOLERANCE...
...INSTEAD OF VINDICATING THOSE PRINCIPLES, TODAY'S DECISION TOSSES THEM ASIDE...
OUR CONSTITUTION DEMANDS, AND OUR COUNTRY DESERVES, A JUDICIARY WILLING TO HOLD THE COORDINATE BRANCHES TO ACCOUNT WHEN THEY DEFY OUR MOST SACRED LEGAL COMMITMENTS. BECAUSE THE COURT'S DECISION TODAY HAS FAILED IN THAT RESPECT, WITH PROFOUND REGRET...
...I DISSENT.

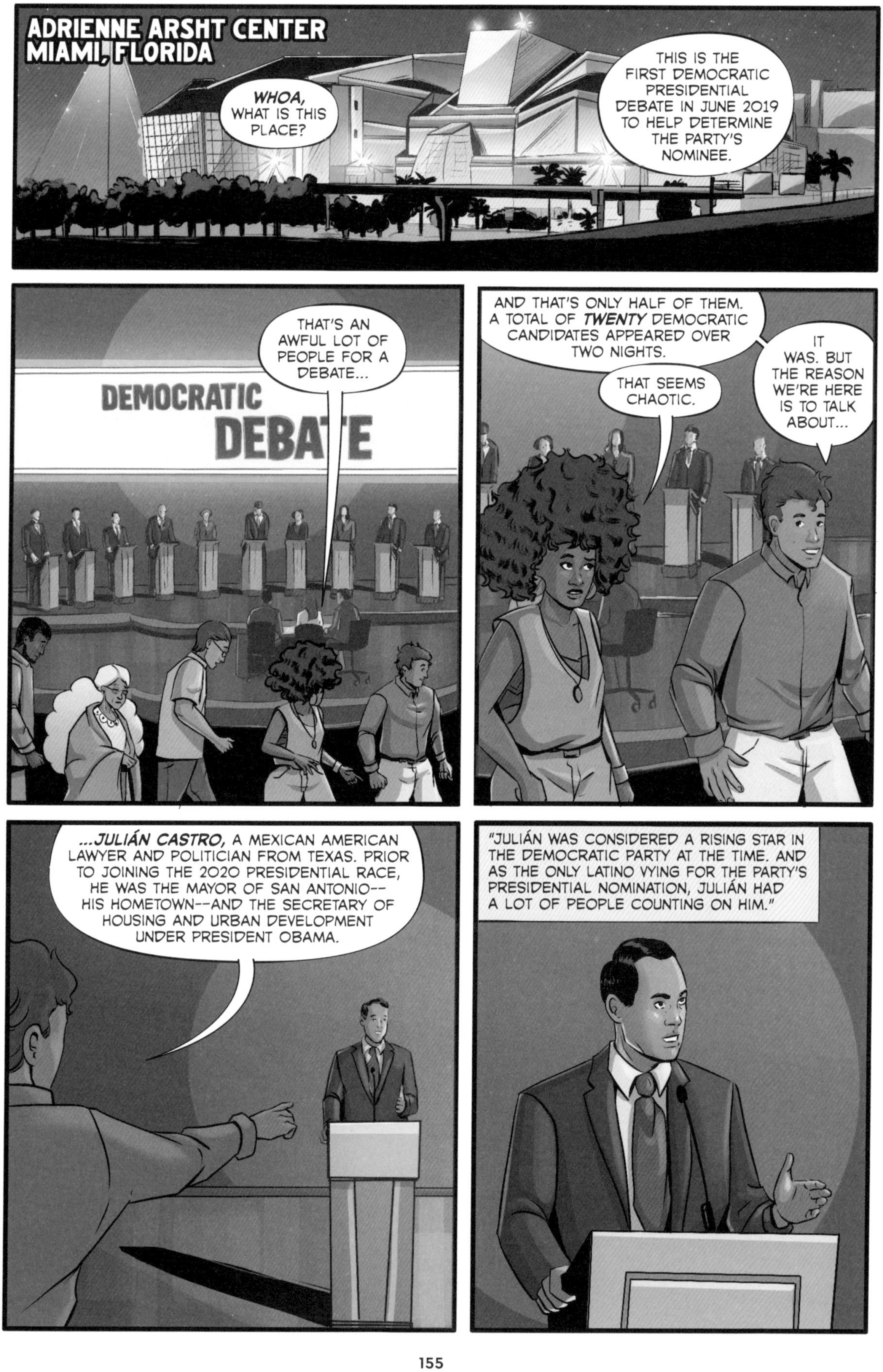
ADRIENNE ARSHT CENTER
MIAMI, FLORIDA
*WHOA,* WHAT IS THIS PLACE?
THIS IS THE FIRST DEMOCRATIC PRESIDENTIAL DEBATE IN JUNE 2019 TO HELP DETERMINE THE PARTY'S NOMINEE.
DEMOCRATIC DEBATE
THAT'S AN AWFUL LOT OF PEOPLE FOR A DEBATE...
AND THAT'S ONLY HALF OF THEM. A TOTAL OF *TWENTY* DEMOCRATIC CANDIDATES APPEARED OVER TWO NIGHTS.
THAT SEEMS CHAOTIC.
IT WAS. BUT THE REASON WE'RE HERE IS TO TALK ABOUT...
...*JULIÁN CASTRO,* A MEXICAN AMERICAN LAWYER AND POLITICIAN FROM TEXAS. PRIOR TO JOINING THE 2020 PRESIDENTIAL RACE, HE WAS THE MAYOR OF SAN ANTONIO--HIS HOMETOWN--AND THE SECRETARY OF HOUSING AND URBAN DEVELOPMENT UNDER PRESIDENT OBAMA.
"JULIÁN WAS CONSIDERED A RISING STAR IN THE DEMOCRATIC PARTY AT THE TIME. AND AS THE ONLY LATINO VYING FOR THE PARTY'S PRESIDENTIAL NOMINATION, JULIÁN HAD A LOT OF PEOPLE COUNTING ON HIM."

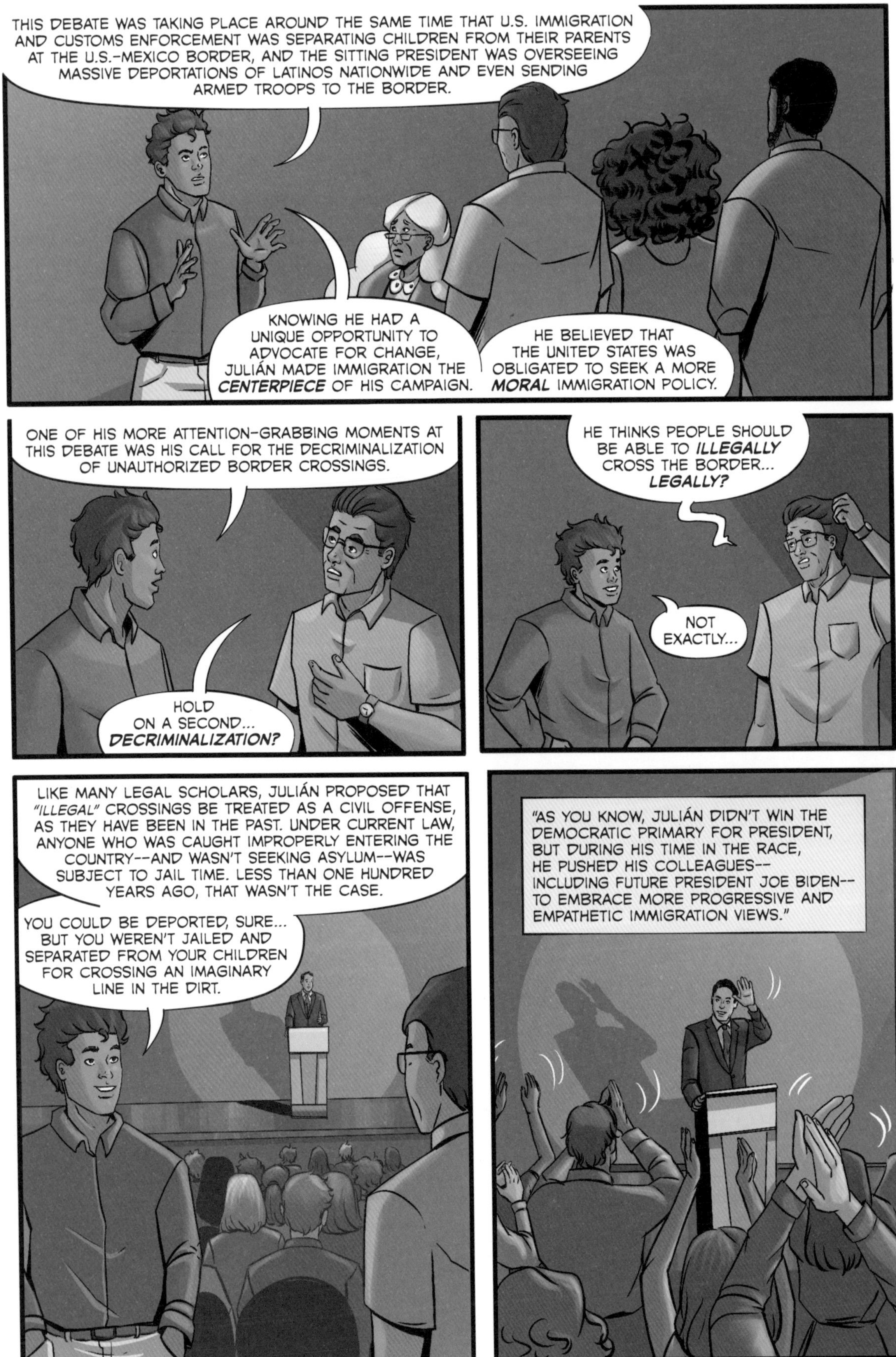
THIS DEBATE WAS TAKING PLACE AROUND THE SAME TIME THAT U.S. IMMIGRATION AND CUSTOMS ENFORCEMENT WAS SEPARATING CHILDREN FROM THEIR PARENTS AT THE U.S.-MEXICO BORDER, AND THE SITTING PRESIDENT WAS OVERSEEING MASSIVE DEPORTATIONS OF LATINOS NATIONWIDE AND EVEN SENDING ARMED TROOPS TO THE BORDER.
KNOWING HE HAD A UNIQUE OPPORTUNITY TO ADVOCATE FOR CHANGE, JULIÁN MADE IMMIGRATION THE *CENTERPIECE* OF HIS CAMPAIGN.
HE BELIEVED THAT THE UNITED STATES WAS OBLIGATED TO SEEK A MORE *MORAL* IMMIGRATION POLICY.
ONE OF HIS MORE ATTENTION-GRABBING MOMENTS AT THIS DEBATE WAS HIS CALL FOR THE DECRIMINALIZATION OF UNAUTHORIZED BORDER CROSSINGS.
HOLD ON A SECOND... *DECRIMINALIZATION?*
HE THINKS PEOPLE SHOULD BE ABLE TO *ILLEGALLY* CROSS THE BORDER... *LEGALLY?*
NOT EXACTLY...
LIKE MANY LEGAL SCHOLARS, JULIÁN PROPOSED THAT *"ILLEGAL"* CROSSINGS BE TREATED AS A CIVIL OFFENSE, AS THEY HAVE BEEN IN THE PAST. UNDER CURRENT LAW, ANYONE WHO WAS CAUGHT IMPROPERLY ENTERING THE COUNTRY--AND WASN'T SEEKING ASYLUM--WAS SUBJECT TO JAIL TIME. LESS THAN ONE HUNDRED YEARS AGO, THAT WASN'T THE CASE.
YOU COULD BE DEPORTED, SURE... BUT YOU WEREN'T JAILED AND SEPARATED FROM YOUR CHILDREN FOR CROSSING AN IMAGINARY LINE IN THE DIRT.
"AS YOU KNOW, JULIÁN DIDN'T WIN THE DEMOCRATIC PRIMARY FOR PRESIDENT, BUT DURING HIS TIME IN THE RACE, HE PUSHED HIS COLLEAGUES--INCLUDING FUTURE PRESIDENT JOE BIDEN--TO EMBRACE MORE PROGRESSIVE AND EMPATHETIC IMMIGRATION VIEWS."

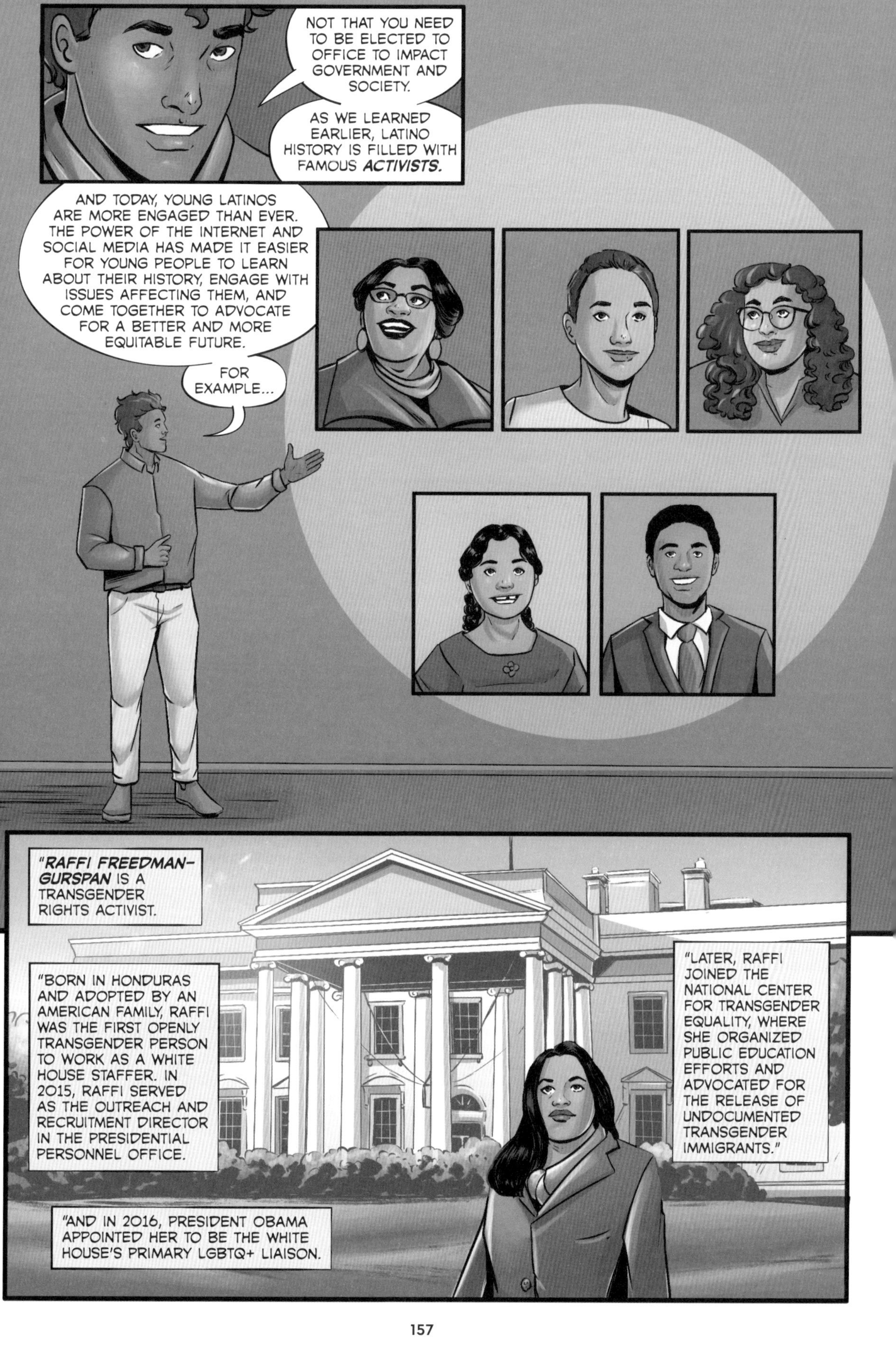
NOT THAT YOU NEED TO BE ELECTED TO OFFICE TO IMPACT GOVERNMENT AND SOCIETY.
AS WE LEARNED EARLIER, LATINO HISTORY IS FILLED WITH FAMOUS ACTIVISTS.
AND TODAY, YOUNG LATINOS ARE MORE ENGAGED THAN EVER. THE POWER OF THE INTERNET AND SOCIAL MEDIA HAS MADE IT EASIER FOR YOUNG PEOPLE TO LEARN ABOUT THEIR HISTORY, ENGAGE WITH ISSUES AFFECTING THEM, AND COME TOGETHER TO ADVOCATE FOR A BETTER AND MORE EQUITABLE FUTURE.
FOR EXAMPLE...
"RAFFI FREEDMAN-GURSPAN IS A TRANSGENDER RIGHTS ACTIVIST.
"BORN IN HONDURAS AND ADOPTED BY AN AMERICAN FAMILY, RAFFI WAS THE FIRST OPENLY TRANSGENDER PERSON TO WORK AS A WHITE HOUSE STAFFER. IN 2015, RAFFI SERVED AS THE OUTREACH AND RECRUITMENT DIRECTOR IN THE PRESIDENTIAL PERSONNEL OFFICE.
"LATER, RAFFI JOINED THE NATIONAL CENTER FOR TRANSGENDER EQUALITY, WHERE SHE ORGANIZED PUBLIC EDUCATION EFFORTS AND ADVOCATED FOR THE RELEASE OF UNDOCUMENTED TRANSGENDER IMMIGRANTS."
"AND IN 2016, PRESIDENT OBAMA APPOINTED HER TO BE THE WHITE HOUSE'S PRIMARY LGBTQ+ LIAISON.

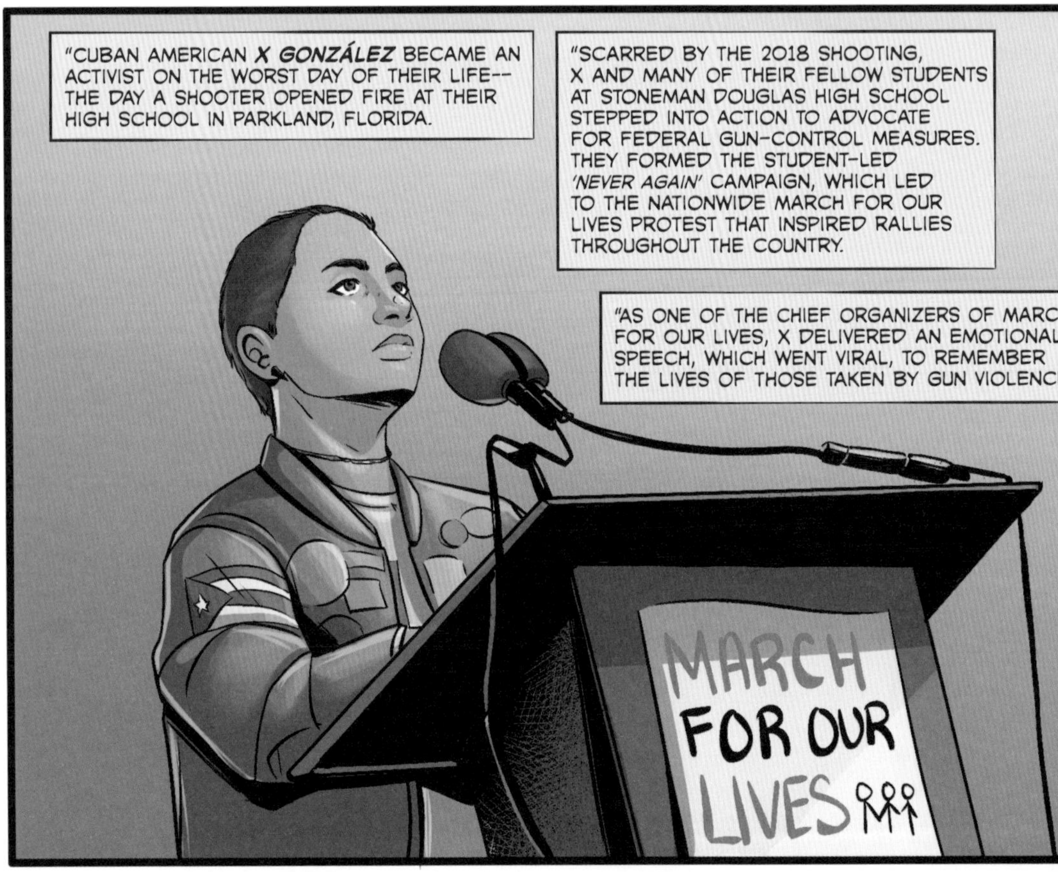
"CUBAN AMERICAN ***X GONZÁLEZ*** BECAME AN ACTIVIST ON THE WORST DAY OF THEIR LIFE-- THE DAY A SHOOTER OPENED FIRE AT THEIR HIGH SCHOOL IN PARKLAND, FLORIDA.
"SCARRED BY THE 2018 SHOOTING, X AND MANY OF THEIR FELLOW STUDENTS AT STONEMAN DOUGLAS HIGH SCHOOL STEPPED INTO ACTION TO ADVOCATE FOR FEDERAL GUN-CONTROL MEASURES. THEY FORMED THE STUDENT-LED *'NEVER AGAIN'* CAMPAIGN, WHICH LED TO THE NATIONWIDE MARCH FOR OUR LIVES PROTEST THAT INSPIRED RALLIES THROUGHOUT THE COUNTRY.
"AS ONE OF THE CHIEF ORGANIZERS OF MARCH FOR OUR LIVES, X DELIVERED AN EMOTIONAL SPEECH, WHICH WENT VIRAL, TO REMEMBER THE LIVES OF THOSE TAKEN BY GUN VIOLENCE."
MARCH FOR OUR LIVES

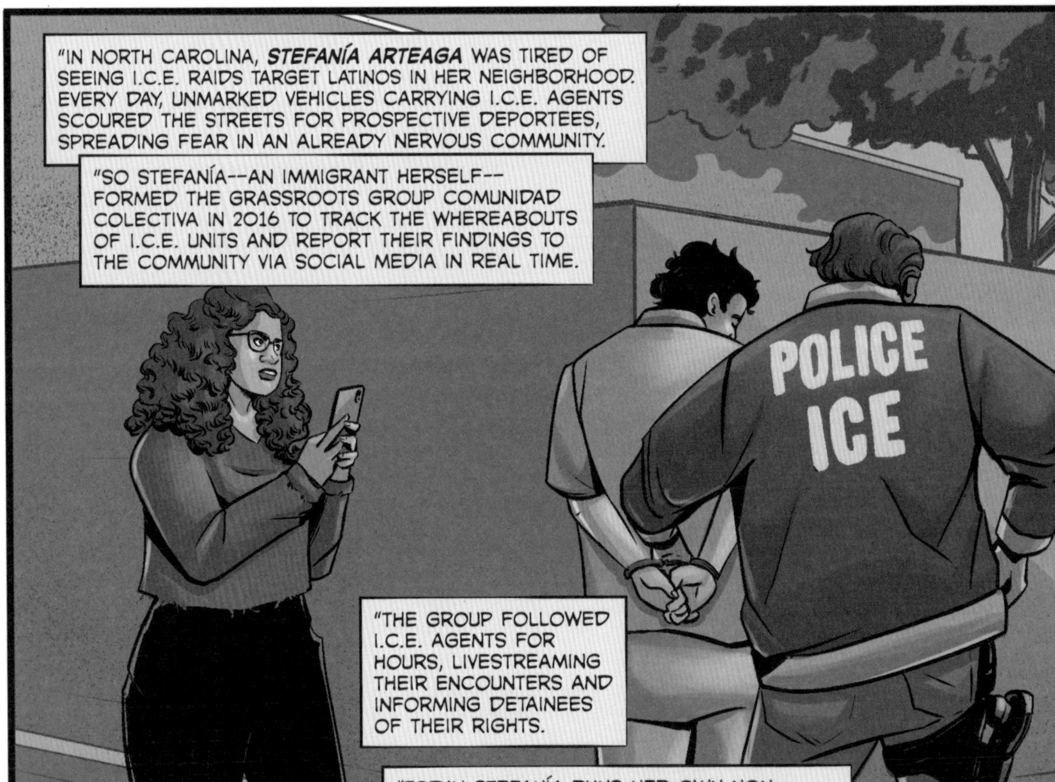
"IN NORTH CAROLINA, ***STEFANÍA ARTEAGA*** WAS TIRED OF SEEING I.C.E. RAIDS TARGET LATINOS IN HER NEIGHBORHOOD. EVERY DAY, UNMARKED VEHICLES CARRYING I.C.E. AGENTS SCOURED THE STREETS FOR PROSPECTIVE DEPORTEES, SPREADING FEAR IN AN ALREADY NERVOUS COMMUNITY.
"SO STEFANÍA--AN IMMIGRANT HERSELF-- FORMED THE GRASSROOTS GROUP COMUNIDAD COLECTIVA IN 2016 TO TRACK THE WHEREABOUTS OF I.C.E. UNITS AND REPORT THEIR FINDINGS TO THE COMMUNITY VIA SOCIAL MEDIA IN REAL TIME.
POLICE ICE
"THE GROUP FOLLOWED I.C.E. AGENTS FOR HOURS, LIVESTREAMING THEIR ENCOUNTERS AND INFORMING DETAINEES OF THEIR RIGHTS.
"TODAY, STEFANÍA RUNS HER OWN NON-PROFIT ORGANIZATION PROVIDING FREE LEGAL AID TO IMMIGRANTS FACING DEPORTATION.

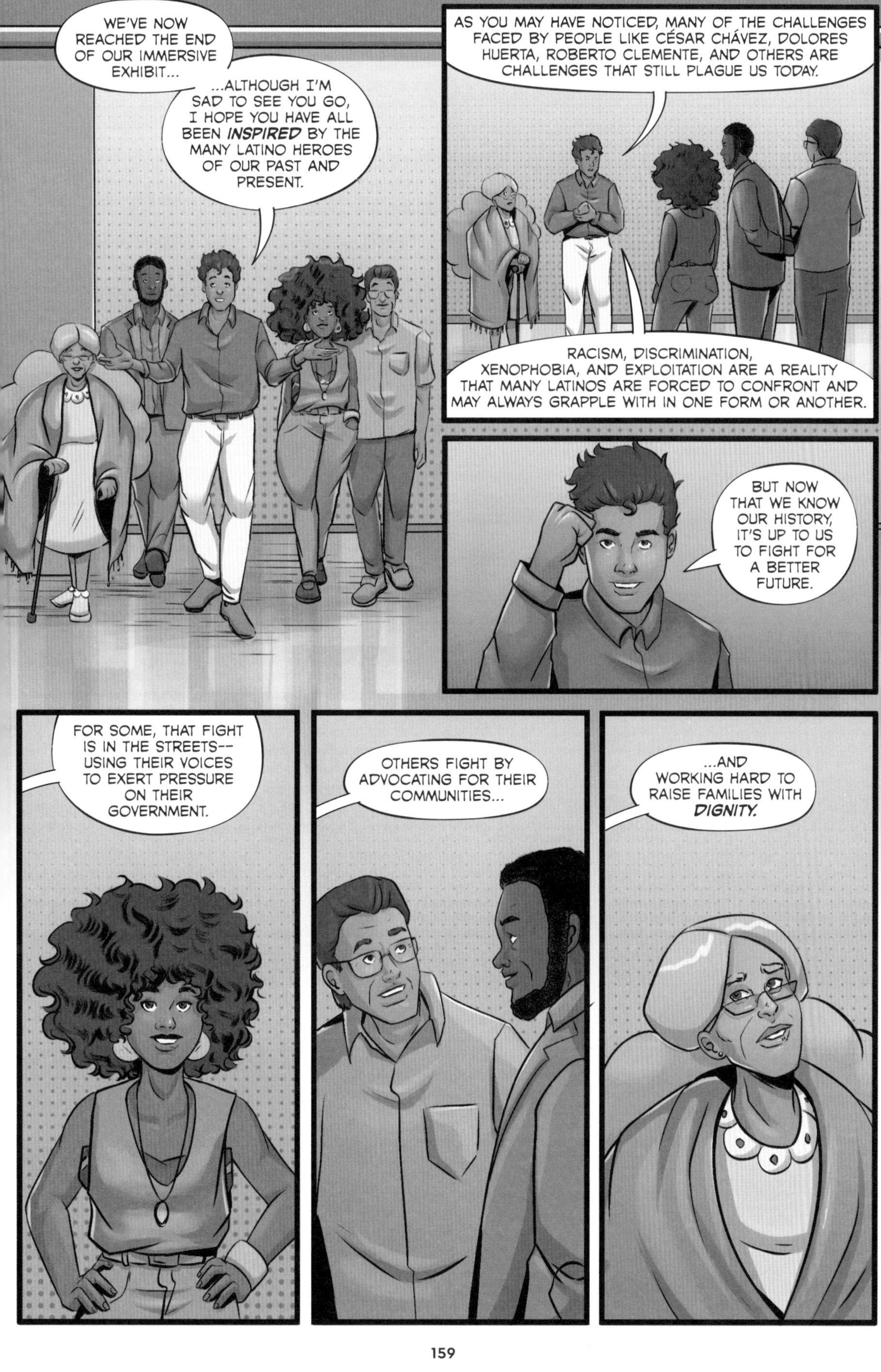
WE'VE NOW REACHED THE END OF OUR IMMERSIVE EXHIBIT...
...ALTHOUGH I'M SAD TO SEE YOU GO, I HOPE YOU HAVE ALL BEEN INSPIRED BY THE MANY LATINO HEROES OF OUR PAST AND PRESENT.
AS YOU MAY HAVE NOTICED, MANY OF THE CHALLENGES FACED BY PEOPLE LIKE CÉSAR CHÁVEZ, DOLORES HUERTA, ROBERTO CLEMENTE, AND OTHERS ARE CHALLENGES THAT STILL PLAGUE US TODAY.
RACISM, DISCRIMINATION, XENOPHOBIA, AND EXPLOITATION ARE A REALITY THAT MANY LATINOS ARE FORCED TO CONFRONT AND MAY ALWAYS GRAPPLE WITH IN ONE FORM OR ANOTHER.
BUT NOW THAT WE KNOW OUR HISTORY, IT'S UP TO US TO FIGHT FOR A BETTER FUTURE.
FOR SOME, THAT FIGHT IS IN THE STREETS-- USING THEIR VOICES TO EXERT PRESSURE ON THEIR GOVERNMENT.
OTHERS FIGHT BY ADVOCATING FOR THEIR COMMUNITIES...
...AND WORKING HARD TO RAISE FAMILIES WITH DIGNITY.

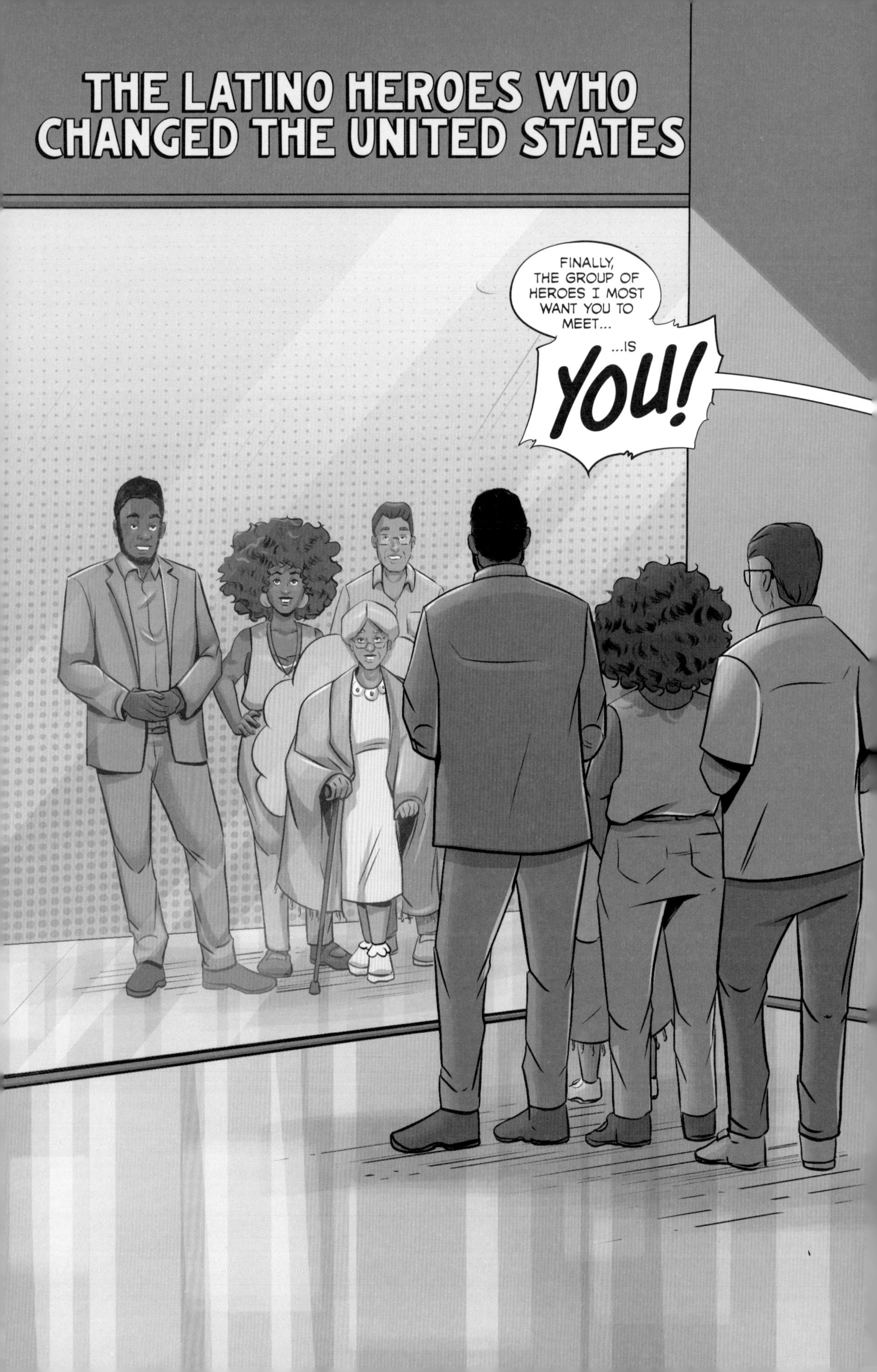
THE LATINO HEROES WHO CHANGED THE UNITED STATES
FINALLY, THE GROUP OF HEROES I MOST WANT YOU TO MEET...
...IS
YOU!

# ADDITIONAL RESOURCES

Learn more about the Latino heroes who changed the United States!

## BOOKS

*A Book*
Author: Desi Arnaz

*Clemente: The Passion and Grace of Baseball's Last Hero*
Author: David Maraniss

*Cuba: An American History*
Author: Ada Ferrer

*Harvest of Empire: A History of Latinos in America*
Author: Juan González

*Inventing Latinos: A New Story of American Racism*
Author: Laura Gómez

*La Voz De M.A.Y.O: Tata Rambo*
Author: Henry Barajas
Illustrator: J. Gonzo

*My Beloved World*
Author: Sonia Sotomayor

*Viva Hollywood: The Legacy of Latin and Hispanic Artists in American Film*
Author: Luis I. Reyes

*The Young Lords: A Radical History*
Author: Johanna Fernández

## DOCUMENTARIES

*Dolores: Rebel. Activist. Feminist. Mother.*
Dir: Peter Bratt

*Immigration Nation*
Dir: Christina Clusiau and Shaul Schwarz

*Knock Down the House*
Dir: Rachel Lears

*The Latin Explosion: A New America*
Dir: Jon Alpert and Matthew O'Neill

*Latino Americans: The 500-Year Legacy That Reshaped a Nation*
Prod: PBS

*Lucy And Desi*
Dir: Amy Poehler

*Rita Moreno: Just a Girl Who Decided to Go for It*
Dir: Mariem Pérez Riera

# ABOUT THE AUTHOR

**JULIO ANTA** is a Cuban and Colombian American author from Miami, Florida. He currently resides in New York City where he works to tell narratively rich stories about diverse Latino characters for readers of all ages. He is best known for his comic book series Home, his young adult graphic novel *Frontera*, and his work at Marvel and DC Comics.

**YASMÍN FLORES MONTAÑEZ** is a comic artist from Puerto Rico. She enjoys crafting diverse cultural stories that are both action-packed and introspective. She earned an MFA in sequential art at SCAD and she's part of the inaugural class of the Milestone Initiative Talent Development Program by DC Comics. Yasmín has illustrated stories for DC Comics, Marvel Comics, IDW Publishing, and more. Her works include *Goosebumps: Secrets of the Swamp, Marvel's Voices: Comunidades,* and the upcoming graphic novel *We Are Pan*.

# INDEX

## E



## F



## G



## H



## I



## J



## K



## L



## M

## N



## O



## P



## Q



## R



## S

## T



## U



## V



## W



## Y

Published in the United States by Ten Speed Graphic, an imprint of the Crown Publishing Group, a division of Penguin Random House LLC, New York.
TenSpeed.com



Typeface: SilverAge by Nate Piekos

Library of Congress Control Number: 2023933478

Trade Paperback ISBN: 978-1-9848-6091-0
eBook ISBN: 978-1-9848-6092-7

Printed in China

Acquiring editor: Shaida Boroumand | Project editor: Vedika Khanna
Production editor: Serena Wang | Editorial assistant: Kausaur Fahimuddin
Art director and designer: Chloe Rawlins | Co-designer: Meggie Ramm
Colorist: Fabi Marques
Letterer: Hassan Otsmane-Elhaou
Project manager: Dan Myers
Copyeditor: Jeff Campbell | Proofreader: Mikayla Butchart
Indexer: Stephen Callahan
Publicist: Felix Cruz | Marketer: Monica Stanton

10 9 8 7 6 5 4 3 2 1

First Edition